Hands-On Deep Learning for Games

Leverage the power of neural networks and reinforcement learning to build intelligent games

Micheal Lanham

BIRMINGHAM - MUMBAI

Hands-On Deep Learning for Games

Commissioning Editor: Kunal Chaudhari
Acquisition Editor: Larissa Pinto
Content Development Editor: Pranay Fereira
Techincal Reviewer: Yosun Chang
Technical Editor: Sachin Sunilkumar
Copy Editor: Safis Editing
Project Coordinator: Kinjal Bari
Proofreader: Safis Editing
Indexer: Rekha Nair
Graphics: Alishon Mendonsa
Production Coordinator: Shraddha Falebhai

First published: March 2019

Production reference: 1290319

Published by Packt Publishing Ltd.
Livery Place
35 Livery Street
Birmingham
B3 2PB, UK.

ISBN 978-1-78899-407-1

`www.packtpub.com`

I would like to dedicate this book to my employers at Geo-Steering Solutions Inc., Neil Tice and Barbara and Darrell Joy who have gone out of their way to assist my research in helping me to finish this insurmountable book.

– Micheal Lanham

Mapt

Contributors

About the author

Micheal Lanham is a proven software and tech innovator with 20 years of experience. During that time, he has developed a broad range of software applications in areas including games, graphics, web, desktop, engineering, artificial intelligence, GIS, and machine learning applications for a variety of industries as an R&D developer. At the turn of the millennium, Micheal began working with neural networks and evolutionary algorithms in game development. He was later introduced to Unity and has been an avid developer, consultant, manager, and author of multiple Unity games, graphic projects, and books ever since.

This book would not be possible if it wasn't for the researchers and contributors. This book has been built on top of, including the development of the ML-Agents toolkit by Unity Technologies, with both Dr. Danny Lange and Dr. Arthur Juliani taking a leading role. This book would also not be possible without the support of my family, friends, Rhonda and my co-workers. I'd like to give a special thanks to those who attend my deep learning tutorials and have given additional feedback.

Packt is searching for authors like you

Table of Contents

Preface

As we enter the 21st century, it is quickly becoming apparent that AI and machine learning technologies will radically change the way we live our lives in the future. We now experience AI daily, from conversational assistants to smart recommendations in a search engine, and the average user/consumer now expects a smarter interface in anything they do. This most certainly includes games, and is likely one of the reasons why you, as a game developer, are considering reading this book.

This book will provide you, with a hands-on approach to building deep learning models for simple encoding for the purpose of building self-driving algorithms, generating music, and creating conversational bots, finishing with an in-depth discovery of deep reinforcement learning (DRL). We will begin with the basics of reinforcement learning (RL) and progress to combining DL and RL in order to create DRL. Then, we will take an in-depth look at ways to optimize reinforcement learning to train agents in order to perform complex tasks, from navigating hallways to playing soccer against zombies. Along the way, we will learn the nuances of tuning hyperparameters through hands-on trial and error, as well as how to use cutting-edge algorithms, including curiosity learning, Curriculum Learning, backplay, and imitation learning, in order to optimize agent training.

Who this book is for

This book is for any game–or budding–game developer who is interested in using deep learning in an aspect of their next game project. In order to be successful in learning this material, you should have knowledge of the Python programming language and another C-based language, such as C#, C, C++, or Java. In addition, a basic knowledge of calculus, statistics, and probability will aid your digestion of the materials and facilitate your learning, but this is not essential.

What this book covers

`Chapter 1`, *Deep Learning for Games,* covers the background of deep learning in games before moving on to cover the basics by building a basic perceptron. From there, we will learn the concepts of network layers and build a simple autoencoder.

`Chapter 2`, *Convolutional and Recurrent Networks*, explores advanced layers, known as convolution and pooling, and how to apply them to building a self-driving deep network. Then, we will look at the concept of learning sequences with recurrent layers in deep networks.

`Chapter 3`, *GAN for Games*, outlines the concept of a GAN, a generative adversarial network or an architectural pattern that pits two competing networks against one another. We will then explore and use various GANs to generate a game texture and original music.

`Chapter 4`, *Building a Deep Learning Gaming Chatbot*, goes into further detail regarding recurrent networks and develops a few forms of conversational chatbot. We will finish the chapter by allowing the chatbot to be chatted with through Unity.

`Chapter 5`, *Introduction DRL*, begins with the basics of reinforcement learning before moving on to cover multi-arm bandits and Q-Learning. We will then quickly move on to integrating deep learning and will explore deep reinforcement learning using the Open AI Gym environment.

`Chapter 6`, *Unity ML-Agents*, begins by exploring the ML-Agents toolkit, which is a powerful deep reinforcement learning platform built on top of Unity. We will then learn how to set up and train various demo scenarios provided with the toolkit.

`Chapter 7`, *Agent and the Environment*, explores how an input state captured from the environment affects training. We will look at ways to improve these issues by building different input state encoders for various visual environments.

`Chapter 8`, *Understanding PPO*, explains how learning to train agents requires some in-depth background knowledge of the various algorithms used in DRL. In this chapter, we will explore in depth the powerhouse of the ML-Agents toolkit, the proximal policy optimization algorithm.

`Chapter 9`, *Rewards and Reinforcement Learning*, explains how rewards are foundational to RL, exploring their importance and how to model their functions. We'll also explore the sparsity of rewards and ways of overcoming these problems in RL with Curriculum Learning and backplay.

`Chapter 10`, *Imitation and Transfer Learning*, explores further advanced methods, imitation and transfer learning, as ways of overcoming the sparsity of rewards and other agent training problems. We will then look at others ways of applying transfer learning i.

`Chapter 11`, *Building Multi-Agent Environments*, explores a number of scenarios that incorporate multiple agents competing against or cooperating with each other.

`Chapter 12`, *Debugging/Testing a Game with DRL*, explains how to build a testing/debugging framework with ML-Agents for use on your next game, which is one new aspect of DRL that is less well covered.

`Chapter 13`, *Obstacle Tower Challenge and Beyond*, explores what is next for you. Are you prepared to take on the Unity Obstacle Tower challenge and build your own game, or perhaps you require further learning?

To get the most out of this book

Some knowledge of Python and some exposure to machine learning will be beneficial, as will a knowledge of a C style language, such as C, C++, C#, or Java. Some understanding of calculus, while not essential, will be helpful, as will an understanding of probability and statistics.

Download the example code files

You can download the example code files for this book from your account at `www.packt.com`. If you purchased this book elsewhere, you can visit `www.packt.com/support` and register to have the files emailed directly to you.

You can download the code files by following these steps:

1. Log in or register at `www.packt.com`.
2. Select the **SUPPORT** tab.
3. Click on **Code Downloads & Errata**.
4. Enter the name of the book in the **Search** box and follow the onscreen instructions.

Once the file is downloaded, please make sure that you unzip or extract the folder using the latest version of:

- WinRAR/7-Zip for Windows
- Zipeg/iZip/UnRarX for Mac
- 7-Zip/PeaZip for Linux

The code bundle for the book is also hosted on GitHub at `https://github.com/PacktPublishing/Hands-On-Deep-Learning-for-Games. In case there's an update to the code, it will be updated on the existing GitHub repository.`

We also have other code bundles from our rich catalog of books and videos available at `https://github.com/PacktPublishing/`. Check them out!

Download the color images

We also provide a PDF file that has color images of the screenshots/diagrams used in this book. You can download it here: `https://www.packtpub.com/sites/default/files/downloads/9781788994071_ColorImages.pdf`.

Conventions used

There are a number of text conventions used throughout this book.

`CodeInText`: Indicates code words in text, database table names, folder names, filenames, file extensions, pathnames, dummy URLs, user input, and Twitter handles. Here is an example: "Mount the downloaded `WebStorm-10*.dmg` disk image file as another disk in your system."

A block of code is set as follows:

```
html, body, #map {
 height: 100%;
 margin: 0;
 padding: 0
}
```

When we wish to draw your attention to a particular part of a code block, the relevant lines or items are set in bold:

```
[default]
exten => s,1,Dial(Zap/1|30)
exten => s,2,Voicemail(u100)
exten => s,102,Voicemail(b100)
exten => i,1,Voicemail(s0)
```

Any command-line input or output is written as follows:

```
$ mkdir css
$ cd css
```

Bold: Indicates a new term, an important word, or words that you see on screen. For example, words in menus or dialog boxes appear in the text like this. Here is an example: "Select **System info** from the **Administration** panel."

Warnings or important notes appear like this.

Tips and tricks appear like this.

Get in touch

Feedback from our readers is always welcome.

General feedback: If you have questions about any aspect of this book, mention the book title in the subject of your message and email us at `customercare@packtpub.com`.

Errata: Although we have taken every care to ensure the accuracy of our content, mistakes do happen. If you have found a mistake in this book, we would be grateful if you would report this to us. Please visit `www.packt.com/submit-errata`, selecting your book, clicking on the Errata Submission Form link, and entering the details.

Piracy: If you come across any illegal copies of our works in any form on the internet, we would be grateful if you would provide us with the location address or website name. Please contact us at `copyright@packt.com` with a link to the material.

If you are interested in becoming an author: If there is a topic that you have expertise in, and you are interested in either writing or contributing to a book, please visit `authors.packtpub.com`.

Reviews

Please leave a review. Once you have read and used this book, why not leave a review on the site that you purchased it from? Potential readers can then see and use your unbiased opinion to make purchase decisions, we at Packt can understand what you think about our products, and our authors can see your feedback on their book. Thank you!

For more information about Packt, please visit `packt.com`.

1
Section 1: The Basics

This section of the book covers the basic concepts of neural networks and deep learning. We'll be looking at everything from the simplest autoencoder, **generative adversarial networks** (**GANs**), and convolutional and recurrent neural networks, all the way to building a working real-world chatbot. This section will give you the basic foundations for building your neural network and deep learning knowledge.

We will include the following chapters in this section:

- `Chapter 1`, *Deep Learning for Games*
- `Chapter 2`, *Convolutional and Recurrent Networks*
- `Chapter 3`, *GAN for Games*
- `Chapter 4`, *Building a Deep Learning Gaming Chatbot*

1
Deep Learning for Games

Welcome to *Hands-on Deep Learning for Games*. This book is for anyone wanting an extremely practical approach to the complexity of **deep learning** (**DL**) for games. Importantly, the concepts discussed in this book aren't solely limited to games. Much of what we'll learn here will easily carry over to other applications/simulations.

Reinforcement learning (**RL**), which will be a core element we talk about in later chapters, is quickly becoming the dominant **machine learning** (**ML**) technology. It has been applied to everything from server optimization to predicting customer activity for retail markets. Our journey in this book will primarily be focused on game development, and our goal will be to build a working adventure game. Keep in the back of your mind how the same principles you discover in this book could be applied to other problems, such as simulations, robotics, and lots more.

In this chapter, we are going to start from the very basics of neural networks and deep learning. We will discuss the background of neural networks, working our way toward building a neural network that can play a simple text game. Specifically, this chapter will cover the following topics:

- The past, present, and future of DL
- Neural networks – the foundation
- Multilayer perceptron in **TensorFlow** (**TF**)
- Understanding TensorFlow
- Training neural networks with backpropagation
- Building an Autoencoder in Keras

This book assumes that you have a working knowledge of Python. You should be able to set up and activate a virtual environment. Later chapters will use Unity 3D, which is limited to Windows and macOS (apologies to those hardcore Linux users).

You might be inclined to skip this chapter if you've already grasped deep learning. Regardless, this chapter is well worth reading and will establish the terminology we use throughout the book. At the very least, do the hands-on exercise—you will thank yourself later!

The past, present, and future of DL

While the term *deep learning* was first associated with neural networks in 2000 by Igor Aizenberg and colleagues, it has only become popular in the last 5 years. Prior to this, we called this type of algorithm an **artificial neural network** (**ANN**). However, deep learning refers to something broader than ANNs and includes many other areas of connected machines. Therefore, to clarify, we will be discussing the ANN form of DL for much of the remainder of this book. However, we will also discuss some other forms of DL that can be used in games, in `Chapter 5`, *Introducing DRL*.

The past

The first form of a **multilayer perceptron** (**MLP**) network, or what we now call an ANN, was introduced by Alexey Ivakhnenko in 1965. Ivakhnenko waited several years before writing about the multilayer perceptron in 1971. The concept took a while to percolate and it wasn't until the 1980s that more research began. This time, image classification and speech recognition were attempted, and they failed, but progress was being made. It took another 10 years, and in the late 90s, it became popular again. So much so that ANNs made their way into some games, again, until better methods came along. Things quietened down and another decade or so passed.

Then, in 2012, Andrew Ng and Jeff Dean used an ANN to recognize cats in videos, and the interest in deep learning exploded. Their stride was one of several trivial (yet entertaining) advancements which made people sit up and take notice of deep learning. Then, in 2015, Google's **DeepMind** team built AlphaGo, and this time the whole world sat up. AlphaGo was shown to solidly beat the best players in the world at the game of Go, and that changed everything. Other techniques soon followed, **Deep Reinforcement Learning** (**DRL**) being one, showing that human performance could be consistently beaten in areas where that was previously not thought of as possible.

While teaching their students about neural networks, there is a humorous and pertinent tale professors enjoy sharing: *The US Army did early research in the '80s using an ANN to recognize enemy tanks. The algorithm worked 100% of the time, and the army organized a big demonstration to showcase its success. Unfortunately, nothing worked at the demonstration, and every test failed miserably. After going back and analyzing things, the army realized the ANN wasn't recognizing enemy tanks at all. Instead, it had been trained on images taken on a cloudy day, and all it was doing was recognizing the clouds.*

The present

At present, at least at the time of writing, we are still in the midst of a deep learning explosion with debris and chaos, and it is our job as developers to make sense of all this. Neural networks are currently the basis for many DL technologies, several of which we will cover in this book. Except, it seems that every day, new and more powerful techniques emerge, and researchers scramble to make sense of them. Now, this rush of ideas can actually stall a technology, as researchers spend more and more time trying to replicate results. It is most certainly a cause for much of the earlier stalling that ANNs (deep learning) previously suffered from. In fact, many skeptics in the industry are predicting yet another hiccup. So, should you be worried, is reading this book worth it? The short answer is *yes*. The long answer is *probably not*, this time things are very different and many deep learning concepts are now generating revenue, which is a good thing. The fact that DL technology is now a proven money-earner puts investors at ease and only encourages new investment and growth. Exactly how much growth is yet to be seen, but the machine and DL space is now ripe with opportunity and growth from all sectors.

So, is it still possible that the game industry will again turn its back on games? That is also unlikely, generally because many of the more recent major advances, like reinforcement learning, were built to play classic Atari games, and use games as the problem. This only encourages more research into deep learning using games. Unity 3D, the game platform, has made a major investment into reinforcement learning for playing games. In fact, Unity is developing some of the most cutting-edge technology in reinforcement learning and we will be working with this platform later. Unity does use C# for scripting but uses Python to build and train deep learning models.

The future

Predicting the future of anything is extremely difficult, but if you watch carefully enough, you may gain some insight into what, where, or how things will develop. Of course, having a crystal ball or a well-trained neural network would certainly help, but a lot of what becomes popular often hinges on the next great achievement. Without any ability to predict that, what can we observe about the current trend in deep learning research and commercial development? Well, the current trend is to use ML to generate DL; that is, a machine essentially assembles itself a neural network that is addressed to solve a problem. Google is currently investing considerable resources into building a technology called **AutoML**, which generates a neural network inference model that can recognize objects/activities in images, speech recognition, or handwriting recognition, and more. Geoffery Hinton, who is often cited as the godfather of the ANN, has recently shown that complex deep network systems can be decomposed into reusable layers. Essentially, you can construct a network using layers extracted from various pre-trained models. This will certainly evolve into more interesting tech and plays well into the DL search but also makes way for the next phase in computing.

Now, programming code is going to become too tedious, difficult, and expensive at some point. We can already see this with the explosion of offshore development, with companies seeking the cheapest developers. It is now estimated that code costs an average of $10-$20 per line, yes, per *line*. So, at what point will the developer start building their code in the form of an ANN or **TensorFlow** (**TF**) inference graph? Well, for most of this book, the DL code we develop will be generated down to a TF inference graph; a brain, if you will. We will then use these brains in the last chapter of the book to build intelligence in our adventure game. The technique of building graph models is quickly becoming mainstream. Many online ML apps now allow users to build models that can recognize things in images, speech, and videos, all by just uploading training content and pressing a button. Does this mean that apps could be developed this way in the future without any programming? The answer is yes, and it is already happening.

Now that we have explored the past, present, and future of deep learning, we can start to dig into more of the nomenclature and how neural networks actually work, in the next section.

Neural networks – the foundation

The inspiration for neural networks or multilayer perceptrons is the human brain and nervous system. At the heart of our nervous system is the neuron pictured above the computer analog, which is a perceptron:

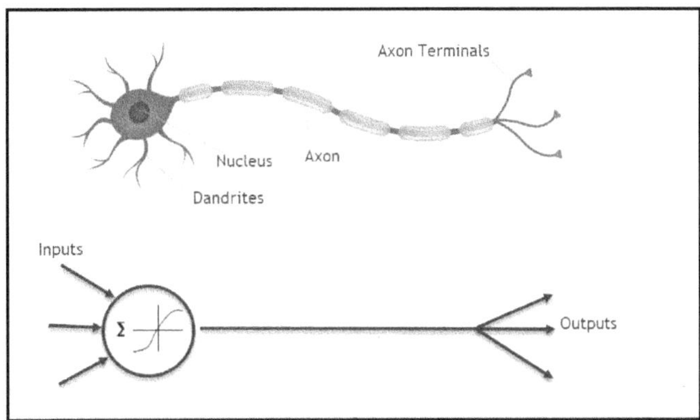

Example of human neuron beside a perceptron

The neurons in our brain collect input, do something, and then spit out a response much like the computer analog, the **perceptron**. A perceptron takes a set of inputs, sums them all up, and passes them through an activation function. That activation function determines whether to send output, and at what level to send it when activated. Let's take a closer look at the perceptron, as follows:

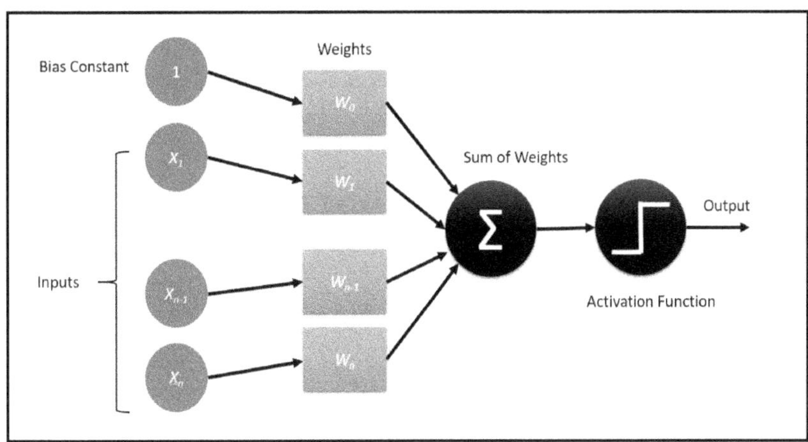

Perceptron

On the left-hand side of the preceding diagram, you can see the set of inputs getting pushed in, plus a constant bias. We will get more into the bias later. Then the inputs are multiplied by a set of individual weights and passed through an activation function. In Python code, it is as simple as the one in `Chapter_1_1.py`:

```
inputs = [1,2]
weights = [1,1,1]

def perceptron_predict(inputs, weights):
    activation = weights[0]
    for i in range(len(inputs)-1):
        activation += weights[i] * input
    return 1.0 if activation >= 0.0 else 0.0

print(perceptron_predict(inputs,weights))
```

Note how the `weights` list has one more element than the `inputs` list; that is to account for the bias (`weights[0]`). Other than that, you can see we just simply loop through the `inputs`, multiplying them by the designated weight and adding the bias. Then the `activation` is compared to `0.0`, and if it is greater than 0, we output. In this very simple example, we are just comparing the value to 0, which is essentially a simple step function. We will spend some time later revisiting various activation functions over and over again; consider this simple model an essential part of carrying out those functions.

What is the output from the preceding block of sample code? See whether you can figure it out, or take the less challenging route and copy and paste it into your favorite Python editor and run it. The code will run as is and requires no special libraries.

In the previous code example, we are looking at one point of input data, `[1,2]`, which is hardly useful when it comes to DL. DL models typically require hundreds, thousands, or even millions of data points or sets of input data to train and learn effectively. Fortunately, with one perceptron, the amount of data we need is less than 10.

Let's expand on the preceding example and run a training set of 10 points through the `perceptron_predict` function by opening up your preferred Python editor and following these steps:

We will use Visual Studio code for most of the major coding sections later in this book. By all means, use your preferred editor, but if you are relatively new to Python, give the code a try. Code is available for Windows, macOS, and Linux.

1. Enter the following block of code in your preferred Python editor or open `Chapter_1_2.py` from the downloaded source code:

```
train =
[[1,2],[2,3],[1,1],[2,2],[3,3],[4,2],[2,5],[5,5],[4,1],[4,4]]
weights = [1,1,1]

def perceptron_predict(inputs, weights):
    activation = weights[0]
    for i in range(len(inputs)-1):
      activation += weights[i+1] * inputs[i]
      return 1.0 if activation >= 0.0 else 0.0

for inputs in train:
  print(perceptron_predict(inputs,weights))
```

2. This code just extends the earlier example we looked at. In this case, we are testing multiple points of data defined in the `train` list. Then we just iterate through each item in the list and print out the predicted value.
3. Run the code and observe the output. If you are unsure of how to run Python code, be sure to take that course first before going any further.

You should see an output of repeating 1.0s, which essentially means all input values are recognized as the same. This is not something that is very useful. The reason for this is that we have not trained or adjusted the input weights to match a known output. What we need to do is train the weights to recognize the data, and we will look at how to do that in the next section.

Training a perceptron in Python

Perfect! We created a simple perceptron that takes input and spits out output but doesn't really do anything. Our perceptron needs to have its weights trained in order to actually do something. Fortunately, there is a well-defined method, known as **gradient descent**, that we can use to adjust each of those weights. Open up your Python editor again and update or enter the following code or open `Chapter_1_3.py` from the code download:

```
def perceptron_predict(inputs, weights):
 activation = weights[0]
 for i in range(len(inputs)-1):
  activation += weights[i + 1] * inputs[i]
 return 1.0 if activation >= 0.0 else 0.0

def train_weights(train, learning_rate, epochs):
 weights = [0.0 for i in range(len(train[0]))]
 for epoch in range(epochs):
  sum_error = 0.0
  for inputs in train:
   prediction = perceptron_predict(inputs, weights)
   error = inputs[-1] - prediction
   sum_error += error**2
   weights[0] = weights[0] + learning_rate * error
   for i in range(len(inputs)-1):
    weights[i + 1] = weights[i + 1] + learning_rate * error * inputs[i]
  print('>epoch=%d, learning_rate=%.3f, error=%.3f' % (epoch,
learning_rate, sum_error))
 return weights

train =
[[1.5,2.5,0],[2.5,3.5,0],[1.0,11.0,1],[2.3,2.3,1],[3.6,3.6,1],[4.2,2.4,0],[
2.4,5.4,0],[5.1,5.1,1],[4.3,1.3,0],[4.8,4.8,1]]

learning_rate = 0.1
epochs = 10
weights = train_weights(train, learning_rate, epochs)
print(weights)
```

The `train_weights` function is new and will be used to train the perceptron using iterative error minimization and will be a basis for when we use gradient descent in more complex networks. There is a lot going on here, so we will break it down piece by piece. First, we initialize the `weights` list to a value of `0.0` with this line:

```
weights = [0.0 for i in range(len(train[0]))]
```

Then we start training each epoch in a `for` loop. An **epoch** is essentially one pass through our training data. The reason we make multiple passes is to allow our weights to converge at a global minimum and not a local one. During each epoch, the weights are trained using the following equation:

$$W_{t+1} = W_t + learningrate \times (expected(t) - predicted(t)) * x(t)$$

Consider the following:

W = weight
$learningrate$ = the rate at which the perceptron learns
$expected$ = the labeled training value
$predicted$ = the value returned from the perceptron
$error$ = $expected$ - $predicted$

The bias is trained in a similar manner, but just recall it is `weight`. Note also how we are labeling our data points now in the `train` list, with an end value of `0.0` or `1.0`. A value of `0.0` means *no match*, while a value of `1.0` means *perfect match*, as shown in the following code excerpt:

```
train =
[[1.5,2.5,0.0],[2.5,3.5,0.0],[1.0,11.0,1.0],[2.3,2.3,1.0],[3.6,3.6,1.0],[4.
2,2.4,0.0],[2.4,5.4,0.0],[5.1,5.1,1.0],[4.3,1.3,0.0],[4.8,4.8,1.0]]
```

This labeling of data is common in training neural networks and is called **supervised training**. We will explore other unsupervised and semi-supervised training methods in later chapters. If you run the preceding code, you will see the following output:

```
>epoch=0, lrate=0.100, error=5.000
>epoch=1, lrate=0.100, error=6.000
>epoch=2, lrate=0.100, error=4.000
>epoch=3, lrate=0.100, error=7.000
>epoch=4, lrate=0.100, error=6.000
>epoch=5, lrate=0.100, error=6.000
>epoch=6, lrate=0.100, error=4.000
>epoch=7, lrate=0.100, error=5.000
>epoch=8, lrate=0.100, error=6.000
>epoch=9, lrate=0.100, error=6.000
[-0.8999999999999999, -0.3900000000000005, 0.6899999999999998]
Press any key to continue . . .
```

Example output from sample training run

Now, if you have some previous ML experience, you will immediately recognize the training wobbling going on around some local minima, making our training unable to converge. You will likely come across this type of wobble several more times in your DL career, so it is helpful to understand how to fix it.

In this case, our issue is likely the choice of the `activation` function, which, as you may recall, was just a simple step function. We can fix this by entering a new function, called a **Rectified Linear Unit** (**ReLU**). An example of the `step` and `ReLU` functions, side by side, are shown in the following diagram:

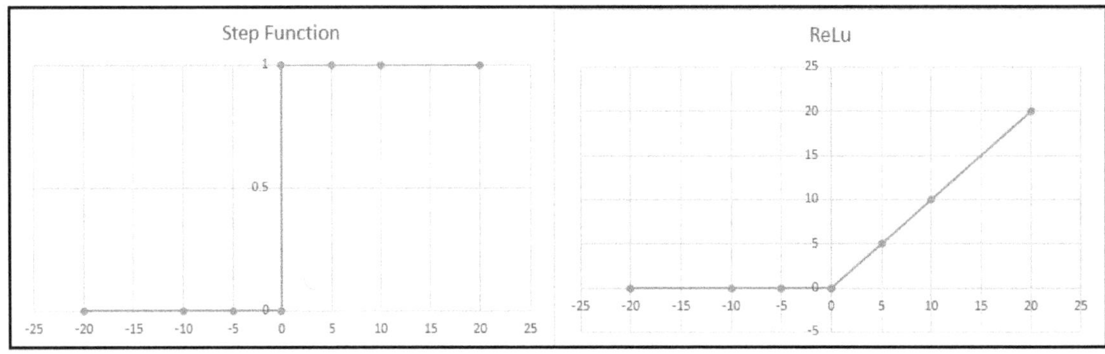

Comparison of step and ReLU activation functions

In order to change the activation function, open up the previous code listing and follow along:

1. Locate the following line of code:

```
return 1.0 if activation >= 0.0 else 0.0
```

2. Modify it, like so:

```
return 1.0 if activation * (activation>0) >= 0.0 else 0.0
```

3. That subtle difference in multiplying the activation function by itself if its value is greater than 0 is the implementation of the `ReLU` function. Yes, it is that deceptively easy.
4. Run the code and observe the change in output.

When you run the code, the values quickly converge and remain stable. This is a tremendous improvement in our training and a cause of changing the activation function to `ReLU`. The reason for this is that now our perceptron weights can more slowly converge to a global maximum, whereas before they just wobbled around a local minimum by using the `step` function. There are plenty of other activation functions we will test through the course of this book. In the next section, we look at how things get much more complicated when we start to combine our perceptrons into multiple layers.

Multilayer perceptron in TF

Thus far, we have been looking at a simple example of a single perceptron and how to train it. This worked well for our small dataset, but as the number of inputs increases, the complexity of our networks increases, and this cascades into the math as well. The following diagram shows a multilayer perceptron, or what we commonly refer to as an ANN:

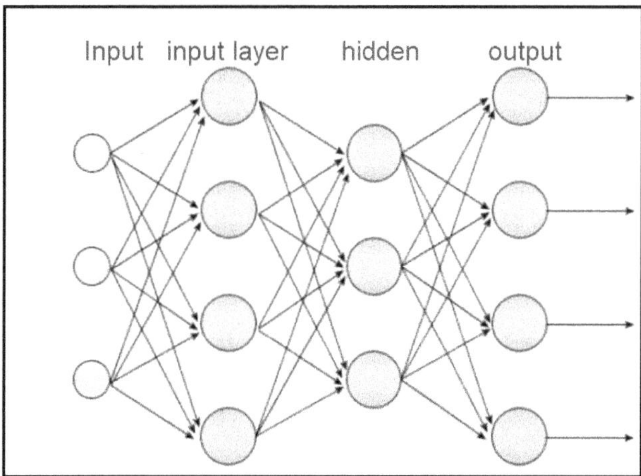

Multilayer perceptron or ANN

In the diagram, we see a network with one input, one hidden, and one output layer. The inputs are now shared across an input layer of neurons. The first layer of neurons processes the inputs, and outputs the results to be processed by the hidden layer and so on, until they finally reach the output layer.

Multilayer networks can get quite complex, and the code for these models is often abstracted away by high-level interfaces such as Keras, PyTorch, and so on. These tools work well for quickly exploring network architecture and understanding DL concepts. However, when it comes to performance, which is key in games, it really requires the models to be built in TensorFlow or an API that supports low-level math operations. In this book, we will swap from Keras, a higher-level SDK, to TensorFlow and back for the introductory DL chapters. This will allow you to see the differences and similarities between working with either interface.

Unity ML-Agents was first prototyped with Keras but has since progressed to TensorFlow. Most certainly, the team at Unity, as well as others, has done this for reasons of performance and, to some extent, control. Working with TensorFlow is akin to writing your own shaders. While it is quite difficult to write shaders and TF code, the ability to customize your own rendering and now learning will make your game be unique, and it will stand out.

There is a great TensorFlow example of a multilayer perceptron next for your reference, listing `Chapter_1_4.py`. In order to run this code using TensorFlow, follow the next steps:

We won't cover the basics of TensorFlow until the next section. This is so you can see TF in action first before we bore you with the details.

1. First, install TensorFlow using the following command from a Python 3.5/3.6 window on Windows or macOS. You can also use an Anaconda Prompt, with administrator rights:

```
pip install tensorflow
OR
conda install tensorflow     //using Anaconda
```

2. Make sure you install TensorFlow suited to the default Python environment. We will worry about creating more structured virtual environments later. If you are not sure what a Python virtual environment is, step away from the book and take a course in Python right away.

In this exercise, we are loading the **MNIST** handwritten digits database. If you have read anything at all about ML and DL, you have most likely seen or heard about this dataset already. If you haven't, just quickly Google *MNIST* to get a sense of what these digits look like.

3. The following Python code is from the `Chapter_1_4.py` listing, with each section explained in the following steps:

```
from tensorflow.examples.tutorials.mnist import input_data
mnist = input_data.read_data_sets("/tmp/data/", one_hot=True)
```

4. We start by loading the `mnist` training set. The `mnist` dataset is a collection of 28 x 28 pixel images showing hand-drawn representations of the digits 0-9, or what we will refer to as 10 classes:

```
import tensorflow as tf
# Parameters
learning_rate = 0.001
training_epochs = 15
batch_size = 100
display_step = 1
# Network Parameters
n_hidden_1 = 256 # 1st layer number of neurons
n_hidden_2 = 256 # 2nd layer number of neurons
n_input = 784 # MNIST data input (img shape: 28*28)
n_classes = 10 # MNIST total classes (0-9 digits)
```

5. Then we import the `tensorflow` library as `tf`. Next, we set a number of parameters we will use later. Note how we are defining the inputs and hidden parameters as well:

```
# tf Graph input
X = tf.placeholder("float", [None, n_input])
Y = tf.placeholder("float", [None, n_classes])

# Store layers weight & bias
weights = {
 'h1': tf.Variable(tf.random_normal([n_input, n_hidden_1])),
 'h2': tf.Variable(tf.random_normal([n_hidden_1, n_hidden_2])),
 'out': tf.Variable(tf.random_normal([n_hidden_2, n_classes]))
}
biases = {
 'b1': tf.Variable(tf.random_normal([n_hidden_1])),
 'b2': tf.Variable(tf.random_normal([n_hidden_2])),
 'out': tf.Variable(tf.random_normal([n_classes]))
}
```

6. Next, we set up a couple of TensorFlow placeholders with `tf.placeholder`, to hold the number of inputs and classes as type `'float'`. Then we create and initialize variables using `tf.Variable`, first doing the weights and then the biases. Inside the variable declaration, we initialize normally distributed data into a 2D matrix or tensor with dimensions equal to `n_input` and `n_hidden_1` using `tf.random_normal`, which fills a tensor with randomly distributed data:

```
# Create model
def multilayer_perceptron(x):
 # Hidden fully connected layer with 256 neurons
 layer_1 = tf.add(tf.matmul(x, weights['h1']), biases['b1'])
 # Hidden fully connected layer with 256 neurons
 layer_2 = tf.add(tf.matmul(layer_1, weights['h2']), biases['b2'])
 # Output fully connected layer with a neuron for each class
 out_layer = tf.matmul(layer_2, weights['out']) + biases['out']
 return out_layer

# Construct model
logits = multilayer_perceptron(X)
```

7. Then we create the model by multiplying the weights and biases for each layer operation. What we are doing here is essentially converting our activation equation into a matrix/tensor of equations. Now instead of doing a single pass, we perform multiple passes in one operation using matrix/tensor multiplication. This allows us to run multiple training images or sets of data at a time, which is a technique we use to better generalize learning.

For each layer in our neural network, we use `tf.add` and `tf.matmul` to add matrix multiplication operations to what we commonly call a **TensorFlow inference graph**. You can see by the code we are creating that there are two hidden layers and one output layer for our model:

```
# Define loss and optimizer
loss_op =
tf.reduce_mean(tf.nn.softmax_cross_entropy_with_logits(logits=logit
s, labels=Y))
optimizer = tf.train.AdamOptimizer(learning_rate=learning_rate)
train_op = optimizer.minimize(loss_op)
```

8. Next, we define a `loss` function and optimizer. `loss_op` is used to calculate the total loss of the network. Then `AdamOptimizer` is what does the optimizing according to the `loss` or `cost` function. We will explain these terms in detail later, so don't worry if things are still fuzzy:

```
# Initializing the variables
init = tf.global_variables_initializer()
with tf.Session() as sess:
 sess.run(init)
 # Training cycle
 for epoch in range(training_epochs):
   avg_cost = 0.
   total_batch = int(mnist.train.num_examples/batch_size)
   # Loop over all batches
   for i in range(total_batch):
     batch_x, batch_y = mnist.train.next_batch(batch_size)
     # Run optimization op (backprop) and cost op (to get loss
value)
     _, c = sess.run([train_op, loss_op], feed_dict={X: batch_x,Y:
batch_y})
     # Compute average loss
     avg_cost += c / total_batch
```

9. Then we initialize a new TensorFlow session by creating a new session and running it. We use that epoch iterative training method again to loop over each batch of images. Remember, an entire batch of images goes through the network at the same time, not just one image. Then, we loop through each batch of images in each epoch and optimize (backpropagate and train) the cost, or minimize the cost if you will:

```
# Display logs per epoch step
 if epoch % display_step == 0:
 print("Epoch:", '%04d' % (epoch+1),
"cost={:.9f}".format(avg_cost))
 print("Optimization Finished!")
```

10. Then we output the results of each epoch run, showing how the network is minimizing the error:

```
# Test model
 pred = tf.nn.softmax(logits) # Apply softmax to logits
 correct_prediction = tf.equal(tf.argmax(pred, 1), tf.argmax(Y, 1))
```

11. Next, we actually run the prediction with the preceding code and determine the percentage of correct values using the optimizer we selected before on the `logits` model:

```
# Calculate accuracy
 accuracy = tf.reduce_mean(tf.cast(correct_prediction, "float"))
 print("Accuracy:", accuracy.eval({X: mnist.test.images, Y:
mnist.test.labels}))
```

12. Finally, we calculate and output the `accuracy` of our model. If you run the exercise, don't just go into how accurate the model is but think of ways the accuracy could be improved.

There is plenty going on in the preceding reference example, and we will break it down further in the next sections. Hopefully, you can see at this point how complex things can get. This is why for most of the fundamental chapters in this book, we will teach the concepts with Keras first. Keras is a powerful and simple framework that will help us build complex networks in no time and makes it much simpler for us to teach and for you to learn. We will also provide duplicate examples developed in TensorFlow and show some of the key differences as we progress through the book.

In the next section, we explain the basic concepts of TensorFlow, what it is, and how we use it.

TensorFlow Basics

TensorFlow (**TF**) is quickly becoming the technology that powers many DL applications. There are other APIs, such as Theano, but it is the one that has gathered the greatest interest and mostly applies to us. Overarching frameworks, such as Keras, offer the ability to deploy TF or Theano models, for instance. This is great for prototyping and building a quick proof of concept, but, as a game developer, you know that when it comes to games, the dominant requirements are always performance and control. TF provides better performance and more control than any higher-level framework such as Keras. In other words, to be a serious DL developer, you likely need and want to learn TF.

TF, as its name suggests, is all about tensors. A tensor is a mathematical concept that describes a set of data organized in *n* dimensions, where *n* could be 1, 2 x 2, 4 x 4 x 4, and so on. A one-dimensional tensor would describe a single number, say (x_1), a 2 x 2 tensor would be $\begin{pmatrix} x_1 & x_2 \\ x_3 & x_4 \end{pmatrix}$ or what you may refer to as a matrix. A 3 x 3 x 3 tensor would describe a cube shape. Essentially, any operation that you would apply on a matrix can be applied to a tensor and everything in TF is a tensor. It is often helpful when you first start working with tensors, as someone with a game development background, to think of them as a matrix or vector.

Tensors are nothing more than multidimensional arrays, vectors, or matrices, and many examples are shown in the following diagram:

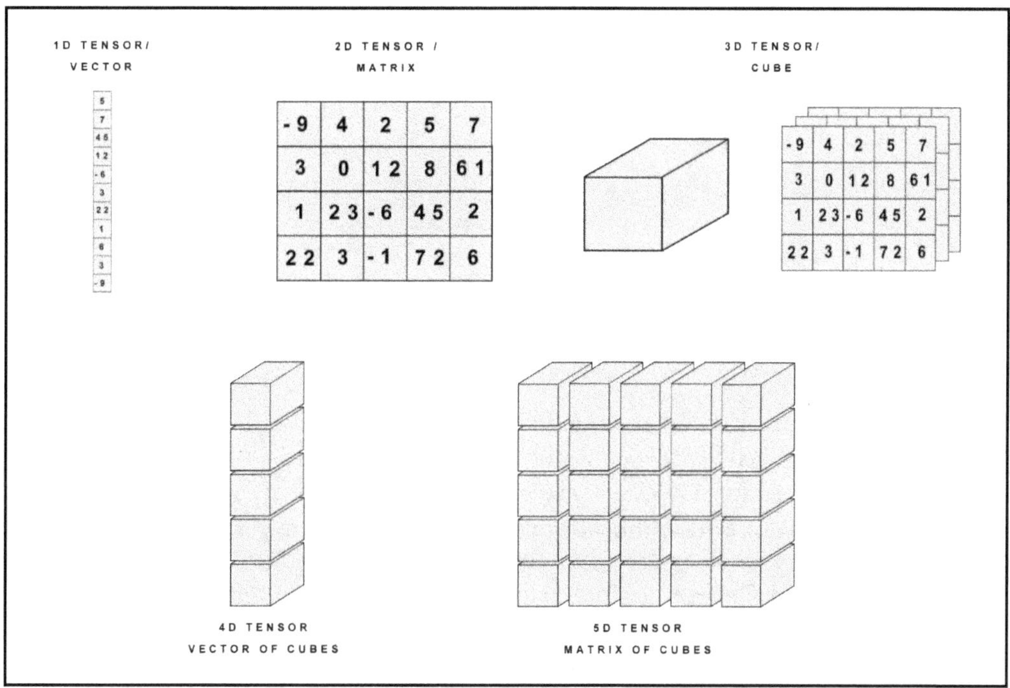

Tensor in many forms (placeholder)

Let's go back and open up `Chapter_1_4.py` and follow the next steps in order to better understand how the TF example runs:

1. First, examine the top section again and pay special attention to where the placeholder and variable is declared; this is shown again in the following snippet:

   ```
   tf.placeholder("float", [None, n_input])
   ...
   tf.Variable(tf.random_normal([n_input, n_hidden_1]))
   ```

2. The `placeholder` is used to define the input and output tensors. `Variable` sets up a variable tensor that can be manipulated while the TF session or program executes. In the case of the example, a helper method called `random_normal` populates the hidden weights with a normally distributed dataset. There are other helper methods such as this that can be used; check the docs for more info.
3. Next, we construct the `logits` model as a function called `multilayer_perceptron`, as follows:

   ```
   def multilayer_perceptron(x):
     layer_1 = tf.add(tf.matmul(x, weights['h1']), biases['b1'])
     layer_2 = tf.add(tf.matmul(layer_1, weights['h2']), biases['b2'])
     out_layer = tf.matmul(layer_2, weights['out']) + biases['out']
     return out_layer

   logits = multilayer_perceptron(X)
   ```

4. Inside the function, we see the definition of three network layers, two input and one output. Each layer is constructed by using the add or + function to add the results of the `matmul (x, weights['h1'])` and the `biases['b1'].Matmul` does a simple matrix multiplication of each weight times the input *x*. Think back to our first example perceptron; this is the same as multiplying all our weights by the input and then adding the bias. Note how the resultant tensors `(layer_1, layer_2)` are used as inputs into the following layer.
5. Skip down to around line 50 and note how we grab references to the `loss`, `optimizer`, and `initialization` functions:

   ```
   loss_op =
   tf.reduce_mean(tf.nn.softmax_cross_entropy_with_logits(logits=logit
   s, labels=Y))
   optimizer = tf.train.AdamOptimizer(learning_rate=learning_rate)
   train_op = optimizer.minimize(loss_op)
   init = tf.global_variables_initializer()
   ```

6. It is important to understand that we are storing references to the functions and not executing them just yet. The loss and optimizer functions have been covered in some depth already, but also pay special attention to the `global_variables_initalizer()` function. This function is where all the variables are initialized, and we are required to run this function first.
7. Next, scroll down to the start of the session initialization and start, as follows:

```
with tf.Session() as sess:
  sess.run(init)
```

8. We construct `Session` in TF as a container of execution or what is called a graph. This is a mathematical graph that describes nodes and connections, not that unlike the networks we are simulating. Everything in TF needs to happen within a session. Then we run the first function, `(init)`, with `run`.
9. As we have already covered the training in some detail, the next element we will look at is the next function, `run`, executed by the following code:

```
_, c = sess.run([train_op, loss_op], feed_dict={X: batch_x,Y:
batch_y})
```

10. A lot is going on in the `run` function. We input as a set the training and loss functions `train_op` and `loss_op` using the current `feed_dict` dictionary as input. The resultant output value, `c`, is equal to the total cost. Note that the input function set is defined as `train_op` then `loss_op`. In this case, the order is defined as `train/loss`, but it could be also reversed if you choose. You would also need to reverse the output values as well, since the output order matches the input order.

The rest of the code has already been defined in some detail, but it is important to understand some of the key differences when building your models with TF. As you can see, it is relatively easy for us to now build complex neural networks quickly. Yet, we are still missing some critical knowledge that will be useful in constructing more complex networks later. What we have been missing is the underlying math used to train a neural network, which we will explore in the next section.

Training neural networks with backpropagation

Calculating the activation of a neuron, the forward part, or what we call **feed-forward propagation**, is quite straightforward to process. The complexity we encounter now is training the errors back through the network. When we train the network now, we start at the last output layer and determine the total error, just as we did with a single perceptron, but now we need to sum up all errors across the output layer. Then we need to use this value to backpropagate the error back through the network, updating each of the weights based on their contribution to the total error. Understanding the contribution of a single weight in a network with thousands or millions of weights could be quite complicated, except thankfully for the help of differentiation and the chain rule. Before we get to the complicated math, we first need to discuss the `Cost` function and how we calculate errors in the next section.

While the math of backpropagation is complicated and may be intimidating, at some point, you will want or need to understand it well. However, for the purposes of this book, you can omit or just revisit this section as needed. All the networks we develop in later chapters will automatically handle backpropagation for us. Of course, you can't run away from the math either; it is everywhere in deep learning.

The Cost function

A `Cost` function describes the average sum of errors for a batch in our entire network and is often defined by this equation:

$$C(w_1, w_2, .., w_n) = C(w)$$

The input is defined as each weight and the output is the total average cost we encountered over the processed batch. Think of this cost as the average sum of errors. Now, our goal here is to minimize this function or the cost of errors to the lowest value possible. In the previous couple of examples, we have seen a technique called **gradient descent** being used to minimize this cost function. Gradient descent works by differentiating the `Cost` function and determining the gradient with respect to each weight. Then, for each weight, or dimension if you will, the algorithm alters the weight based on the calculated gradient that minimizes the `Cost` function.

Before we get into the heavy math that explains the differentiation, let's see how gradient descent works in two dimensions, with the following diagram:

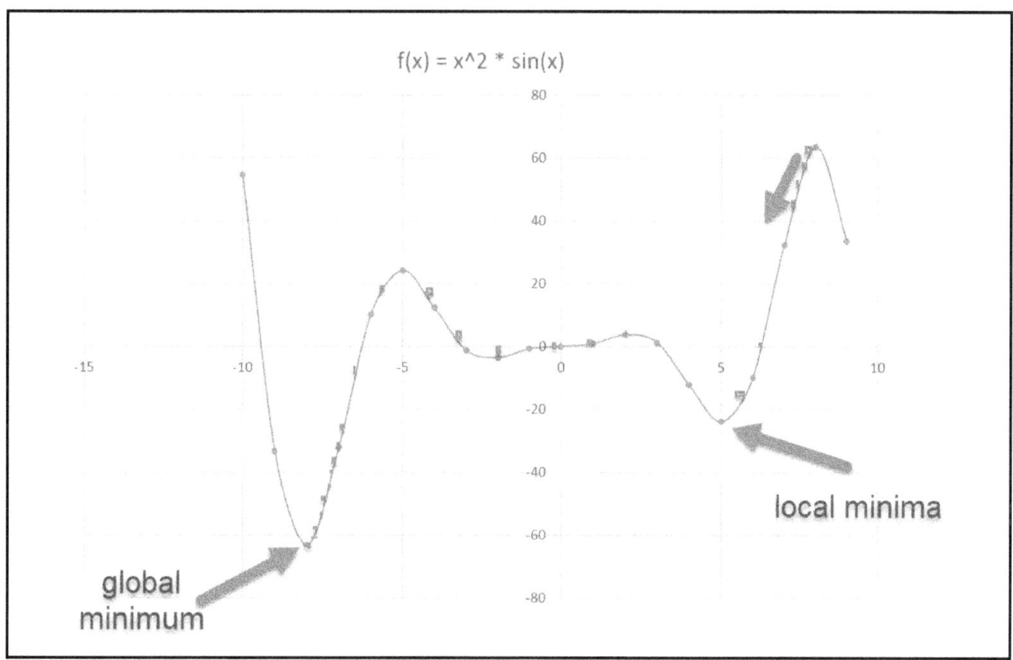

Example of gradient descent finding a global minimum

In simpler terms, all that the algorithm is doing is just trying to find the minimum in slow gradual steps. We use small steps in order to avoid overshooting the minimum, which as you have seen earlier can happen (remember the wobble). That is where the term **learning rate** also comes in, which determines how fast we want to train. The slower the training, the more confident you will be in your results, but usually at a cost of time. The alternative is to train quicker, using a higher learning rate, but, as you can see now, it may be easy to overshoot any global minimum.

Gradient descent is the simplest form we will talk about, but keep in mind that there are also several advanced variations of other optimization algorithms we will explore. In the TF example, for instance, we used `AdamOptimizer` to minimize the `Cost` function, but there are several other variations. For now, though, we will focus on how to calculate the gradient of the `Cost` function and understand the basics of backpropagation with gradient descent in the next section.

Partial differentiation and the chain rule

Before we get into the details of calculating each weight, let's review a little bit of calculus and differentiation. If you recall your favorite math class, calculus, you can determine the slope of change for any point on a function by differentiating. A calculus refresher is shown in the following diagram:

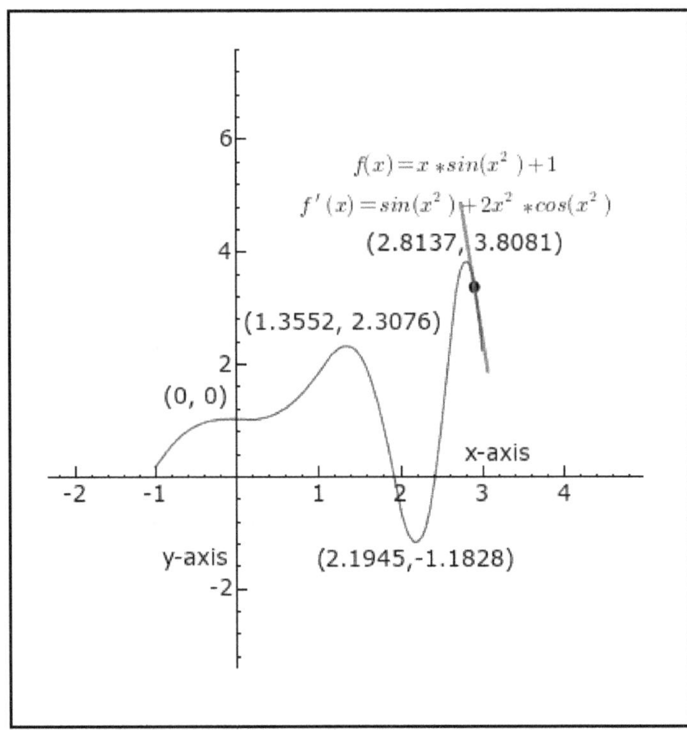

A review of basic calculus equations

In the diagram, we have a nonlinear function, **f**, that describes the equation of the blue line. We can determine the slope (rate of change) on any point by differentiating to **f'** and solving. Recall that we can also determine the functions of local and global minimum or maximum using this new function and as shown in the diagram. Simple differentiation allows us to solve for one variable, but we need to solve for multiple weights, so we will use partial derivatives or differentiating with respect to one variable.

As you may recall, partial differentiation allows us to derive for a single variable with respect to the other variables, which we then treat as constants. Let's go back to our `Cost` function and see how to differentiate that with respect to a single weight:

1. C is our cost function described by the following:

$$C(w_1, w_2, \ldots w_{n-1}, w_n) = C(w)$$

2. We can differentiate this function with respect to a single variable weight as follows:

$$C'(w_1) = \frac{\partial C}{\partial w_1}$$

$$C'(w_2) = \frac{\partial C}{\partial w_2}$$

3. If we collect all of these partial derivatives together, we get the vector gradient for our `Cost` function, C, denoted by the following:

$$\Delta C = \begin{bmatrix} \frac{\partial C}{\partial w_1} \\ \frac{\partial C}{\partial w_2} \\ \ldots \\ \frac{\partial C}{\partial w_{n-1}} \\ \frac{\partial C}{\partial w_n} \end{bmatrix}$$

4. This gradient defines a vector direction that we want to negate and use to minimize the `Cost` function. In the case of our previous example, there are over 13,000 components to this vector. These correspond to over 13,000 weights in the network that we need to optimize. That is a lot of partial derivatives we need to combine in order to calculate the gradient. Fortunately, the chain rule in calculus can come to our rescue and greatly simplify the math. Recall that the chain rule is defined by the following:

$$\frac{\partial z}{\partial x} = \frac{\partial z}{\partial y} \times \frac{\partial y}{\partial x}$$

5. This now allows us to define the gradient for a single weight using the chain rule as such:

$$\nabla w_{ij} = \frac{\partial C}{\partial w_{ij}}$$

$$\nabla w_{ij} = \frac{\partial C}{\partial w_{ij}} = \frac{\partial C}{\partial a_i} \times \frac{\partial a_i}{\partial w_{ij}}$$

6. Here, i represents the input number and j the neuron position. Note how we now need to take the partial derivative of the activation function, *a*, for the given neuron, and that is again summarized by the following:

$$a_i^{(l)} = \sum_{i=0}^{N} w_{ij}^{(l)} z_j^{(l-1)}$$

The superscript notation (l) denotes the current layer and $(l-1)$ denotes the previous layer. z denotes either the input or the output from the previous layer. σ denotes the activation function, recall that we previously used the `Step` and `ReLU` functions for this role.

7. Then, we take the partial derivative of this function, like so:

$$\frac{\partial a_i}{\partial w_{ij}} = \frac{\sum_{k=0}^{M} w_{kj}^{(l)} z_k^{(l-1)}}{\partial w_{ij}} = z_i^{(l-1)}$$

For convenience, we define the following:

$$\delta_j^{(l)} \equiv \frac{\partial C}{\partial a_j^{(l)}}$$

8. At this point, things may look a lot more complicated than they are. Try to understand all the subtleties of the notation and remember all we are looking at is essentially the partial derivative of the activation with respect to the `Cost` function. All that the extra notation does is allow us to index the individual weight, neuron, and layer. We can then express this as follows:

$$\Delta w_{ij}^{(l)} = \frac{\partial C}{\partial w_{ij}^{(l)}} = \delta_j^{(l)} z_i^{(l-1)}$$

9. Again, all we are doing is defining the gradient (Δ) for the weight at the ith input, j^{th} neuron, and layer 1. Along with gradient descent, we need to backpropagate the adjustment to the weights using the preceding base formula. For the output layer (last layer), this now can be summarized as follows:

$$\delta_j = \frac{\partial C}{\partial a_j} = \frac{\partial C}{\partial y_j} = \frac{\partial}{\partial y_j}\left(\frac{1}{2}\sum_{i=0}^{M}(\hat{y}_i - y_i)^2\right) = \hat{y}_j - y_j$$

10. For an internal or a hidden layer, the equation comes out to this:

$$\delta_j^{(l-1)} = \frac{\partial C}{\partial a_j^{(l-1)}} = \sum_k \frac{\partial C}{\partial a_k^{(l)}} \frac{\partial a_k^{(l)}}{\partial a_j^{(l-1)}}$$

11. And with a few more substitutions and manipulations of the general equation, we end up with this:

$$\delta_j^{(l-1)} = \sum_k \frac{\partial C}{\partial a_k^{(l)}} \frac{\partial a_k^{(l)}}{\partial a_j^{(l-1)}} = \sum_k \delta_k^{(l)} w_{kj}^{(l)} f'(a_j^{(l-1)}) = f'(a_j^{(l-1)}) \sum_k \delta_k^{(l)} w_{kj}^{(l)}$$

    Here, f' denotes the derivative of the activation function.

The preceding equation allows us to run the network and backpropagate the errors back through, using the following procedure:

1. You first calculate the activations a_j and z_j for each layer starting with the input layer and propagate forward.
2. We then evaluate the term $\delta_j^{(l)}$ at the output layer using $\hat{y}_j - y_j$.

3. We do this by using the remainder to evaluate each layer using $\delta_j^{(l-1)} = f'(a_j^{(l-1)}) \sum_k \delta_k^{(l)} w_{kj}^{(l)}$, starting with the output layer and propagating backward.
4. Again, we are using the partial derivative $\frac{\partial C}{\partial w_{ij}^{(l)}} = \delta_j^{(l)} z_i^{(l-1)}$ to obtain the required derivatives in each layer.

It may take you a few reads through this section in order to grasp all the concepts. What can also be useful is to run the previous examples and watch the training, trying to imagine how each of the weights is getting updated. We are by no means completely done here, and there are a couple more steps—using automatic differentiation being one of them. Unless you are developing your own low-level networks, just having a basic understanding of that math should give you a better understanding of the needs in training a neural network. In the next section, we get back to some more hands-on basics and put our new knowledge to use by building a neural network agent.

Learning does not and likely should not all come from the same source. Be sure to diversify your learning to other books, videos, and courses. You will not only be more successful in learning but likely also understand more in the process.

Building an autoencoder with Keras

While we have covered a lot of important ground we will need for understanding DL, what we haven't done yet is build something that can really do anything. One of the first problems we tackle when starting with DL is to build autoencoders to encode and reform data. Working through this exercise allows us to confirm that what goes into a network can also come back out of a network and essentially reassures us that an ANN is not a complete black box. Building and working with autoencoders also allows us to tweak and test various parameters in order to understand their function. Let's get started by opening up the `Chapter_1_5.py` listing and following these steps:

1. We will go through the listing section by section. First, we input the base layers `Input` and `Dense`, then `Model`, all from the `tensorflow.keras` module, with the following imports:

```
from tensorflow.keras.layers import Input, Dense
from tensorflow.keras.models import Model
```

2. Instead of single neurons, we define our DL model in Keras using layers or neurons. The `Input` and `Dense` layers are the most common ones we use, but we will see others as well. As their name suggests, `Input` layers deal with input, while `Dense` layers are more or less your typical fully connected neuron layer, which we have already looked at.

We are using the embedded version of Keras here. The original sample was taken from the Keras blog and converted to TensorFlow.

3. Next, we set the number of `encoding` dimensions with the following line:

```
encoding_dim = 32
```

4. This is the number of dimensions we want to reduce our sample down to. In this case, it is just 32, which is just around 24 times the compression for an image with 784 input dimensions. Remember, we get `784` input dimensions because our input images are 28 x 28, and we flatten them to a vector of length 784, with each pixel representing a single value or dimension. Next, we set up the `Input` layer with the 784 input dimensions with the following:

```
input_img = Input(shape=(784,))
```

5. That line creates an `Input` layer with a shape of 784 inputs. Then we are going to encode those 784 dimensions into our next `Dense` layer using the following line:

```
encoded = Dense(encoding_dim, activation='ReLU')(input_img)
encoder = Model(input_img, encoded)
```

6. The preceding code simply creates our fully connected hidden (`Dense`) layer of 32 (`encoding_dim`) neurons and builds the encoder. You can see that the `input_img`, the `Input` layer, is used as input and our activation function is `ReLU`. The next line constructs a `Model` using the `Input` layer (`input_img`) and the `Dense` (`encoded`) layer. With two layers, we encode the image from 784 dimensions to 32.

7. Next, we need to decode the image using more layers with the following code:

```
decoded = Dense(784, activation='sigmoid')(encoded)
autoencoder = Model(input_img, decoded)
encoded_input = Input(shape=(encoding_dim,))

decoder_layer = autoencoder.layers[-1]
decoder = Model(encoded_input, decoder_layer(encoded_input))

autoencoder.compile(optimizer='adadelta',
loss='binary_crossentropy')
```

8. The next set of layers and model we build will be used to decode the images back to 784 dimensions. The last line of code at the bottom is where we compile the `autoencoder` model with an `adadelta` optimizer call, using a `loss` function of `binary_crossentropy`. We will spend more time on the types of loss and optimization parameters later, but for now just note that when we compile a model, we are in essence just setting it up to do backpropagation and use an optimization algorithm. Remember, all of this is automatically done for us, and we don't have to deal with any of that nasty math.

That sets up the main parts of our models, the encoder, decoder, and full autoencoder model, which we further compiled for later training. In the next section, we deal with training the model and making predictions.

Training the model

Next, we need to train our model with a sample set of data. We will again be using the MNIST set of handwritten digits; this is easy, free, and convenient. Get back into the code listing and continue the exercise as follows:

1. Pick up where we left off and locate the following section of code:

```
from tensorflow.keras.datasets import mnist
import numpy as np
(x_train, _), (x_test, _) = mnist.load_data()
```

2. We start by importing the `mnist` library and `numpy` then loads the data into `x_train` and `x_test` sets of data. As a general rule in data science and machine learning, you typically want a training set for learning and then an evaluation set for testing. These datasets are often generated by randomly splitting the data into `80` percent for training and `20` percent for testing.
3. Then we further define our training and testing inputs with the following code:

```
x_train = x_train.astype('float32') / 255.
x_test = x_test.astype('float32') / 255.
x_train = x_train.reshape((len(x_train),
np.prod(x_train.shape[1:])))
x_test = x_test.reshape((len(x_test), np.prod(x_test.shape[1:])))
print( x_train.shape)
print( x_test.shape)
```

4. The first two lines are normalizing our input gray scale pixel color values and a number from `0` to `255`, by dividing by `255`. This gives us a number from `0` to `1`. We generally want to try to normalize our inputs. Next, we reshape the training and testing sets into an input `Tensor`.
5. With the models all built and compiled, it is time to start training. The next few lines are where the network will learn how to encode and decode the images:

```
autoencoder.fit(x_train, x_train, epochs=50, batch_size=256,
 shuffle=True, validation_data=(x_test, x_test))

encoded_imgs = encoder.predict(x_test)
decoded_imgs = decoder.predict(encoded_imgs)
```

6. You can see in our code that we are setting up to fit the data using `x_train` as input and output. We are using `50 epochs` with a `batch size` of `256` images. Feel free to play with these parameters on your own later to see what effect they have on training. After that, the `encoder` and then the `decoder` models are used to predict test images.

That completes the model and training setup we need for this model, or models if you will. Remember, we are taking a 28 x 28 image, decompressing it to essentially 32 numbers, and then rebuilding the image using a neural network. With our model complete and trained this time, we want to review the output and we will do that in the next section.

Examining the output

Our final step this time around will be to see what is actually happening with the images. We will finish this exercise by outputting a small sample of images in order to get our success rate. Follow along in the next exercise in order to finish the code and run the autoencoder:

1. Continuing from the last exercise, locate the following last section of code:

```
import matplotlib.pyplot as plt
n = 10 # how many digits we will display
plt.figure(figsize=(20, 4))
for i in range(n):
 # display original
 ax = plt.subplot(2, n, i + 1)
 plt.imshow(x_test[i].reshape(28, 28))
 plt.gray()
 ax.get_xaxis().set_visible(False)
 ax.get_yaxis().set_visible(False)

# display reconstruction
 ax = plt.subplot(2, n, i + 1 + n)
 plt.imshow(decoded_imgs[i].reshape(28, 28))
 plt.gray()
 ax.get_xaxis().set_visible(False)
 ax.get_yaxis().set_visible(False)
plt.show()
```

2. In this section of code, we are just outputting the input and resultant auto-encoded images after all the training is done. This section of code starts with importing `mathplotlib` for plotting, and then we loop through a number of images to display the results. The rest of the code just outputs the images.
3. Run the Python code as you normally would, and this time expect the training to take several minutes. After everything is done, you should see an image similar to the following:

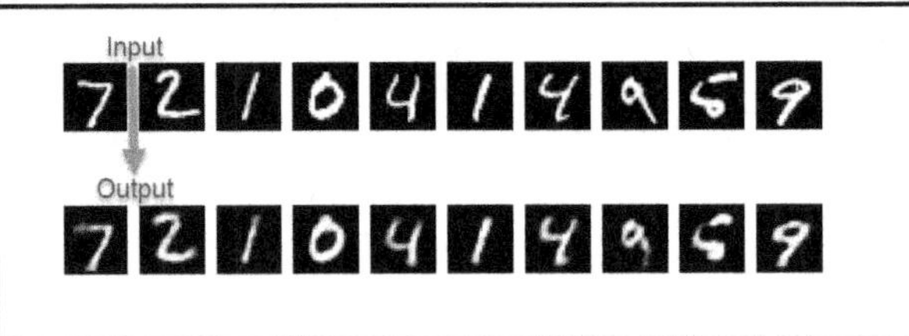

Example of raw input images compared to encoded and decoded output images

That completes our look into building a simple Keras model that can encode and then decode images. This allows us to see how each small piece of a multilayer neural network is written in Keras functions. In the final section, we invite you, the reader, to undertake some additional exercises for further learning.

Exercises

Use these additional exercises to assist in your learning and test your knowledge further.

Answer the following questions:

1. Name three different activation functions. Remember, Google is your friend.
2. What is the purpose of a bias?
3. What would you expect to happen if you reduced the number of epochs in one of the chapter samples? Did you try it?
4. What is the purpose of backpropagation?
5. Explain the purpose of the Cost function.
6. What happens when you increase or decrease the number of encoding dimensions in the Keras autoencoder example?
7. What is the name of the layer type that we feed input into?
8. What happens when you increase or decrease the batch size?
9. What is the shape of the input `Tensor` for the Keras example? Hint: we already have a print statement displaying this.
10. In the last exercise, how many MNIST samples do we train and test with?

As we progress in the book, the additional exercises will certainly become more difficult. For now, though, take some time to answer the questions and test your knowledge.

Summary

In this chapter, we explored the foundations of DL from the basics of the simple single perceptron to more complex multilayer perceptron models. We started with the past, present, and future of DL and, from there, we built a basic reference implementation of a single perceptron so that we could understand the raw simplicity of DL. Then we built on our knowledge by adding more perceptrons into a multiple layer implementation using TF. Using TF allowed us to see how a raw internal model is represented and trained with a much more complex dataset, MNIST. Then we took a long journey through the math, and although a lot of the complex math was abstracted away from us with Keras, we took an in-depth look at how gradient descent and backpropagation work. Finally, we finished off the chapter with another reference implementation from Keras that featured an autoencoder. Auto encoding allows us to train a network with multiple purposes and extends our understanding of how network architecture doesn't have to be linear.

For the next chapter, we will build on our current level of knowledge and discover **convolutional** and **recurrent** neural networks. These extensions provide additional capabilities to the base form of a neural network and have played a significant part in our most recent DL advances.

For the next chapter, we will begin our journey into building components for games when we look at another element considered foundational to DL—the GAN. GANs are like a Swiss Army knife in DL and, as we will see in the next chapter, they offer us plenty of uses.

2
Convolutional and Recurrent Networks

The human brain is often the main inspiration and comparison we make when building AI and is something deep learning researchers often look to for inspiration or reassurance. By studying the brain and its parts in more detail, we often discover neural sub-processes. An example of a neural sub-process would be our visual cortex, the area or region of our brain responsible for vision. We now understand that this area of our brain is wired differently and responds differently to input. This just so happens to be analogous to analog what we have found in our previous attempts at using neural networks to classify images. Now, the human brain has many sub-processes all with specific mapped areas in the brain (sight, hearing, smell, speech, taste, touch, and memory/temporal), but in this chapter, we will look at how we model just sight and memory by using advanced forms of deep learning called **convolutional and recurrent networks**. The two-core sub-processes of sight and memory are used extensively by us for many tasks including gaming and form the focus of research of many deep learners.

Researchers often look to the brain for inspiration, but the computer models they build often don't entirely resemble their biological counterpart. However, researchers have begun to identify almost perfect analogs to neural networks inside our brains. One example of this is the ReLU activation function. It was recently found that the excitement level in our brains' neurons, when plotted, perfectly matched a ReLU graph.

In this chapter, we will explore, in some detail, convolutional and recurrent neural networks. We will look at how they solve the problem of replicating accurate vision and memory in deep learning. These two new network or layer types are a fairly recent discovery but have been responsible in part for many advances in deep learning. This chapter will cover the following topics:

- Convolutional neural networks
- Understanding convolution

- Building a self-driving CNN
- Memory and recurrent networks
- Playing rock, paper, scissors with LSTMs

Be sure you understand the fundamentals outlined in the previous chapter reasonably well before proceeding. This includes running the code samples, which install this chapter's required dependencies.

Convolutional neural networks

Sight is hands-down the most-used sub-process. You are using it right now! Of course, it was something researchers attempted to mimic with neural networks early on, except that nothing really worked well until the concept of convolution was applied and used to classify images. The concept of convolution is the idea behind detecting, sometimes grouping, and isolating common features in an image. For instance, if you cover up 3/4 of a picture of a familiar object and show it to someone, they will almost certainly recognize the image by recognizing just the partial features. Convolution works the same way, by blowing up an image and then isolating the features for later recognition.

Convolution works by dissecting an image into its feature parts, which makes it easier to train a network. Let's jump into a code sample that extends from where we left off in the previous chapter but that now introduces convolution. Open up the `Chapter_2_1.py` listing and follow these steps:

1. Take a look at the first couple of lines doing the import:

```
import tensorflow as tf
from tensorflow.keras.layers import Input, Dense, Conv2D,
MaxPooling2D, UpSampling2D
from tensorflow.keras.models import Model
from tensorflow.keras import backend as K
```

2. In this example, we import new layer types: `Conv2D`, `MaxPooling2D`, and `UpSampling2D`.
3. Then we set the `Input` and build up the encoded and decoded network sections using the following code:

```
input_img = Input(shape=(28, 28, 1)) # adapt this if using
`channels_first` image data format

x = Conv2D(16, (3, 3), activation='relu',
padding='same')(input_img)
```

```
x = MaxPooling2D((2, 2), padding='same')(x)
x = Conv2D(8, (3, 3), activation='relu', padding='same')(x)
x = MaxPooling2D((2, 2), padding='same')(x)
x = Conv2D(8, (3, 3), activation='relu', padding='same')(x)
encoded = MaxPooling2D((2, 2), padding='same')(x)

x = Conv2D(8, (3, 3), activation='relu', padding='same')(encoded)
x = UpSampling2D((2, 2))(x)
x = Conv2D(8, (3, 3), activation='relu', padding='same')(x)
x = UpSampling2D((2, 2))(x)
x = Conv2D(16, (3, 3), activation='relu')(x)
x = UpSampling2D((2, 2))(x)
decoded = Conv2D(1, (3, 3), activation='sigmoid',
padding='same')(x)
```

4. The first thing to note is that we are now preserving the dimensions of the image, in this case, 28 x 28 pixels wide and 1 layer or channel. This example uses an image that is in grayscale, so there is only a single color channel. This is vastly different from before, when we just unraveled the image into a single 784-dimension vector.

   The second thing to note is the use of the `Conv2D` layer or two-dimensional convolutional layer and the following `MaxPooling2D` or `UpSampling2D` layers. Pooling or sampling layers are used to gather or conversely unravel features. Note how we use pooling or down-sampling layers after convolution when the image is encoded and then up-sampling layers when decoding the image.

5. Next, we build and train the model with the following block of code:

```
autoencoder = Model(input_img, decoded)
autoencoder.compile(optimizer='adadelta',
loss='binary_crossentropy')

from tensorflow.keras.datasets import mnist
import numpy as np

(x_train, _), (x_test, _) = mnist.load_data()

x_train = x_train.astype('float32') / 255.
x_test = x_test.astype('float32') / 255.
x_train = np.reshape(x_train, (len(x_train), 28, 28, 1))
x_test = np.reshape(x_test, (len(x_test), 28, 28, 1))

from tensorflow.keras.callbacks import TensorBoard

autoencoder.fit(x_train, x_train,
 epochs=50,
```

```
    batch_size=128,
    shuffle=True,
    validation_data=(x_test, x_test),
    callbacks=[TensorBoard(log_dir='/tmp/autoencoder')])

decoded_imgs = autoencoder.predict(x_test)
```

6. The training of the model in the preceding code mirrors what we did at the end of the previous chapter, but note the selection of training and testing sets now. We no longer squish the image but rather preserve its spatial properties as inputs into the convolutional layer.
7. Finally, we output the results with the following code:

```
n = 10
plt.figure(figsize=(20, 4))
for i in range(n):
  ax = plt.subplot(2, n, i)
  plt.imshow(x_test[i].reshape(28, 28))
  plt.gray()
  ax.get_xaxis().set_visible(False)
  ax.get_yaxis().set_visible(False)
  ax = plt.subplot(2, n, i + n)
  plt.imshow(decoded_imgs[i].reshape(28, 28))
  plt.gray()
  ax.get_xaxis().set_visible(False)
  ax.get_yaxis().set_visible(False)
plt.show()
```

8. Run the code, as you have before, and you'll immediately notice that it is about 100 times slower to train. This may or may not require you to wait, depending on your machine; if it does, go get a beverage or three and perhaps a meal.

Training our simple sample now takes a large amount of time, which may be quite noticeable on older hardware. In the next section, we look at how we can start to monitor the training sessions, in great detail.

Monitoring training with TensorBoard

TensorBoard is essentially a mathematical graph or calculation engine that performs very well at crunching numbers, hence our use of it in deep learning. The tool itself is still quite immature, but there are some very useful features for monitoring training exercises.

Follow these steps to start monitoring training on our sample:

1. You can monitor the training session by entering the following command into a new **Anaconda** or command window from the same directory/folder that you are running the sample from:

```
//first change directory to sample working folder
tensorboard --logdir=/tmp/autoencoder
```

2. This will launch a TensorBoard server, and you can view the output by navigating your browser to the URL in italics, as shown in the window you are running `TensorBoard` from. It will typically look something like the following:

```
TensorBoard 1.10.0 at http://DESKTOP-V2J9HRG:6006 (Press CTRL+C to
quit)
or use
http://0.0.0.0:6000
```

3. Note, the URL should use your machine name, but if that doesn't work, try the second form. Be sure to allow ports `6000`, and `6006` and/or the **TensorBoard** application through your firewall if prompted.
4. When the sample is done running, you should see the following:

Auto-encoding digits using convolution

5. Go back and compare the results from this example and the last example from `Chapter 1`, *Deep Learning for Games*. Note the improvement in performance.

Your immediate thought may be, "*Is the increased training time we experienced worth the effort?*" After all, the decoded images look quite similar in the previous example, and it trained much faster, except, remember we are training the network weights slowly by adjusting each weight over each iteration, which we can then save as a model. That model or brain can then be used to perform the same task again later, without training. Works scarily enough! Keep this concept in mind as we work through this chapter. In `Chapter 3`, *GAN for Games*, we will start saving and moving our brain models around.

In the next section, we take a more in-depth look at how convolution works. Convolution can be tricky to understand when you first encounter it, so take your time. It is important to understand how it works, as we will use it extensively later.

Understanding convolution

Convolution is a way of extracting features from an image that may allow us to more easily classify it based on known features. Before we get into convolution, let's first take a step back and understand why networks, and our vision for that matter, need to isolate features in an image. Take a look at the following; it's a sample image of a dog, called Sadie, with various image filters applied:

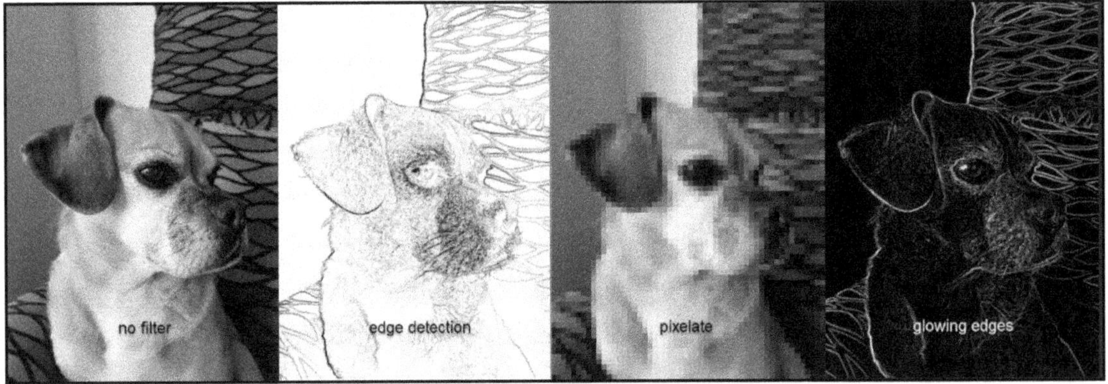

Example of an image with different filters applied

The preceding shows four different versions with no filter, edge detection, pixelate, and glowing edges filters applied. In all cases, though, you as a human can clearly recognize it is a picture of a dog, regardless of the filter applied, except note that in the edge detection case, we have eliminated the extra image data that is unnecessary to recognize a dog. By using a filter, we can extract just the required features our NN needs to recognize a dog. This is all a convolution filter does, and in some cases, one of those filters could be just a simple edge detection.

A convolution filter is a matrix or kernel of numbers that defines a single math operation. The process starts by being multiplied by the upper-left corner pixel value, with the results of the matrix operation summed and set as the output. The kernel is slid across the image in a step size called a **stride**, and this operation is demonstrated:

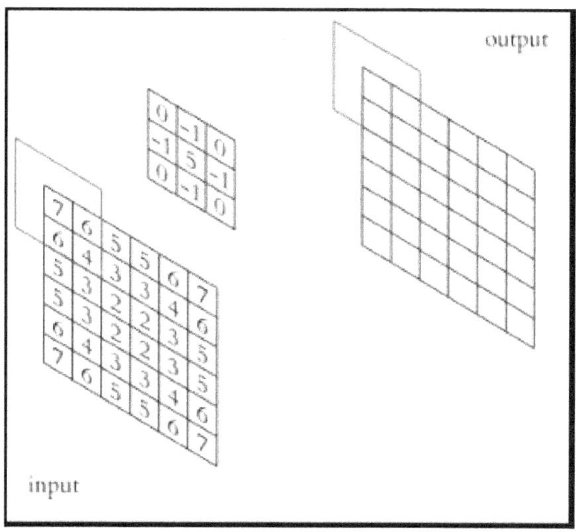

Applying a convolution filter

In the preceding diagram, a stride of 1 is being used. The filter being applied in the convolution operation is essentially an edge detection filter. If you look at the result of the final operation, you can see the middle section is now filled with OS, greatly simplifying any classification task. The less information our networks need to learn, the quicker they will learn and with less data. Now, the interesting part of this is that the convolution learns the filter, the numbers,or the weights it needs to apply in order to extract the relevant features. This is not so obvious and may be confusing, so let's go over it again. Go back to our previous example and look at how we define the first convolution layer:

```
x = Conv2D(16, (3, 3), activation='relu', padding='same')(input_img)
```

In that line of code, we define the first convolution layer as having `16` output filters, meaning our output from this layer is actually 16 filters. We then set the kernel size to `(3,3)`, which represents a `3x3` matrix , just as in our example. Note how we don't specify the values of the various kernel filter weights, as that is after all what the network is training to do.

Let's see how this looks when everything is put together in the following diagram:

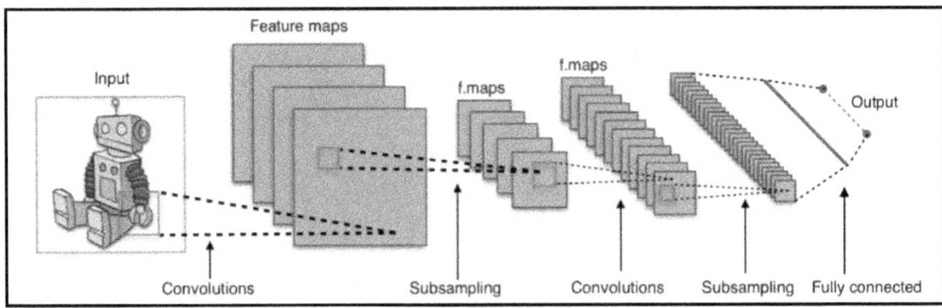

Full convolution operation

The output from the first step in convolution is the feature map. One feature map represents a single convolution filter being applied and is generated by applying the learned filter/kernel. In our example, the first layer produces **16 kernels**, which in turn produce **16 feature maps**; remember that the value of `16` is for the number of filters.

After convolution, we then apply pooling or subsampling in order to collect or gather features into sets. This subsampling further creates new concentrated feature maps that highlight the image's important features we are training for. Take a look back at how we defined the first pooling layer in our previous example:

```
x = MaxPooling2D((2, 2), padding='same')(x)
```

In the code, we are subsampling using a `pool_size` of `(2,2)`. The size indicates the factor by which to down-sample the image by width and height. So a 2 x 2 pool size will create four feature maps at half the size in width and height. This results in a total of 64 feature maps after our first layer of convolution and pooling. We get this by multiplying 16 (convolution feature maps) x 4 (pooling feature maps) = 64 feature maps. Consider how many total feature maps we build in our simple example:

$$TotalFeatureMaps = Conv2D_1 \times Pooling_1 \times Conv2D_2 \times Pooling_2 \times Conv2D_3 \times Pooling_3$$

$$TotalFeatureMaps = 16 \times 4 \times 8 \times 4 \times 8 \times 4$$

$$TotalFeatureMaps = 65536$$

That is 65,536 feature maps of 4 x 4 images. This means we now train our network on 65,536 smaller images; for each image, we attempt to encode or classify. This is obviously the cause for the increased training time, but also consider the amount of extra data we are now using to classify our images. Now our network is learning how to identify parts or features of our image, just as we humans identify objects.

For instance, if you were just shown the nose of a dog, you could likely recognize that as a dog. Consequently, our sample network now is identifying parts of the handwritten digits, which as we know now, dramatically improves performance.

As we have seen, convolution works well for identifying images, but the process of pooling can have disruptive consequences to preserving spatial relationships. Therefore, when it comes to games or learning requiring some form of spatial understanding, we prefer to limit pooling or eliminate altogether. Since it is important to understand when to use and not to use pooling, we will cover that in more detail in the next section.

Building a self-driving CNN

Nvidia created a multi-layer CNN called **PilotNet**, in 2017, that was able to steer a vehicle by just showing it a series of images or video. This was a compelling demonstration of the power of neural networks, and in particular the power of convolution. A diagram showing the neural architecture of PilotNet is shown here:

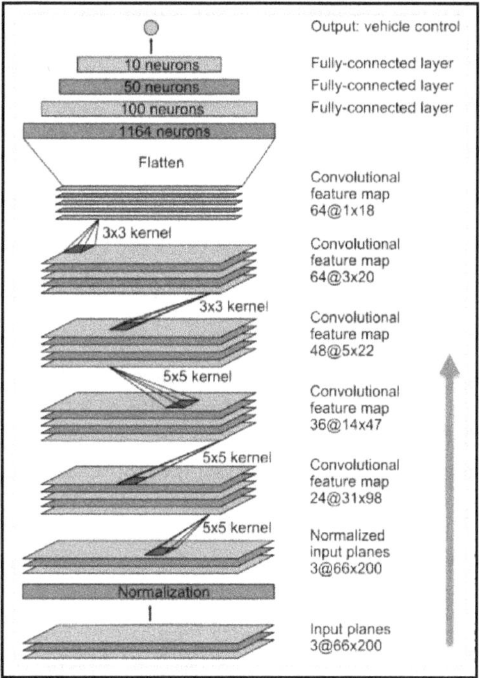

PilotNet neural architecture

The diagram shows the input of the network moving up from the bottom where the results of a single input image output to a single neuron represent the steering direction. Since this is such a great example, several individuals have posted blog posts showing an example of PilotNet, and some actually work. We will examine the code from one of these blog posts to see how a similar architecture is constructed with Keras. Next is an image from the original PilotNet blog, showing a few of the types of images our self-driving network will use to train:

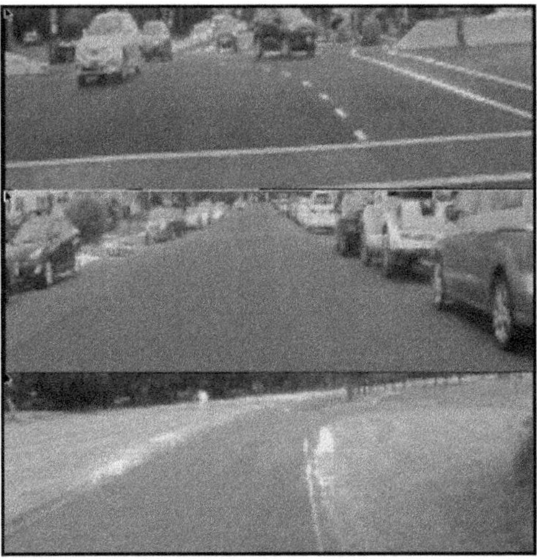

Example of PilotNet training images

The goal of training in this example is to output the degree to which the steering wheel should be turned in order to keep the vehicle on the road. Open up the code listing in `Chapter_2_2.py` and follow these steps:

1. We will now switch to using Keras for a few samples. While the TensorFlow embedded version of Keras has served us well, there are a couple of features we need that are only found in the full version. To install Keras and other dependencies, open a shell or Anaconda window and run the following commands:

```
pip install keras
pip install pickle
pip install matplotlib
```

2. At the start of the code file (`Chapter_2_2.py`), we begin with some imports and load the sample data using the following code:

```
import os
import urllib.request
import pickle
import matplotlib
import matplotlib.pyplot as plt

#downlaod driving data (450Mb)
data_url =
'https://s3.amazonaws.com/donkey_resources/indoor_lanes.pkl'
file_path, headers = urllib.request.urlretrieve(data_url)
print(file_path)

with open(file_path, 'rb') as f:
  X, Y = pickle.load(f)
```

3. This code just does some imports and then downloads the sample driving frames from the author's source data. The original source of this blog was written in a notebook by **Roscoe's Notebooks** and can be found at `https://wroscoe.github.io/keras-lane-following-autopilot.html`.
   `pickle` is a decompression library that unpacks the data in datasets `X` and `Y` at the bottom of the previous listing.
4. Then we shuffle the order of the frames around or essentially randomize the data. We often randomize data this way to make our training stronger. By randomizing the data order, the network needs to learn an absolute steering value for an image, rather than a possible relative or incremental value. The following code does this shuffle:

```
import numpy as np
def unison_shuffled_copies(X, Y):
  assert len(X) == len(Y)
  p = np.random.permutation(len(X))
  return X[p], Y[p]

shuffled_X, shuffled_Y = unison_shuffled_copies(X,Y)
len(shuffled_X)
```

5. All this code does is use `numpy` to randomly shuffle the image frames. Then it prints out the length of the first shuffled set `shuffled_X` so we can confirm the training data is not getting lost.

6. Next, we need to create a training and test set of data. The training set is used to train the network (weights), and the test, or validation, set is used to confirm the accuracy on new or raw data. As we have seen before, this is a common theme when using supervised training or labeled data. We often break the data into 80% training and 20% test. The following code is what does this:

```
test_cutoff = int(len(X) * .8) # 80% of data used for training
val_cutoff = test_cutoff + int(len(X) * .2) # 20% of data used for
validation and test data
train_X, train_Y = shuffled_X[:test_cutoff],
shuffled_Y[:test_cutoff]
val_X, val_Y = shuffled_X[test_cutoff:val_cutoff],
shuffled_Y[test_cutoff:val_cutoff]
test_X, test_Y = shuffled_X[val_cutoff:], shuffled_Y[val_cutoff:]

len(train_X) + len(val_X) + len(test_X)
```

7. After creating the training and test sets, we now want to augment or expand the training data. In this particular case, the author augmented the data just by flipping the original images and adding those to the dataset. There are many other ways of augmenting data that we will discover in later chapters, but this simple and effective method of flipping is something to add to your belt of machine learning tools. The code to do this flip is shown here:

```
X_flipped = np.array([np.fliplr(i) for i in train_X])
Y_flipped = np.array([-i for i in train_Y])
train_X = np.concatenate([train_X, X_flipped])
train_Y = np.concatenate([train_Y, Y_flipped])
len(train_X)
```

8. Now comes the heavy lifting part. The data is prepped, and it is time to build the model as shown in the code:

```
from keras.models import Model, load_model
from keras.layers import Input, Convolution2D, MaxPooling2D,
Activation, Dropout, Flatten, Dense

img_in = Input(shape=(120, 160, 3), name='img_in')
angle_in = Input(shape=(1,), name='angle_in')

x = Convolution2D(8, 3, 3)(img_in)
x = Activation('relu')(x)
x = MaxPooling2D(pool_size=(2, 2))(x)

x = Convolution2D(16, 3, 3)(x)
x = Activation('relu')(x)
x = MaxPooling2D(pool_size=(2, 2))(x)
```

```
x = Convolution2D(32, 3, 3)(x)
x = Activation('relu')(x)
x = MaxPooling2D(pool_size=(2, 2))(x)

merged = Flatten()(x)

x = Dense(256)(merged)
x = Activation('linear')(x)
x = Dropout(.2)(x)

angle_out = Dense(1, name='angle_out')(x)

model = Model(input=[img_in], output=[angle_out])
model.compile(optimizer='adam', loss='mean_squared_error')
model.summary()
```

9. The code to build the model at this point should be fairly self-explanatory. Take note of the variation in the architecture and how the code is written from our previous examples. Also note the two highlighted lines. The first one uses a new layer type called `Flatten`. All this layer type does is flatten the 2 x 2 image into a vector that is then input into a standard `Dense` hidden fully connected layer. The second highlighted line introduces another new layer type called `Dropout`. This layer type needs a bit more explanation and will be covered in more detail at the end of this section.
10. Finally comes the training part, which this code sets up:

```
import os
from keras import callbacks

model_path = os.path.expanduser('~/best_autopilot.hdf5')

save_best = callbacks.ModelCheckpoint(model_path,
monitor='val_loss', verbose=1,
 save_best_only=True, mode='min')

early_stop = callbacks.EarlyStopping(monitor='val_loss',
min_delta=0, patience=5,
 verbose=0, mode='auto')

callbacks_list = [save_best, early_stop]

model.fit(train_X, train_Y, batch_size=64, epochs=4,
validation_data=(val_X, val_Y), callbacks=callbacks_list)
```

11. This last piece of code sets up a set of `callbacks` to update and control the training. We have already used callbacks to update the TensorBoard server with logs. In this case, we use the callbacks to resave the model after every checkpoint (epoch) and check for an early exit. Note the form in which we are saving the model – an `hdf5` file. This file format represents a hierarchical data structure.
12. Run the code as you have already been doing. This sample can take a while, so again be patient. When you are done, there will be no output, but pay special attention to the minimized loss value.

At this point in your deep learning career, you may be realizing that you need much more patience or a better computer or perhaps a TensorFlow-supported GPU. If you want to try the latter, feel free to download and install the TensorFlow GPU library and the other required libraries for your OS, as this will vary. Plenty of documentation can be found online. After you have the GPU version of TensorFlow installed, Keras will automatically try to use that. If you have a supported GPU, you should notice a performance increase, and if not, then consider buying one.

While there is no output for this example, in order to keep it simple, try to appreciate what is happening. After all, this could just as easily be set up as a driving game, where the network drives the vehicle by just looking at screenshots. We have omitted the results from the author's original blog post, but if you want to see how this performs further, go back and check out the `source link`.

One thing the author did in his blog post was to use pooling layers, which, as we have seen, is quite standard when working with convolution. However, when and how to use pooling layers is a bit contentious right now and requires further detailed discussion, which is provided in the next section.

Spatial convolution and pooling

Geoffrey Hinton and his team have recently strongly suggested that using pooling with convolution removes spatial relationships in the image. Hinton instead suggests the use of **CapsNet**, or **Capsule Networks**. Capsule Networks are a method of pooling that preserves the spatial integrity of the data. Now, this may not be a problem in all cases. For handwritten digits, spatial relationships don't matter that much. However, self-driving cars or networks tasked with spatial tasks, a prime example of which is games, often don't perform as well when using pooling. In fact, the team at Unity do not use pooling layers after convolution; let's understand why.

Pooling or down-sampling is a way of augmenting data by collecting its common features together. The problem with this is that any relationship in the data often gets lost entirely. The following diagram demonstrates **MaxPooling(2,2)** over a convolution map:

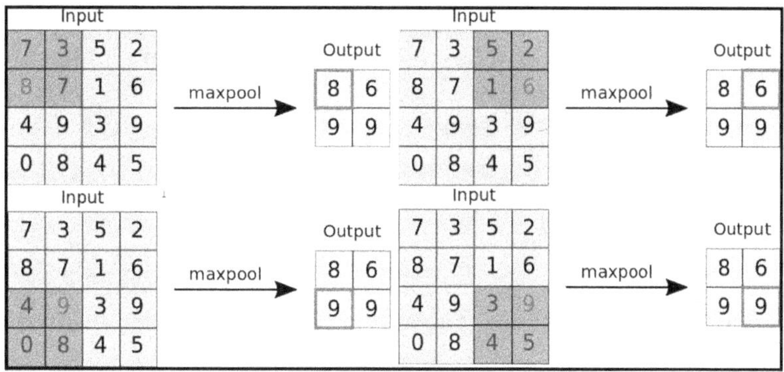

Max pooling at work

Even in the simple preceding diagram, you can quickly appreciate that pooling loses the spatial relationship of the corner (upper-left, bottom-left, lower-right and upper-right) the pooled value started in. Note that, after a couple layers of pooling, any sense of spatial relation will be completely gone.

We can test the effect of removing pooling layers from the model and test this again by following these steps:

1. Open the `Chapter_2_3.py` file and note how we commented out a couple of pooling layers, or you can just delete the lines as well, like so:

```
x = Convolution2D(8, 3, 3)(img_in)
x = Activation('relu')(x)
x = MaxPooling2D(pool_size=(2, 2))(x)

x = Convolution2D(16, 3, 3)(x)
x = Activation('relu')(x)
#x = MaxPooling2D(pool_size=(2, 2))(x)

x = Convolution2D(32, 3, 3)(x)
x = Activation('relu')(x)
#x = MaxPooling2D(pool_size=(2, 2))(x)
```

2. Note how we didn't comment out (or delete) all the pooling layers and left one in. In some cases, you may still want to leave a couple of pooling layers in, perhaps to identify features that are not spatially important. For example, when recognizing digits, space is less important with respect to the overall shape. However, if we consider recognizing a face, then the distance between a person's eyes, mouth, and so on, is what distinguishes a face from another face. However, if you just wanted to identify a face, with eyes, mouth, and so on, then just applying pooling could be quite acceptable.
3. Next, we also increase the dropout rate on our `Dropout` layer like so:

```
x = Dropout(.5)(x)
```

4. We will explore dropout in some detail in the next section. For now, though, just realize that this change will have a more positive effect on our model.
5. Lastly, we bump up the number of epochs to `10` with the following code:

```
model.fit(train_X, train_Y, batch_size=64, epochs=10,
validation_data=(val_X, val_Y), callbacks=callbacks_list)
```

6. In our previous run, if you were watching the loss rate when training, you would realize the last example more or less started to converge at four epochs. Since dropping the pooling layers also reduces the training data, we need to also bump up the number of epochs. Remember, pooling or down-sampling increases the number of feature maps, and fewer maps means the network needs more training runs. If you are not training on a GPU, this model will take a while, so be patient.
7. Finally, run the example, again with those minor changes. One of the first things you will notice is that the training time shoots up dramatically. Remember, this is because our pooling layers do facilitate quicker training, but at a cost. This is one of the reasons we allow for a single pooling layer.
8. When the sample is finished running, compare the results for the `Chapter_2_2.py` sample we ran earlier. Did it do what you expected it to?

We only focus on this particular blog post because it is extremely well presented and well written. The author obviously knew his stuff, but this example just shows how important it is to understand the fundamentals of these concepts in as much detail as you can handle. This is not such an easy task with the flood of information, but this also reinforces the fact that developing working deep learning models is not a trivial task, at least not yet.

Now that we understand the cost/penalty of pooling layers, we can move on to the next section, where we jump back to understanding `Dropout`. It is an excellent tool you will use over and over again.

The need for Dropout

Now, let's go back to our much-needed discussion about `Dropout`. We use dropout in deep learning as a way of randomly cutting network connections between layers during each iteration. An example showing an iteration of dropout being applied to three network layers is shown in the following diagram:

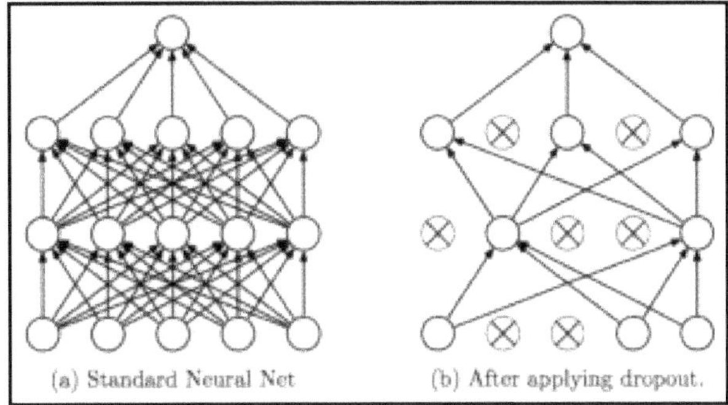

Before and after dropout

The important thing to understand is that the same connections are not always cut. This is done to allow the network to become less specialized and more generalized. Generalizing a model is a common theme in deep learning, and we often do this so our models can learn a broader set of problems, more quickly. Of course, there may be times where generalizing a network limits a network's ability to learn.

If we go back to the previous sample now and look at the code, we see a `Dropout` layer being used like so:

```
x = Dropout(.5)(x)
```

That simple line of code tells the network to drop out or disconnect 50% of the connections randomly after every iteration. Dropout only works for fully connected layers (**Input** -> **Dense** -> **Dense**) but is very useful as a way of improving performance or accuracy. This may or may not account for some of the improved performance from the previous example.

In the next section, we will look at how deep learning mimics the memory sub-process or temporal scent.

Memory and recurrent networks

Memory is often associated with **Recurrent Neural Network** (**RNN**), but that is not entirely an accurate association. An RNN is really only useful for storing a sequence of events or what you may refer to as a **temporal sense**, a sense of time if you will. RNNs do this by persisting state back onto itself in a recursive or recurrent loop. An example of how this looks is shown here:

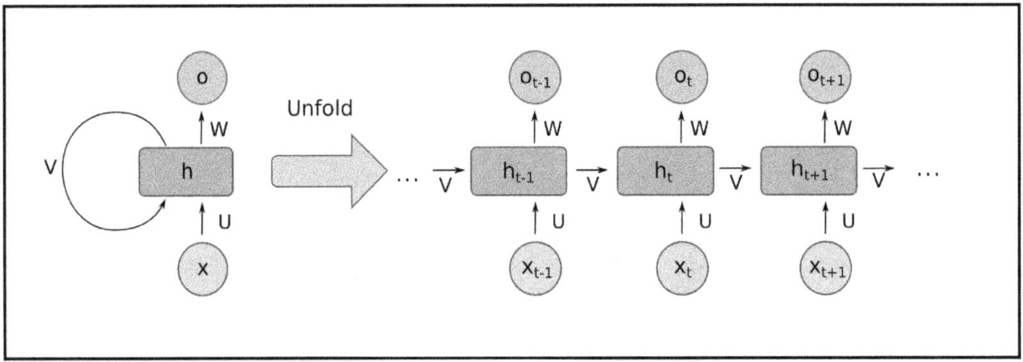

Unfolded recurrent neural network

What the diagram shows is the internal representation of a recurrent neuron that is set to track a number of time steps or iterations where **x** represents the input at a time step and **h** denotes the state. The network weights of **W**, **U**, and **V** remain the same for all time steps and are trained using a technique called **Backpropagation Through Time** (**BPTT**). We won't go into the math of BPTT and leave that up the reader to discover on their own, but just realize that the network weights in a recurrent network use a cost gradient method to optimize them.

A recurrent network allows a neural network to identify sequences of elements and predict what elements typically come next. This has huge applications in predicting text, stocks, and of course games. Pretty much any activity that can benefit from some grasp of time or sequence of events will benefit from using RNN, except standard RNN, the type shown previously, which fails to predict longer sequences due to a problem with gradients. We will get further into this problem and the solution in the next section.

Vanishing and exploding gradients rescued by LSTM

The problem the RNN suffers from is either vanishing or exploding gradients. This happens because, over time, the gradient we try to minimize or reduce becomes so small or big that any additional training has no effect. This limits the usefulness of the RNN, but fortunately this problem was corrected with **Long Short-Term Memory** (**LSTM**) blocks, as shown in this diagram:

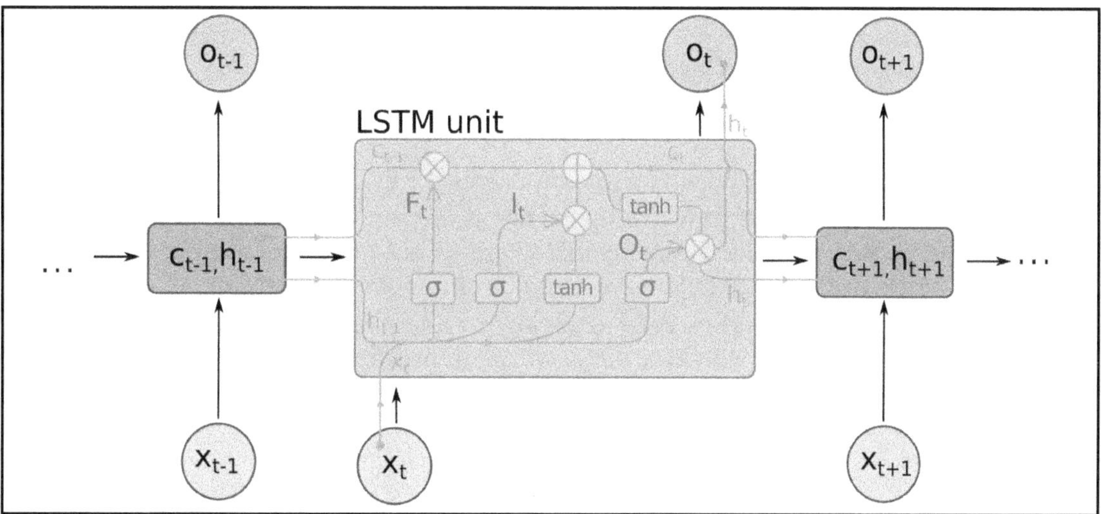

Example of an LSTM block

LSTM blocks overcome the vanishing gradient problem using a few techniques. Internally, in the diagram where you see a **x** inside a circle, it denotes a gate controlled by an activation function. In the diagram, the activation functions are **σ** and **tanh**. These activation functions work much like a step or ReLU do, and we may use either function for activation in a regular network layer. For the most part, we will treat an LSTM as a black box, and all you need to remember is that LSTMs overcome the gradient problem of RNN and can remember long-term sequences.

Let's take a look at a working example to see how this comes together. Open up `Chapter_2_4.py` and follow the these steps:

1. We begin as per usual by importing the various Keras pieces we need, as shown:

This example was pulled from `https://machinelearningmastery.com/understanding-stateful-lstm-recurrent-neural-networks-python-keras/`. This is a site hosted by **Dr. Jason Brownlee**, who has plenty more excellent examples explaining the use of LSTM and recurrent networks.

```
import numpy
from keras.models import Sequential
from keras.layers import Dense
from keras.layers import LSTM
from keras.utils import np_utils
```

2. This time we are importing two new classes, `Sequential` and `LSTM`. Of course we know what `LSTM` is for, but what about `Sequential`? `Sequential` is a form of model that defines the layers in a sequence one after another. We were less worried about this detail before, since our previous models were all sequential.
3. Next, we set the random seed to a known value. We do this so that our example can replicate itself. You may have noticed in previous examples that not all runs perform the same. In many cases, we want our training to be consistent, and hence we set a known seed value by using this code:

```
numpy.random.seed(7)
```

4. It is important to realize that this just sets the `numpy` random seed value. Other libraries may use different random number generators and require different seed settings. We will try to identify these inconsistencies in the future when possible.
5. Next, we need to identify a sequence we will train to; in this case, we will just use the `alphabet` as shown in this code:

```
alphabet = "ABCDEFGHIJKLMNOPQRSTUVWXYZ"

char_to_int = dict((c, i) for i, c in enumerate(alphabet))
int_to_char = dict((i, c) for i, c in enumerate(alphabet))

seq_length = 1
dataX = []
dataY = []

for i in range(0, len(alphabet) - seq_length, 1):
  seq_in = alphabet[i:i + seq_length]
  seq_out = alphabet[i + seq_length]
```

```
    dataX.append([char_to_int[char] for char in seq_in])
    dataY.append(char_to_int[seq_out])
    print(seq_in, '->', seq_out)
```

6. The preceding code builds our sequence of characters as integers and builds a map of each character sequence. It builds a `seq_in` and `seq_out` showing the forward and reverse positions. Since the length of a sequence is defined by `seq_length = 1`, then we are only concerned about a letter of the alphabet and the character that comes after it. You could, of course, do longer sequences.
7. With the sequence data built, it is time to shape the data and normalize it with this code:

```
X = numpy.reshape(dataX, (len(dataX), seq_length, 1))
# normalize
X = X / float(len(alphabet))
# one hot encode the output variable
y = np_utils.to_categorical(dataY)
```

8. The first line in the preceding code reshapes the data into a tensor with a size length of `dataX`, the number of steps or sequences, and the number of features to identify. We then normalize the data. Normalizing the data comes in many forms, but in this case we are normalizing values from 0 to 1. Then we one hot encode the output for easier training.

One hot encoding is where we you set the value to 1 where you have data or a response, and to zero everywhere else. In the example, our model output is 26 neurons, which could also be represented by 26 zeros, one zero for each neuron, like so:
00000000000000000000000000

Where each zero represents the matching character position in the alphabet. If we wanted to denote a character **A**, we would output the one hot encoded value as this:
10000000000000000000000000

9. Then we construct the model, using a slightly different form of code than we have seen before and as shown here:

```
model = Sequential()
model.add(LSTM(32, input_shape=(X.shape[1], X.shape[2])))
model.add(Dense(y.shape[1], activation='softmax'))
model.compile(loss='categorical_crossentropy', optimizer='adam',
metrics=['accuracy'])
model.fit(X, y, epochs=500, batch_size=1, verbose=2)
```

```
scores = model.evaluate(X, y, verbose=0)
print("Model Accuracy: %.2f%%" % (scores[1]*100))
```

10. The critical piece to the preceding code is the highlighted line that shows the construction of the `LSTM` layer. We construct an `LSTM` layer by setting the number of units, in this case `32`, since our sequence is 26 characters long and we want our units disable by `2`. Then we set the `input_shape` to match the previous tensor, `X`, that we created to hold our training data. In this case, we are just setting the shape to match all the characters (26) and the sequence length, in this case `1`.
11. Finally, we output the model with the following code:

```
for pattern in dataX:
  x = numpy.reshape(pattern, (1, len(pattern), 1))
  x = x / float(len(alphabet))
  prediction = model.predict(x, verbose=0)
  index = numpy.argmax(prediction)
  result = int_to_char[index]
  seq_in = [int_to_char[value] for value in pattern]
  print(seq_in, "->", result)
```

12. Run the code as you normally would and examine the output. You will notice that the accuracy is around 80%. See whether you can improve the accuracy of the model for predicting the next sequence in the alphabet.

This simple example demonstrated the basic use of an LSTM block for recognizing a simple sequence. In the next section, we look at a more complex example: using LSTM to play Rock, Paper, Scissors.

Playing Rock, Paper, Scissors with LSTMs

Remembering sequences of data have huge applications in many areas, not the least of which includes gaming. Of course, producing a simple, clean example is another matter. Fortunately, examples abound on the internet and `Chapter_2_5.py` shows an example of using an LSTM to play Rock, Paper, Scissors.

Open up that sample file and follow these steps:

This example was pulled from `https://github.com/hjpulkki/RPS`, but the code needed to be tweaked in several places to get it to work for us.

1. Let's start as we normally do with the imports. For this sample, be sure to have Keras installed as we did for the last set of exercises:

```
import numpy as np
from keras.utils import np_utils
from keras.models import Sequential
from keras.layers import Dense, LSTM
```

2. Then, we set some constants as shown:

```
EPOCH_NP = 100
INPUT_SHAPE = (1, -1, 1)
OUTPUT_SHAPE = (1, -1, 3)
DATA_FILE = "data.txt"
MODEL_FILE = "RPS_model.h5"
```

3. Then, we build the model, this time with three LSTM layers, one for each element in our sequence (rock, paper and scissors), like so:

```
def simple_model():
  new_model = Sequential()
  new_model.add(LSTM(output_dim=64, input_dim=1,
return_sequences=True, activation='sigmoid'))
  new_model.add(LSTM(output_dim=64, return_sequences=True,
activation='sigmoid'))
  new_model.add(LSTM(output_dim=64, return_sequences=True,
activation='sigmoid'))
  new_model.add(Dense(64, activation='relu'))
  new_model.add(Dense(64, activation='relu'))
  new_model.add(Dense(3, activation='softmax'))
  new_model.compile(loss='categorical_crossentropy',
optimizer='adam', metrics=['accuracy', 'categorical_crossentropy'])
  return new_model
```

4. Then we create a function to extract our data from the `data.txt` file. This file holds the sequences of training data using the following code:

```
def batch_generator(filename):
  with open('data.txt', 'r') as data_file:
    for line in data_file:
      data_vector = np.array(list(line[:-1]))
      input_data = data_vector[np.newaxis, :-1, np.newaxis]
      temp = np_utils.to_categorical(data_vector, num_classes=3)
      output_data = temp[np.newaxis, 1:]
      yield (input_data, output_data)
```

5. In this example, we are training each block of training through 100 epochs in the same order as they are in the file. A better method would be to train each training sequence in a random order.
6. Then we create the model:

```
# Create model
np.random.seed(7)
model = simple_model()
```

7. Train the data using a loop, with each iteration pulling a batch from the `data.txt` file:

```
for (input_data, output_data) in batch_generator('data.txt'):
  try:
    model.fit(input_data, output_data, epochs=100, batch_size=100)
  except:
    print("error")
```

8. Finally, we evaluate the results with a validation sequence as shown in this code:

```
print("evaluating")
validation =
'100101000110221110101002201101101101002201011012222210221011011101
011122110010101010101'
input_validation =
np.array(list(validation[:-1])).reshape(INPUT_SHAPE)
output_validation =
np_utils.to_categorical(np.array(list(validation[1:]))).reshape(OUT
PUT_SHAPE)
loss_and_metrics = model.evaluate(input_validation,
output_validation, batch_size=100)

print("\n Evaluation results")

for i in range(len(loss_and_metrics)):
```

```
    print(model.metrics_names[i], loss_and_metrics[i])

input_test = np.array([0, 0, 0, 1, 1, 1, 2, 2,
2]).reshape(INPUT_SHAPE)
res = model.predict(input_test)
prediction = np.argmax(res[0], axis=1)
print(res, prediction)

model.save(MODEL_FILE)
del model
```

9. Run the sample as you normally would. Check the results at the end and note how accurate the model gets at predicting the sequence.

Be sure to run through this simple example a few times and understand how the LSTM layers are set up. Pay special attention to the parameters and how they are set.

That concludes our quick look at understanding how to use recurrent aka LSTM blocks for recognizing and predicting sequences of data. We will of course use this versatile layer type many more times throughout the course of this book.

In the final section of this chapter, we again showcase a number of exercises you are encouraged to undertake for your own benefit.

Exercises

Complete the following exercises in your own time and to improve your own learning experience. Improving your understanding of the material will make you a more successful deep learner, and you will likely enjoy this book better as well:

1. In the `Chapter_2_1.py` example, change the `Conv2D` layers to use a different filter size. Run the sample again, and see what effect this has on training performance and accuracy.
2. Comment out or delete a couple of the `MaxPooling` layers and corresponding `UpSampling` layers in the `Chapter_2_1.py` example. Remember, if you remove a pooling layer between layers 2 and 3, you likewise need to remove the up-sampling to remain consistent. Run the sample again, and see what effect this has on training time, accuracy, and performance.
3. Alter the **Conv2D** layers in the `Chapter_2_2.py` example using a different filter size. See what effect this has on training.

4. Alter the **Conv2D** layers in the `Chapter_2_2.py` example by using a stride value of **2**. You may need to consult the **Keras** docs in order to do this. See what effect this has on training.
5. Alter the **MaxPooling** layers in the `Chapter_2_2.py` example by altering the pooling dimensions. See what effect this has on training.
6. Remove all or comment out different **MaxPooling** layers used in the `Chapter_2_3.py` example. What happens if all the pooling layers are commented out? Do you need to increase the training epochs now?
7. Alter the use of **Dropout** in the various examples used throughout this chapter. This includes adding dropout. Test the effects of using different levels of dropout.
8. Modify the sample in `Chapter_2_4.py` so that the model produces better accuracy. What do you need to do in order to improve training performance?
9. Modify the sample in `Chapter_2_4.py` to predict more than one character in the sequence. If you need help, go back and review the original blog post for more information.
10. What happens if you change the number of units that the three **LSTM** layers use in the `Chapter_2_5.py` example? What if you increase the value to 128, 32, or 16? Try these values to understand the effect they have.

Feel free to expand on these exercises on your own. Try to write a new example on your own as well, even if it is just a simple one. There really is no better way to learn to code than to write your own.

Summary

For this chapter and the last, we took a deep dive into the core elements of deep learning and neural networks. While our review in the last couple chapters was not extensive, it should give you a good base for continuing through the rest of the book. If you had troubles with any of the material in the first two chapters, turn back now and spend more time reviewing the previous material. It is important that you understand the basics of neural network architecture and the use of various specialized layers, as we covered in this chapter (CNN and RNN). Be sure you understand the basics of CNN and how to use it effectively in picking features and what the trade—offs are when using pooling or sub sampling. Also understand the concept of RNN and how and when to use LSTM blocks for predicting or detecting temporal events. Convolutional layers and LSTM blocks are now fundamental components of deep learning, and we will use them in several networks we build going forward.

In the next chapter, we start to build out our sample game for this book and introduce GANs, or generative adversarial networks. We will explore GANs and how they can be used to generate game content.

3
GAN for Games

Thus far, in our deep learning exploration, we have trained all our networks using a technique called **supervised training**. This training technique works well for when you have taken the time to identify and label your data. All of our previous example exercises used supervised training, because it is the simplest form of teaching. However, supervised learning tends to be the most cumbersome and tedious method, largely because it requires some amount of data labeling or identification before training. There have been attempts to use this form of training for machine learning or deep learning in gaming and simulation, but they have proven to be unsuccessful.

This is why, for most of this book, we will look at other forms of training, starting with a form of unsupervised training called a **generative adversarial network** (**GAN**). GANs are able to train themselves using, in essence, a two-player game. This makes them an ideal next step in our learning and a perfect way to actually start generating content for games.

In this chapter, we explore GANs and their use in developing game content. Along the way, we will learn more fundamentals of deep learning techniques. In this chapter, we will cover the following content:

- Introducing GANs
- Coding a GAN in Keras
- Wasserstein GAN
- GAN for creating textures
- Generating music with a GAN
- Exercises

GANs are notoriously hard to train and build successfully. Therefore, it is recommended you take your time with this chapter and go through the exercises a couple of times if you need to. The techniques we learn to make effective GANs will provide you with a better overall understanding of training networks and the many other options available. We also still need to cover many fundamental concepts about training networks, so please work through this chapter thoroughly.

Introducing GANs

The concept of GANs is typically introduced using the analogy of a two-player game. In this game, there is typically an art expert and an art forger. The goal of the art forger or counterfeiter is to make a convincing-enough fake to fool the art expert and thus win the game. An example of how this was first portrayed as a neural network is as follows:

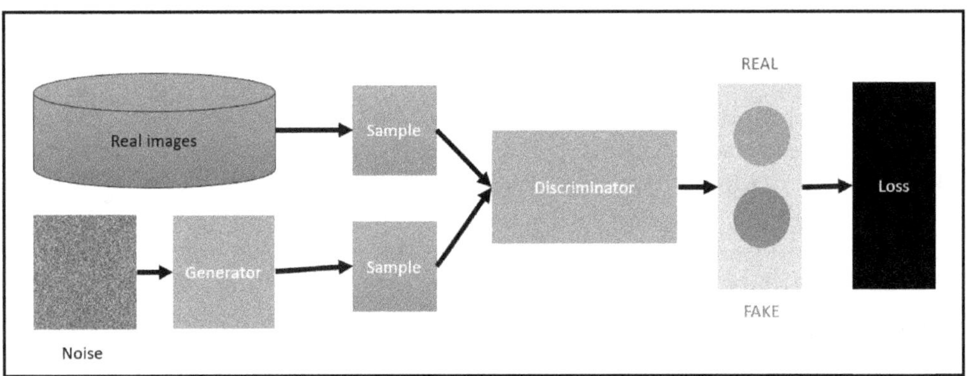

GAN by Ian and others

In the preceding diagram, the **Generator** takes the place of the art forger, the one trying to best the art expert, shown as the **Discriminator**. The **Generator** uses random noise as a source to generate an image, with a goal that the image is convincing enough to fool the **Discriminator**. The **Discriminator** is trained on both real and fake images, and all it does is classify the image as real or fake. The **Generator** is then trained to build a convincing-enough fake that will fool the **Discriminator**. While this concept seems simple enough as a way of self-training a network, in the last few years, the implementation of this adversarial technique has proven exceptional in many areas.

GANs were first developed by Ian Goodfellow and others at the University of Montreal in 2014. In only a few short years, this technique has exploded into many wide and varied applications, from generating images and text to animating static images, all in a very short time. The following is a short summary of some of the more impressive GAN improvements/implementations currently turning heads in the deep learning community:

- **Deep convolutional GANs** (**DCGANs**): These were the first major improvement to the standard architecture we just covered. We will explore this as our first form of GAN in the next section of this chapter.

- **Adversarial Autoencoder GAN**: This variation of an autoencoder uses the adversarial GAN technique to isolate attributes or properties of your data. It has interesting applications for determining latent relationships in data, such as being able to tell the difference in style versus content for a set of handwritten digits, for instance.
- **Auxiliary Classifier GAN**: This is another enhanced GAN that relates to conditioned or conditional GANs. It has been shown to synthesize higher-resolution images and is certainly worth exploring more in gaming.
- **CycleGAN**: This is a variation that is impressive in that it allows the translation of style from one image to another. There are plenty of examples of this form of GAN being used to style a picture as if Van Gogh painted it, to swapping celebrity faces. If this chapter piques your interest in GANs and you want to explore this form, check out this post: `https://hardikbansal.github.io/CycleGANBlog/`.
- **Conditional GANS**: These use a form of semi-supervised learning. This means that the training data is labeled but with meta data or attributes. So, instead of labeling a handwritten digit from the MNIST data set as a 9, you may instead label the writing style (cursive or print). Then, this new form of conditioned GAN can learn not only the digits, but also whether they are cursive or print. This form of GAN has shown some interesting applications and it is one we will explore further when we speak to specific applications in gaming.
- **DiscoGAN**: This is yet another form of GAN showing fun results, from swapping celebrity hairstyles to genders. This GAN extracts features or domains and allows you to transfer them to other images or data spaces. This GAN has numerous applications in gaming and is certainly worth exploring further for the interested reader.
- **DualGAN**: This uses dual GANs to train two generators against two discriminators in order to transfer images or data to other styles. This would be very useful as a way of restyling multiple assets and would work nicely for generating different forms of art content for games.
- **Least squares GAN** (**LSGAN**): This uses a different form of calculating loss and has been shown to be more effective than the DCGAN.
- **pix2pixGAN**: This is an extension to conditional GANs that allows it to transfer or generate multiple features from one image to another. This allows for images of the sketch of an object to return an actual 3D-rendered image of the same object or vice versa. While this is a very powerful GAN, it still is very much research-driven and may not be ready for use in games. Perhaps you will just have to wait six months or a year.

- **InfoGANs**: These types of GANs are, as of yet, used extensively to explore features or information about the training data. They can be used to identify the rotation of a digit in the MNIST dataset, for instance. Also, they are often used as a way of identifying attributes for conditioned GAN training.
- **Stacked or SGAN**: This is a form of GAN that breaks itself into layers where each layer is a generator and discriminator battling it out. This makes the overall GAN easier to train but also requires you to understand each stage or layer in some detail. If you are just starting, this is not the GAN for you, but as you build more complex networks, revisit this model again.
- **Wasserstein GANs**: This is a state-of-the-art GAN, and it will also get attention in its own section in this chapter. The calculation of loss is the improvement in this form of GAN.
- **WassGANs**: This uses the Wasserstein distance to determine loss, which dramatically helps with model convergence.

We will explore further instances of specific GAN implementations as we work through this chapter. Here, we will look at how to generate game textures and music with a GAN. For now, though, let's move on to the next section and learn how to code a GAN in Keras.

Coding a GAN in Keras

Of course, the best way to learn is by doing, so let's jump in and start coding our first GAN. In this example, we will be building the basic DCGAN and then modifying it later for our purposes. Open up `Chapter_3_2.py` and follow these steps:

This code was originally pulled from `https://github.com/eriklindernoren/Keras-GAN`, which is the best representation of GANs in Keras anywhere, and is all thanks to Erik Linder-Norén. Great job, and thanks for the hard work, Erik.

An alternate listing a vanilla GAN has been added as `Chapter_3_1.py` for your learning pleasure.

1. We start by importing libraries:

```
from __future__ import print_function, division
from keras.datasets import mnist
from keras.layers import Input, Dense, Reshape, Flatten, Dropout
from keras.layers import BatchNormalization, Activation,
ZeroPadding2D
from keras.layers.advanced_activations import LeakyReLU
```

```
from keras.layers.convolutional import UpSampling2D, Conv2D
from keras.models import Sequential, Model
from keras.optimizers import Adam
import matplotlib.pyplot as plt
import sys
import numpy as np
```

2. There are a few highlighted new types introduced in the preceding code: `Reshape`, `BatchNormalization`, `ZeroPadding2D`, `LeakyReLU`, `Model`, and `Adam`. We will explore each of these types in more detail next.
3. Most of our previous examples worked with basic scripts. We are now at a point where we want types (classes) of our own built for further use later. That means we now start by defining our class like so:

```
class DCGAN():
```

4. So, we create a new class (type) called `DCGAN` for our implementation of a deep convolutional GAN.
5. Next, we would normally define our `init` function by Python convention. However, for our purposes, let's first look at the `generator` function:

```
def build_generator(self):
  model = Sequential()
  model.add(Dense(128 * 7 * 7, activation="relu",
input_dim=self.latent_dim))
  model.add(Reshape((7, 7, 128)))
  model.add(UpSampling2D())
  model.add(Conv2D(128, kernel_size=3, padding="same"))
  model.add(BatchNormalization(momentum=0.8))
  model.add(Activation("relu"))
  model.add(UpSampling2D())
  model.add(Conv2D(64, kernel_size=3, padding="same"))
  model.add(BatchNormalization(momentum=0.8))
  model.add(Activation("relu"))
  model.add(Conv2D(self.channels, kernel_size=3, padding="same"))
  model.add(Activation("tanh"))
  model.summary()

  noise = Input(shape=(self.latent_dim,))
  img = model(noise)
  return Model(noise, img)
```

6. The `build_generator` function builds the art-forger model, which means it takes that sample set of noise and tries to convert it into an image the discriminator will believe is real. In this form, it uses the principle of convolution to make it more efficient, except, in this case, it generates a feature map of noise that it then turns into a real image. Essentially, the generator is doing the opposite of recognizing an image, but instead trying to generate an image based on feature maps.
   In the preceding block of code, note how the input starts with `128, 7x7` feature maps of noise then uses a `Reshape` layer to turn it into the proper image layout we want to create. It then up-samples (the reverse of pooling or down-sampling) the feature map into 2x size (14 x 14), training another layer of convolution followed by more up-sampling (2x to 28 x 28) until the correct image size (28x28 for the MNIST) is generated. We also see the use of a new layer type called `BatchNormalization`, which we will cover in more detail shortly.
7. Next, we will build the `build_discriminator` function like so:

```
def build_discriminator(self):
  model = Sequential()
  model.add(Conv2D(32, kernel_size=3, strides=2,
input_shape=self.img_shape, padding="same"))
  model.add(LeakyReLU(alpha=0.2))
  model.add(Dropout(0.25))
  model.add(Conv2D(64, kernel_size=3, strides=2, padding="same"))
  model.add(ZeroPadding2D(padding=((0,1),(0,1))))
  model.add(BatchNormalization(momentum=0.8))
  model.add(LeakyReLU(alpha=0.2))
  model.add(Dropout(0.25))
  model.add(Conv2D(128, kernel_size=3, strides=2, padding="same"))
  model.add(BatchNormalization(momentum=0.8))
  model.add(LeakyReLU(alpha=0.2))
  model.add(Dropout(0.25))
  model.add(Conv2D(256, kernel_size=3, strides=1, padding="same"))
  model.add(BatchNormalization(momentum=0.8))
  model.add(LeakyReLU(alpha=0.2))
  model.add(Dropout(0.25))
  model.add(Flatten())
  model.add(Dense(1, activation='sigmoid'))
  model.summary()

  img = Input(shape=self.img_shape)
  validity = model(img)
  return Model(img, validity)
```

8. This time, the discriminator is testing the image inputs and determining whether they are fake. It uses convolution to identify features, but in this example it uses `ZeroPadding2D` to place a buffer of zeros around the images in order to help identification. The opposite form of this layer would be `Cropping2D`, which crops an image. Note how this model does not use down-sampling or pooling with the convolution. We will explore the other new special layers `LeakyReLU` and `BatchNormalization` in the coming sections. Note how we have not used any pooling layers in our convolution. This is done to increase the spatial dimensionality through the fractionally strided convolutions. See how inside the convolution layers we are using an odd kernel and stride size.
9. We will now circle back and define the `init` function like so:

```
def __init__(self):
  self.img_rows = 28
  self.img_cols = 28
  self.channels = 1
  self.img_shape = (self.img_rows, self.img_cols, self.channels)
  self.latent_dim = 100
  optimizer = Adam(0.0002, 0.5)

  self.discriminator = self.build_discriminator()
  self.discriminator.compile(loss='binary_crossentropy',
  optimizer=optimizer, metrics=['accuracy'])

  self.generator = self.build_generator()
  z = Input(shape=(self.latent_dim,))
  img = self.generator(z)
  self.discriminator.trainable = False
  valid = self.discriminator(img)
  self.combined = Model(z, valid)
  self.combined.compile(loss='binary_crossentropy',
optimizer=optimizer)
```

10. This initialization code sets up the sizes for our input images (28 x 28 x 1, one channel for grayscale). It then sets up an `Adam` optimizer, something else we will review in another section on optimizers. After this, it builds the `discriminator` and then the `generator`. Then it combines the two models or sub networks (`generator` and `discriminator`) together. This allows the networks to work in tandem and optimize training across an entire network. Again, this is a concept we will look at more closely under optimizers.
11. Before we get too deep, take some time to run this example. This sample can take an extensive amount of time to run, so return to the book after it starts and keep it running.

12. As the sample runs, you will be able to see the generated output get placed into a folder called `images` within the same folder as your running Python file. Go ahead and watch as every 50 epochs a new image is saved, which is shown in the following diagram:

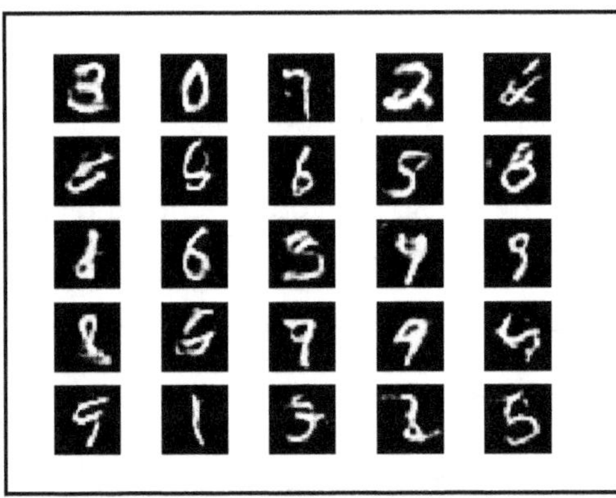

Example of output generated from a GAN

The preceding shows the results after 3,900 epochs or so. When you start training, it will take a while to get results this good.

That covers the basics of setting up the models, except all the work that is in the training, which we will cover in the next section.

Training a GAN

Training a GAN requires a fair bit more attention to detail and an understanding of more advanced optimization techniques. We will walk through each section of this function in detail in order to understand the intricacies of training. Let's open up `Chapter_3_1.py` and look at the `train` function and follow these steps:

1. At the start of the `train` function, you will see the following code:

```
def train(self, epochs, batch_size=128, save_interval=50):
  (X_train, _), (_, _) = mnist.load_data()
  X_train = X_train / 127.5 - 1.
  X_train = np.expand_dims(X_train, axis=3)

  valid = np.ones((batch_size, 1))
  fake = np.zeros((batch_size, 1))
```

2. The data is first loaded from the MNIST training set and then rescaled to the range of `-1` to `1`. We do this in order to better center that data around 0 and to accommodate our activation function, `tanh`. If you go back to the generator function, you will see that the bottom activation is `tanh`.
3. Next, we build a `for` loop to iterate through the epochs like so:

```
for epoch in range(epochs):
```

4. Then we randomly select half of the *real* training images, using this code:

```
idx = np.random.randint(0, X_train.shape[0], batch_size)
imgs = X_train[idx]
```

5. After that, we sample `noise` and generate a set of forged images with the following code:

```
noise = np.random.normal(0, 1, (batch_size, self.latent_dim))
gen_imgs = self.generator.predict(noise)
```

6. Now, half of the images are real and the other half are faked by our `generator`.
7. Next, the `discriminator` is trained against the images generating a loss for incorrectly predicted fakes and correctly identified real images as shown:

```
d_loss_real = self.discriminator.train_on_batch(imgs, valid)
d_loss_fake = self.discriminator.train_on_batch(gen_imgs, fake)
d_loss = 0.5 * np.add(d_loss_real, d_loss_fake)
```

8. Remember, this block of code is running across a set or batch. This is why we use the `numpy` `np.add` function to add the `d_loss_real`, and `d_loss_fake`. `numpy` is a library we will often use to work on sets or tensors of data.
9. Finally, we train the generator using the following code:

```
g_loss = self.combined.train_on_batch(noise, valid)

print ("%d [D loss: %f, acc.: %.2f%%] [G loss: %f]" % (epoch,
d_loss[0], 100*d_loss[1], g_loss))

if epoch % save_interval == 0:
  self.save_imgs(epoch)
```

10. Note how the `g_loss` is calculated based on training the combined model. As you may recall, the combined model takes the input from real and fake images and backpropagates the training back through the entire model. This allows us to train both the `generator` and `discriminator` together as a combined model. An example of how this looks is shown next, but just note that the image sizes are a little different than ours:

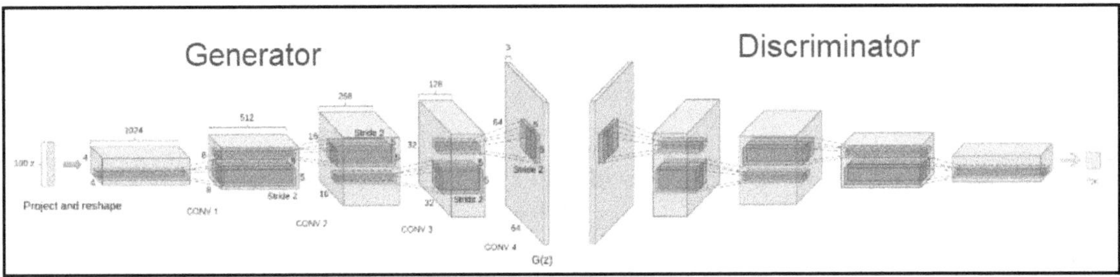

Layer architecture diagram of DCGAN

Now that we have a better understanding of the architecture, we need to go back and understand some details about the new layer types and the optimization of the combined model. We will look at how we can optimize a joined model such as our GAN in the next section.

Optimizers

An **optimizer** is really nothing more than another way to train the backpropagation of error through a network. As we learned back in `Chapter 1`, *Deep Learning for Games*, the base algorithm we use for backpropagation is the gradient descent and the more advanced **stochastic gradient descent** (**SGD**).

SGD works by altering the evaluation of the gradient by randomly picking the batch order during each training iteration. While SGD works well for most cases, it does not perform well in a GAN, due to a problem known as the **vanishing / exploding gradient**, which happens when trying to train multiple, but combined, networks. Remember, we are directly feeding the results of our generator into the discriminator. Instead, we look to more advanced optimizers. A graph showing the performance of the typical best optimizers is shown in the following diagram:

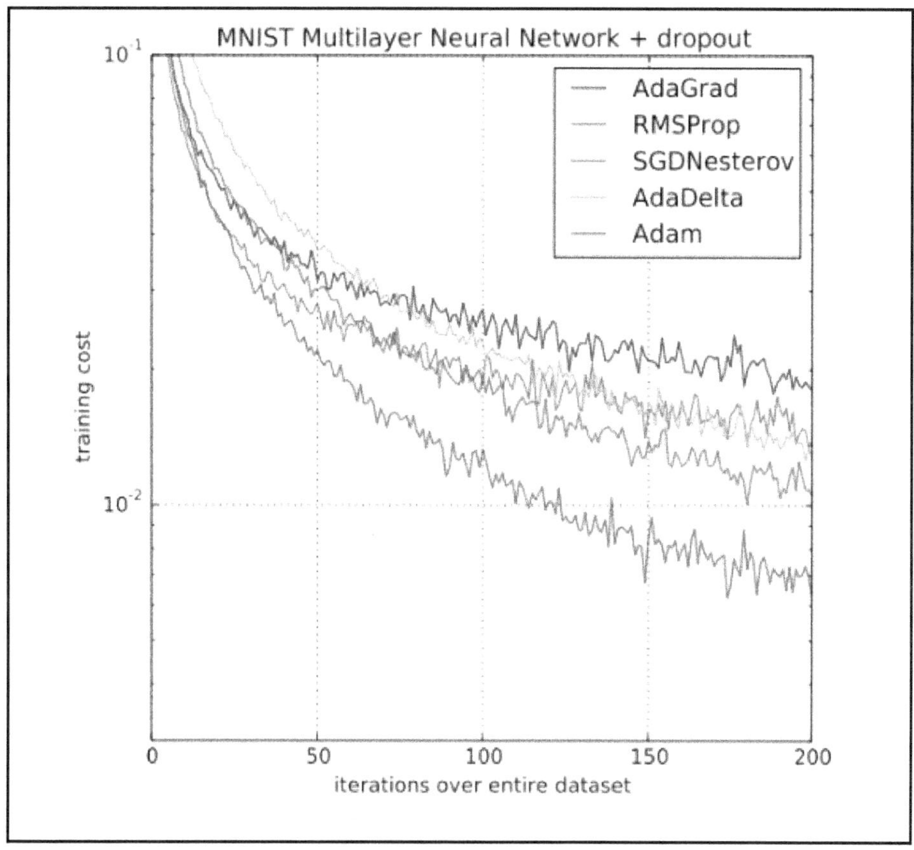

Performance comparison of various optimizers

All of the methods in the graph have their origin in SGD, but you can clearly see the winner in this instance is **Adam**. There are cases where this is not the case, but the current favorite optimizer is Adam. It is something we have used extensively before, as you may have noticed, and you will likely continue using it in the future. However, let's take a look at each of the optimizers in a little more detail, as follows:

- **SGD**: This is one of the first models we looked at and it will often be our baseline to train against.

- **SGD with Nesterov**: The problem SGD often faces is that wobble effect we saw in network loss, in one of the earlier training examples. Remember, during training, our network loss would fluctuate between two values, almost as if it was a ball going up and down a hill. In essence, that is exactly what is happening, but we can correct that by introducing a term we call **momentum**. An example of the effect momentum has on training is shown in the following diagram:

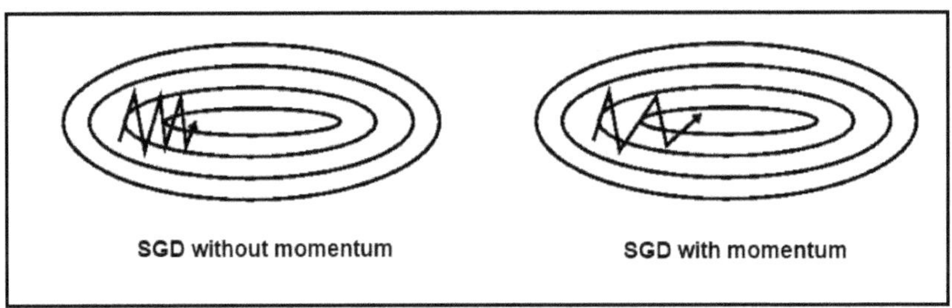

SGD with and without momentum

  So, now, instead of just letting the ball blindly roll around, we control its speed. We give it a push to get over some of those annoying bumps or wobbles, and more efficiently get to the lowest point.

  As you may recall from studying the math of backpropagation, we control the gradient in SGD to train the network to minimize error or loss. By introducing momentum, we try to control the gradient to be more efficient by approximating what the values should be. The **Nesterov technique**, or it may just be referred to as **Momentum**, uses an accelerated momentum term to further optimize the gradient.

- **AdaGrad**: This method optimizes the individual training parameters based on the frequency of the updates, which makes it ideal for working with smaller datasets. The other main benefit is that it allows you to not have to tune the learning rate. However, a big weakness with this method is squared gradients causing the learning rate to become so small that the network stops learning.
- **AdaDelta**: This method is an extension to AdaGrad, which deals with the squared gradients and vanishing learning rate. It does this by fixing the learning rate window to a particular minimum.
- **RMSProp**: Developed by Geoff Hinton, the grandfather of deep learning, this is a technique to manage the vanishing learning rate problem in AdaGrad. As you can see in the graph, it is on par with AdaDelta for the sample shown.

- **Adaptive Moment Estimation** (**Adam**): This is another technique that attempts to control that gradient using a more controlled version of Momentum. It is often described as Momentum plus RMSProp, since it combines the best of both techniques.
- **AdaMax**: This method is not shown on the performance graph but is worth mentioning. It is an extension to Adam that generalizes each iteration of an update applied to the momentum.
- **Nadam**: This is another method not on the graph; it is a combination of Nesterov-accelerated Momentum and Adam. The vanilla Adam just uses a Momentum term that is not accelerated.
- **AMSGrad**: This is a variation of Adam that works best when Adam is shown to be unable to converge or wobble. This is caused by the algorithm failing to adapt learning rates and is fixed by taking a maximum rather than an average of previously squared gradients. The difference is subtle and tends to prefer smaller datasets. Keep this option in the back of your mind as a possible future tool.

That completes our short overview of optimizers; be sure to refer to the exercises at the end of the chapter for ways you can explore them further. In the next section, we build our own GAN that can generate textures we can use in games.

Wasserstein GAN

As you can most certainly appreciate by now, GANs have wide and varied applications, several of which apply very well to games. One such application is the generation of textures or texture variations. We often want slight variations in textures to give our game worlds a more convincing look. This is and can be done with **shaders**, but for performance reasons, it is often best to create **static assets**.

Therefore, in this section, we will build a GAN project that allows us to generate textures or height maps. You could also extend this concept using any of the other cool GANs we briefly touched on earlier. We will be using a default implementation of the Wasserstein GAN by Erik Linder-Norén and converting it for our purposes.

One of the major hurdles you will face when first approaching deep learning problems is shaping data to the form you need. In the original sample, Erik used the MNIST dataset, but we will convert the sample to use the CIFAR100 dataset. The CIFAR100 dataset is a set of color images classified by type, as follows:

CIFAR 100 dataset

For now, though, let's open up `Chapter_3_wgan.py` and follow these steps:

1. Open the Python file and review the code. Most of the code will look the same as the DCGAN we already looked at. However, there are a few key differences we want to look at, as follows:

```
def train(self, epochs, batch_size=128, sample_interval=50):
  (X_train, _), (_, _) = mnist.load_data()

  X_train = (X_train.astype(np.float32) - 127.5) / 127.5
  X_train = np.expand_dims(X_train, axis=3)

  valid = -np.ones((batch_size, 1))
  fake = np.ones((batch_size, 1))

  for epoch in range(epochs):
    for _ in range(self.n_critic):
      idx = np.random.randint(0, X_train.shape[0], batch_size)
      imgs = X_train[idx]
      noise = np.random.normal(0, 1, (batch_size, self.latent_dim))
```

```
            gen_imgs = self.generator.predict(noise)

            d_loss_real = self.critic.train_on_batch(imgs, valid)
            d_loss_fake = self.critic.train_on_batch(gen_imgs, fake)
            d_loss = 0.5 * np.add(d_loss_fake, d_loss_real)
            for l in self.critic.layers:
              weights = l.get_weights()
              weights = [np.clip(w, -self.clip_value, self.clip_value)
for
              w in weights]
              l.set_weights(weights)

          g_loss = self.combined.train_on_batch(noise, valid)
          print ("%d [D loss: %f] [G loss: %f]" % (epoch, 1 - d_loss[0],
1
          - g_loss[0]))\

          if epoch % sample_interval == 0:
            self.sample_images(epoch)
```

2. The Wasserstein GAN uses a distance function in order to determine the cost or loss for each training iteration. Along with this, this form of GAN uses multiple critics rather than a single discriminator to determine cost or loss. Training multiple critics together improves performance and handles the vanishing gradient problem we often see plaguing GANs. An example of a different form of GAN training is as follows:

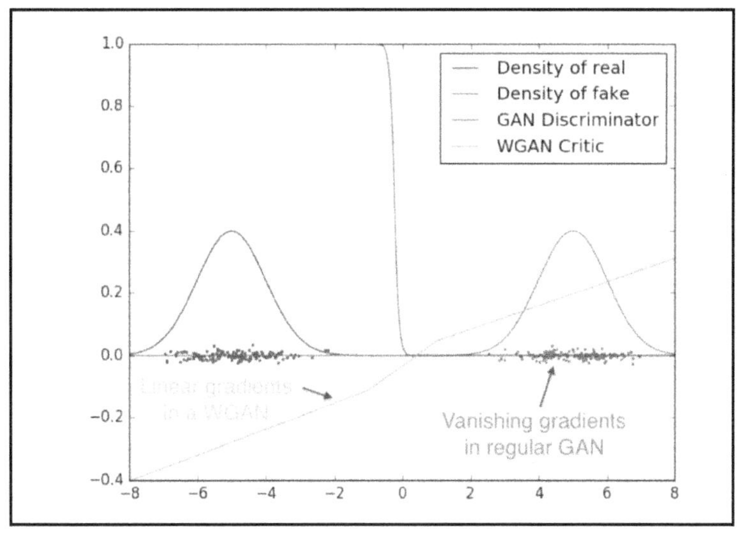

Training performance across GAN implementations (https://arxiv.org/pdf/1701.07875.pdf)

3. A WGAN overcomes the gradient problem by managing cost through a distance function that determines the cost of moving, rather than a difference in error values. A linear cost function could be as simple as the number of moves a character needs to take in order to spell a word correctly. For example, the word *SOPT* would have a cost of 2, since the *T* character needs to move two places to spell *STOP* correctly. The word *OTPS* has a distance cost of *3 (S) + 1 (T) = 4* to spell *STOP* correctly.
4. The Wasserstein distance function essentially determines the cost of transforming one probability distribution to another. As you can imagine, the math to understand this can be quite complex, so we will defer that to the more interested reader.
5. Run the example. This sample can take a significant time to run, so be patient. Also, this sample has been shown to have trouble training on some GPU hardware. If you find this to be the case, just disable the use of GPU.
6. As the sample runs, open the `images` folder from the same folder as the Python file and watch the training images generate.

Run the sample for as long as you feel the need to in order to understand how it works. This sample can take several hours even on advanced hardware. When you are done, move on to the next section, and we will see how to modify this sample for generating textures.

Generating textures with a GAN

One of the things so rarely covered in advanced deep learning books is the specifics of shaping data to input into a network. Along with shaping data is the need to alter the internals of a network to accommodate the new data. The final version of this example is `Chapter_3_3.py`, but for this exercise, start with the `Chapter_3_wgan.py` file and follow these steps:

1. We will start by changing the training set of data from MNIST to CIFAR by swapping out the imports like so:

```
from keras.datasets import mnist  #remove or leave
from keras.datasets import cifar100  #add
```

2. At the start of the class, we will change the image size parameters from 28 x 28 grayscale to 32 x 32 color like so:

```
class WGAN():
  def __init__(self):
    self.img_rows = 32
    self.img_cols = 32
    self.channels = 3
```

3. Now, move down to the `train` function and alter the code as follows:

```
#(X_train, _), (_, _) = mnist.load_data() or delete me
(X_train, y), (_, _) = cifar100.load_data(label_mode='fine')
Z_train = []
cnt = 0
for i in range(0,len(y)):
  if y[i] == 33:  #forest images
  cnt = cnt + 1
  z = X_train[i]
  Z_train.append(z)
#X_train = (X_train.astype(np.float32) - 127.5) / 127.5 or delete
me
#X_train = np.expand_dims(X_train, axis=3)
Z_train = np.reshape(Z_train, [500, 32, 32, 3])
Z_train = (Z_train.astype(np.float32) - 127.5) / 127.5

#X_train = (X_train.astype(np.float32) - 127.5) / 127.5
#X_train = np.expand_dims(X_train, axis=3)
```

4. This code loads the images from the CIFAR100 dataset and sorts through them by label. Labels are stored in the `y` variable, and the code loops through all the downloaded images and isolates those to one specific set. In this case, we are using the label `33`, which corresponds to forest images. There are 100 categories in the CIFAR100, and we are selecting one category that holds 500 images. Feel free to try to generate other textures from other categories.
   The rest of the code is fairly straightforward, except for the `np.reshape` call where we reshape the data into a list of 500 images `32x32` pixels by three channels. You may also want to note that we do not need to expand the axis to three as we did before. This is because our image is already scaled to three channels.

5. We now need to go back to the generator and critic models and alter that code slightly. First, we will change the generator like so:

```
def build_generator(self):
  model = Sequential()
  model.add(Dense(128 * 8 * 8, activation="relu",
input_dim=self.latent_dim))
  model.add(Reshape((8, 8, 128)))
  model.add(UpSampling2D())
  model.add(Conv2D(128, kernel_size=4, padding="same"))
  model.add(BatchNormalization(momentum=0.8))
  model.add(Activation("relu"))
  model.add(UpSampling2D())
  model.add(Conv2D(64, kernel_size=4, padding="same"))
  model.add(BatchNormalization(momentum=0.8))
  model.add(Activation("relu"))
  model.add(Conv2D(self.channels, kernel_size=4, padding="same"))
  model.add(Activation("tanh"))
  model.summary()
  noise = Input(shape=(self.latent_dim,))
  img = model(noise)
  return Model(noise, img)
```

6. The boldface code denotes the changes. All we are doing for this model is converting the `7x7` original feature map to `8x8`. Recall that the original full image size is `28x28`. Our convolution starts with a `7x7` feature map, doubled twice, which equals `28x28`. Since our new image size is `32x32`, we need to convert our network to start with `8x8` feature maps, which doubled twice equals `32x32`, the same size as the CIFAR100 images. Fortunately, we can leave the critic model as it is.
7. Next, we add a new function to save samples of the original CIFAR images, and this is shown here:

```
def save_images(self, imgs, epoch):
  r, c = 5, 5
  gen_imgs = 0.5 * imgs + 1
  fig, axs = plt.subplots(r, c)
  cnt = 0
  for i in range(r):
    for j in range(c):
      axs[i,j].imshow(gen_imgs[cnt, :,:,0],cmap='gray')
      axs[i,j].axis('off')
      cnt += 1

  fig.savefig("images/cifar_%d.png" % epoch)
  plt.close()
```

8. The `save_images` function outputs a sampling of the original images and is called by the following code in the `train` function:

```
idx = np.random.randint(0, Z_train.shape[0], batch_size)
imgs = Z_train[idx]
if epoch % sample_interval == 0:
  self.save_images(imgs, epoch)
```

9. The new code is in boldface and just outputs what a sampling of the originals looks like, as follows:

Example of the original images

10. Run the sample and observe the output in the `images` folder again labeled `cifar`, showing the result of training. Again, this sample can take some time to run, so read on to the next section.

As the sample runs, you can observe how the GAN is training to match the images. The benefit here is that you can generate various textures easily using a variety of techniques. You can use these as textures or height maps in Unity or another game engine. Before we finish up this section, let's jump into some normalization and other parameters.

Batch normalization

Batch normalization, as its name suggests, normalizes the distribution of weights in a layer around some mean of 0. This allows for the network to use a higher learning while still avoiding a vanishing or exploding gradient problem. It is due to the weights being normalized, which allows for fewer shifts or training wobble, as we have seen before.

By normalizing the weights in a layer, we allow for the network to use a higher learning rate and thus train faster. Also, we can avoid or reduce the need to use `DropOut`. You will see that we use the standard term, shown here, to normalize the layers:

```
model.add(BatchNormalization(momentum=0.8))
```

Recall from our discussions of optimizers that momentum controls how quickly or slowly we want to decrease the training gradient. In this case, momentum refers to the amount of change of the mean or center of the normalized distribution.

In the next section, we look at another special layer called LeakyReLU.

Leaky and other ReLUs

LeakyReLU adds an activation layer that allows for negative values to have a small slope, rather than just 0, as in the case of the standard ReLU activation function. The standard ReLU encourages sparsity in the network by only allowing neurons with positive activation to fire. However, this also creates a dead neuron state, where parts of the network essentially die off or become untrainable. To overcome this issue, we introduce a leaky form of ReLU activation called LeakyReLU. An example of how this activation works is shown here:

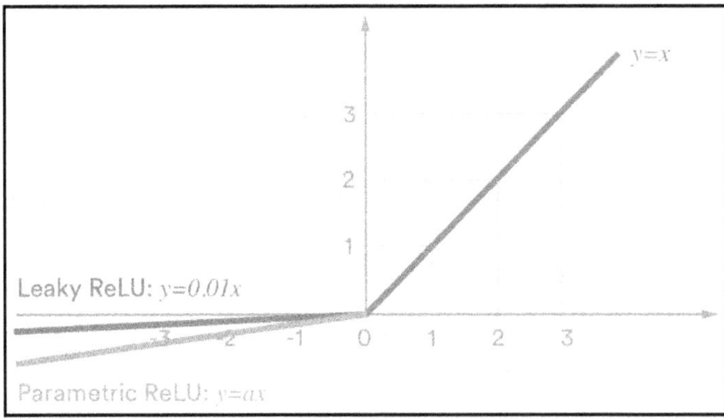

Example of a leaky and parametric ReLU

Pictured in the preceding diagram is **Parametric ReLU**, which is similar to Leaky, but it allows the network to train the parameter itself. This allows the network to adjust on its own, but it will take longer to train.

The other ReLU variants you can use are summarized here:

- **Exponential Linear** (**ELU, SELU**): These forms of ReLU activate as shown in the diagram as follows:

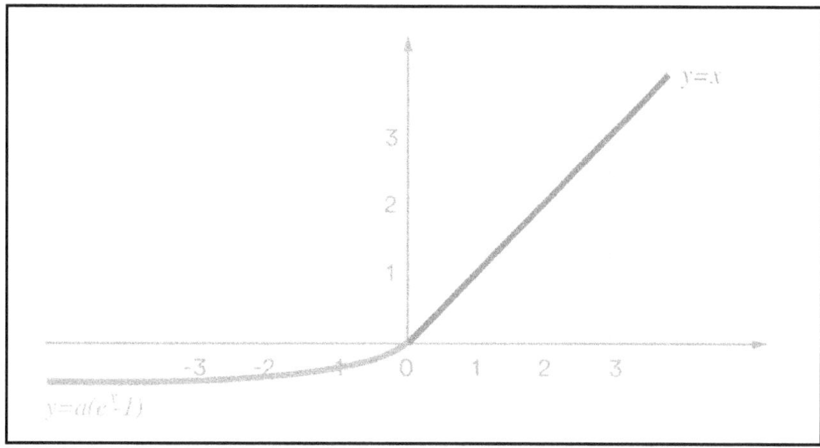

ELU and SELU

- **Concatenated ReLU** (**CReLU**): This joins the regular and leaky form together to provide a new function that produces two output values. For positive values, it generates *[0,x]*, while for negative values, it returns *[x,0]*. One thing to note about this layer is the doubling of output, since two values are generated per neuron.
- **ReLU-6**: The value of 6 is arbitrary but allows for the network to train sparse neurons. Sparsity is of value because it encourages the network to learn or build stronger weights or bonds. The human brain has been shown to function in a sparse state, with only a few activated neurons at a time. You will often hear the myth that we only use 10% of our brain at a time at most. This may very well be true, but the reasons for this are more mathematical than us being able to use our entire brain. We do use our entire brain, just not all of it at the same time. Stronger individual weights, encouraged by sparsity, allow for the network to make better/stronger decisions. Fewer weights also encourage less overfitting or memorization of data. This can often happen in deep networks with thousands of neurons.

Regularization is another technique we will often use to trim or reduce unneeded or weights and create sparse networks. We will have a few opportunities to look at regularization and sparsity later in the coming chapters.

In the next section, we use what we have learned to build a working music GAN that can generate game music.

A GAN for creating music

In our final grand example of this chapter, we are going to look at generating music with GANs for games. Music generation is not especially difficult, but it does allow us to see a whole variation of a GAN that uses LSTM layers to identify sequences and patterns in music. Then it attempts to build that music back from random noise to a passable sequence of notes and melodies. This sample becomes ethereal when you listen to those generated notes and realize the tune originates from a computer brain.

The origins of this sample are pulled from GitHub, `https://github.com/megis7/musegen`, and developed by Michalis Megisoglou. The reason we look at these code examples is so that we can see the best of what others have produced and learn from those. In some cases, these samples are close to the original, and others not so much. We did have to tweak a few things. Michalis also produced a nice GitHub README on the code he built for his implementation of **museGAN**, music generation with GAN. If you are interested in building on this example further, be sure to check out the GitHub site as well. There are a few implementations of museGAN available using various libraries; one of them is TensorFlow.

We use Keras in this example in order to make this example easier to understand. If you are serious about using TensorFlow, then be sure to take a look at the TensorFlow version of museGAN as well.

This example trains the discriminator and generator separately, which means it needs to have the discriminator trained first. For our first run, we will run this example with the author's previously generated models, but we still need some setup; let's follow these steps:

1. We first need to install a couple of dependencies. Open an Anaconda or Python window as an admin and run the following commands:

```
pip install music21
pip install h5py
```

2. `Music21` is a Python library for loading MIDI files. **MIDI** is a music interchange format used to describe, as you might have guessed, music/notes. The original models were trained on a collection of MIDI files that describe 300 chorales of Bach's music. You can locate the project by navigating to the `musegen` folder and running the script.
3. Navigate to the project folder and execute the script that runs the previously trained models like so:

```
cd musegen
python musegen.py or python3 musegen.py
```

4. This will load the previously saved models and use those models to train the generator and generate music. You could, of course, train this GAN on other MIDI files of your choosing later as needed. There are plenty of free sources for MIDI files from classical music, to TV theme music, games, and modern pop. We use the author's original models in this example, but the possibilities are endless.
5. Loading the music files and training can take a really long time, as training typically does. So, take this opportunity to look at the code. Open up the `musegen.py` file located in the project folder. Take a look at around line 39, as follows:

```
print('loading networks...')
dir_path = os.path.dirname(os.path.realpath(__file__))
generator = loadModelAndWeights(os.path.join(dir_path,
note_generator_dir, 'model.json'),
                               os.path.join(dir_path,
note_generator_dir, 'weights-{:02d}.hdf5'.format(generator_epoch)))
```

6. This section of code loads the previously trained model from an `hdf5` or hierarchical data file. The preceding code sets up a number of variables that define the notes to a vocabulary we will use to generate new notes.
7. Locate the `notegenerator.py` file located in the same project folder. Take a look at the creation of the model code, as follows:

```
x_p = Input(shape=(sequence_length, pitch_dim,),
name='pitches_input')
h = LSTM(256, return_sequences=True, name='h_lstm_p_1')(x_p)
h = LSTM(512, return_sequences=True, name='h_lstm_p_2')(h)
h = LSTM(256, return_sequences=True, name='h_lstm_p_3')(h)

# VAE for pitches
z_mean_p = TimeDistributed(Dense(latent_dim_p,
kernel_initializer='uniform'))(h)
z_log_var_p = TimeDistributed(Dense(latent_dim_p,
```

```
kernel_initializer='uniform'))(h)

z_p = Lambda(sampling)([z_mean_p, z_log_var_p])
z_p = TimeDistributed(Dense(pitch_dim,
kernel_initializer='uniform', activation='softmax'))(z_p)

x_d = Input(shape=(sequence_length, duration_dim, ),
name='durations_input')
h = LSTM(128, return_sequences=True)(x_d)
h = LSTM(256, return_sequences=True)(h)
h = LSTM(128, return_sequences=True)(h)

# VAE for durations
z_mean_d = TimeDistributed(Dense(latent_dim_d,
kernel_initializer='uniform'))(h)
z_log_var_d = TimeDistributed(Dense(latent_dim_d,
kernel_initializer='uniform'))(h)

z_d = Lambda(sampling)([z_mean_d, z_log_var_d])
z_d = TimeDistributed(Dense(duration_dim,
kernel_initializer='uniform', activation='softmax'))(z_d)
conc = Concatenate(axis=-1)([z_p, z_d])
latent = TimeDistributed(Dense(pitch_dim + duration_dim,
kernel_initializer='uniform'))(conc)
latent = LSTM(256, return_sequences=False)(latent)

o_p = Dense(pitch_dim, activation='softmax', name='pitches_output',
kernel_initializer='uniform')(latent)
o_d = Dense(duration_dim, activation='softmax',
name='durations_output', kernel_initializer='uniform')(latent)
```

8. Note how we have changed from using `Conv2D` layers to `LSTM` layers, since we have gone from image recognition to sequence or note pattern recognition. We have also gone from using more straightforward layers to a complex time-distributed architecture. Also, the author used a concept known as **variational auto encoding** in order to determine the distribution of notes in a sequence. This network is the most complex we have looked at so far, and there is a lot going on here. Don't fret too much about this example, except to see how the code flows. We will take a closer look at more of these type of advanced time- distributed networks in `Chapter 4`, *Building a Deep Learning Gaming Chatbot*.
9. Let the sample run and generate some music samples into the `samples/note-generator` folder. As we get into more complex problems, our training time will go from hours to days for very complex problems or more. It is possible that you could easily generate a network that you would not have the computing power to train in a reasonable time.

10. Open the folder and double-click on one of the sample files to listen to the generated MIDI file. Remember, this music was just generated by a computer brain.

There is a lot of code that we did not cover in this example. So, be sure to go back and go through the `musegen.py` file to get a better understanding of the flow and types of layers used to build the network generator. In the next section, we explore how to train this GAN.

Training the music GAN

Before we get into training this network, we will look at the overall architecture as depicted in the author's original GitHub source:

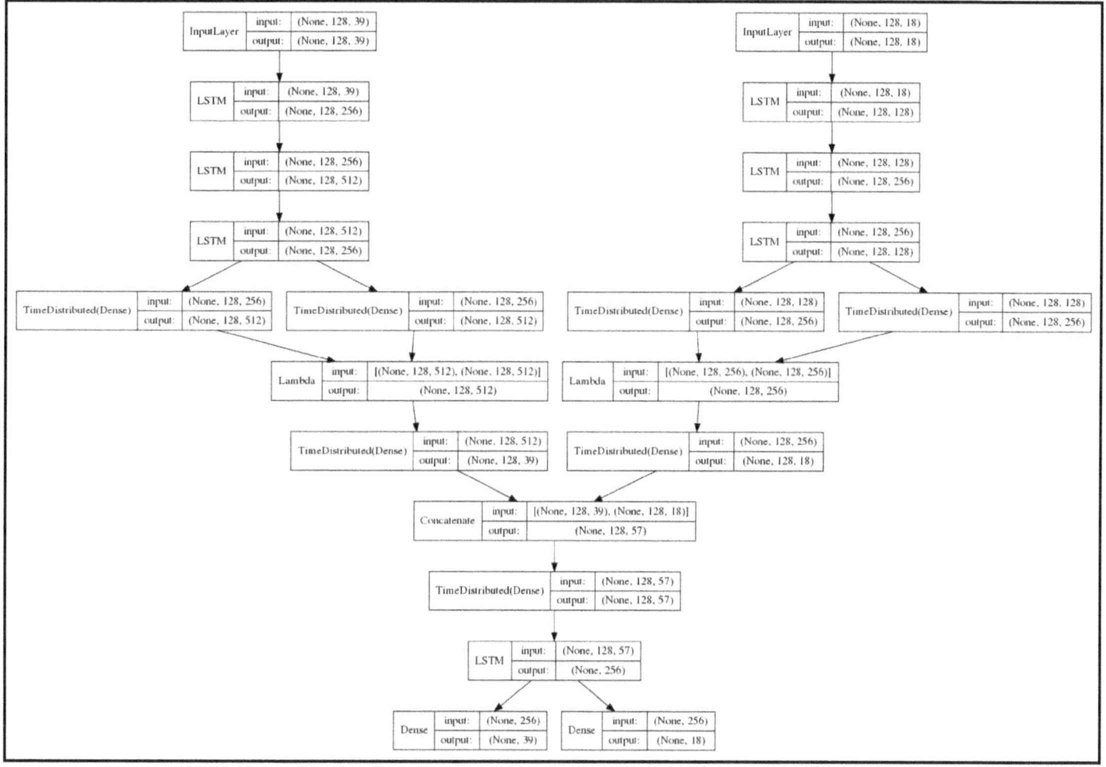

Overview of museGAN network architecture

The networks are almost identical until you look closer and see the subtle differences in the LSTM layers. Note how one set uses double the units as the other model.

We can generate music models by running the following command at the Python or Anaconda prompt:

```
python note-generator.py
or
python3 note-generator.py
```

This script loads the sample data and generates the models we use in the `musegen.py` file later when we create original music. Open up the `note-generator.py` file with the main parts shown here:

The code was modified from the original to make it more Windows-compatible and cross-platform. Again, this is certainly not a criticism of the author's excellent work.

```
def loadChorales():
    notes = []
    iterator = getChoralesIterator()

    # load notes of chorales
    for chorale in iterator[1:maxChorales]: # iterator is 1-based
        transpose_to_C_A(chorale.parts[0])
        notes = notes + parseToFlatArray(chorale.parts[0])
        notes.append((['end'], 0.0)) # mark the end of the piece
    return notes
```

This code uses the Music21 library to read the MIDI notes and other music forms from the corpus of music you can use for your own testing. This training dataset is an excellent way to generate other sources of music and is composed of the following: `http://web.mit.edu/music21/doc/moduleReference/moduleCorpus.html`.

You can further modify this example by modifying the contents or adding additional configuration options in the `config.py` file as shown:

```
# latent dimension of VAE (used in pitch-generator)
latent_dim = 512

# latent dimensions for pitches and durations (used in note-generator)
latent_dim_p = 512
latent_dim_d = 256

# directory for saving the note embedding network model --- not used
anymore
note_embedding_dir = "models/note-embedding"
```

```
# directory for saving the generator network model
pitch_generator_dir = 'models/pitch-generator'

# directory for saving the note generator network model
note_generator_dir = 'models/note-generator'

# directory for saving generated music samples
output_dir = 'samples'
```

The previous sample is great for exploring the generation of music. A more practical and potentially useful example will be introduced in the next section.

Generating music via an alternative GAN

Another example of music generation is also included in the `Chapter_3` source folder, called **Classical-Piano-Composer**, with the source located at `https://github.com/Skuldur/Classical-Piano-Composer`, developed by Sigurður Skúli. This example uses a full set of Final Fantasy MIDI files as source inspiration for the music generation and is a great practical example for generating your own music.

In order to run this sample, you need to run the `lstm.py` first using the following command from the `Classical-Piano-Composer` project folder:

```
python lstm.py
or
python3 lstm.py
```

This sample can take a substantial time to train, so be sure to open the file and read through what it does.

After the models are trained, you can run the generator by running the following:

```
python predict.py
or
python3 predict.py
```

This script loads the trained model and generates the music. It does this by encoding the MIDI notes into network input in terms of sequences or sets of notes. What we are doing here is breaking up the music files into short sequences, or a music snapshot if you will. You can control the length of these sequences by adjusting the `sequences_length` property in the code file.

The great thing about this second example is the ability to download your own MIDI files and put them in the appropriate input folder for training. It is also interesting to see how both projects use a similar three-layer LSTM structure but vary quite widely in other forms of execution.

If you want to learn more about audio or music development for games and especially for Unity, check out the book *Game Audio Development with Unity 5.x*, by Micheal Lanham. This book can show you many more techniques for working with audio and music in games.

Both music samples can take some time to train and then generate music, but it is certainly worth the effort to run through both examples and understand how they work. GANs have innovated the way we think of training neural networks and what type of output they are able to produce. As such, they certainly have a place in generating content for games.

Exercises

Take some time to reinforce your learning by undertaking the following exercises:

1. What type of GAN would you use to transfer styles on an image?
2. What type of GAN would you use to isolate or extract the style?
3. Modify the number of critics used in the Wasserstein GAN example and see the effect it has on training.
4. Modify the first GAN, the DCGAN, to improve training performance using any technique you learned in this chapter. How did you increase training performance?
5. Modify the BatchNormalization momentum parameter and see what effect it has on training.
6. Modify a few of the samples by changing the activation from LeakyReLU to another advanced form of activation.
7. Modify the Wasserstein GAN example to use your own textures. There is a sample data loader available in the downloaded code sample for the chapter.
8. Download one of the other reference GANs from `https://github.com/eriklindernoren/Keras-GAN` and modify that to use your own dataset.
9. Alter the first music generation GAN to use a different corpus.
10. Use your own MIDI files to train the second music generation GAN example.
11. (BONUS) Which music GAN generated better music? Is it what you expected?

You certainly don't have to work through all these exercises, but give a few a try. Putting this knowledge to practice right away can substantially improve your understanding of the material. Practice does make perfect, after all.

Summary

In this chapter, we looked at generative adversarial networks, or GANs, as a way to build DNNs that can generate unique content based on copying or extracting features from other content. This also allowed us to explore unsupervised training, a method of training that requires no previous data classification or labeling. In the previous chapter, we used supervised training. We started with looking at the many variations of GANs currently making an impression in the DL community. Then we coded up a deep convolutional GAN in Keras, followed by the state-of-the-art Wasserstein GAN. From there, we looked at how to generate game textures or height maps using sample images. We finished the chapter off by looking at two music-generating GANs that can generate original MIDI music from sampled music.

For the final sample, we looked at music generation with GANs that relied heavily on RNNs (LSTM). We will continue our exploration of RNNs when we look at how to build DL chatbots for games.

4
Building a Deep Learning Gaming Chatbot

Chatbots, or conversational agents, are an exploding trend in AI and are seen as the next human interface with the computer. From Siri, Alexa, and Google Home, there has been an explosion of commercial growth in this area, and you most likely already have interfaced with a computer in this manner. Therefore, it only seems natural that we cover how to build conversational agents for games. For our purposes, however, we are going to look at the class of bots called **neural conversational agents**. Their name follows from the fact that they are developed with neural networks. Now, chatbots don't have to just chat; we will also look at other ways conversational bots can be used in gaming.

In this chapter, we learn how to build neural conversational agents and how to apply these techniques to games. The following is a summary of the main topics we will cover:

- Neural conversational agents
- Sequence-to-sequence learning
- DeepPavlov
- Building the bot server
- Running the bot in Unity
- Exercises

We will now start building more practical real-world working examples of the projects. While not all of your training is complete, it is time we started to build pieces you can use. This means we will begin working with Unity in this chapter and things may start to get complicated quickly. Just remember to take your time and, if you need to, go over the material a few times. Again, the exercises at the end of the chapter are an excellent resource for additional learning.

In the next section, we explore the basics of neural conversational agents.

Neural conversational agents

The concept of communicating with a computer via natural language first became popular as far back as Star Trek (1966 to 1969). In the series, we can often see Kirk, Scotty, and the gang issuing commands to the computer. Since then, many attempts have been made to build chatbots that can converse naturally with a human. During this often unsuccessful journey over the years, several linguistic methods have been developed. These methods are often grouped together and referred to as **natural language processing**, or **NLP**. Now, NLP still is the foundation for most chatbots, including the deep learning variety we will get to shortly.

We often group conversational agents by purpose or task. Currently, we categorize chatbots into two main types:

- **Goal-oriented**: These bots are the kind Kirk would use or the ones you likely communicate with on a daily basis, and a good example is Siri or Alexa.
- **General conversationalist**: These chatbots are designed to converse with people regarding a wide range of topics, and a good example would be **Microsoft Tay**. Unfortunately, the Tay bot was perhaps a little too impressionable and picked up bad language, much like a two-year-old does.

Gaming is certainly no stranger to chatbots, and attempts have been made to use both forms with varying success. While you may think goal-oriented bots make perfect sense, in reality the vocal/text is too slow and tedious for most repetitive gaming tasks. Even simple vocal commands (grunts or groans) are just too slow, at least currently. Therefore, we will look at the often under utilized conversational chatbots and how they can be used in gaming.

The following is a summary of the gaming tasks these bots could undertake:

- **Non-player characters** (**NPCs**): This is an obvious first choice. NPCs are often scripted and become repetitive. How about an NPC that can converse naturally about a topic, perhaps revealing information when the right combination of words or phrases are used? The possibilities are endless here, and some NLP is already used in gaming for this matter.

- **Player character**: How about a game where you could converse with yourself? Perhaps the character has amnesia and is trying to remember information or learn a backstory.
- **Promotion/hints**: Perhaps as a way to promote your game, you build a bot that can hint at how to complete some difficult tasks or just as a way to talk about your game.
- **MMO virtual character**: What if, while you were away from your favorite MMO game, your character stayed in the game, unable to do actions, but still able to converse as you? This is the example we will look at in this chapter, and we will get to the action part later, when we explore **reinforcement learning**.

There are likely dozens more uses that will evolve over time, but for now the preceding list should give you some great ideas regarding how to use chatbots in gaming. In the next section, we get into the background of what makes a conversationalist bot.

General conversational models

Conversational chatbots can be broken down further into two main forms: **generative** and **selective**. The method we will look at is called generative. Generative models learn by being fed a sequence of words and dialog in context/reply pairs. Internally, these models use RNN (LSTM) layers to learn and predict those sequences back to the conversant. An example of how this system works is as follows:

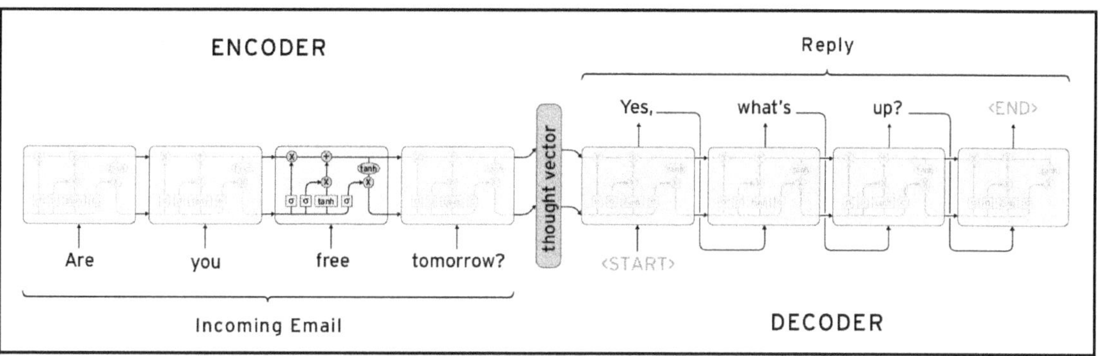

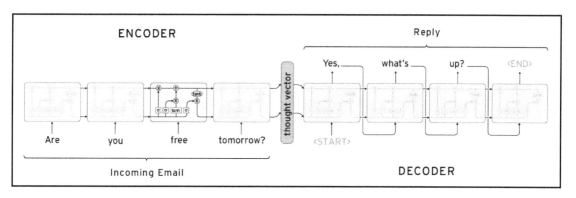

Example of the generative conversational model

Note that each block in the diagram represents one LSTM cell. Each cell then remembers the sequence that text was part of. What may not be clear from the preceding diagram is that both sides of the conversation text were fed into the model before training. Thus, this model is not unlike the GANs we covered in `Chapter 3`, *GAN for Games*. In the next section, we will get into the details of setting up this type of model.

Sequence-to-sequence learning

In the previous section, we saw a high-level overview of our network model. In this section, we want to look at a Keras implementation of a generative conversational model that uses sequence-to-sequence learning. Before we get into the theory of this form of generative model, let's get the sample running, since it can take a while. The sample we will explore is the Keras reference sample for sequence-to-sequence machine translation. It is currently configured to do English-to-French translation.

Open up the `Chapter_4_1.py` sample code listing and get it running using these steps:

1. Open up a shell or Anaconda window. Then run the following command:

   ```
   python3 Chapter_4_1.py
   ```

2. This will run the sample, and it may take several hours to run. The sample can also consume a substantial amount of memory and this may force memory paging on lower memory systems. Paging memory to disk will take additional time to train, especially if you are not running an SSD. If you find that you are unable to complete training on this sample, reduce the number of `epochs` and/or `num_samples` parameters as follows:

   ```
   batch_size = 64 # Batch size for training.
   epochs = 100 # Number of epochs to train for.
   latent_dim = 256 # Latent dimensionality of the encoding space.
   num_samples = 10000 # Number of samples to train on.
   ```

3. Decrease the `epochs` or `num_samples` parameters if you are unable to train on the original values.

4. After the sample has completed training, it will run through a test set of data. As it does so, it will output the results and you can see how well it is translating from English to French.
5. Open the `fra-eng` folder located in the chapter source code.
6. Open the `fra.txt` file and the top few lines are as follows:

```
Go. Va !
Hi. Salut !
Run! Cours !
Run! Courez !
Wow! Ça alors !
Fire! Au feu !
Help! À l'aide !
Jump. Saute.
Stop! Ça suffit !
Stop! Stop !
Stop! Arrête-toi !
Wait! Attends !
Wait! Attendez !
Go on. Poursuis.
Go on. Continuez.
Go on. Poursuivez.
Hello! Bonjour !
Hello! Salut !
```

7. Notice how the training text (English/French) is split on punctuation and spaces. Also, note how the sequences vary in length. The sequences we input do not have to match the length of the output, and vice versa.

The sample we just looked at uses sequence-to-sequence character encoding to translate text from English to French. Typically, chat generation is done with word-to-word encoding, but this sample uses a finer-grained character-to-character model. This has an advantage in games because the language we attempt to generate may not always be human. Keep in mind that while we are only generating translated text in this sample, the text paired with an input could be any response you deem appropriate. In the next section, we will break down the code and understand in some detail how this sample works.

Breaking down the code

As we progress through the book, we will begin to only focus on important sections of code, sections that help us understand a concept or how a method is implemented. This will make it more important for you to open up the code and at least pursue it on your own. In the next exercise, we take a look at the important sections of the sample code:

1. Open `Chapter_4_1.py` and scroll down to the comment `Vectorize the data`, as follows:

```
# Vectorize the data.
input_texts = []
target_texts = []
input_characters = set()
target_characters = set()
with open(data_path, 'r', encoding='utf-8') as f:
    lines = f.read().split('\n')
for line in lines[: min(num_samples, len(lines) - 1)]:
    input_text, target_text = line.split('\t')
    # We use "tab" as the "start sequence" character
    # for the targets, and "\n" as "end sequence" character.
    target_text = '\t' + target_text + '\n'
    input_texts.append(input_text)
    target_texts.append(target_text)
    for char in input_text:
        if char not in input_characters:
            input_characters.add(char)
    for char in target_text:
        if char not in target_characters:
            target_characters.add(char)

input_characters = sorted(list(input_characters))
target_characters = sorted(list(target_characters))
num_encoder_tokens = len(input_characters)
num_decoder_tokens = len(target_characters)
max_encoder_seq_length = max([len(txt) for txt in input_texts])
max_decoder_seq_length = max([len(txt) for txt in target_texts])

print('Number of samples:', len(input_texts))
print('Number of unique input tokens:', num_encoder_tokens)
print('Number of unique output tokens:', num_decoder_tokens)
print('Max sequence length for inputs:', max_encoder_seq_length)
print('Max sequence length for outputs:', max_decoder_seq_length)
```

2. This section of code inputs the training data and encodes it into the character sequences it uses to vectorize. Note how the `num_encoder_tokens` and `num_decoder_tokens` parameters being set here are dependent on the number of characters in each set and not the number of samples. Finally, the maximum length of the encoding and decoding sequences are set on the maximum length of the encoded characters in both.
3. Next, we want to take a look at the vectorization of the input data. Vectorization of the data reduces the number of characters for each response match and is also the memory-intensive part, except, when we align this data, we want to keep the responses or targets to be one step ahead of the original input. This subtle difference allows our sequence-learning LSTM layers to predict the next patterns in the sequence. A diagram of how this works follows:

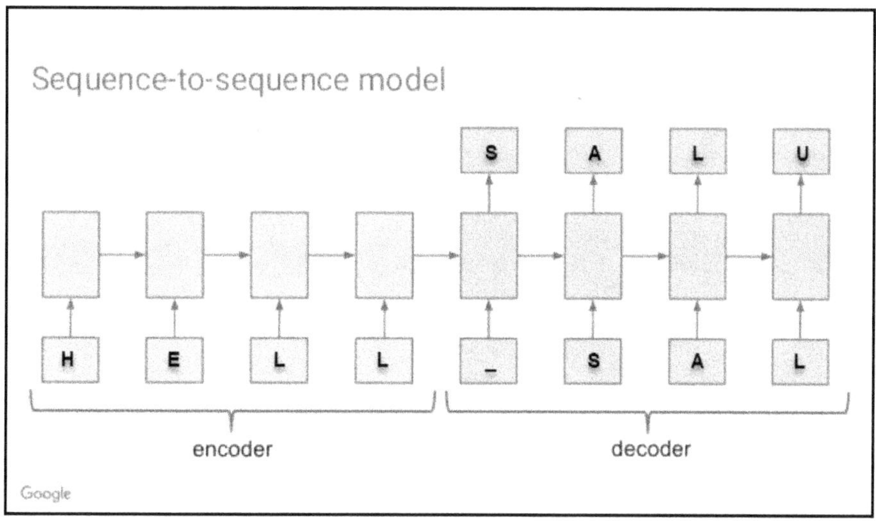

Sequence-to-sequence model

4. In the diagram, we can see how the start of the text **HELLO** is being translated one step behind the response phrase **SALUT** (*hello* in French). Pay attention to how this works in the preceding code.

5. We then build the layers that will map to our network model with the code as follows:

```
# Define an input sequence and process it.
encoder_inputs = Input(shape=(None, num_encoder_tokens))
encoder = LSTM(latent_dim, return_state=True)
encoder_outputs, state_h, state_c = encoder(encoder_inputs)
# We discard `encoder_outputs` and only keep the states.
encoder_states = [state_h, state_c]

# Set up the decoder, using `encoder_states` as initial state.
decoder_inputs = Input(shape=(None, num_decoder_tokens))
# We set up our decoder to return full output sequences,
# and to return internal states as well. We don't use the
# return states in the training model, but we will use them in
inference.
decoder_lstm = LSTM(latent_dim, return_sequences=True,
return_state=True)
decoder_outputs, _, _ = decoder_lstm(decoder_inputs,
                                     initial_state=encoder_states)
decoder_dense = Dense(num_decoder_tokens, activation='softmax')
decoder_outputs = decoder_dense(decoder_outputs)

# Define the model that will turn
# `encoder_input_data` & `decoder_input_data` into
`decoder_target_data`
model = Model([encoder_inputs, decoder_inputs], decoder_outputs)

# Run training
model.compile(optimizer='rmsprop', loss='categorical_crossentropy')
model.fit([encoder_input_data, decoder_input_data],
decoder_target_data,
          batch_size=batch_size,
          epochs=epochs,
          validation_split=0.2)
# Save model
model.save('s2s.h5')
```

6. Note how we are creating encoder and decoder inputs along with decoder outputs. This code builds and trains the `model` and then saves it for later use in inference. We use the term *inference* to mean that a model is inferring or generating an answer or response to some input. A diagram of this sequence-to-sequence model in layer architecture follows:

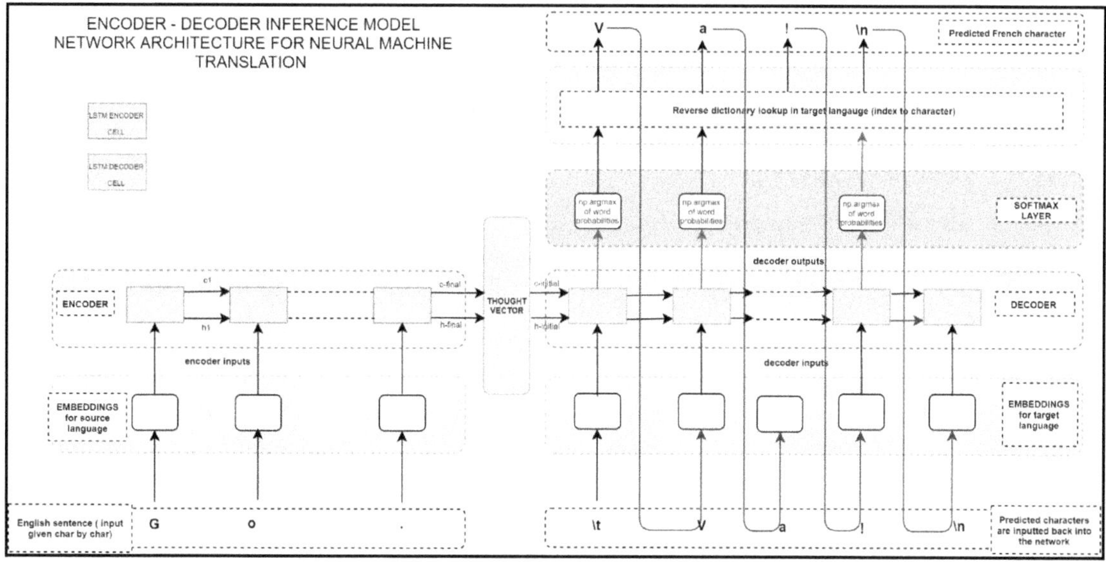

Encoder/decoder inference model

7. This model is quite complex and there is a lot going on here. We have just covered the first part of the model. Next, we need to cover the building of the thought vector and generating the sampling models. The final code to do this follows:

```
encoder_model = Model(encoder_inputs, encoder_states)

decoder_state_input_h = Input(shape=(latent_dim,))
decoder_state_input_c = Input(shape=(latent_dim,))
decoder_states_inputs = [decoder_state_input_h,
decoder_state_input_c]
decoder_outputs, state_h, state_c = decoder_lstm(
    decoder_inputs, initial_state=decoder_states_inputs)
decoder_states = [state_h, state_c]
decoder_outputs = decoder_dense(decoder_outputs)
decoder_model = Model(
    [decoder_inputs] + decoder_states_inputs,
    [decoder_outputs] + decoder_states)

# Reverse-lookup token index to decode sequences back to
# something readable.
reverse_input_char_index = dict(
    (i, char) for char, i in input_token_index.items())
reverse_target_char_index = dict(
    (i, char) for char, i in target_token_index.items())
```

Look over this code and see whether you can understand the structure. We are still missing a critical piece of the puzzle and we will cover that in the next section.

Thought vectors

At the middle of the encoding and decoding text process is the generation of a thought vector. The **thought vector**, popularized by the godfather himself, Dr. Geoffrey Hinton, represents a vector that shows the context of one element in relation to many other elements.

For instance, the word *hello* could have a high relational context to many words or phrases, such as *hi, how are you?, hey, goodbye,* and so on. Likewise, words such as *red, blue, fire,* and *old* would have a low context when associated with the word *hello, at* least in regular day-to-day speech. The word or character contexts are based on the pairings we have in the machine translation file. In this example, we are using the French translation pairings, but the pairings could be anything.

This process takes place as part of the first encoding model into the thought vector or, in this case, a vector of probabilities. The LSTM layer calculates the probability or context of how the words/characters are related. You will often come across the following equation, which describes this transformation:

$$p(y_1, \ldots, y_{T}{'} | x_1, \ldots, x_T) = \prod_{t=1}^{T'} p(y_t | v, y_1 \ldots, y_{t-1})$$

Consider the following:

- $y_1, \ldots, y_{T'}$= output sequence
- $x_1, \ldots, x_T$ = input sequence
- v= Vector representation

The Π represents the multiplication form of sigma (Σ) and is used to pool the probabilities into the thought vector. This is a big simplification of the whole process, and the interested reader is encouraged to Google more about sequence-to-sequence learning on their own. For our purposes, the critical thing to remember is that each word/character has a probability or context that relates it to another. Generating this thought vector can be time consuming and memory-intensive, as you may have already noticed. Therefore, for our purposes, we will look at a more comprehensive set of natural language tools in order to create a neural conversational bot in the next section.

DeepPavlov

DeepPavlov is a comprehensive open source framework for building chatbots and other conversational agents for a variety of purposes and tasks. While this bot is designed for more goal-oriented bots, it will suit us well, as it is full-featured and includes several sequence-to-sequence model variations. Let's take a look at how to build a simple pattern (sequence-to-sequence) recognition model in the following steps:

1. Up until now, we have kept our Python environment loose, but that has to change. We now want to isolate our development environment so that we can easily replicate it to other systems later. The best way to do this is working with Python virtual environments. Create a new environment and then activate it with the following commands at an Anaconda window:

```
#Anaconda virtual environment
conda create --name dlgames
#when prompted choose yes
activate dlgames
```

2. If you don't use Anaconda, the process is a bit more involved, as follows:

```
#Python virtual environment
pip install virtualenv
virutalenv dlgames

#on Mac
source dlgames/bin/activate

#on Windows
dlgames\Scripts\activate
```

3. Then we need to install DeepPavlov with the following command at a shell or an Anaconda window:

```
pip install deeppavlov
```

4. This framework will attempt to install several libraries and may disrupt any existing Python environments. This is the other reason we are now using virtual environments.

5. For our purposes, we are just going to look at the basic `Hello World` sample that is very simple to follow now that we have covered the background. We first do our imports as per standard as follows:

```
from deeppavlov.skills.pattern_matching_skill import
PatternMatchingSkill
from deeppavlov.agents.default_agent.default_agent import
DefaultAgent
from deeppavlov.agents.processors.highest_confidence_selector
import HighestConfidenceSelector
```

6. Now, DeepPavlov is based on Keras, but as you can see, the types we are using here wrap the functionality of a sequence-to-sequence pattern-matching model. The `PatternMatchingSkill` represents the sequence-to-sequence model we want to give our chatbot agent. Next, we import the `DefaultAgent` type, which is just the basic agent. After that, we introduce a confidence selector called `HighestConfidenceSelector`. Remember that the thought vector we generate is a vector of probabilities. The `HighestConfidenceSelector` selector always chooses the highest value relation or context that matches the corresponding word.
7. Next, we generate three sets of patterns with corresponding responses, shown in the following code:

```
hello = PatternMatchingSkill(responses=['Hello world!'],
patterns=["hi", "hello", "good day"])
bye = PatternMatchingSkill(['Goodbye world!', 'See you around'],
patterns=["bye", "ciao", "see you"])
fallback = PatternMatchingSkill(["I don't understand, sorry", 'I
can say "Hello world!"'])
```

8. Each `PatternMatchingSkill` represents a set of pattern/response-contextual pairs. Note how there may be multiple responses and patterns for each. The other great thing about this framework is the ability to interchange and add skills. In this case, we are using just pattern matching, but there are plenty of other skills the reader is encouraged to explore.
9. Finally, we build the agent and run it by simply printing the results with the final bit of code:

```
HelloBot = DefaultAgent([hello, bye, fallback],
skills_selector=HighestConfidenceSelector())

print(HelloBot(['Hello!', 'Boo...', 'Bye.']))
```

10. This last section of code creates a `DefaultAgent` with the three skills (`hello`, `bye`, and `fallback`) using the `HighestConfidenceSelector`. Then it runs the agent by feeding a set of three inputs nested inside the `print` statement.
11. Run the code as you normally would and look at the output. Is it what you expected?

The simplicity of DeepPavlov makes it an excellent tool to build up various conversational chatbots for your games or other purposes if you so choose. The framework itself is very broad-featured and provides multiple natural language processing tools for a variety of tasks, including goal-oriented chatbots. Whole books could and probably should be written about Pavlov; if you have an interest in this, look more for NLP and DeepPavlov.

With our new tool in hand, we now need a platform in which to serve up our bots with great conversational abilities. In the next section, we explore how to build a server for our bot.

Building the chatbot server

Python is a great framework and it provides a number of great tools for game development. However, we are going to focus on using Unity for our purposes. Unity is an excellent and very user-friendly game engine that will make setting up complex examples in later chapters a breeze. Don't worry if you don't know C#, the language of Unity, since we will be manipulating the engine through Python in many cases. This means we want the ability to run our Python code outside Unity and we want to do it on a server.

If you are developing your game in Python, using a server then becomes optional, except that there are very compelling reasons to set up your AI bots as services or microservices. Microservices are self-contained succinct applications or services that only interface through some form of well-known communication protocol. **AI Microservices** or **AI as a Service** (**AIaaS**) are quickly outpacing other forms of SaaS, and it will only be a matter of time untill this same business model converts to gaming as well. In any case, for now, the benefit we gain from creating our chatbot as a microservice is **decoupling**. Decoupling will allow you to easily convert this bot to other platforms in the future.

Microservices also introduce a new communication pattern into the mix. Typically, when a client app connects to a server, the communication is direct and immediate. But what if your connection is broken or the communication needs to be filtered, duplicated, or stored for later analysis or reuse? Then using a direct communication protocol becomes burdened by adding these additional functions, when it doesn't need to be. Instead, microservices introduce the concept of a **message hub**. This is essentially a container or post office where all the message traffic passes through. This allows for incredible flexibility and offlines the need for our communication protocol to manage extra tasks. We will take a look at how to install a very easy-to-use message hub in the next section.

Message hubs (RabbitMQ)

If you have never come across the concept of microservices or message hubs before, you may be somewhat daunted by what is coming next. Don't be. Message hubs and microservices are designed to make it easier to connect, route, and troubleshoot issues with multiple services that need to talk to one another. As such, these systems are designed to be easy to set up, and easier to use. Let's see how easy it is to set up an excellent message queue platform called RabbitMQ in the next exercise:

1. Navigate your browser over to `https://www.rabbitmq.com/#getstarted`.
2. Download and install **RabbitMQ** for your platform. There is typically a download button near the top of the page. You may be prompted to install **Erlang**, as follows:

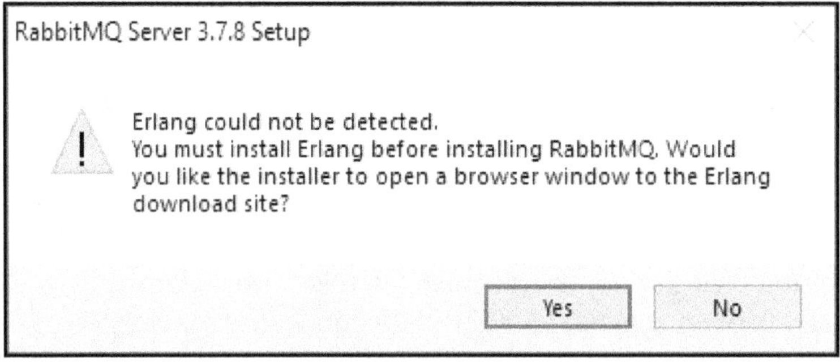

Erlang warning dialog

3. **Erlang** is a concurrent functional programming language and perfect for writing messaging hubs. If you don't have it on your system, just download and install it, again for your platform; next, restart the **RabbitMQ** installation.

4. For the most part, follow the installation choosing the defaults, except for the installation path. Make sure to keep the installation path short and memorable, as we will want to find it later. An example of setting the path in the installer for Windows as follows:

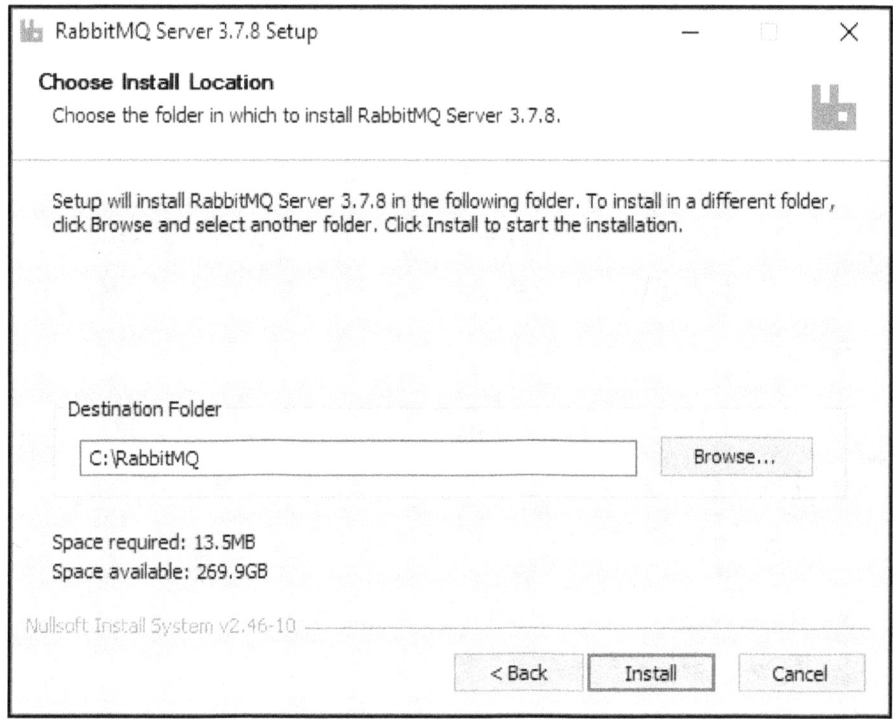

Example of setting the installation path on Windows

5. **RabbitMQ** will install itself as a service on your platform. Depending on your system, you may get a number of security prompts requesting firewall or admin access. Just allow all these exceptions, as the hub needs full access. When the installation completes, RabbitMQ should be running on your system. Be sure to check the documentation for your platform if you have any concerns on the configuration or setup. RabbitMQ is designed to use secure communication but keeps itself fairly open for development. Please avoid installing the hub in a production system, and expect to do some security configuration.

6. Next, we want to activate the RabbitMQ management tool so that we can get a good overview of how the hub works. Open up a Command Prompt and navigate to the `RabbitMQ` installation server folder (the one marked server). Then navigate to the `sbin` folder. When you are there, run the following command to install the management plugin (Windows or macOS):

```
rabbitmq-plugins enable rabbitmq_management
```

7. An example of how this looks in a Windows Command Prompt follows:

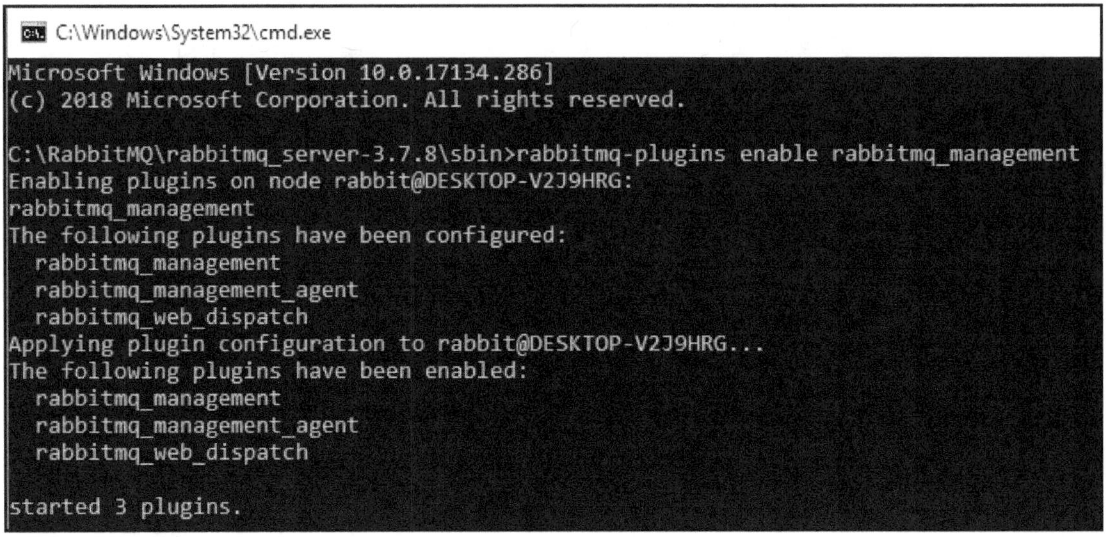

```
C:\Windows\System32\cmd.exe
Microsoft Windows [Version 10.0.17134.286]
(c) 2018 Microsoft Corporation. All rights reserved.

C:\RabbitMQ\rabbitmq_server-3.7.8\sbin>rabbitmq-plugins enable rabbitmq_management
Enabling plugins on node rabbit@DESKTOP-V2J9HRG:
rabbitmq_management
The following plugins have been configured:
  rabbitmq_management
  rabbitmq_management_agent
  rabbitmq_web_dispatch
Applying plugin configuration to rabbit@DESKTOP-V2J9HRG...
The following plugins have been enabled:
  rabbitmq_management
  rabbitmq_management_agent
  rabbitmq_web_dispatch

started 3 plugins.
```

Installing the RabbitMQ management plugin

That completes the installation of the hub on your system. In the next section, we will see how to inspect the hub with the management interface.

Managing RabbitMQ

RabbitMQ is a full-featured message hub that is very powerful and flexible in what it can do. There is a lot to RabbitMQ and it may be intimidating to some users less familiar with networking. Fortunately, we only need to use a few pieces right now, and in the future we will explore more functionality.

For now, though, open up a browser and follow along these steps to explore the hub's management interface:

1. Navigate your browser to `http://localhost:15672/` and you should see a login dialog.
2. Enter the **username** as `guest` and the **password** as `guest`. These are the default credentials and should work unless you've configured it otherwise.
3. After you log in, you will see the RabbitMQ interface:

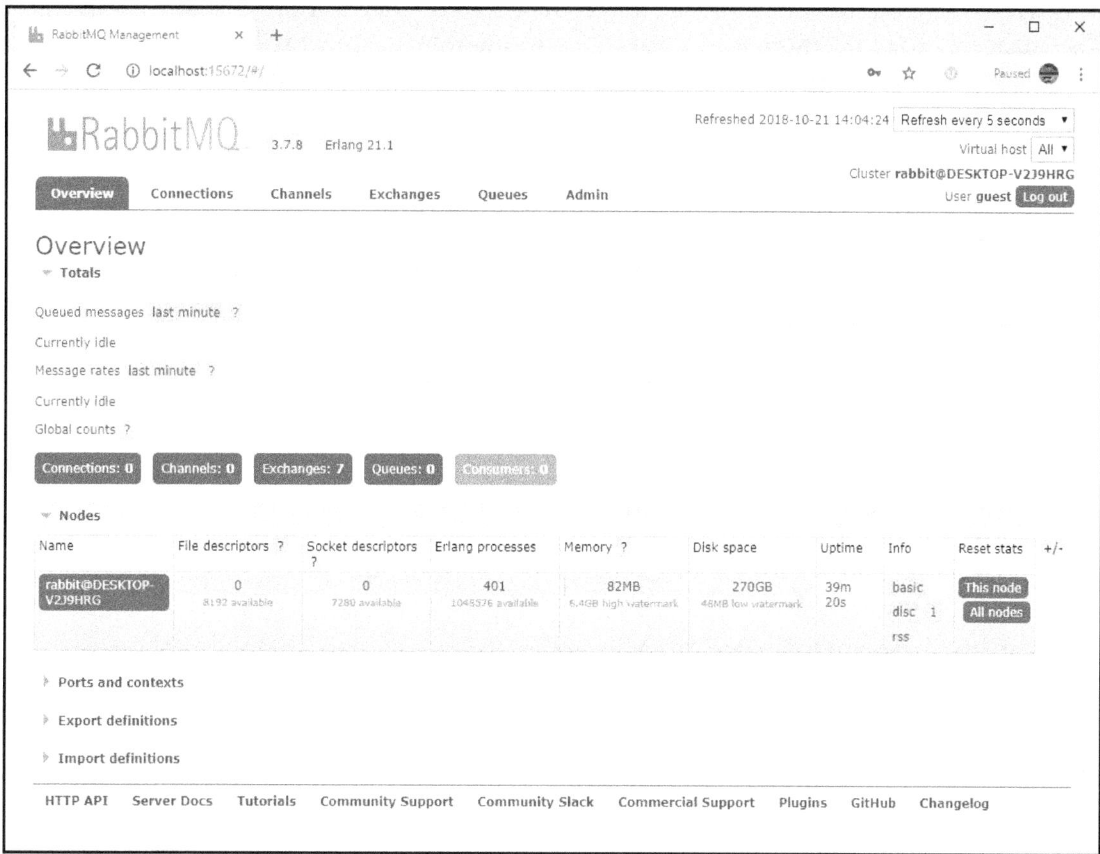

RabbitMQ management interface

4. There is a lot going on here, so for now just click around and explore the various options. Avoid changing any settings, at least for now and until requested to do so. RabbitMQ is very powerful, but we all know that with great power comes great responsibility.

Now, currently, your message queue is empty, so you won't see a lot of activity, but we will soon resolve that in the next section, where we learn how to send and receive messages to and from the queue.

Sending and receiving to/from the MQ

RabbitMQ uses a protocol called **Advanced Message Queuing Protocol** (**AMQP**) for communication, which is a standard for all messaging middleware. This means that we can effectively swap out RabbitMQ for a more robust system, such as Kafka, in the future. This also means that, for the most part, all of the concepts we cover here will likely apply to similar messaging systems.

The first thing we will do is put a message on the queue from a very simple Python client. Open up the source file `Chapter_4_3.py` and follow these steps:

1. Open the source code file and take a look:

```
import pika

connection =
pika.BlockingConnection(pika.ConnectionParameters(host='localhost')
)
channel = connection.channel()
channel.queue_declare(queue='hello')
channel.basic_publish(exchange='',
                      routing_key='hello',
                      body='Hello World!')
print(" [x] Sent 'Hello World!'")
connection.close()
```

2. The code is taken from the RabbitMQ reference tutorial and shows how to connect. It first connects to the hub and opens a `queue` called `hello`. A queue is like a mailbox or stack of messages. A hub may have several different queues. Then the code publishes a message to the `hello` queue with the body of `Hello World!`.
3. Before we can run the sample, we first need to install `Pika`. Pika is an AMQP connection library and can be installed with the following command:

```
pip install pika
```

4. Then run the code file as you normally would and watch the output. It's not very exciting, is it?
5. Go to the RabbitMQ management interface again at `http://localhost:15672/` and see that we now have a single message in the hub, as follows:

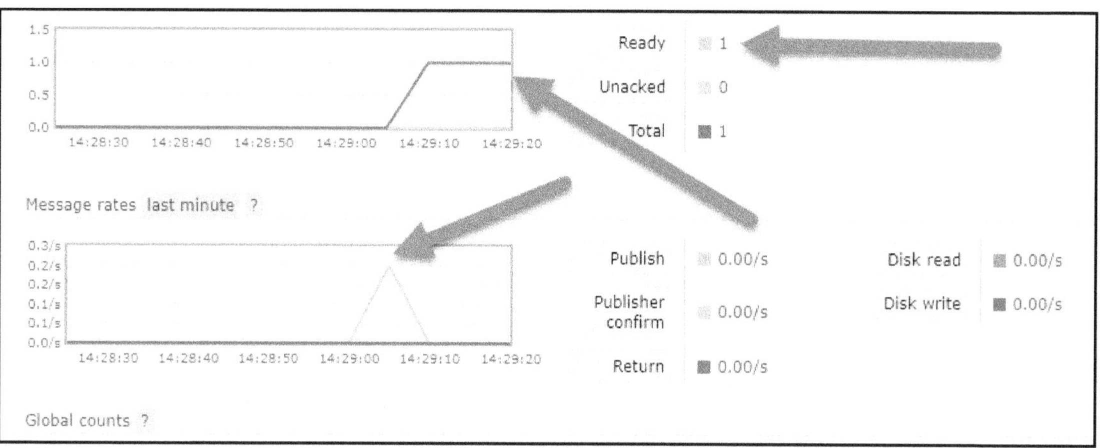

RabbitMQ interface showing the addition of a message

6. The message we just sent will stay on the hub until we collect it later. This single feature will allow us to run individual services and make sure they are communicating correctly without having to worry about other consumers or publishers.

For the purposes of RabbitMQ, we just wrote a publisher. In some cases, you many want a service or app to just publish messages, while in others you may want them to consume them. In the next exercise, `Chapter_4_4_py`, we will write a hub consumer or client:

1. Open the source file `Chapter_4_4.py` and look at the code:

```
import pika

connection =
pika.BlockingConnection(pika.ConnectionParameters(host='localhost')
)
channel = connection.channel()

channel.queue_declare(queue='hello')

def callback(ch, method, properties, body):
```

```
        print(" [x] Received %r" % body)

    channel.basic_consume(callback,
                          queue='hello',
                          no_ack=True)

    print(' [*] Waiting for messages. To exit press CTRL+C')
    channel.start_consuming()
```

2. The preceding code is almost identical to the previous example, except that this time it only consumes from the queue using an internal `callback` function to receive the response. In this example, also note how the script blocks itself and waits for the message. In most cases, the client will register a callback with the queue in order to register an event. That event is triggered when a new message enters the particular queue.
3. Run the code as you normally would and watch the first `Hello World` message get pulled from the queue and output on the client window.
4. Keep the client running and run another instance of the `Chapter_4_3.py` (publish) script and note how the client quickly consumes it and outputs it to the window.

This completes the simple send and receive communication to/from the message hub. As you can see, the code is fairly straightforward and the configuration works out of the box, for the most part. If you do experience any issues with this setup, be sure to consult the RabbitMQ tutorials, which are an additional excellent resource for extra help. In the next section, we look at how to build the working chatbot server example.

Writing the message queue chatbot

The chatbot server we want to create is essentially a combination of the three previous examples. Open up `Chapter_4_5.py` and follow the next exercise:

1. The complete server code as follows:

```
import pika
from deeppavlov.skills.pattern_matching_skill import
PatternMatchingSkill
from deeppavlov.agents.default_agent.default_agent import
DefaultAgent
from deeppavlov.agents.processors.highest_confidence_selector
import HighestConfidenceSelector

hello = PatternMatchingSkill(responses=['Hello world!'],
```

```
patterns=["hi", "hello", "good day"])
bye = PatternMatchingSkill(['Goodbye world!', 'See you around'],
patterns=["bye", "chao", "see you"])
fallback = PatternMatchingSkill(["I don't understand, sorry", 'I
can say "Hello world!"'])

HelloBot = DefaultAgent([hello, bye, fallback],
skills_selector=HighestConfidenceSelector())

connection =
pika.BlockingConnection(pika.ConnectionParameters(host='localhost')
)
channelin = connection.channel()
channelin.exchange_declare(exchange='chat', exchange_type='direct',
durable=True)
channelin.queue_bind(exchange='chat', queue='chatin')

channelout = connection.channel()
channelout.exchange_declare(exchange='chat', durable=True)

def callback(ch, method, properties, body):
    global HelloBot, channelout
    response = HelloBot([str(body)])[0].encode()
    print(body,response)
    channelout.basic_publish(exchange='chat',
                      routing_key='chatout',
                      body=response)
    print(" [x] Sent response %r" % response)

channelin.basic_consume(callback,
                      queue='chatin',
                      no_ack=True)

print(' [*] Waiting for messages. To exit press CTRL+C')
channelin.start_consuming()
```

2. We essentially have a complete working `Hello World` chatbot server in fewer than 25 lines of code. Of course, the functionality is still limited, but by now you can certainly understand how to add other pattern-matching skills to the bot. The important thing to note here is that we are consuming from a queue called `chatin` and publishing to a queue called `chatout`. These queues are now wrapped in an exchange called `chat`. You can think of an exchange as a routing service. Exchanges provide for additional functionality around queues, and the great thing is that they are optional. For use, though, we want to use exchanges, because they provide us with better global control of our services. There are four types of exchanges used in RabbitMQ and they are summarized here:
    - **Direct**: Messages are sent directly to the queue marked in the message transmission.
    - **Fanout**: Duplicate the message to all queues wrapped by the exchange. This is great when you want to add logging or historical archiving.
    - **Topic**: This allows you to send messages to queues identified by matching the message queue. For instance, you could send a message to the queue `chat` and any queue wrapped in the same exchange containing the word *chat* receives the message. The topic exchange allows you to group like messages.
    - **Headers**: This works similar to the topic exchange but instead filters based on the headers in the message itself. This is a great exchange to use for dynamic routing of messages with the appropriate headers.
3. Run the `Chapter_4_5.py` server example and keep it running.
4. Next, open the `Chapter_4_6.py` file and look at the code shown:

```
import pika

connection =
pika.BlockingConnection(pika.ConnectionParameters(host='localhost')
)
channelin = connection.channel()

channelin.exchange_declare(exchange='chat')

chat = 'boo'

channelin.basic_publish(exchange='chat',
                        routing_key='chatin',
                        body=chat)
print(" [x] Sent '{0}'".format(chat))
connection.close()
```

5. The preceding code is just a sample client we can use to test the chatbot server. Note how the message variable `chat` is set to `'boo'`. When you run the code, check the output window of the chatbot server; this is the `Chapter_4_5.py` file we ran earlier. You should see a response message logged in the window that is appropriate to the chat message we just sent.

At this point, you could write a full chat client that could communicate with our chatbot in Python. However, we want to connect our bot up to Unity and see how we can use our bot as a microservice in the next section.

Running the chatbot in Unity

Unity is quickly becoming the standard game engine for learning to develop games, virtual reality, and augmented reality applications. Now it is quickly becoming the standard platform for developing AI and ML applications as well, partly due to the excellent reinforcement learning platform the team at Unity has built. This Unity ML platform is a key component in our desire to use the tool, since it currently is at the cutting edge of advanced AI for games.

The AI team at Unity, led by Dr. Danny Lange and their senior developer Dr. Arthur Juliani, have made numerous suggestions and contributions to ideas for content in this book, both directly and indirectly. This, of course, has had a huge impact on using Unity for major portions of this book.

Installing Unity is quite straightforward, but we want to make sure we get the installation just right the first time. Therefore, follow these steps to install a version of Unity on your system:

1. Navigate your browser to `https://store.unity.com/download` and accept the terms, and then download the Unity Download Assistant. This is the tool that downloads and installs the pieces we need.

2. Run the **Download Assistant** and select the following minimum components to install, as shown in the dialog as follows:

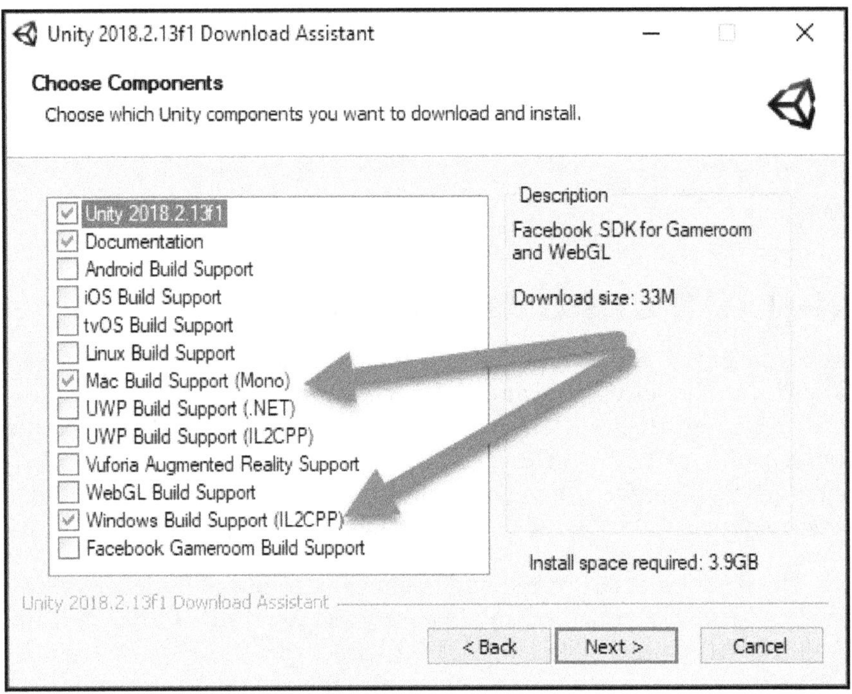

Selecting the installation components for Unity

3. Just be sure to install the latest version of Unity and select the components that match your preferred OS, as shown in the preceding screenshot. You may, of course, select other components at your discretion, but those are the minimum you will need for this book.
4. Next, set the path to install Unity to a well-known folder. A good choice is to set the folder name equal to the version. This allows you to have multiple versions of Unity on the same system that you can easily find. The following screenshot shows how you may do this on Windows:

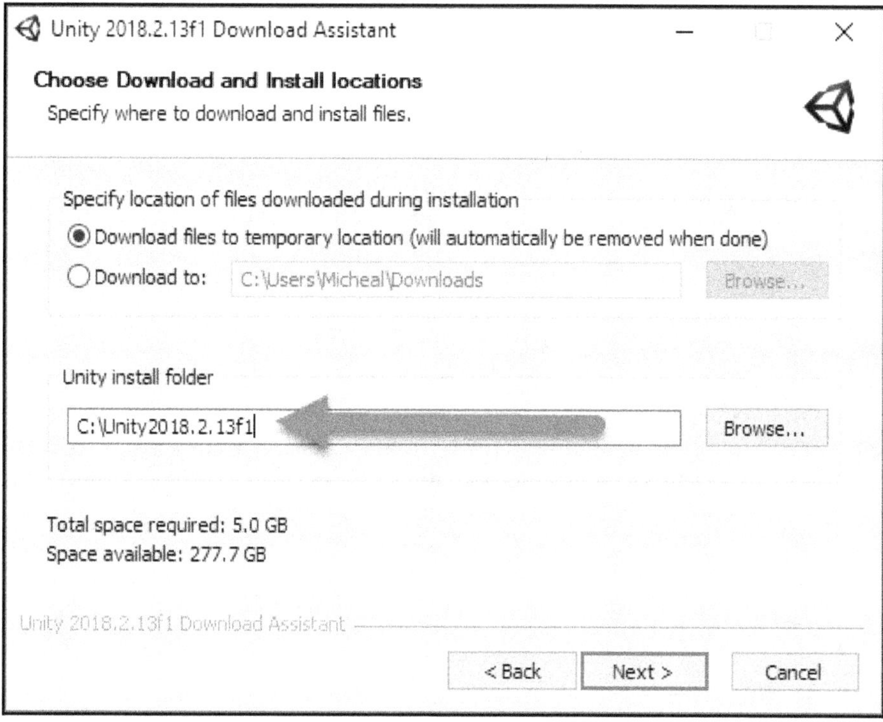

Setting the installation path to Unity

5. Those are the only critical parts to the installation and you can continue installing the software using the defaults.
6. Launch the Unity editor after it installs and you will be prompted to log in. Unity requires you to have an account, regardless of whether you are using the free version. Go back to `unity.com` and just create an account. After you are done setting up the account, go back in and log in to the editor.
7. After you log in, create a empty project called `Chatbot` and let the editor open to a blank scene.

Unity is a full-featured game engine and may be intimidating if this is your first visit. There are plenty of online tutorials and videos that can get you up to speed on the interface. We will do our best to demonstrate concepts simply, but if you get lost, just take your time and work through the exercise a few times.

With Unity installed, we now have to install the components or assets that will allow us to easily connect to the chatbot server we just created. In the next section, we install the AMQP asset for Unity.

Installing AMQP for Unity

RabbitMQ has an excellent resource for plenty of cross-platform libraries that allow you to connect to the hub with ease. The library for C# does work well outside Unity but is problematic to set up. Fortunately, the good folks at Cymantic Labs have built and open sourced a version for Unity on GitHub. Let's see how to install this code in the next exercise:

1. Download and unpack the code using `git` or as a ZIP file from `https://github.com/CymaticLabs/Unity3D.Amqp`:

   ```
   git clone https://github.com/CymaticLabs/Unity3D.Amqp.git
   ```

2. Switch to Unity from the menu, and select **File | Open Project** and navigate to the `Unity3D.Amqp\unity\CymaticLabs.UnityAmqp` folder where you installed the code. This will open the asset in its own project. Wait for the project to load.
3. Open the `Assets/CymanticLabs/Amqp/Scenes` folder in the **Project** window (typically at the bottom).
4. Double-click on the **AmqpDemo** scene to open it in the editor.
5. Press the **Play** button at the top of the editor to run the scene. After you run the scene, you should see the following:

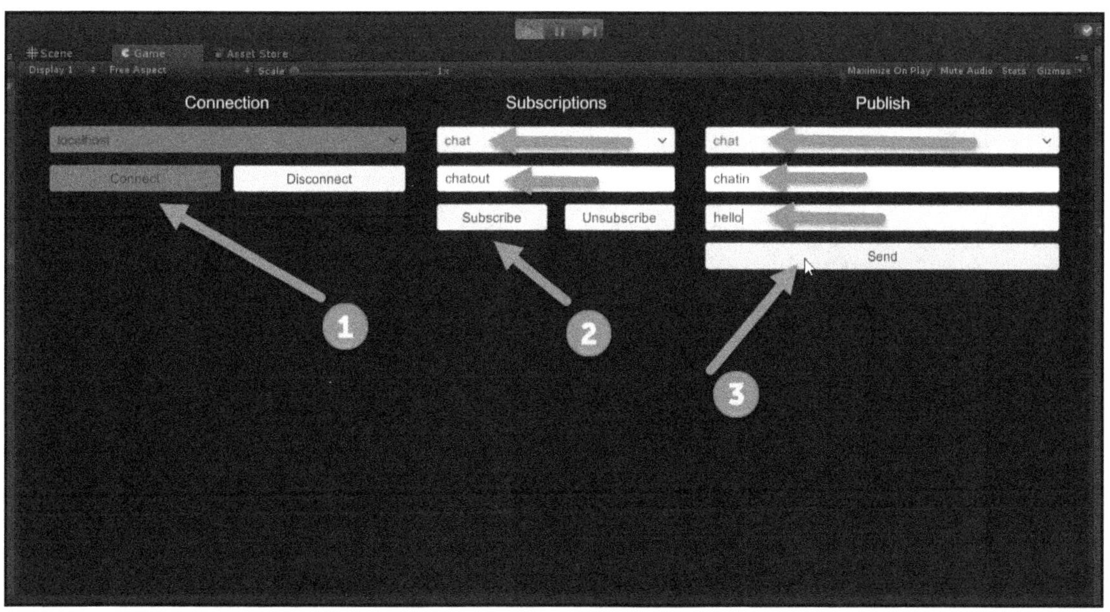

Setting the Amqp connection and sending a message

6. Press the **Connect** button to connect to the local RabbitMQ.
7. Next, under **Subscriptions**, set the exchange to **chat**, and the queue to **chatout**, and click **Subscribe**. This will subscribe to the queue so we can see any return message in the Unity console window.
8. Finally, under **Publish**, set the exchange to **chat**, and the queue to **chatin**, and type a message such as `hello`. Click the **Send** button and you should see a response from the bot in the console window.

That sets up our working chatbot. Of course, this is just the start of what is possible and the reader is certainly encouraged to explore further, but keep in mind we will revisit this code later and make use of it in a later section of the book.

That completes this chapter, and now you can take advantage of it for further learning in the next section.

Exercises

Use the following exercises to expand your learning and get more confident with the material in this chapter:

1. Go back to the first exercise and load another set of translations. Train the bot on those and see what responses are generated after training. There are plenty of other language files available for training.
2. Set up your own conversational training file using the English/French translation one as an example. Remember, the matching responses can be anything and not just translated text.
3. Add additional pattern-matching skills to the DeepPavlov bot. Either the simple test one and/or the chatbot server.
4. The DeepPavlov chatbot uses a highest-value selection criteria for selecting a response. DeepPavlov does have a random selector as well. Change the response selector on the chatbot to use random.
5. Change the exchange type in the example to use **Fanout** and create a log queue to log messages.
6. Change the exchange type to **Topic** and see how you can group messages. Warning: this will likely break the example; see whether you can fix it.
7. Write a RabbitMQ publisher in Python that publishes to one or more different types of queues.
8. Create an entire set of conversation skills using the pattern-matching skill. Then, see how well your bot converses with you.
9. Add additional skills of other types to the chatbot server. This may require some additional homework on your part.
10. Write or run two chatbots over RabbitMQ and watch them converse with each other.

Work through at least two or three of these exercises.

Summary

In this chapter, we looked at building chatbots or neural conversational agents using neural networks and deep learning. We first saw what makes a chatbot and the main forms in use today: goal-oriented and conversational bots. Then we looked at how to build a basic machine translation conversational chatbot that used sequence-to-sequence learning.

After getting a background in sequence learning, we looked at the open source tool DeepPavlov. DeepPavlov is a powerful chat platform built on top of Keras and designed for many forms of neural agent conversation and tasks. This made it ideal for us to use the chatbot server as a base. Then we installed RabbitMQ, a microservices message hub platform that will allow our bot and all manner of other services to talk together later on.

Finally, we installed Unity and then quickly installed the AMQP plugin asset and connected to our chatbot server.

This completes our introductory section to deep learning, and, in the next section, we begin to get more into game AI by diving into **deep reinforcement learning**.

2

Section 2: Deep Reinforcement Learning

In this section, we will study deep reinforcement learning in detail, using various frameworks and technologies to explore multiple interesting examples.

We will cover the following chapters in this section:

- `Chapter 5`, *Introducing DRL*
- `Chapter 6`, *Unity ML-Agents*
- `Chapter 7`, *Agent and the Environment*
- `Chapter 8`, *Understanding PPO*
- `Chapter 9`, *Rewards and Reinforcement Learning*
- `Chapter 10`, *Imitation and Transfer Learning*
- `Chapter 11`, *Building Multi-Agent Environments*

5 Introducing DRL

Deep reinforcement learning (**DRL**) is currently taking the world by storm and is seen as the "it" of machine learning technologies, the it goal of reaching some form of general AI. Perhaps it is because DRL approaches the cusp of general AI or what we perceive as general intelligence. It is also likely to be one of the main reasons you are reading this book. Fortunately, this chapter, and the majority of the rest of the book, focuses deeply on **reinforcement learning** (**RL**) and its many variations. In this chapter, we start learning the basics of RL and how it can be adapted to **deep learning** (**DL**). We will explore the **OpenAI Gym** environment, a great RL playground, and see how to use it with some simple DRL techniques.

Keep in mind, this is a hands-on book, so we will be keeping technical theory to a minimum, and instead we will explore plenty of working examples. Some readers may feel lost without the theoretical background and feel the need to explore the more theoretical side of RL on their own.

For other readers not familiar with the theoretical background of RL, we will cover several core concepts, but this is the abridged version, so it is recommended you seek theoretical knowledge from other sources when you are ready.

In this chapter, we will start learning about DRL, a topic that will carry through to many chapters. We will start with the basics and then look to explore some working examples adapted to DL. Here is what we will cover in this chapter:

- Reinforcement learning
- The Q-learning model
- Running the OpenAI gym
- The first DRL with Deep Q-Network
- RL experiments

For those of you who like to jump around books: yes, it is OK to start this book from this chapter. However, you may need to go back to previous chapters in order to complete some exercises. We will also assume that your Python environment is configured with TensorFlow and Keras, but if you are unsure, check out the `requirements.txt` file in the project folder.

All the projects in this book are built with Visual Studio 2017 (Python), and it is the recommended editor for the examples in this book. If you use VS 2017 with Python, you can easily manage the samples by opening the chapter solution file. Of course, there are plenty of other excellent Python editors and tools, so use what you are comfortable with.

Reinforcement learning

RL currently leads the pack in advances compared to other machine learning methodologies. Note the use of the word *methodology* and not *technology*. RL is a methodology or algorithm that applies a principle we can use with neural networks, whereas, neural networks are a machine learning technology that can be applied to several methodologies. Previously, we looked at other methodologies that blended with DL, but we focused more on the actual implementation. However, RL introduces a new methodology that requires us to understand more of the inner and outer workings before we understand how to apply it.

RL was popularized by Richard Sutton, a Canadian, and current professor at the University of Alberta. Sutton has also assisted in the development of RL at Google's DeepMind, and is quite often regarded as the father of RL.

At the heart of any machine learning system is the need for training. Often, the AI agent/brain knows nothing, and then we feed it data through some automated process for it to learn. As we have seen, the most common way of doing this is called **supervised training**. This is when we first label our training data. We have also looked at **unsupervised training**, where our **Generative Adversarial Networks** (**GANs**) were trained by competing against each other. However, neither system replicated the type of learning or training we see in **Biology**, and that is often referred to as **rewards** or RL: the type of learning that lets you teach your dog to bark for a treat, fetch the paper, and use the outdoors for nature's calling, a type of learning that lets an agent explore its own environment and learn for itself. This is not unlike the type of learning a general AI would be expected to use; after all, RL is likely similar to the system we use, or so we believe.

David Silver, a former student of Prof Sutton's and now head of DeepMind, has an excellent video series on the theoretical background of RL. The first five videos are quite interesting and recommended viewing, but the later content gets quite deep and may not be for everyone. Here's the link for the videos: `https://www.youtube.com/watch?v=2pWv7GOvuf0`

RL defines its own type of training called by the same name. This form of reward-based training is shown in the following diagram:

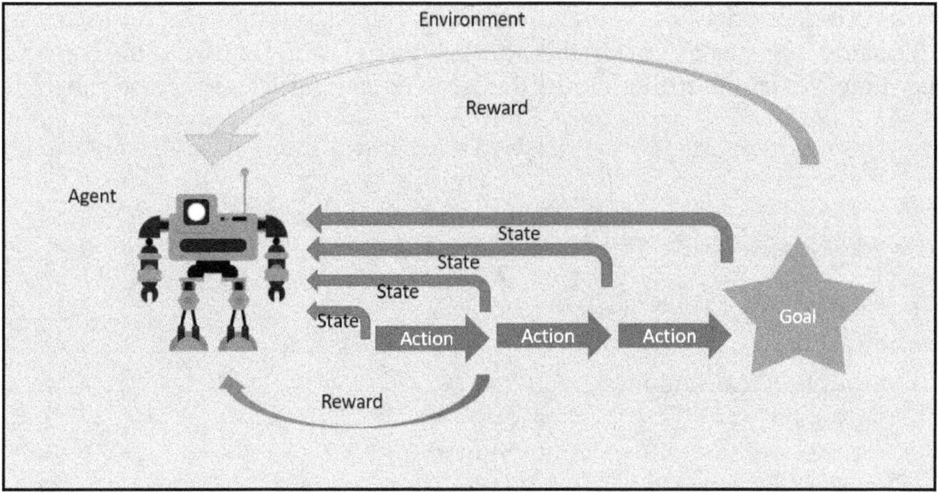

Reinforcement learning

The diagram shows an agent in an environment. That agent reads the state of the environment and then decides and performs an action. This action may, or may not, give a reward, and that reward could be good or bad. After each action and possible reward, the agent collects the state of the environment again. The process repeats itself until the agent reaches a terminal or end state. That is, until it reaches the goal; perhaps it dies or just gets tired. It is important to note a couple of subtle things about the preceding diagram. First, the agent doesn't always receive a reward, meaning rewards could be delayed, until some future goal is reached. This is quite different from the other forms of learning we explored earlier, which provided immediate feedback to our training networks. Rewards can be good or bad, and it is often just as effective to negatively train agents this way, but less so for humans.

Now, as you might expect with any powerful learning model, the mathematics can be quite complex and certainly daunting to the newcomer. We won't go too far into the theoretical details other than to describe some of the foundations of RL in the next section.

The multi-armed bandit

The diagram we saw earlier describes the full RL problem as we will use for most of the rest of this book. However, we often teach a simpler one-step variation of this problem called the **multi-armed bandit**. The armed bandit is in reference to the Vegas slot machine and nothing more nefarious. We use these simpler scenarios in order to explain the basics of RL in the form of a one-step or one-state problem.

In the case of the multi-armed bandit, picture a fictional multi-armed Vegas slot machine that awards different prizes based on which arm is pulled, but the prize for each arm is always the same. The agent's goal in this scenario would be to figure out the correct arm to pull every time. We could further model this in an equation such as the one shown here:

$$V(a) = V(a) + \alpha(r - V(a))$$

Consider the following equation:

- $V(a)$ = vector of values (1,2,3,4)
- a = action
- α = alpha = learning rate
- r = reward

This equation calculates the value (*V*), a vector, for each action the agent takes. Then, it feeds back these values into itself, subtracted from the reward and multiplied by a learning rate. This calculated value can be used to determine which arm to pull, but first the agent needs to pull each arm at least once. Let's quickly model this in code, so as game/simulation programmers, we can see how this works. Open the `Chapter_5_1.py` code and follow these steps:

1. The code for this exercise is as follows:

```
alpha = .9
arms = [['bronze' , 1],['gold', 3], ['silver' , 2], ['bronze' , 1]]
v = [0,0,0,0]

for i in range(10):
    for a in range(len(arms)):
        print('pulling arm '+ arms[a][0])
        v[a] = v[a] + alpha * (arms[a][1]-v[a])

print(v)
```

2. This code creates the required setup variables, the `arms` (`gold`, `silver`, and `bronze`), and the value vector `v` (all zeros). Then, the code loops through a number of iterations (`10`) where each arm is pulled and the value, `v`, is calculated and updated based on the equation. Note that the reward value is replaced by the value of the arm pull, which is the term `arms[a][1]`.
3. Run the example, and you will see the output generated showing the value for each action, or in this case an arm pull.

As we saw, with a simple equation, we were able to model the multi-armed bandit problem and arrive at a solution that will allow an agent to consistently pull the correct arm. This sets the foundation for RL, and in the next section, we take the next step and look at **contextual bandits**.

Contextual bandits

We can now elevate the single multi-armed bandit problem into a problem with multiple multi-armed bandits, each with its own set of arms. Now our problem introduces context or state into the equation. With each bandit defining its own context/state, now we evaluate our equation in terms of quality and action. Our modified equation is shown here:

$$Q[s,a] = Q[s,a] + \alpha \times (r - Q[s,a])$$

Consider the following equation:

- $Q[s,a]$ = table/matrix of values

  [1,2,3,4
  2,3,4,5
  4,2,1,4]

- s = state
- a = action
- α = alpha = learning rate
- r = reward

Let's open up `Chapter_5_2.py` and observe the following steps:

1. Open the code up, as follows, and follow the changes made from the previous sample:

```
import random

alpha = .9
bandits = [[['bronze' , 1],['gold', 3], ['silver' , 2], ['bronze' ,
1]],
            [['bronze' , 1],['gold', 3], ['silver' , 2], ['bronze' ,
1]],
            [['bronze' , 1],['gold', 3], ['silver' , 2], ['bronze' ,
1]],
            [['bronze' , 1],['gold', 3], ['silver' , 2], ['bronze' ,
1]]]
q = [[0,0,0,0],
     [0,0,0,0],
     [0,0,0,0],
     [0,0,0,0]]

for i in range(10):
    for b in range(len(bandits)):
        arm = random.randint(0,3)
        print('pulling arm {0} on bandit {1}'.format(arm,b))
        q[b][arm] = q[b][arm] + alpha * (bandits[b][arm][1]-
q[b][arm])

print(q)
```

2. This code sets up a number of multi-armed bandits, each with its own set of arms. It then iterates through a number of iterations, but this time as it loops, it also loops through each bandit. During each loop, it picks a random arm to pull and evaluates the quality.
3. Run the sample and look at the output of `q`. Note how, even after selecting random arms, the equation again consistently selected the gold arm, the arm with the highest reward, to pull.

Feel free to play around with this sample some more and look to the exercises for additional inspiration. We will expand on the complexity of our RL problems when we discuss Q-Learning. However, before we get to that section, we will take a quick diversion and look at setting up the OpenAI Gym in order to conduct more RL experiments.

RL with the OpenAI Gym

RL has become so popular that there is now a race to just build tools that help build RL algorithms. The two major competitors in this area right now are **OpenAI Gym** and **Unity**. Unity has quickly become the RL racing machine we will explore extensively later. For now, we will put our training wheels on and run OpenAI Gym to explore the fundamentals of RL further.

We need to install the OpenAI Gym toolkit before we can continue, and installation may vary greatly depending on your operating system. As such, we will focus on the Windows installation instructions here, as it is likely other OS users will have less difficulty. Follow the next steps to install OpenAI Gym on Windows:

1. Install a C++ compiler; if you have Visual Studio 2017 installed, you may already have a recommended one. You can find other supported compilers here: `https://wiki.python.org/moin/WindowsCompilers`.
2. Be sure to have Anaconda installed, and open an Anaconda command prompt and run the following commands:

```
conda create -n gym
conda activate gym
conda install python=3.5  # reverts Python, for use with TensorFlow
later
pip install tensorflow
pip install keras
pip install gym
```

3. For our purposes, in the short term, we don't need to install any other Gym modules. Gym has plenty of example environments, Atari games and MuJoCo (robotics simulator) being some of the most fun to work with. We will take a look at the Atari games module later in this chapter.

That should install the Gym environment for your system. Most of what we need will work with minimal setup. If you decide to do more with Gym, then you will likely want to install other modules; there are several. In the next section, we are going to test this new environment as we learn about Q-Learning.

A Q-Learning model

RL is deeply entwined with several mathematical and dynamic programming concepts that could fill a textbook, and indeed there are several. For our purposes, however, we just need to understand the key concepts in order to build our DRL agents. Therefore, we will choose not to get too burdened with the math, but there are a few key concepts that you will need to understand to be successful. If you covered the math in the `Chapter 1`, *Deep Learning for Games*, this section will be a breeze. For those that didn't, just take your time, but you can't miss this one.

In order to understand the Q-Learning model, which is a form of RL, we need to go back to the basics. In the next section, we talk about the importance of the **Markov decision process** and the **Bellman equation**.

Markov decision process and the Bellman equation

At the heart of RL is the **Markov decision process** (**MDP**). An MDP is often described as a discrete time stochastic control process. In simpler terms, this just means it is a control program that functions by time steps to determine the probability of actions, provided each action leads to a reward. This process is already used for most automation control of robotics, drones, networking, and of course RL. The classic way we picture this process is shown in the following diagram:

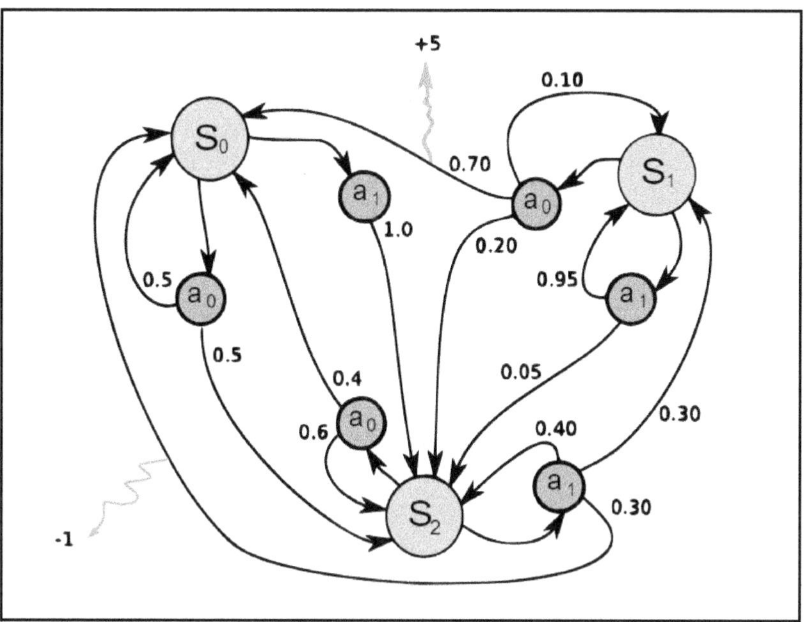

The Markov decision process

Where represent an MDP as a tuple or vector (S, A, P_a, R, γ), using the following variables:

- S - being a finite set of states,
- A - being a finite set of actions,
- P_a - the probability that action A in state S at time t will lead to state S_{t+1} at time $t+1$,
- R - is the immediate reward
- γ - gamma is a discount factor we apply in order to discount the significance or provide significance to future rewards

The diagram works by picturing yourself as an agent in one of the states. You then determine actions based on the probability, always taking a random action. As you move to the next state, the action gives you a reward and you update the probability based on the reward. Again, David Silver covers this piece very well in his lectures.

Now, the preceding process works, but another variation came along that provided for better future reward evaluation, and that was done by introducing the **Bellman Equation** and the concept of a policy/value iteration. Whereas before we had a value, V, we now have a policy (π) for a value called V^{π}, and this yields us a new equation, shown here:

$$V^{\pi} = R(s, \pi(s)) + \gamma \sum_{s'} P(s'|s, a)V^{\pi}(s')$$

We won't cover much more about this equation other than to say to keep the concept of quality iteration in mind. In the next section, we will see how we can reduce this equation back to a quality indicator of each action and use that for Q-Learning.

Q-learning

With the introduction of quality iteration methods, the derivation of a finite state method called **Q-learning** or **quality learning** was derived. Q uses the technique of quality iteration for a given finite state problem to determine the best course of action for an agent. The equation we saw in the previous section can now be represented as the following:

$$Q^{new}(s_t, a_t) = Q(s_t, a_t) + \alpha \times (r_t + \gamma \times max(Q(s_{t+1}, a))$$

Consider the following equation:

- $s_t =$ current state
- $a_t =$ current action
- $a =$ next action
- $r_t =$ current reward
- $\alpha =$ learning rate (alpha)
- $\gamma =$ reward discount factor (gamma)

The Q value is now updated alliteratively, as the agent roams through its environment. Nothing demonstrates these concepts better than an example. Open up `Chapter_5_3.py` and follow these steps:

1. We start with the various imports and set them up as shown in the following code:

```
from collections import deque
import numpy as np
import os
```

```
clear = lambda: os.system('cls') #linux/mac use 'clear'
import time
import gym
from gym import wrappers, logger
```

2. These imports just load the basic libraries we need for this example. Remember, you will need to install `Gym` to run this sample.
3. Next, we set up a new environment; in this example, we use the basic `FrozenLake-v0` sample, a perfect example to test on Q-learning:

```
environment = 'FrozenLake-v0'
env = gym.make(environment)
```

4. Then we set up the AI environment (`env`) and a number of other parameters:

```
outdir = os.path.join('monitor','q-learning-
{0}'.format(environment))
env = wrappers.Monitor(env, directory=outdir, force=True)
env.seed(0)
env.is_slippery = False
q_table = np.zeros([env.observation_space.n, env.action_space.n])

#parameters
wins = 0
episodes = 40000
delay = 1

epsilon = .8
epsilon_min = .1
epsilon_decay = .001
gamma = .9
learning_rate = .1
```

5. In this section of the code, we set up a number of variables that we will get to shortly. For this sample, we are using a wrapper tool to monitor the environment, and this is useful for determining any potential training issues. The other thing to note is the setup of the `q_table` array, defined by the environment `observation_space` (state) and `action_space` (action); spaces define arrays and not just vectors. In this particular example, the `action_space` is a vector, but it could be a multi-dimensional array or tensor.

6. Pass over the next section of functions and skip to the end, where the training iteration occurs and is shown in the following code:

```
for episode in range(episodes):
    state = env.reset()
    done = False
    while not done:
        action = act(env.action_space,state)
        next_state, reward, done, _ = env.step(action)
        clear()
        env.render()
        learn(state, action, reward, next_state)
        if done:
            if reward > 0:
                wins += 1
            time.sleep(3*delay)
        else:
            time.sleep(delay)

print("Goals/Holes: %d/%d" % (wins, episodes - wins))
env.close()
```

7. Most of the preceding code is relatively straightforward and should be easy to follow. Look at how the `env` (environment) is using the `action` generated from the `act` function; this is used to step or conduct an action on the agent. The output of the `step` function is `next_state`, `reward`, and `done`, which we use to determine the optimum Q policy by using the `learn` function.
8. Before we get into the action and learning functions, run the sample and watch how the agent trains. It may take a while to train, so feel free to return to the book.

The following is an example of the OpenAI Gym FrozenLake environment running our Q-learning model:

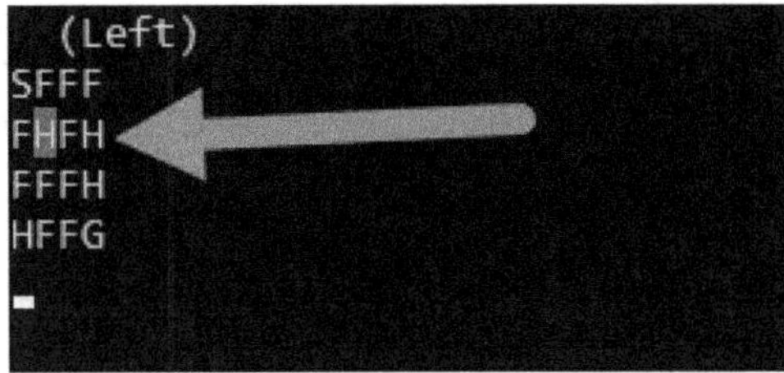

FrozenLake Gym environment

As the sample runs, you will see a simple text output showing the environment. `S` represents the start, `G` the goal, `F` a frozen section, and `H` a hole. The goal for the agent is to find its way through the environment, without falling in a hole, and reach the goal. Pay special attention to how the agent moves and finds it way around the environment. In the next section, we unravel the `learn` and `act` functions and understand the importance of exploration.

Q-learning and exploration

One problem we face with the policy iterative models such as Q-learning is the problem of exploration versus exploitation. The Q-model equation assumes the use of maximum quality to determine an action and we refer to this as exploitation (exploiting the model). The problem with this is that it can often corner an agent into a solution that only looks for the best short-term benefits. Instead, we need to allow the agent some flexibility to explore the environment and learn on its own. We do this by introducing a dissolving exploration factor into the training. Let's see how this looks by again opening up the `Chapter_5_3.py` example:

1. Scroll down to the `act` and `is_explore` functions as shown:

```
def is_explore():
    global epsilon, epsilon_decay, epsilon_min
    epsilon = max(epsilon-epsilon_decay,epsilon_min)
    if np.random.rand() < epsilon:
        return True
    else:
        return False

def act(action_space, state):
    # 0 - left, 1 - Down, 2 - Right, 3 - Up
    global q_table
    if is_explore():
        return action_space.sample()
    else:
        return np.argmax(q_table[state])
```

2. Note that in the `act` function, it first tests whether the agent wants to or needs to explore with `is_explore()`. In the `is_explore` function, we can see that the global `epsilon` value is decayed over each iteration with `epsilon_decay` to a global minimum value, `epsilon_min`. When the agent starts an episode, their exploration `epsilon` is high, making them more probable to explore. Over time, as the episode progresses, the `epsilon` decreases. We do in with the assumption that over time the agent will need to explore less and less. This trade-off between exploration and exploitation is quite important and something to understand with respect to the size of the environment state. We will see this trade-off explored more throughout this book.
   Note that the agent uses an exploration function and just selects a random action.
3. Finally, we get to the `learn` function. This function is where the `Q` value is calculated, as follows:

```
def learn(state, action, reward, next_state):
    # Q(s, a) += alpha * (reward + gamma * max_a' Q(s', a') - Q(s,
a))
    global q_table
    q_value = gamma * np.amax(q_table[next_state])
    q_value += reward
    q_value -= q_table[state, action]
    q_value *= learning_rate
    q_value += q_table[state, action]
    q_table[state, action] = q_value
```

4. Here, the equation is broken up and simplified, but this is the step that calculates the value the agent will use when exploiting.

Keep the agent running until it finishes. We just completed the first full reinforcement learning problem, albeit the one that had a finite state. In the next section, we greatly expand our horizons and look at deep learning combined with reinforcement learning.

First DRL with Deep Q-learning

Now that we understand the reinforcement learning process in detail, we can look to adapt our Q-learning model to work with deep learning. This, as you could likely guess, is the culmination of our efforts and where the true power of RL shines. As we learned through earlier chapters, deep learning is essentially a complex system of equations that can map inputs through a non-linear function to generate a trained output.

A neural network is just another, simpler method of solving a non-linear equation. We will look at how to use DNN to solve other equations later, but for now we will focus on using it to solve the Q-learning equation we saw in the previous section.

We will use the **CartPole** training environment from the OpenAI Gym toolkit. This environment is pretty much the standard used to learn **Deep Q-learning** (**DQN**).

Open up `Chapter_5_4.py` and follow the next steps to see how we convert our solver to use deep learning:

1. As usual, we look at the imports and some initial starting parameters, as follows:

```
import random
import gym
import numpy as np
from collections import deque
from keras.models import Sequential
from keras.layers import Dense
from keras.optimizers import Adam

EPISODES = 1000
```

2. Next, we are going to create a class this time to contain the functionality of the DQN agent. The `__init__` function is as follows:

```
class DQNAgent:
    def __init__(self, state_size, action_size):
        self.state_size = state_size
        self.action_size = action_size
        self.memory = deque(maxlen=2000)
        self.gamma = 0.95 # discount rate
        self.epsilon = 1.0 # exploration rate
        self.epsilon_min = 0.01
        self.epsilon_decay = 0.995
        self.learning_rate = 0.001
        self.model = self._build_model()
```

3. Most of the parameters have already been covered, but note a new one called `memory`, which is a **deque** collection that holds that last 2,000 steps. This allows us to batch train our neural network in a sort of replay mode.

4. Next, we look at how the neural network model is built with the `_build_model` function, as follows:

```
def _build_model(self):
    # Neural Net for Deep-Q learning Model
    model = Sequential()
    model.add(Dense(24, input_dim=self.state_size,
activation='relu'))
    model.add(Dense(24, activation='relu'))
    model.add(Dense(self.action_size, activation='linear'))
    model.compile(loss='mse',
                  optimizer=Adam(lr=self.learning_rate))
    return model
```

5. This builds a fairly simple model, compared to others we have already seen, with three **dense** layers outputting a value for each action. The input into this network is the state.
6. Jump down to the bottom of the file and look at the training iteration loop, shown as follows:

```
if __name__ == "__main__":
    env = gym.make('CartPole-v1')
    state_size = env.observation_space.shape[0]
    action_size = env.action_space.n
    agent = DQNAgent(state_size, action_size)
    # agent.load("./save/cartpole-dqn.h5")
    done = False
    batch_size = 32

    for e in range(EPISODES):
        state = env.reset()
        state = np.reshape(state, [1, state_size])
        for time in range(500):
            # env.render()
            action = agent.act(state)
            env.render()
            next_state, reward, done, _ = env.step(action)
            reward = reward if not done else -10
            next_state = np.reshape(next_state, [1, state_size])
            agent.remember(state, action, reward, next_state, done)
            state = next_state
            if done:
                print("episode: {}/{}, score: {}, e: {:.2}"
                      .format(e, EPISODES, time, agent.epsilon))
                break
            if len(agent.memory) > batch_size:
                agent.replay(batch_size)
```

7. In this sample, our training takes place in a real-time `render` loop. The important sections of the code are highlighted, showing the reshaping of the state and calling the `agent.remember` function. The `agent.replay` function at the end is where the network trains. The `remember` function is as follows:

```
def remember(self, state, action, reward, next_state, done):
    self.memory.append((state, action, reward, next_state, done))
```

8. This function just stores the `state`, `action`, `reward`, `next_state`, and `done` parameters for the replay training. Scroll down more to the `replay` function, as follows:

```
def replay(self, batch_size):
    minibatch = random.sample(self.memory, batch_size)
    for state, action, reward, next_state, done in minibatch:
        target = reward
        if not done:
            target = (reward+self.gamma*
                      np.amax(self.model.predict(next_state)[0]))
            target_f = self.model.predict(state)
            target_f[0][action] = target
            self.model.fit(state, target_f, epochs=1, verbose=0)
        if self.epsilon > self.epsilon_min:
            self.epsilon *= self.epsilon_decay
```

9. The `replay` function is where the network training occurs. We first define a `minibatch`, which is defined from a random sampling of previous experiences grouped by `batch_size`. Then, we loop through the batches setting `reward` to the `target` and if not `done` calculating a new target based on the model prediction on the `next_state`. After that, we use the `model.predict` function on the `state` to determine the final target. Finally, we use the `model.fit` function to backpropagate the trained target back into the network.
   As this section is important, let's reiterate. Note the line where the variable `target` is calculated and set. These lines of code may look familiar, as they match the Q value equation we saw earlier. This `target` value is the value that should be predicted for the current action. This is the value that is backpropagated back for the current action and set by the returned `reward`.

10. Run the sample and watch the agent train to balance the pole on the cart. The following shows the environment as it is being trained:

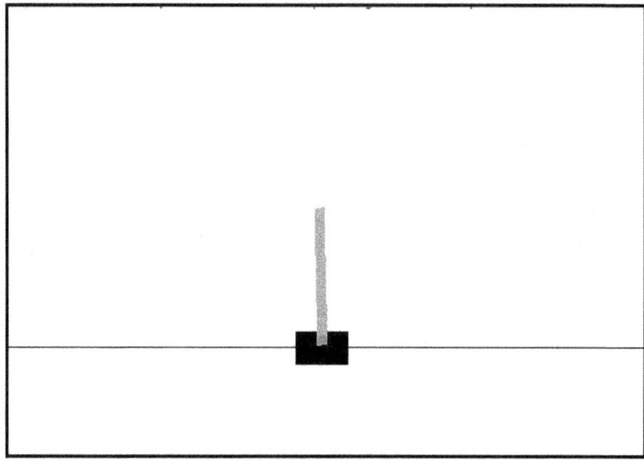

CartPole OpenAI Gym environment

The example environment uses the typical first environment, CartPole, we use to learn to build our first DRL model. In the next section, we will look at how to use the DQNAgent in other scenarios and other models supplied through the Keras-RL API.

RL experiments

Reinforcement learning is quickly advancing, and the DQN model we just looked at has quickly become outpaced by more advanced algorithms. There are several variations and advancements in RL algorithms that could fill several chapters, but most of that material would be considered academic. As such, we will instead look at some more practical examples of the various RL models the Keras RL API provides.

The first simple example we can work with is changing our previous example to work with a new `gym` environment. Open up `Chapter_5_5.py` and follow the next exercise:

1. Change the environment name in the following code:

```
if __name__ == "__main__":
    env = gym.make('MountainCar-v0')
```

2. In this case, we are going to use the `MountainCar` environment, as shown:

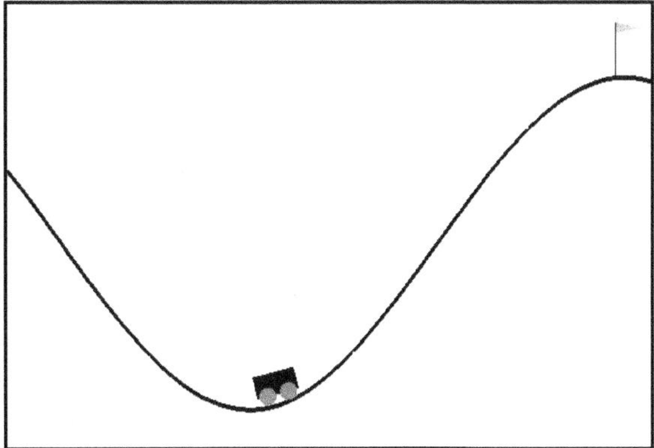

Example of MountainCar environment

3. Run the code as you normally would and see how the DQNAgent solves the hill-climbing problem.

You can see how quickly we were able to switch environments and test the DQNAgent in another environment. In the next section, we look at training Atari games with the various RL algorithms that the Keras-RL API provides.

Keras RL

Keras provides a very useful RL API that wraps several variations such as DQN, DDQN, SARSA, and so on. We won't get into the details of those various RL variations right now, but we will cover the important parts later, as we get into more complex models. For now, though, we are going to look at how you can quickly build a DRL model to play Atari games. Open up `Chapter_5_6.py` and follow these steps:

1. We first need to install several dependencies with `pip`; open a command shell or Anaconda window, and enter the following commands:

```
pip install Pillow
pip install keras-rl

pip install gym[atari] # on Linux or Mac
pip install --no-index -f
https://github.com/Kojoley/atari-py/releases atari_py  # on Windows
thanks to Nikita Kniazev
```

2. This will install the Keras RL API, `Pillow`, an image framework, and the Atari environment for `gym`.
3. Run the example code as you normally would. This sample does take script arguments, but we don't need to use them here. An example of the rendered Atari Breakout environment follows:

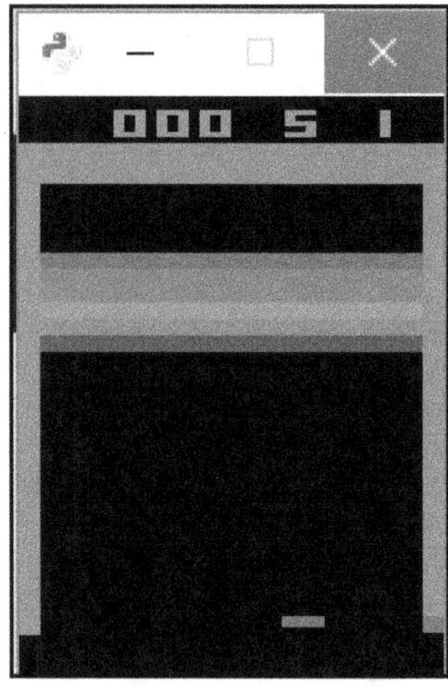

Atari Breakout environment

Unfortunately, you cannot see the game run as the agent plays, because all the action takes place in the background, but let the agent run until it completes and saves the model. Here's how we would run the sample:

1. You can rerun the sample using `--mode test` as an argument to let the agent run over 10 episodes and see the results.
2. As the sample runs, look through the code and pay special attention to the model, as follows:

```
model = Sequential()
if K.image_dim_ordering() == 'tf':
    # (width, height, channels)
    model.add(Permute((2, 3, 1), input_shape=input_shape))
elif K.image_dim_ordering() == 'th':
    # (channels, width, height)
    model.add(Permute((1, 2, 3), input_shape=input_shape))
else:
    raise RuntimeError('Unknown image_dim_ordering.')
model.add(Convolution2D(32, (8, 8), strides=(4, 4)))
model.add(Activation('relu'))
```

```
model.add(Convolution2D(64, (4, 4), strides=(2, 2)))
model.add(Activation('relu'))
model.add(Convolution2D(64, (3, 3), strides=(1, 1)))
model.add(Activation('relu'))
model.add(Flatten())
model.add(Dense(512))
model.add(Activation('relu'))
model.add(Dense(nb_actions))
model.add(Activation('linear'))
print(model.summary())
```

3. Note how our model is using `Convolution`, with pooling. This is because this example reads each screen/frame of the game as input (state) and responds accordingly. In this case, the model state is massive, and this demonstrates the real power of DRL. In this case, we are still training to a state model, but in future chapters, we will look at training a policy, rather than a model.

This was a simple introduction to RL, and we have omitted several details that can get lost on newcomers. As we plan to cover several more chapters on RL, and in particular the **Proximal Policy Optimization** (**PPO**) in more detail in `Chapter 8`, *Understanding PPO*, don't fret too much about differences such as policy and model-based RL.

There is an excellent example of this same DQN in TensorFlow at this GitHub link: `https://github.com/floodsung/DQN-Atari-Tensorflow`. The code may be a bit dated, but it is a simple and excellent example that is worth taking a look at.

We won't look any further at the code, but the reader is certainly invited to. Now let's try some exercises.

Exercises

As always, use the exercises in this section to get a better understanding of the material you learn. Try to work through at least two or three exercises in this section:

1. Return to the example `Chapter_5_1.py` and change the **alpha** (`learning_rate`) variable and see what effect this has on the values calculated.
2. Return to the example `Chapter_5_2.py` and alter the arm positions on the various bandits.
3. Change the learning rate on the example `Chapter_5_2.py` and see what effect this has on the Q results output.

4. Alter the gamma reward discount factor in the `Chapter_5_3.py` example, and see what effect this has on agent training.
5. Change the exploration epsilon in the `Chapter_5_3.py` to different values and rerun the sample. See what effect altering the various exploration parameters has on training the agent.
6. Alter the various parameters (**exploration**, **alpha**, and **gamma**) in the `Chapter_5_4.py` example and see what effect this has on training.
7. Alter the size of the memory in the `Chapter_5_4.py` example, either higher or lower, and see what effect this has on training.
8. Try to use different Gym environments in the DQNAgent example from `Chapter_5_5.py`. You can do a quick Google search to see the other possible environments you can choose from.
9. The `Chapter_5_6.py` example currently uses a form-exploration policy called `LinearAnnealedPolicy`; change the policy to use the `BoltzmannQPolicy` policy as mentioned in the code comments.
10. Be sure to download and run other Keras-RL examples from `https://github.com/keras-rl/keras-rl`. Again, you may have to install other Gym environments to get them working.

There are plenty of other examples, videos, and other materials to study with respect to RL. Learn as much as you can, as this material is extensive and complex and not something you will pick up overnight.

Summary

RL is the machine learning technology currently dominating the interest of many researchers. It is typically appealing to us, because it fits well with games and simulations. In this chapter, we covered some of the foundations of RL by starting with the fundamental introductory problems of the multi-armed and contextual bandits. Then, we quickly looked at installing the OpenAI Gym RL toolkit. We then looked at Q-learning and how to implement that in code and train it on an OpenAI Gym environment. Finally, we looked at how we could conduct various other experiments with Gym by loading a couple of other environments, including the Atari games simulator.

In the next chapter, we look at the quickly evolving a cutting-edge RL platform that Unity is currently developing.

6
Unity ML-Agents

Unity has embraced machine learning, and deep reinforcement learning in particular, with determination and vigor with the aim of producing a working **seep reinforcement learning** (**DRL**) SDK for game and simulation developers. Fortunately, the team at Unity, led by Danny Lange, has succeeded in developing a robust cutting-edge DRL engine capable of impressive results. This engine is the top of the line and outclasses the DQN model we introduced earlier in many ways. Unity uses a **proximal policy optimization** (**PPO**) model as the basis for its DRL engine. This model is significantly more complex and may differ in some ways, but, fortunately, this is at the start of many more chapters, and we will have plenty of time to introduce the concepts as we go—this is a hands-on book, after all.

In this chapter, we introduce the **Unity ML-Agents** tools and SDK for building DRL agents to play games and simulations. While this tool is both powerful and cutting-edge, it is also easy to use and provides a few tools to help us learn concepts as we go. In this chapter, we will cover the following topics:

- Installing ML-Agents
- Training an agent
- What's in a brain?
- Monitoring training with TensorBoard
- Running an agent

We would like to thank the team members at Unity for their great work on ML-Agents; here are the team members at the time of writing:

- Danny Lange (`https://arxiv.org/search/cs?searchtype=authorquery=Lange%2C+D`)
- Arthur Juliani (`https://arxiv.org/search/cs?searchtype=authorquery=Juliani%2C+A`)
- Vincent-Pierre Berges (`https://arxiv.org/search/cs?searchtype=authorquery=Berges%2C+V`)
- Esh Vckay (`https://arxiv.org/search/cs?searchtype=authorquery=Vckay%2C+E`)
- Yuan Gao (`https://arxiv.org/search/cs?searchtype=authorquery=Gao%2C+Y`)
- Hunter Henry (`https://arxiv.org/search/cs?searchtype=authorquery=Henry%2C+H`)
- Marwan Mattar (`https://arxiv.org/search/cs?searchtype=authorquery=Mattar%2C+M`)
- Adam Crespi (`https://arxiv.org/search/cs?searchtype=authorquery=Crespi%2C+A`)
- Jonathan Harper (`https://arxiv.org/search/cs?searchtype=authorquery=Harper%2C+J`)

Be sure you have Unity installed as per the section in `Chapter 4`, *Building a Deep Learning Gaming Chatbot,* before proceeding with this chapter.

Installing ML-Agents

In this section, we cover a high-level overview of the steps you will need to take in order to successfully install the ML-Agents SDK. This material is still in beta and has already changed significantly from version to version. As such, if you get stuck going through these high-level steps, just go back to the most recent Unity docs; they are very well written.

Jump on your computer and follow these steps; there may be many sub steps, so expect this to take a while:

1. Be sure you have **Git** installed on your computer; it works from the command line. Git is a very popular source code management system, and there is a ton of resources on how to install and use Git for your platform. After you have installed Git, just be sure it works by test cloning a repository, any repository.
2. Open a command window or a regular shell. Windows users can open an Anaconda window.
3. Change to a working folder where you want to place the new code, and enter the following command (Windows users may want to use `C:\ML-Agents`):

```
git clone https://github.com/Unity-Technologies/ml-agents
```

4. This will clone the `ml-agents` repository onto your computer and create a new folder with the same name. You may want to take the extra step of also adding the version to the folder name. Unity, and pretty much the whole AI space, is in continuous transition, at least at the moment. This means new and constant changes are always happening. At the time of writing, we will clone to a folder named `ml-agents.6`, like so:

```
git clone https://github.com/Unity-Technologies/ml-agents ml-agents.6
```

The author of this book previously wrote a book on ML-Agents and had to rewrite several chapters over the course of a short time in order to accommodate the major changes. In fact, this chapter has had to be also rewritten a few times to account for more major changes.

5. Create a new virtual environment for `ml-agents` and set it to `3.6`, like so:

```
#Windows
conda create -n ml-agents python=3.6

#Mac
Use the documentation for your preferred environment
```

6. Activate the environment, again, using Anaconda:

```
activate ml-agents
```

7. Install TensorFlow. With Anaconda, we can do this by using the following:

```
pip install tensorflow==1.7.1
```

8. Install the Python packages. On Anaconda, enter the following:

```
cd ML-Agents #from root folder
cd ml-agents or cd ml-agents.6  #for example
cd ml-agents
pip install -e . or pip3 install -e .
```

9. This will install all the required packages for the Agents SDK and may take several minutes. Be sure to leave this window open, as we will use it shortly.

This is the basic installation of TensorFlow and does not use a GPU. Consult the Unity documentation in order to learn how to install the GPU version. This may or may not have a dramatic impact on your training performance, depending on the power of your GPU.

This should complete the setup of the Unity Python SDK for ML-Agents. In the next section, we will learn how to set up and train one of the many example environments provided by Unity.

Training an agent

For much of this book, we have spent our time looking at code and the inner depths of **deep learning** (**DL**) and **reinforcement learning** (**RL**). With that knowledge established, we can now jump in and look at examples where **deep reinforcement learning** (**DRL**) is put to use. Fortunately, the new agent's toolkit provides several examples to demonstrate the power of the engine. Open up Unity or the Unity Hub and follow these steps:

1. Click the **Open** project button at the top of the **Project** dialog.
2. Locate and open the `UnitySDK` project folder as shown in the following screenshot:

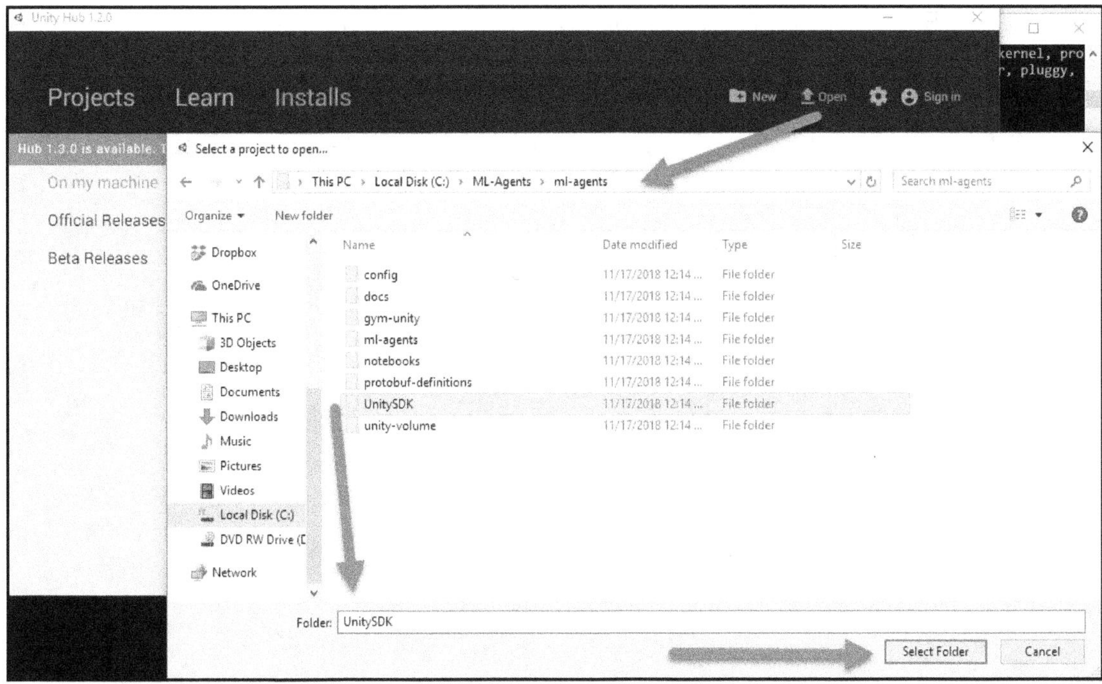

Opening the UnitySDK project

3. Wait for the project to load and then open the **Project** window at the bottom of the editor. If you are asked to update the project, just be sure to say **yes** or **continue**. Thus far, all of the agent code has been designed to be backward compatible.

4. Locate and open the **GridWorld** scene as shown in this screenshot:

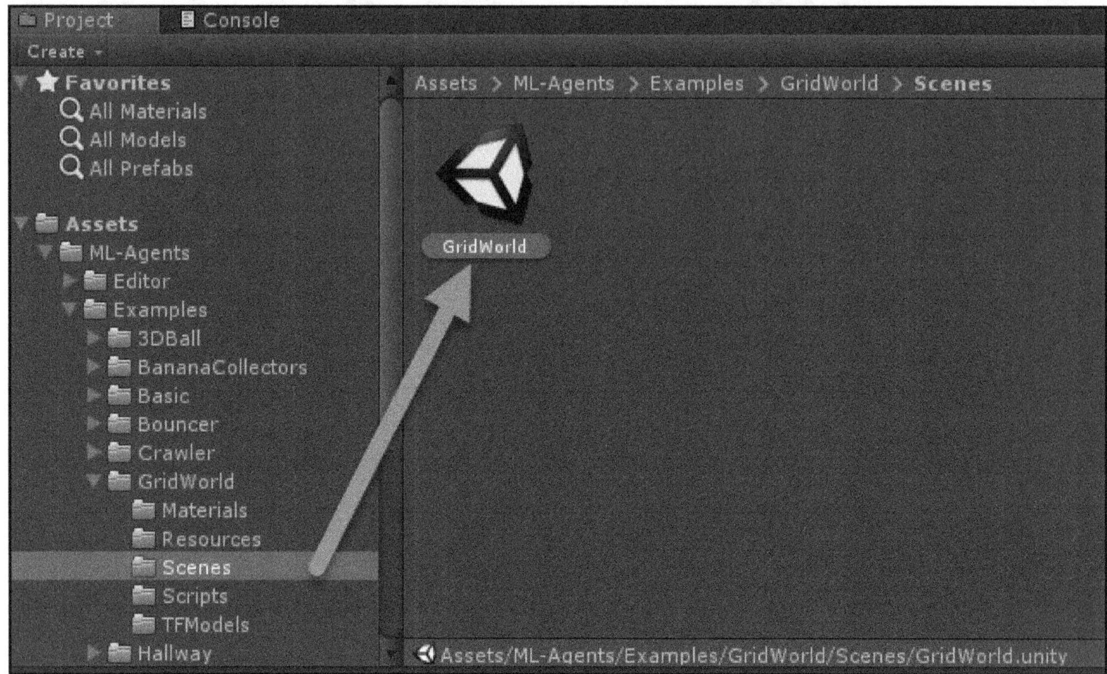

Opening the GridWorld example scene

5. Select the **GridAcademy** object in the **Hierarchy** window.

6. Then direct your attention to the **Inspector** window, and beside the Brains, click the target icon to open the Brain selection dialog:

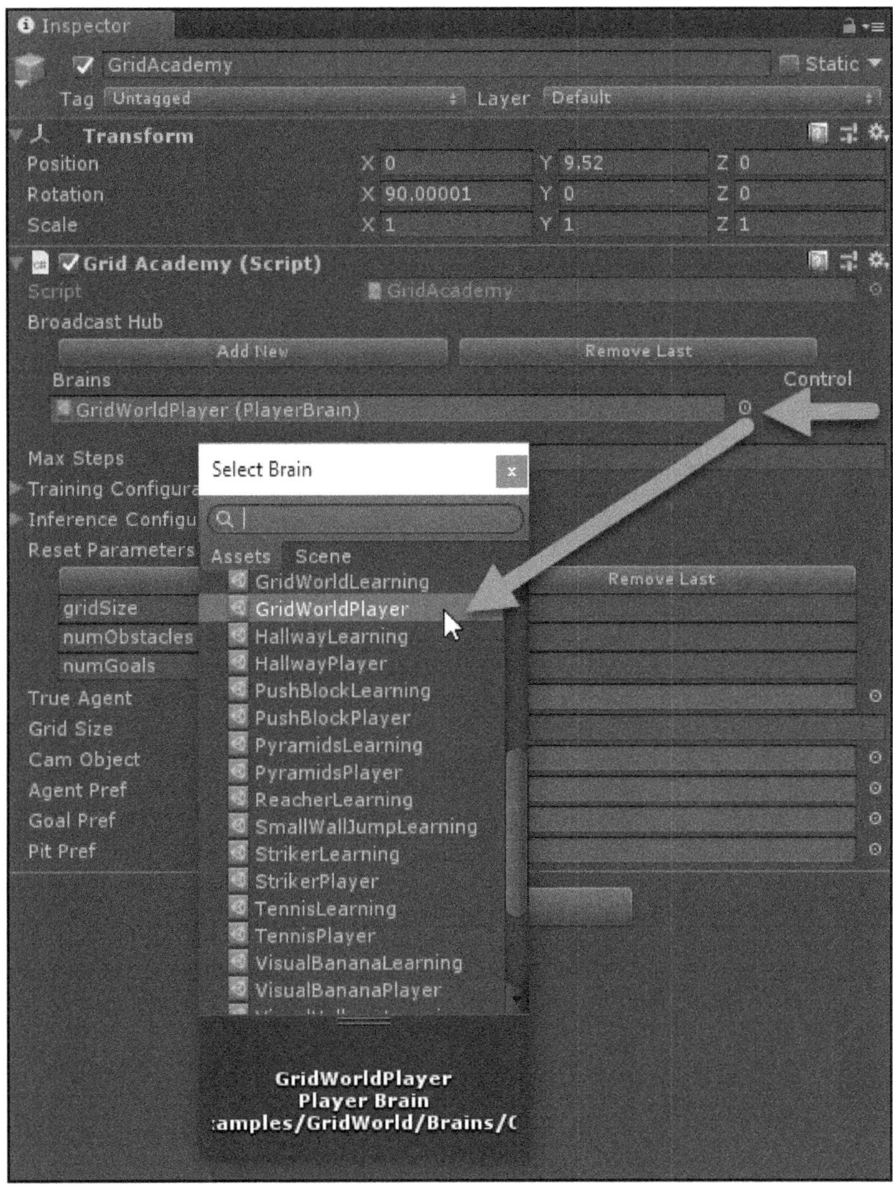

Inspecting the GridWorld example environment

7. Select the **GridWorldPlayer** brain. This brain is a *player* brain, meaning that a player, you, can control the game. We will look at this brain concept more in the next section.
8. Press the **Play** button at the top of the editor and watch the grid environment form. Since the game is currently set to a player, you can use the **WASD** controls to move the cube. The goal is much like the FrozenPond environment we built a DQN for earlier. That is, you have to move the blue cube to the green + symbol and avoid the red X.

Feel free to play the game as much as you like. Note how the game only runs for a certain amount of time and is not turn-based. In the next section, we will learn how to run this example with a DRL agent.

What's in a brain?

One of the brilliant aspects of the ML-Agents platform is the ability to switch from player control to AI/agent control very quickly and seamlessly. In order to do this, Unity uses the concept of a **brain**. A brain may be either player-controlled, a player brain, or agent-controlled, a learning brain. The brilliant part is that you can build a game and test it, as a player can then turn the game loose on an RL agent. This has the added benefit of making any game written in Unity controllable by an AI with very little effort. In fact, this is such a powerful workflow that we will spend an entire chapter, `Chapter 12`, *Debugging/Testing a Game with DRL*, on testing and debugging your games with RL.

Training an RL agent with Unity is fairly straightforward to set up and run. Unity uses Python externally to build the learning brain model. Using Python makes far more sense, since as we have already seen, several DL libraries are built on top of it. Follow these steps to train an agent for the GridWorld environment:

1. Select the **GridAcademy** again and switch the **Brains** from **GridWorldPlayer** to **GridWorldLearning** as shown:

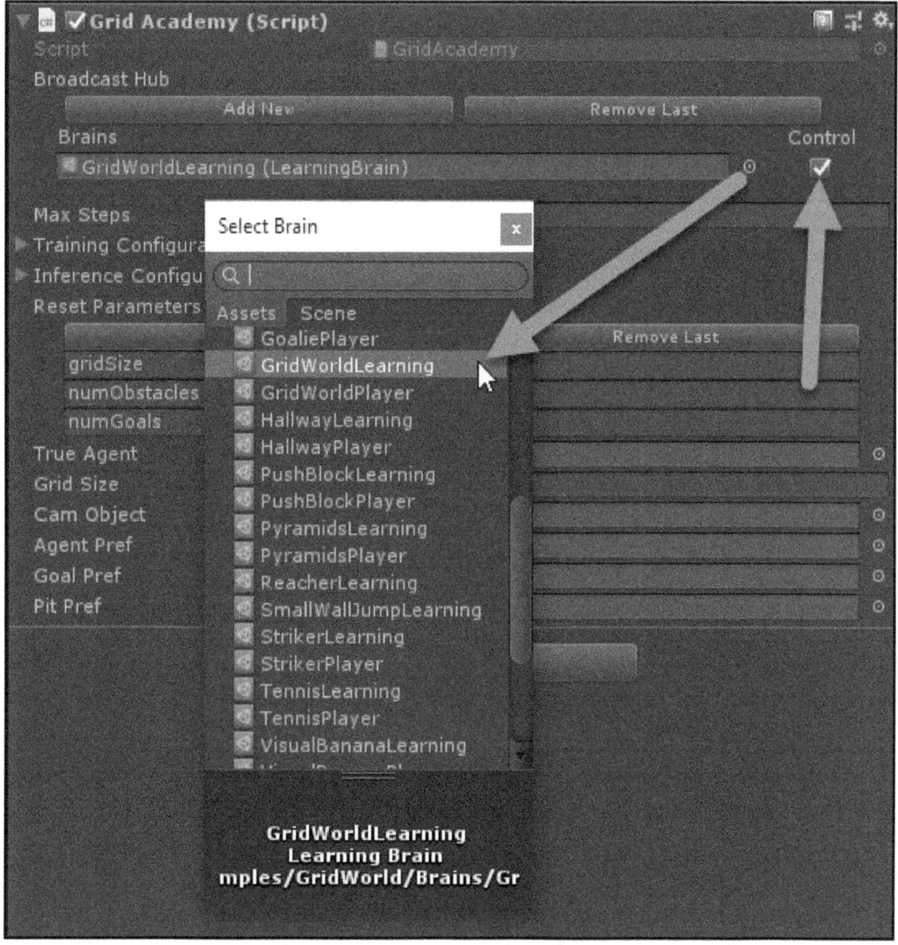

Switching the brain to use GridWorldLearning

2. Make sure to click the **Control** option at the end. This simple setting is what tells the brain it may be controlled externally. Be sure to double-check that the option is enabled.
3. Select the **trueAgent** object in the **Hierarchy** window, and then, in the **Inspector** window, change the **Brain** property under the **Grid Agent** component to a **GridWorldLearning** brain:

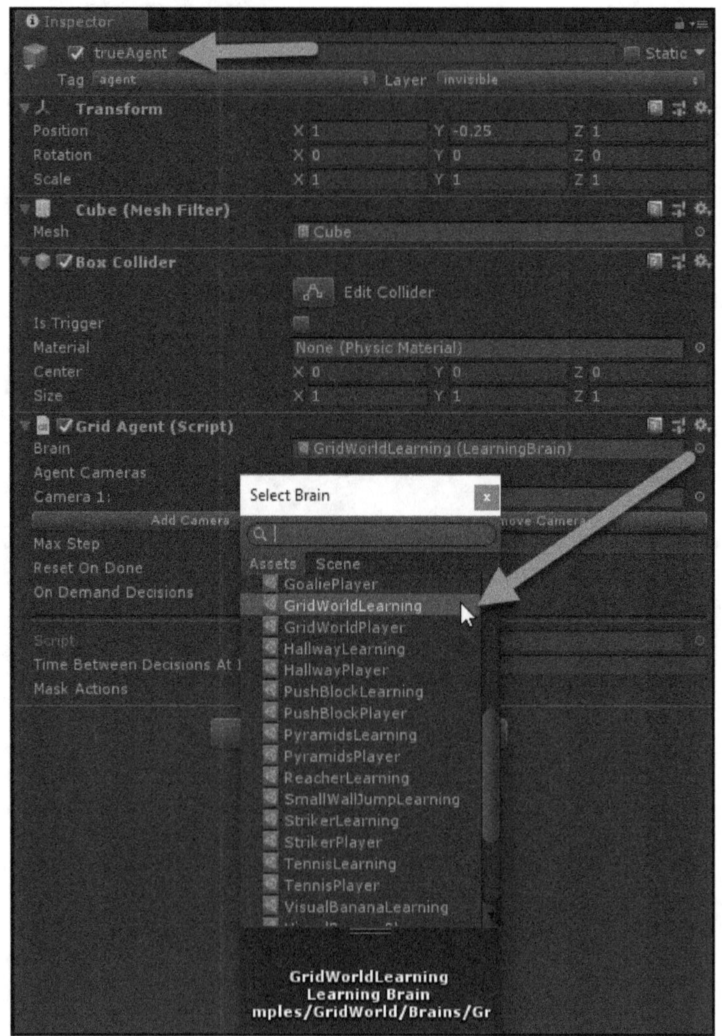

Setting the brain on the agent to GridWorldLearning

4. For this sample, we want to switch our **Academy** and **Agent** to use the same brain, **GridWorldLearning**. In more advanced cases we will explore later, this is not always the case. You could of course have a player and an agent brain running in tandem, or many other configurations.
5. Be sure you have an Anaconda or Python window open and set to the `ML-Agents/ml-agents` folder or your versioned `ml-agents` folder.
6. Run the following command in the Anaconda or Python window using the `ml-agents` virtual environment:

```
mlagents-learn config/trainer_config.yaml --run-id=firstRun --train
```

7. This will start the Unity PPO trainer and run the agent example as configured. At some point, the command window will prompt you to run the Unity editor with the environment loaded.
8. Press **Play** in the Unity editor to run the **GridWorld** environment. Shortly after, you should see the agent training with the results being output in the Python script window:

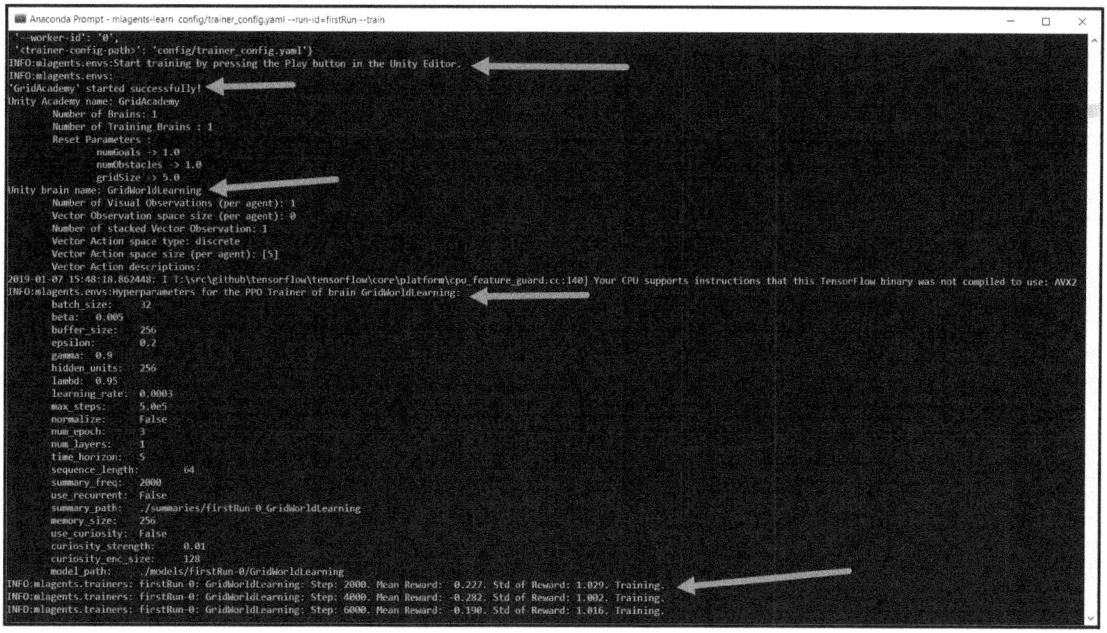

Running the GridWorld environment in training mode

9. Note how the `mlagents-learn` script is the Python code that builds the RL model to run the agent. As you can see from the output of the script, there are several parameters, or what we refer to as **hyper-parameters**, that need to be configured. Some of these parameters may sound familiar, and they should, but several may be unclear. Fortunately, for the rest of this chapter and this book, we will explore how to tune these parameters in some detail.
10. Let the agent train for several thousand iterations and note how quickly it learns. The internal model here, called **PPO**, has been shown to be a very effective learner at multiple forms of tasks and is very well suited for game development. Depending on your hardware, the agent may learn to perfect this task in less than an hour.

Keep the agent training, and we will look at more ways to inspect the agent's training progress in the next section.

Monitoring training with TensorBoard

Training an agent with RL, or any DL model for that matter, while enjoyable, is not often a simple task and requires some attention to detail. Fortunately, TensorFlow ships with a set of graph tools called **TensorBoard** we can use to monitor training progress. Follow these steps to run TensorBoard:

1. Open an Anaconda or Python window. Activate the `ml-agents` virtual environment. Don't shut down the window running the trainer; we need to keep that going.
2. Navigate to the `ML-Agents/ml-agents` folder and run the following command:

```
tensorboard --logdir=summaries
```

3. This will run TensorBoard with its own built-in web server. You can load the page by using the URL that is shown after you run the previous command.
4. Enter the URL for TensorBoard as shown in the window, or use `localhost:6006` or `machinename:6006` in your browser. After an hour or so, you should see something similar to the following:

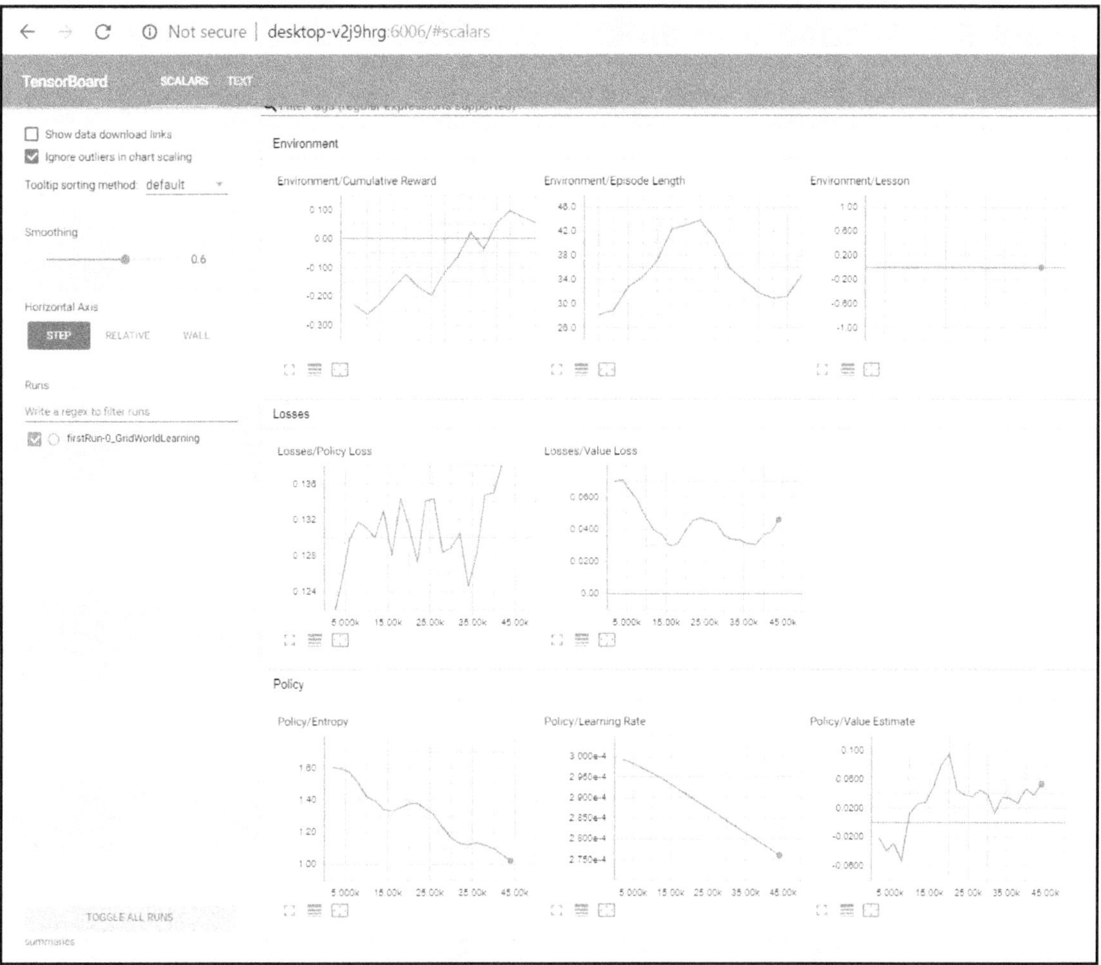

The TensorBoard graph window

5. In the preceding screenshot, you can see each of the various graphs denoting an aspect of training. Understanding each of these graphs is important to understanding how your agent is training, so we will break down the output from each section:
    - **Environment**: This section shows how the agent is performing overall in the environment. A closer look at each of the graphs is shown in the following screenshot with their preferred trend:

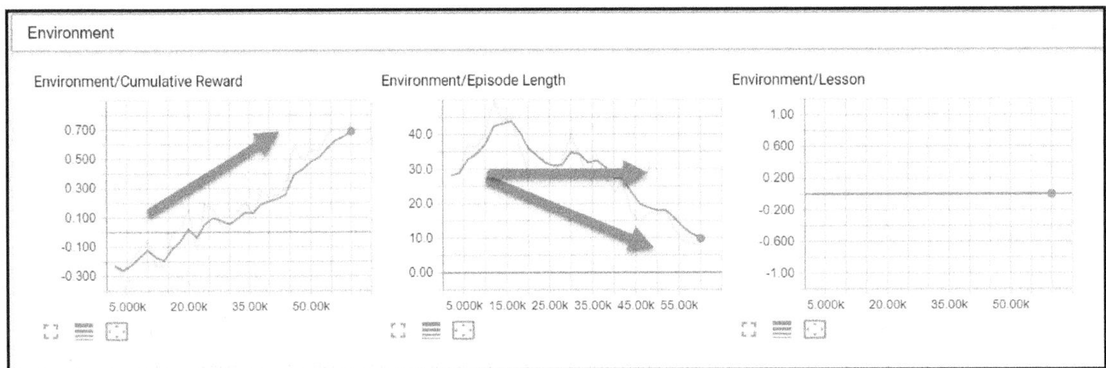

Closer look at the Environment section plots

- **Cumulative Reward**: This is the total reward the agent is maximizing. You generally want to see this going up, but there are reasons why it may fall. It is always best to maximize rewards in the range of 1 to -1. If you see rewards outside this range on the graph, you also want to correct this as well.
- **Episode Length**: It usually is a better sign if this value decreases. After all, shorter episodes mean more training. However, keep in mind that the episode length could increase out of need, so this one can go either way.
- **Lesson**: This represents which lesson the agent is on and is intended for Curriculum Learning. We will learn more about Curriculum Learning in `Chapter 9`, *Rewards and Reinforcement Learning*.

- **Losses**: This section shows graphs that represent the calculated loss or cost of the policy and value. Of course, we haven't spent much time explaining PPO and how it uses a policy, so, at this point, just understand the preferred direction when training. A screenshot of this section is shown next, again with arrows showing the optimum preferences:

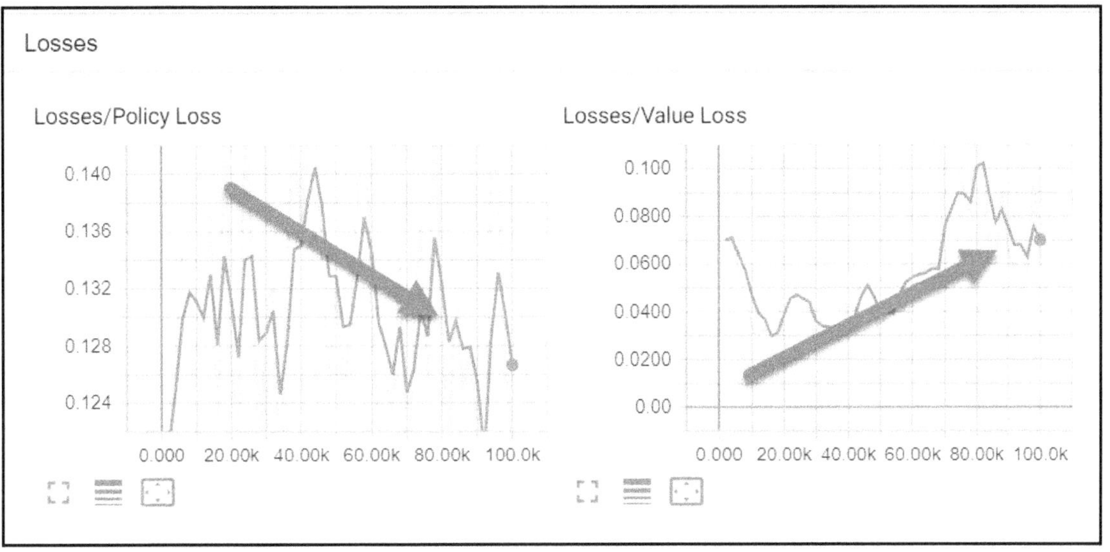

Losses and preferred training direction

- **Policy Loss**: This determines how much the policy is changing over time. The policy is the piece that decides the actions, and in general this graph should be showing a downward trend, indicating that the policy is getting better at making decisions.
- **Value Loss**: This is the mean or average loss of the `value` function. It essentially models how well the agent is predicting the value of its next state. Initially, this value should increase, and then after the reward is stabilized, it should decrease.

- **Policy**: PPO uses the concept of a policy rather than a model to determine the quality of actions. Again, we will spend more time on this in `Chapter 8`, *Understanding PPO,* where we will uncover further details about PPO. The next screenshot shows the policy graphs and their preferred trend:

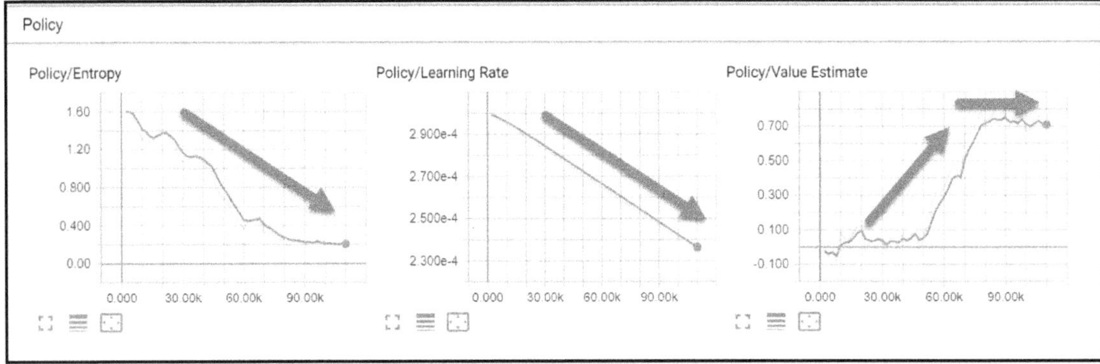

Policy graphs and preferred trends

- **Entropy**: This represents how much the agent is exploring. You want this value to decrease as the agent learns more about its surroundings and needs to explore less.
- **Learning Rate**: Currently, this value is set to decrease linearly over time.
- **Value Estimate**: This is the mean or average value visited by all states of the agent. This value should increase in order to represent a growth of the agent's knowledge and then stabilize.

These graphs are all designed to work with the implementation of the PPO method Unity is based on. Don't worry too much about understanding these new terms just yet. We will explore the foundations of PPO in `Chapter 7`, *Agent and the Environment.*

6. Let the agent run to completion and keep TensorBoard running.
7. Go back to the Anaconda/Python window that was training the brain and run this command:

```
mlagents-learn config/trainer_config.yaml --run-id=secondRun --
train
```

8. You will again be prompted to press **Play** in the editor; be sure to do so. Let the agent start the training and run for a few sessions. As you do so, monitor the TensorBoard window and note how the `secondRun` is shown on the graphs. Feel free to let this agent run to completion as well, but you can stop it now, if you want to.

In previous versions of ML-Agents, you needed to build a Unity executable first as a game-training environment and run that. The external Python brain would still run the same. This method made it very difficult to debug any code issues or problems with your game. All of these difficulties were corrected with the current method; however, we may need to use the old executable method later for some custom training.

Now that we have seen how easy it is to set up and train an agent, we will go through the next section to see how that agent can be run without an external Python brain and run directly in Unity.

Running an agent

Using Python to train works well, but it is not something a real game would ever use. Ideally, what we want to be able to do is build a TensorFlow graph and use it in Unity. Fortunately, a library was constructed, called TensorFlowSharp, that allows .NET to consume TensorFlow graphs. This allows us to build offline TFModels and later inject them into our game. Unfortunately, we can only use trained models and not train in this manner, at least not yet.

Let's see how this works by using the graph we just trained for the **GridWorld** environment and use it as an internal brain in Unity. Follow the exercise in the next section to set up and use an internal brain:

1. Download the TFSharp plugin from this link: `https://s3.amazonaws.com/unity-ml-agents/0.5/TFSharpPlugin.unitypackage`.

If this link does not work, consult the Unity docs or the Asset Store for a new one. The current version is described as experimental and subject to change.

2. From the editor menu, select **Assets** | **Import Package** | **Custom Package...**
3. Locate the asset package you just downloaded and use the import dialogs to load the plugin into the project. If you need help with these basic Unity tasks, there is plenty of help online that can guide you further.

4. From the menu, select **Edit** | **Project Settings**. This will open the **Settings** window (new in 2018.3)
5. Locate under the **Player** options the **Scripting Define Symbols** and set the text to `ENABLE_TENSORFLOW` and enable **Allow Unsafe Code**, as shown in this screenshot:

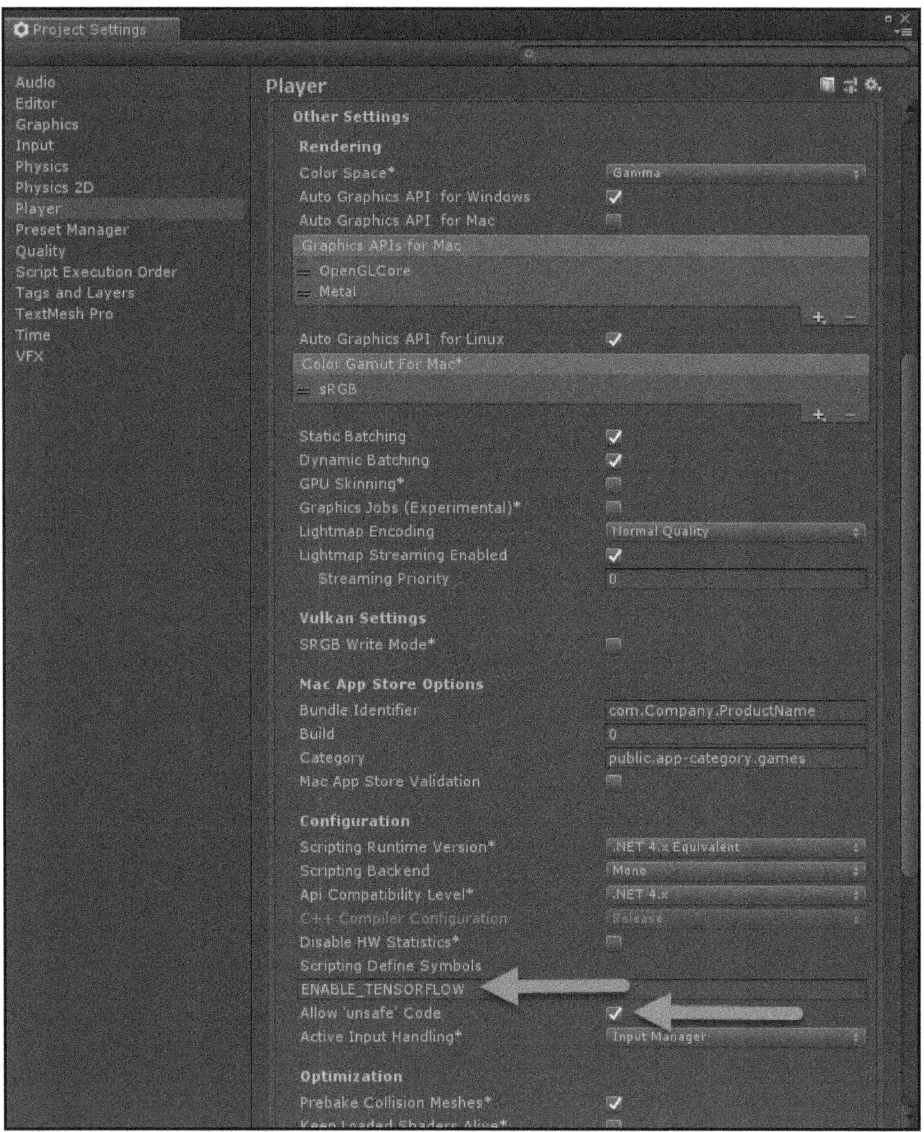

Setting the ENABLE_TENSORFLOW flag

6. Locate the **GridWorldAcademy** object in the **Hierarchy** window and make sure it is using the **Brains** | **GridWorldLearning**. Turn the **Control** option off under the **Brains** section of the **Grid Academy** script.
7. Locate the **GridWorldLearning** brain in the `Assets/Examples/GridWorld/Brains` folder and make sure the **Model** parameter is set in the **Inspector** window, as shown in this screenshot:

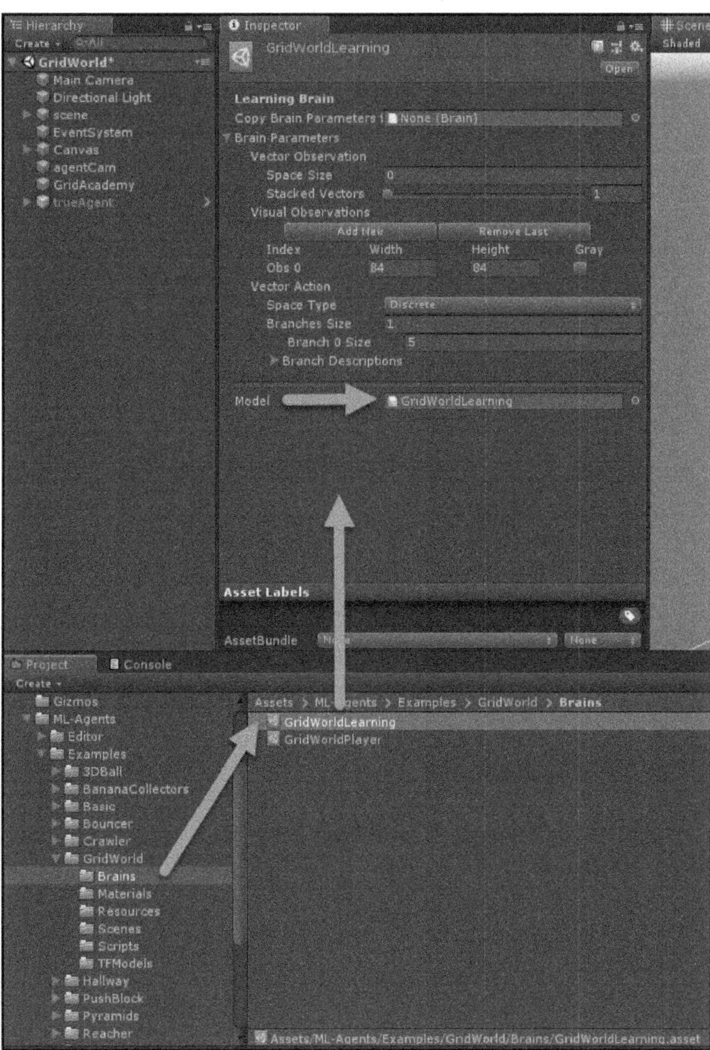

Setting the model for the brain to use

8. The **Model** should already be set to the **GridWorldLearning** model. In this example, we are using the TFModel that is shipped with the **GridWorld** example. You could also easily use the model we had trained from the earlier example by just importing it into the project and then setting it as the model.
9. Press **Play** to run the editor and watch the agent control the cube.

Right now, we are running the environment with the pre-trained Unity brain. In the next section, we will look at how to use the brain we trained in the previous section.

Loading a trained brain

All of the Unity samples come with pre-trained brains you can use to explore the samples. Of course, we want to be able to load our own TF graphs into Unity and run them. Follow the next steps in order to load a trained graph:

1. Locate the `ML-Agents/ml-agents/models/firstRun-0` folder. Inside this folder, you should see a file named `GridWorldLearning.bytes`. Drag this file into the Unity editor into the `Project/Assets/ML-Agents/Examples/GridWorld/TFModels` folder, as shown:

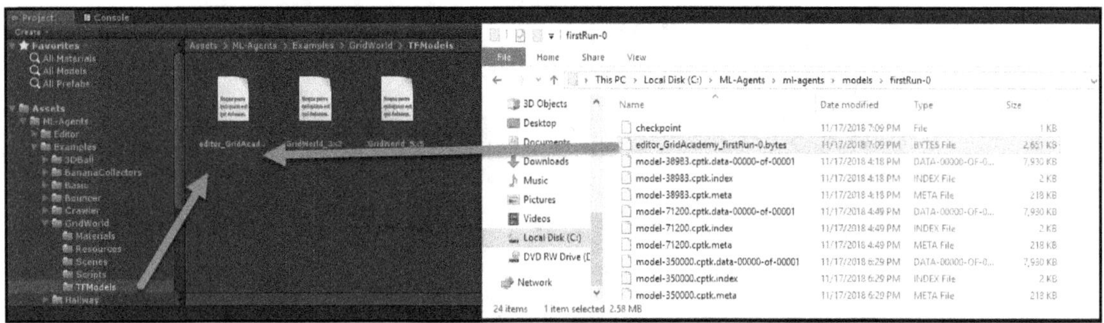

Dragging the bytes graph into Unity

2. This will import the graph into the Unity project as a resource and rename it `GridWorldLearning 1`. It does this because the default model already has the same name.

3. Locate the `GridWorldLearning` from the `brains` folder and select it in the **Inspector** windows and drag the new **GridWorldLearning 1** model onto the **Model** slot under the **Brain Parameters**:

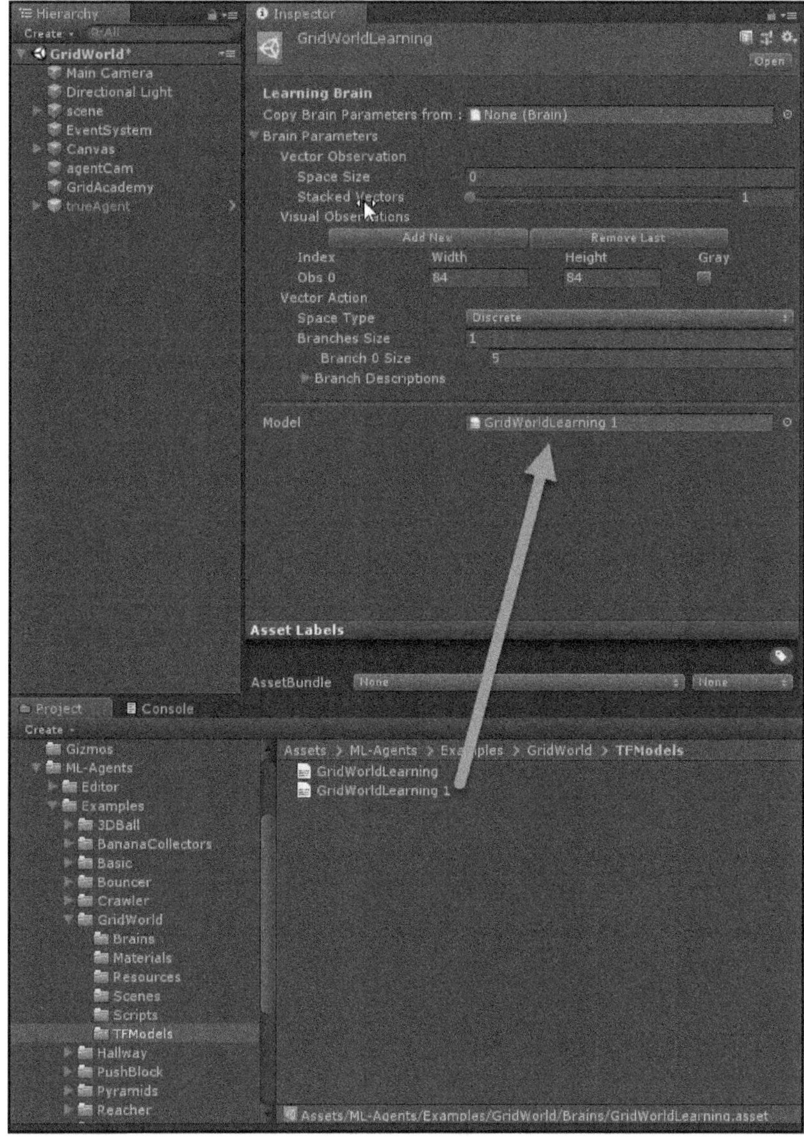

Loading the Graph Model slot in the brain

4. We won't need to change any other parameters at this point, but pay special attention to how the brain is configured. The defaults will work for now.
5. Press **Play** in the Unity editor and watch the agent run through the game successfully.
6. How long you trained the agent for will really determine how well it plays the game. If you let it complete the training, the agent should be equal to the already trained Unity agent.

There are plenty of Unity samples that you can now run and explore on your own. Feel free to train several of the examples on your own or as listed in the exercises in the next section.

Exercises

Use the exercises in this section to enhance and reinforce your learning. Attempt at least a few of these exercises on your own, and remember this is really for your benefit:

1. Set up and run the **3DBall** example environment to train a working agent. This environment uses multiple games/agents to train.
2. Set the **3DBall** example to let half of the games use an already trained brain and the other to use training or external learning.
3. Train the **PushBlock** environment agents using external learning.
4. Train the **VisualPushBlock** environment. Note how this example uses a visual camera to capture the environment state.
5. Run the **Hallway** scene as a player and then train the scene using an external learning brain.
6. Run the **VisualHallway** scene as a player and then train the scene using an external learning brain.
7. Run the **WallJump** scene and then run it under training conditions. This example uses Curriculum Training, which we will look at further in `Chapter 9`, *Rewards and Reinforcement Learning*.
8. Run the **Pyramids** scene and then set it up for training.
9. Run the **VisualPyramids** scene and set it up for training.
10. Run the **Bouncer** scene and set it up for training.

While you don't have to run all these exercises/examples, it can be helpful to familiarize yourself with them. They can often be the basis for creating new environments, as we will see in the next chapter.

Summary

As you have learned, the workflow for training RL and DRL agents in Unity is much more integrated and seamless than in OpenAI Gym. We didn't have to write a line of code to train an agent in a grid world environment, and the visuals are just plain better. For this chapter, we started by installing the ML-Agents toolkit. Then we loaded up a **GridWorld** environment and set it up to train with an RL agent. From there, we looked at TensorBoard for monitoring agent training and progress. After we were done training, we first loaded up a Unity pre-trained brain and ran that in the **GridWorld** environment. Then we used a brain we just trained and imported that into Unity as an asset and then as the **GridWorldLearning** brain's model.

In the next chapter, we will explore how to construct a new RL environment or game we can use an agent to learn and play. This will allow us to peek under the covers further about the various details we skimmed over in this chapter.

7 Agent and the Environment

Playing with and exploring experimental reinforcement learning environments is all well and good, but, at the end of the day, most game developers want to develop their own learning environment. To do that, we need to understand a lot more about training deep reinforcement learning environments, and, in particular, how an agent receives and processes input. Therefore, in this chapter, we will take a very close look at training one of the more difficult sample environments in Unity. This will help us understand many of the intricate details of how important input and state is to training an agent, and the many features in the Unity ML-Agents toolkit that make it easy for us to explore multiple options. This will be a critical chapter for anyone wanting to build their own environments and use the ML-Agents in their game. So, if you need to work through this chapter a couple of times to understand the details, please do so.

In this chapter, we are going to cover many details related to how agents process input/state, and how you can adapt this to fit your agent training. Here is a summary of what we will cover in this chapter:

- Exploring the training environment
- Understanding state
- Understanding visual state
- Convolution and visual state
- Recurrent networks

Ensure that you have read, understood, and ran some of the sample exercises from the last chapter, `Chapter 6`, *Unity ML-Agents*. It is essential that you have Unity and the ML-Agents toolkit configured and running correctly before continuing.

Exploring the training environment

One of the things that often pushes us to success, or pushes us to learn, is failure. As humans, when we fail, one of two things happens: we try harder or we quit. Interestingly, this is not unlike a negative reward in reinforcement learning. In RL, an agent that gets a negative reward may quit exploring a path if it sees no future value, or that it predicts will not give enough benefit. However, if the agent feels like more exploration is needed, or it hasn't exhausted the path fully, it will push on and, often, this leads it to the right path. Again, this is certainly not unlike us humans. Therefore, in this section, we are going to train one of the more difficult example agents to push ourselves to learn how to fail and fix training failures.

Unity is currently in the process of building a multi-level bench marking tower environment that features multiple levels of difficulty. This will allow DRL enthusiasts, practitioners, and researchers to test their skills/models on baseline environments. The author has been told, on reasonably good authority, that this environment should be completed by early/mid 2019.

We will need to use many of the advanced features of the Unity ML-Agents toolkit ultimately get this example working. This will require you to have a good understanding of the first five chapters of this book. If you skipped those chapters to get here, please go back and review them as needed. In many places in this chapter, helpful links have been provided to previous relevant chapters.

The training sample environment we will focus on is the **VisualHallway**, not to be confused with the standard **Hallway** example. The **VisualHallway** differs in that it uses the camera as the complete input state into the model, while the other Unity examples we previously looked at used some form of multi-aware sensor input, often allowing the agent to see 90 to 360 degrees at all times, and be given other useful information. This is fine for most games, and, in fact, many games still allow such cheats or intuition for NPC or computer opponents as part of their AI. Putting these cheats in for a game's AI has been an accepted practice for many years, but perhaps that will soon change.

After all, good games are fun to play, and make sense to the player. Games of the not so distant past could get away with giving the AI cheats. However, now, players are expecting more, they want their AI to play by the same rules as them. The previous perception that computer AI was hindered by technological limitations is gone, and now a game AI must play by the same rules as the player, which makes our focus on getting the **VisualHallway** sample working/training more compelling.

There is, of course, another added benefit to teaching an AI to play/learn like a player, and that is the ability to transfer that capability to play in other environments using a concept called transfer learning. We will explore transfer learning in `Chapter 10`, *Imitation and Transfer Learning*, where we will learn how to adapt pretrained models/parameters and apply them to other environments.

The **VisualHallway/Hallway** samples start by dropping the agent into a long room or hallway at random. In the center of this space is a colored block, and at one end of the hallway in each corner is a colored square covering the floor. The block is either red or gold (orange/yellow) and is used to inform the agent of the target square that is the same color. The goal is for the agent to move to the correct colored square. In the standard Hallway example, the agent is given 360 degree sensor awareness. In the Visual Hallway example, the agent is only shown a camera view of the room, exactly as the player version of the game would see. This puts our agent on equal footing with a player.

Before we get to training, let's open up the example and play it as a player would, and see how we do. Follow this exercise to open the **VisualHallway** sample:

1. Ensure you have a working installation of ML-Agents and can train a brain externally in Python before continuing. Consult the previous chapter if you need help.
2. Open the **VisualHallway** scene from the **Assets** | **ML-Agents** | **Examples** | **Hallway** | **Scenes** folder in the **Project** window.

3. Make sure that **Agent** | **Hallway Agent** | **Brain** is set to **VisualHallwayPlayer**, as shown in the following screenshot:

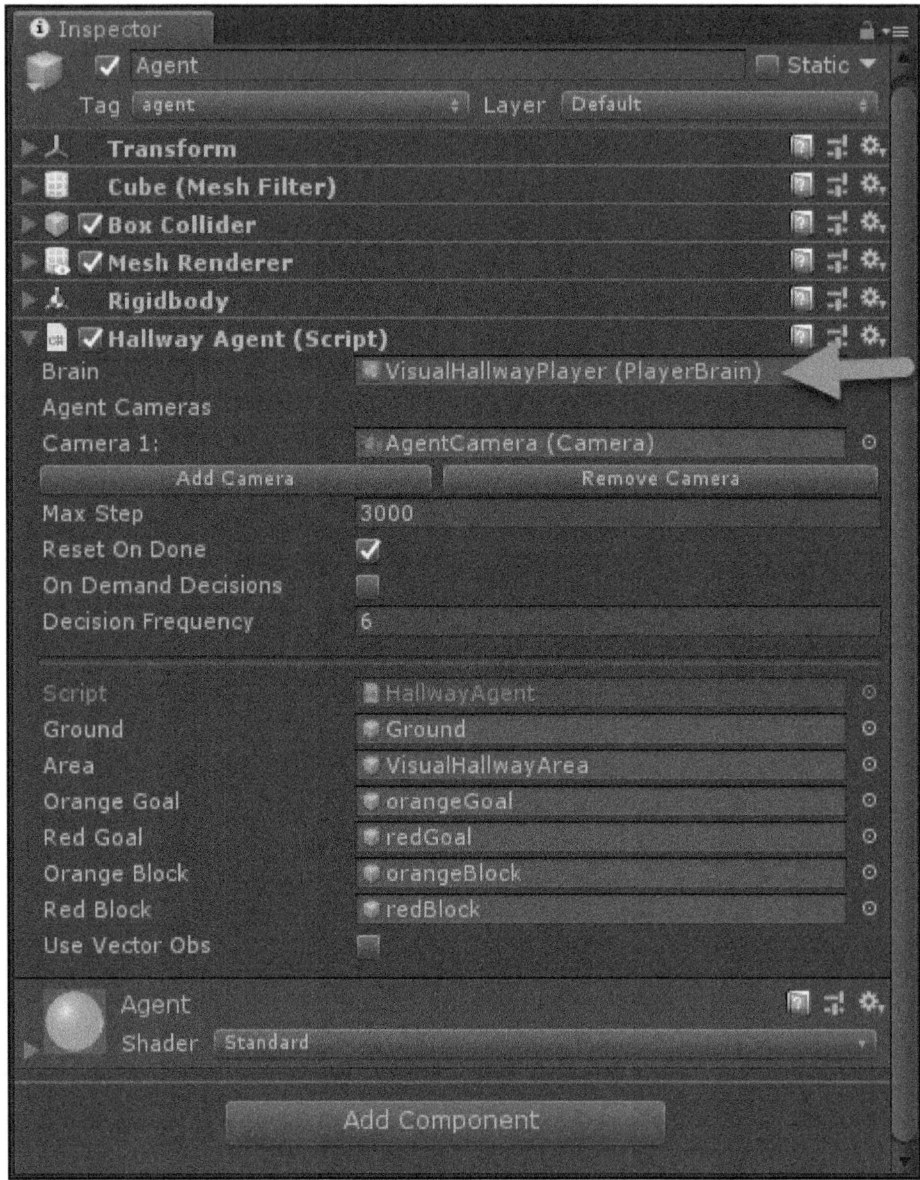

Hallway Agent | Brain set to player

4. Press **Play** in the editor to run the scene, and use the *W*, *A*, *S*, and *D* keys to control the agent. Remember, the goal is to move to the square that is the same color as the center square.
5. Play the game and move to both color squares to see what happens when a reward is given, either negative or positive. The game screen will flash with green or red when a reward square is entered.

This game environment is typical of a first person shooter, and perfect for training an agent to play in first person as well. Training an agent to play as a human would be the goal of many an AI practitioner, and one you may or may not strive to incorporate in your game. As we will see, depending on the complexity of your game, this type of learning/training may not even be a viable option. At this point, we should look at how to set up and train the agent visually.

Training the agent visually

Fortunately, setting up the agent to train it visually is quite straightforward, especially if you worked through the exercises in the last chapter. Open the Unity editor to the **VisualHallway** scene, have a Python command or Anaconda window ready, and let's begin:

1. In Unity, change **Agent** | **Hallway Agent** | **Brain** to **VisualHallwayLearning**, as shown in the following screenshot:

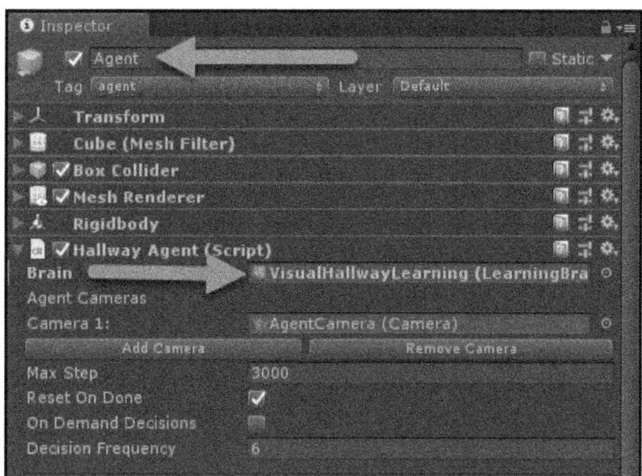

Changing that the Brain to learning

2. Click on the **VisualHallwayLearning** brain to locate it in the **Project** window.
3. Click on the **VisualHallwayLearning** brain to view its properties in the **Inspector** window, and as shown in the following screen excerpt:

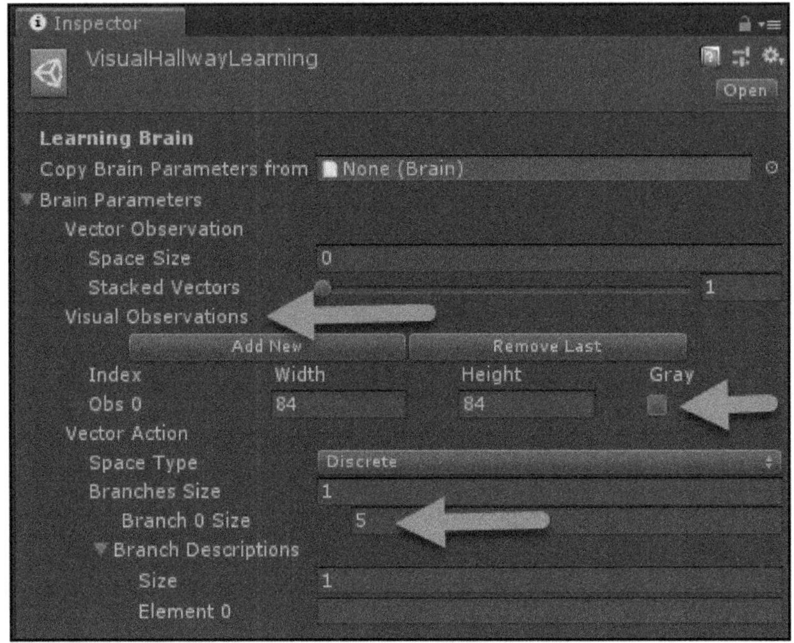

Confirming the properties are set correctly on the learning brain

4. Make sure that the **Brain** parameters are set to accept a single **Visual Observation** at a resolution of `84` x `84` pixels, and are not using **Gray** scale. Gray is simply the removal of the color channels, which makes the input one channel instead of three. Recall our discussion of CNN layers in `Chapter 2`, *Convolutional and Recurrent Networks*. Also, be sure that the **Vector Observation** | **Space Size** is **0**, as shown in the preceding screenshot.
5. From the **Menu**, select **File** | **Save** and **File** | **Save Project** to save all your changes.
6. Switch to your Python window or Anaconda prompt, make sure you are in the `ML-Agents/ml-agents` directory, and run the following command:

```
mlagents-learn config/trainer_config.yaml --run-id=visualhallway --
train
```

7. After the command runs, wait for the prompt to start the editor. Then, run the editor when prompted and let the sample run to completion, or however long you have the patience for.
8. After you run the sample to completion, you should see something like the following:

```
Anaconda Prompt
NFO:mlagents.trainers: visualhallway2-0: VisualHallwayLearning: Step: 471000. Mean Reward: -1.000. Std of Reward: 0.000. Training.
NFO:mlagents.trainers: visualhallway2-0: VisualHallwayLearning: Step: 472000. Mean Reward: -1.000. Std of Reward: 0.000. Training.
NFO:mlagents.trainers: visualhallway2-0: VisualHallwayLearning: Step: 473000. Mean Reward: -1.000. Std of Reward: 0.000. Training.
NFO:mlagents.trainers: visualhallway2-0: VisualHallwayLearning: Step: 474000. Mean Reward: -1.000. Std of Reward: 0.000. Training.
NFO:mlagents.trainers: visualhallway2-0: VisualHallwayLearning: Step: 475000. Mean Reward: -1.000. Std of Reward: 0.000. Training.
NFO:mlagents.trainers: visualhallway2-0: VisualHallwayLearning: Step: 476000. Mean Reward: -1.000. Std of Reward: 0.000. Training.
NFO:mlagents.trainers: visualhallway2-0: VisualHallwayLearning: Step: 477000. Mean Reward: -1.000. Std of Reward: 0.000. Training.
NFO:mlagents.trainers: visualhallway2-0: VisualHallwayLearning: Step: 478000. Mean Reward: -1.000. Std of Reward: 0.000. Training.
NFO:mlagents.trainers: visualhallway2-0: VisualHallwayLearning: Step: 479000. Mean Reward: -1.000. Std of Reward: 0.000. Training.
NFO:mlagents.trainers: visualhallway2-0: VisualHallwayLearning: Step: 480000. Mean Reward: -1.000. Std of Reward: 0.000. Training.
NFO:mlagents.trainers: visualhallway2-0: VisualHallwayLearning: Step: 481000. Mean Reward: -1.000. Std of Reward: 0.000. Training.
NFO:mlagents.trainers: visualhallway2-0: VisualHallwayLearning: Step: 482000. Mean Reward: -1.000. Std of Reward: 0.000. Training.
NFO:mlagents.trainers: visualhallway2-0: VisualHallwayLearning: Step: 483000. Mean Reward: -1.000. Std of Reward: 0.000. Training.
NFO:mlagents.trainers: visualhallway2-0: VisualHallwayLearning: Step: 484000. Mean Reward: -1.000. Std of Reward: 0.000. Training.
NFO:mlagents.trainers: visualhallway2-0: VisualHallwayLearning: Step: 485000. Mean Reward: -1.000. Std of Reward: 0.000. Training.
NFO:mlagents.trainers: visualhallway2-0: VisualHallwayLearning: Step: 486000. Mean Reward: -1.000. Std of Reward: 0.000. Training.
NFO:mlagents.trainers: visualhallway2-0: VisualHallwayLearning: Step: 487000. Mean Reward: -1.000. Std of Reward: 0.000. Training.
NFO:mlagents.trainers: visualhallway2-0: VisualHallwayLearning: Step: 488000. Mean Reward: -1.000. Std of Reward: 0.000. Training.
NFO:mlagents.trainers: visualhallway2-0: VisualHallwayLearning: Step: 489000. Mean Reward: -1.000. Std of Reward: 0.000. Training.
NFO:mlagents.trainers: visualhallway2-0: VisualHallwayLearning: Step: 490000. Mean Reward: -1.000. Std of Reward: 0.000. Training.
NFO:mlagents.trainers: visualhallway2-0: VisualHallwayLearning: Step: 491000. Mean Reward: -1.000. Std of Reward: 0.000. Training.
NFO:mlagents.trainers: visualhallway2-0: VisualHallwayLearning: Step: 492000. Mean Reward: -1.000. Std of Reward: 0.000. Training.
NFO:mlagents.trainers: visualhallway2-0: VisualHallwayLearning: Step: 493000. Mean Reward: -1.000. Std of Reward: 0.000. Training.
NFO:mlagents.trainers: visualhallway2-0: VisualHallwayLearning: Step: 494000. Mean Reward: -1.000. Std of Reward: 0.000. Training.
NFO:mlagents.trainers: visualhallway2-0: VisualHallwayLearning: Step: 495000. Mean Reward: -1.000. Std of Reward: 0.000. Training.
NFO:mlagents.trainers: visualhallway2-0: VisualHallwayLearning: Step: 496000. Mean Reward: -1.000. Std of Reward: 0.000. Training.
NFO:mlagents.trainers: visualhallway2-0: VisualHallwayLearning: Step: 497000. Mean Reward: -1.000. Std of Reward: 0.000. Training.
NFO:mlagents.trainers: visualhallway2-0: VisualHallwayLearning: Step: 498000. Mean Reward: -1.000. Std of Reward: 0.000. Training.
NFO:mlagents.trainers: visualhallway2-0: VisualHallwayLearning: Step: 499000. Mean Reward: -1.000. Std of Reward: 0.000. Training.
NFO:mlagents.envs:Saved Model
NFO:mlagents.trainers: visualhallway2-0: VisualHallwayLearning: Step: 500000. Mean Reward: -1.000. Std of Reward: 0.000. Training.
NFO:mlagents.envs:Saved Model
NFO:mlagents.trainers:List of nodes to export for brain :VisualHallwayLearning
NFO:mlagents.trainers: is_continuous_control
NFO:mlagents.trainers: version_number
NFO:mlagents.trainers: memory_size
NFO:mlagents.trainers: action_output_shape
NFO:mlagents.trainers: recurrent_out
NFO:mlagents.trainers: action_probs
NFO:mlagents.trainers: action
NFO:mlagents.trainers: value_estimate
NFO:tensorflow:Restoring parameters from ./models/visualhallway2-0/VisualHallwayLearning\model-500001.cptk
NFO:tensorflow:Froze 15 variables.
onverted 15 variables to const ops.
```

Full training run to completion

Assuming you trained your agent to the end of the run that is, for 500 K iterations, then you can confirm that the agent does, in fact, learn nothing. So, why would Unity put an example like that in their samples? Well, you could argue that it was an intentional challenge, or perhaps just an oversight on their part. Either way, we will take it as a challenge to better understand reinforcement learning.

Before we tackle this challenge, let's take a step back and reaffirm our understanding of this environment by looking at the easier to train Hallway example in the next section.

Reverting to the basics

Often, when you get stuck on a problem, it helps to go back to the beginning and reaffirm that your understanding of everything works as expected. Now, to be fair, we have yet to explore the internals of ML-Agents and really understand DRL, so we never actually started at the beginning, but, for the purposes of this example, we will take a step back and look at the **Hallway** example in more detail. Jump back into the editor and follow this exercise:

1. Open the **Hallway** sample scene in the editor. Remember, the scene is located in the **Assets** | **ML-Agents** | **Examples** | **Hallway** | **Scenes** folder.
2. This example is configured to use several concurrent training environments. We are able to train multiple concurrent training environments with the same brain, because **Proximal Policy Optimization** (**PPO**), the RL algorithm powering this agent, trains to a policy and not a model. We will cover the fundamentals of policy and model-based learning when we get to the internals of PPO in `Chapter 8`, *Understanding PPO,* for RL. For our purposes and for simplicity, we will disable these additional environments for now.
3. Press *Shift* and then select all the numbered **HallwayArea** (1-15) objects in the **Hierarchy**.
4. With all the extra **HallwayArea** objects selected, disable them all by clicking the **Active** checkbox, as shown in the following screenshot:

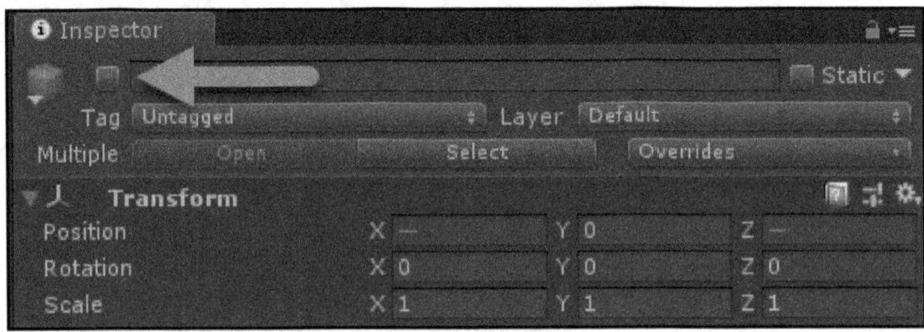

Disabling all the extra training hallways

5. Open the remaining active **HallwayArea** in the **Hierarchy** window and select the **Agent**.
6. Set the **Brain** agents to use the **HallwayLearning** brain. It may be set to use the player brain by default.
7. Select the **Academy** object back in the **Hierarchy** window, and make sure the **Hallway Academy** component has its brain set to **Learning** and that the **Control** checkbox is enabled.
8. Open a Python or Anaconda window to the `ML-Agents/ml-agents` folder. Make sure your ML-Agents virtual environment is active and run the following command:

```
mlagents-learn config/trainer_config.yaml --run-id=hallway --train
```

9. Let the trainer start up and prompt you to click **Play** in the editor. Watch the agent run and compare its performance to the **VisualHallway** example.

Generally, you will notice some amount of training activity from the agent before 50,000 iterations, but this may vary. By training activity, we mean the agent is responding with a Mean Reward greater than -1.0 and a Standard Reward not equal to zero. Even if you let the example run to completion, that is, 500,000 iterations again, it is unlikely that the sample will train to a positive Mean Reward. We generally want our rewards to range from -1.0 to +1.0, with some amount of variation to show learning activity. If you recall from the VisualHallway example, the agent showed no learning activity for the duration of the training. We could have extended the training iterations, but it is unlikely we would have seen any stable training emerge. The reason for this has to do with the increased state space and handling of rewards. We will expand our understanding of state and how it pertains to RL in the next section.

Understanding state

The **Hallway** and **VisualHallway** examples are essentially the same game problem, but provide a different perspective, or what we may refer to in reinforcement learning as environment or game state. In the **Hallway** example, the agent learns by sensor input, which is something we will look at shortly, while in the **VisualHallway** example, the agent learns by a camera or player view. What will be helpful at this point is to understand how each example handles state, and how we can modify it.

In the following exercise, we will modify the **Hallway** input state and see the results:

1. Jump back into the **Hallway** scene with learning enabled as we left it at the end of the last exercise.
2. We will need to modify a few lines of C# code, nothing very difficult, but it may be useful to install Visual Studio (Community or another version) as this will be our preferred editor. You can, of course, use any code editor you like as long as it works with Unity.
3. Locate the **Agent** object in the **Hierarchy** window, and then, in the **Inspector** window, click the Gear icon over the **Hallway Agent** component, as shown in the following screenshot:

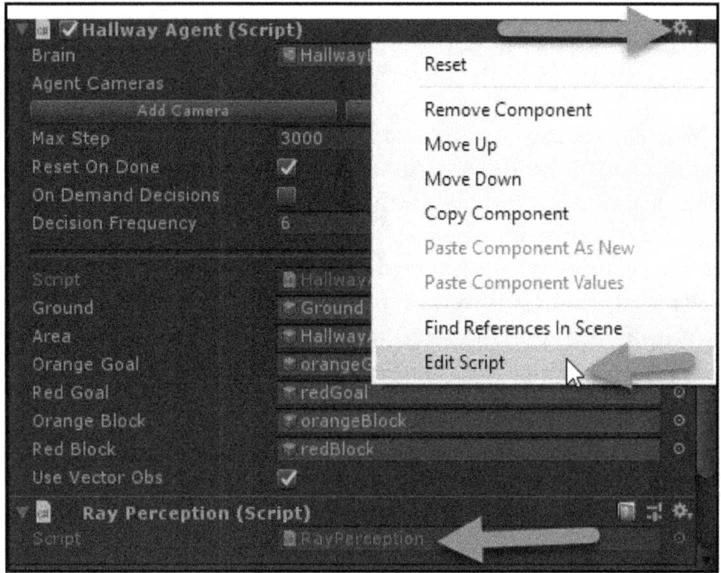

Opening the HallwayAgent.cs script

4. From the context menu, select the **Edit Script** option, as shown in the previous screenshot. This will open the script in your code editor of choice.

5. Locate the following section of C# code in your editor:

```
public override void CollectObservations()
{
  if (useVectorObs)
  {
    float rayDistance = 12f;
    float[] rayAngles = { 20f, 60f, 90f, 120f, 160f };
    string[] detectableObjects = { "orangeGoal", "redGoal",
"orangeBlock", "redBlock", "wall" };
    AddVectorObs(GetStepCount() / (float)agentParameters.maxStep);
    AddVectorObs(rayPer.Perceive(rayDistance, rayAngles,
detectableObjects, 0f, 0f));
  }
}
```

6. The `CollectObservations` method is where the agent collects its observations or inputs its state. In the Hallway example, the agent has `useVectorObs` set to `true`, meaning that it detects state by using the block of code that's internal to the `if` statement. All this code does is cast a ray or line from the agent in angles of `20f`, `60f`, `120f`, and `160f` degrees at a distance defined by `rayDistance` and detect objects defined in `detectableObjects`. The ray perception is done with a helper component called `rayPer` of the `RayPerception` type, and it executes `rayPer.Percieve` to collect the environment state it perceives. This, along with the ratio of steps, is added to the vector observations or state the agent will input. At this point, the state is 36 vectors in length. As of this version, this needs to be constructed in code, but this will likely change in the future.
7. Alter the `rayAngles` line of code so that it matches the following:

```
float[] rayAngles = { 20f, 60f };
```

8. This has the effect of narrowing the agent's vision or perception dramatically from 180 to 60 degrees. Another way to think of it is reducing the input state.
9. After you finish the edit, save the file and return to Unity. Unity will recompile the code when you return to the editor.

10. Locate the **HallwayLearning** brain in the **Assets** | **ML-Agents** | **Examples** | **Hallway** | **Brains** folder and change the **Vector Observation** | **Space Size** to `15`, as shown in the following screenshot:

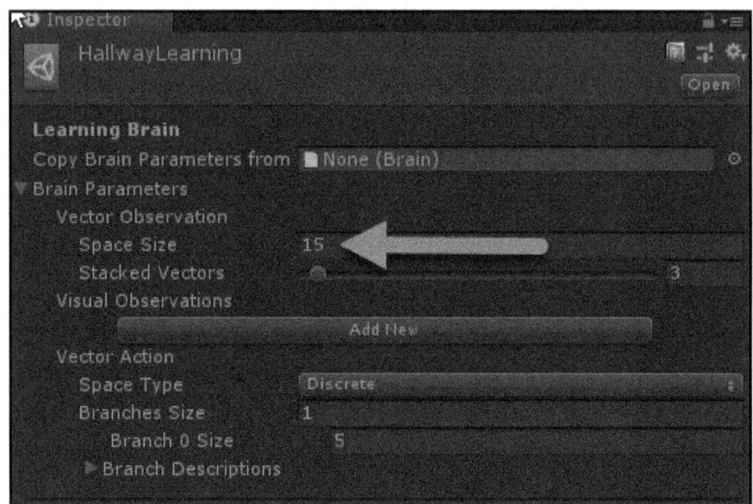

Setting the Vector Observation Space Size

11. The reason we reduce this to 15 is that the input now consists of two angle inputs, plus one steps input. Each angle input consists of five detectable objects, plus two boundaries for seven total perceptions or inputs. Thus, two angles times seven perceptions plus one for steps, equals 15. Previously, we had five angles times seven perceptions plus one step, which equals 35.
12. Make sure that you save the project after modifying the **Brain** scriptable objects.
13. Run the example again in training and watch how the agent trains. Take some time and pay attention to the actions the agent takes and how it learns. Be sure to let this example run as long as you let the other Hallway sample run for, hopefully to completion.

Were you surprised by the results? Yes, our agent with a smaller view of the world actually trained quicker. This may seem completely counter-intuitive, but think about this in terms of mathematics. A smaller input space or state means the agent has less paths to explore, and so should train quicker. This is indeed what we saw in this example when we reduced the input space by more than half. At this point, we definitely need to see what happens when we reduce the visual state space in the VisualHallway example.

Understanding visual state

RL is a very powerful algorithm, but can become very computationally complex when we start to look at massive state inputs. To account for massive states, many powerful RL algorithms use the concept of model-free or policy-based learning, something we will cover in a later chapter. As we already know, Unity uses a policy-based algorithm that allows it to learn any size of state space by generalizing to a policy. This allows us to easily input a state space of 15 vectors in the example we just ran to something more massive, as in the VisualHallway example.

Let's open up Unity to the VisualHallway example scene and look at how to reduce the visual input space in the following exercise:

1. With the **VisualHallway** scene open, locate the **HallwayLearningBrain** in the **Assets** | **ML-Agents** | **Examples** | **Hallway** | **Brains** folder and select it.
2. Modify the **Brain Parameters** | **Visual Observation** first camera observable to an input of `32` x `32` **Gray** scale. An example of this is shown in the following screenshot:

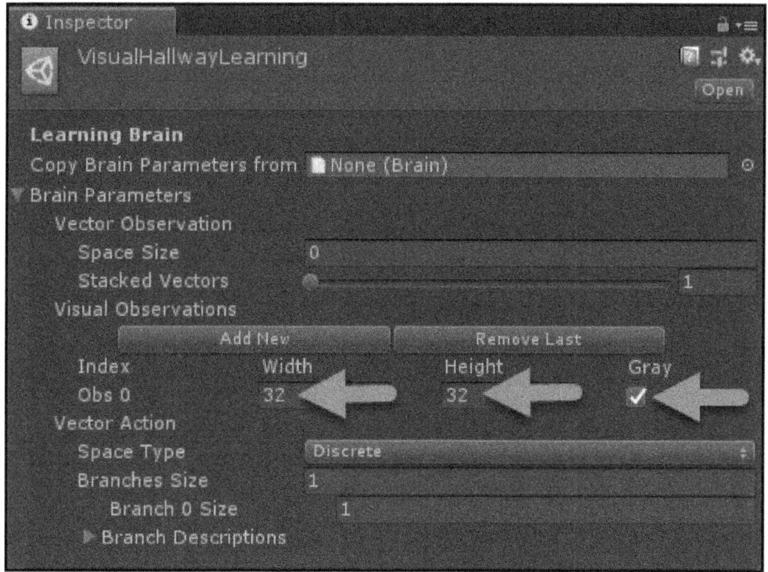

Setting up the visual observation space for the agent

3. When **Visual Observations** are set on a brain, then every frame is captured from the camera at the resolution selected. Previously, the captured image was 84 x 84 pixels large, by no means as large as the game screen in player mode, but still significantly larger than 35 vector inputs. By reducing our image size and making it **gray**, scale we reduced one input frame from 84 x 84 x 3 = 20,172 inputs to 32 x 32 x 1 =1,024. In turn, this greatly reduces our required model input space and the complexity of the network that's needed to learn.
4. Save the project and the scene.
5. Run the VisualHallway in learning mode again using the following command:

```
mlagents-learn config/trainer_config.yaml --run-id=vh_reduced --
train
```

6. Notice how we are changing the `--run-id` parameter with every run. Recall that, if we want to use TensorBoard, then each of our runs needs a unique name, otherwise it just writes over previous runs.
7. Let the sample train for as long as you ran the earlier VisualHallway exercise, as this will give you a good comparison of the change we made in state.

Are the results what you expected? Yeah, the agent still doesn't learn, even after reducing the state. The reason for this is because the smaller visual state actually works against the agent in this particular case. Not unlike the results, we would expect us humans to have when trying to solve a task by looking through a pinhole. However, there is another way to reduce visual state into feature sets using convolution. As you may recall, we covered convolution and CNN in `Chapter 2`, *Convolutional and Recurrent Networks*, at some length. In the next section, we will look at how we can reduce the visual state of our example by adding convolutional layers.

Convolution and visual state

The visual state an agent uses in the ML-Agents toolkit is defined by a process that takes a screenshot at a specific resolution and then feeds that into a convolutional network to train some form of embedded state. In the following exercise, we will open up the ML-Agents training code and enhance the convolution code for better input state:

1. Use a file browser to open the ML-Agents `trainers` folder located at `ml-agents.6\ml-agents\mlagents\trainers`. Inside this folder, you will find several Python files that are used to train the agents. The file we are interested in is called `models.py`.

2. Open the `models.py` file in your Python editor of choice. Visual Studio with the Python data extensions is an excellent platform, and also provides the ability to interactively debug code.
3. Scroll down in the file to locate the `create_visual_observation_encoder` function, which looks as follows:

```
def create_visual_observation_encoder(self, image_input, h_size,
activation, num_layers, scope,reuse):
  #comments removed
  with tf.variable_scope(scope):
    conv1 = tf.layers.conv2d(image_input, 16, kernel_size=[8, 8],
strides=[4, 4],activation=tf.nn.elu, reuse=reuse, name="conv_1")
    conv2 = tf.layers.conv2d(conv1, 32, kernel_size=[4, 4],
strides=[2, 2],activation=tf.nn.elu, reuse=reuse, name="conv_2")
    hidden = c_layers.flatten(conv2)

    with tf.variable_scope(scope + '/' + 'flat_encoding'):
      hidden_flat = self.create_vector_observation_encoder(hidden,
h_size, activation, num_layers, scope, reuse)
 return hidden_flat
```

4. The code is Python using TensorFlow, but you should be able to identify the `conv1` and `conv2` convolution layers. Notice how the kernel and stride is defined for layers and the missing pooling layers as well. Unity does not use pooling in order to avoid loss of spatial relationships in data. However, as we discussed earlier, this is not always so cut-and-dry, and really varies by the type of visual features you are trying to identify.
5. Add the following lines of code after the two convolution layers and modify the `hidden` layer setup, as follows:

```
conv1 = tf.layers.conv2d(image_input, 16, kernel_size=[8, 8],
strides=[4, 4], activation=tf.nn.elu, reuse=reuse, name="conv_1")
conv2 = tf.layers.conv2d(conv1, 32, kernel_size=[4, 4], strides=[2,
2], activation=tf.nn.elu, reuse=reuse, name="conv_2")
conv3 = tf.layers.conv2d(image_input, 64, kernel_size=[2, 2],
strides=[2, 2], activation=tf.nn.elu, reuse=reuse, name="conv_3")

hidden = c_layers.flatten(conv3)
```

6. This will have the effect of adding another layer of convolution to extract finer details in the agents game view. As we saw in `Chapter 2`, *Convolutional and Recurrent Networks*, adding extra layers of convolution will increase training time, but does increase training performance – at least on image classifiers, anyway.
7. Jump back to your command or Anaconda window and run the sample in learning mode with the following command:

```
mlagents-learn config/trainer_config.yaml --run-id=vh_conv1 --train
```

8. Observe the training and watch how the agent performs—be sure to watch the agent's movements in the **Game** window as the sample runs. Is the agent doing what you expected? Compare your results with the previous runs and notice the differences.

One thing you will certainly notice is the agent becoming slightly more graceful and being able to perform finer movements. While the training may take much longer overall, this agent will be able to observe finer changes in the environment, and so will make finer movements. You could, of course, swap the entire CNN architecture of ML-Agents to use more well-defined architectures. However, be aware that most image classification networks ignore spatial relevance that, as we will see in the next section, is very relevant to game agents.

To pool or not to pool

As we discussed in `Chapter 2`, *Convolutional and Recurrent Networks*, ML-Agents does not use any pooling in order to avoid any loss of spatial relationships in data. However, as we saw in our self-driving vehicle example, a single pooling layer or two up at the higher feature level extraction (convolutional layers) can in fact help. Although our example was tested on a much more complex network, it will be helpful to see how this applies to a more complex ML-Agents CNN embedding. Let's try this out, and apply a layer of pooling to the last example by completing the following exercise:

1. Open the `models.py` file in your Python editor of choice. Visual Studio with the Python data extensions is an excellent platform, and also provides the ability to interactively debug code.
2. Locate the following block of code, which is as we last left it in the previous exercise:

```
conv1 = tf.layers.conv2d(image_input, 16, kernel_size=[8, 8],
strides=[4, 4], activation=tf.nn.elu, reuse=reuse, name="conv_1")
conv2 = tf.layers.conv2d(conv1, 32, kernel_size=[4, 4], strides=[2,
2], activation=tf.nn.elu, reuse=reuse, name="conv_2")
```

```
conv3 = tf.layers.conv2d(image_input, 64, kernel_size=[2, 2],
strides=[2, 2], activation=tf.nn.elu, reuse=reuse, name="conv_3")

hidden = c_layers.flatten(conv3)
```

3. We will now inject a layer of pooling by modifying the block of code, like so:

```
conv1 = tf.layers.conv2d(image_input, 16, kernel_size=[8, 8],
strides=[4, 4], activation=tf.nn.elu, reuse=reuse, name="conv_1")
#################### ADD POOLING
conv2 = tf.layers.conv2d(conv1, 32, kernel_size=[4, 4], strides=[2,
2], activation=tf.nn.elu, reuse=reuse, name="conv_2")
conv3 = tf.layers.conv2d(image_input, 64, kernel_size=[2, 2],
strides=[2, 2], activation=tf.nn.elu, reuse=reuse, name="conv_3")

hidden = c_layers.flatten(conv3)
```

4. This now sets up our previous sample to use a single layer of pooling. You can think of this as extracting all the upper features, such as the sky, wall, or floor, and pooling the results together. When you think about it, how much spatial information does the agent need to know regarding one sky patch versus another? All the agent really needs to know is that the sky is always up.
5. Open your command shell or Anaconda window and train the sample by running the following code:

```
mlagents-learn config/trainer_config.yaml --run-id=vh_conv_wpool1 -
-train
```

6. As always, watch the performance of the agent and notice how the agent moves as it trains. Watch the training until completion, or as much as you observed others.

Now, depending on your machine or environment you may have noticed a substantial improvement in training time, but actual performance suffered slightly. This means that each training iteration executed much quicker, two to three times or more, but the agent needs slightly more interactions. In this case, the agent will train quicker time-wise, but in other environments, pooling at higher levels maybe more detrimental. When it comes down to it, it will depend on the visuals of your environment, how well you want your agent to perform, and, ultimately, your patience.

In the next section, we will look at another characteristic of state – memory, or sequencing. We will look at how recurrent networks are used to capture the importance of remembering sequences or event series.

Recurrent networks for remembering series

The sample environments we have been running in this chapter use a form of recurrent memory by default to remember past sequences of events. This recurrent memory is constructed of **Long Short-Term Memory** (**LSTM**) layers that allow the agent to remember beneficial sequences that may encourage some amount of future reward. Remember that we extensively covered LSTM networks in `Chapter 2`, *Convolutional and Recurrent Networks*. For example, an agent may see the same sequence of frames repeatedly, perhaps moving toward the target goal, and then associate that sequence of states with an increased reward. A diagram showing the original form of this network, taken from the paper *Training an Agent for FPS Doom Game using Visual Reinforcement Learning and VizDoom* by *Khan Aduil et al.*, is as follows:

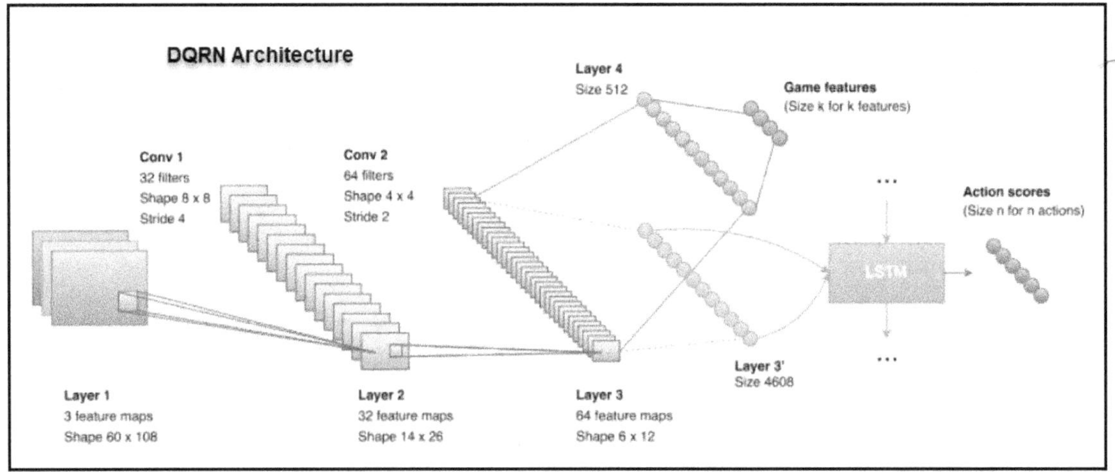

DQRN Architecture

The authors referred to the network architecture as DQRN, which stands for deep Q recurrent network. It is perhaps strange they did not call it DQCRN, since the diagram clearly shows the addition of convolution. While the ML-Agents implementation is slightly different, the concept is very much the same. Either way, the addition of LSTM layers can be a huge benefit to agent training, but, at this stage, we have yet to see the affect of not being used in training.

Therefore, in the following exercise, we will learn how to disable recurrent networks and see what effect this has on training:

1. Open the standard Hallway example scene, the one without visual learning, from the `Assets/ML-Agents/Examples/Hallway/Scenes` folder.
2. Open a command shell or Anaconda window and make sure your ML-Agent's virtual Python environment is active.
3. Locate and open the `trainer_config.xml` file located in the `ML-Agents/ml-agents/config` folder in a text or XML editor of your choice.
4. Locate the configuration block, as follows:

```
HallwayLearning:
    use_recurrent: true
    sequence_length: 64
    num_layers: 2
    hidden_units: 128
    memory_size: 256
    beta: 1.0e-2
    gamma: 0.99
    num_epoch: 3
    buffer_size: 1024
    batch_size: 128
    max_steps: 5.0e5
    summary_freq: 1000
    time_horizon: 64
```

5. The named configuration block, called `HallwayLearning`, matches the name of the brain we set up in the **Academy** within the scene. If you need to confirm this, go ahead.
6. We generally refer to all these configuration parameters as hyperparameters, and they can have a considerable effect on training, especially if set incorrectly. If you scroll to the top of the file, you will notice a set of default parameters, followed by exceptions for each of the named brains. Each section of brain parameters for each brain override the default settings.
7. Disable the `use_recurrent` networks by modifying the code, as follows:

```
HallwayLearning:
    use_recurrent: false
```

8. Setting `use_recurrent` to `false` disables the use of recurrent encoding. We can now see what effect this has on training.

9. Save the configuration file.
10. Run the sample on learning as you normally would. You should be able to run a training sample in your sleep by now.
11. As always, watch how the agent performs and be sure to pay attention to the agent's movements as well.

As you can see, the agent performs considerably worse in this example, and it is obvious that the use of recurrent networks to capture sequences of important moves made a big difference. In fact, in most repetitive game environments, such as the Hallway and VisualHallway, the addition of recurrent state works quite well. However, there will be other environments that may not benefit, or may indeed suffer, from the use of state sequencing. Environments that feature extensive exploration or new content may, in fact, suffer. Since the agent may prefer shorter action sequences, this is limited by the amount of memory that is configured for the agent. Try to keep that in mind when you develop a new environment.

Now that we have a comparison for how our samples run without recurrent or LSTM layers, we can test the sample again by tweaking some of the relevant recurrent hyperparameters in the next section.

Tuning recurrent hyperparameters

As we learned in our discussion of recurrent networks, LSTM layers may receive variable input, but we still need to define a maximum sequence length that we want the network to remember. There are two critical hyperparameters we need to play with when using recurrent networks. A description of these parameters, at the time of writing, and as listed in the ML-Agents docs, is as follows:

- `sequence_length`: Corresponds to the length of the sequences of experience that are passed through the network during training. This should be long enough to capture whatever information your agent might need to remember over time. For example, if your agent needs to remember the velocity of objects, then this can be a small value. If your agent needs to remember a piece of information that's given only once at the beginning of an episode, then this should be a larger value:
    - Typical Range: 4 – 128

- `memory_size`: Corresponds to the size of the array of floating point numbers that are used to store the hidden state of the recurrent neural network. This value must be a multiple of four, and should scale with the amount of information you expect the agent will need to remember to successfully complete the task:
    - Typical Range: 64 – 512

The description of the recurrent `sequence_length` and `memory_size` hyperparameters was extracted directly from the Unity ML-Agents documentation.

If we look at our VisualHallway example configuration in the `trainer_config.yaml` file, we can see that the parameters are defined as follows:

```
VisualHallwayLearning:
    use_recurrent: true
    sequence_length: 64
    num_layers: 1
    hidden_units: 128
    memory_size: 256
    beta: 1.0e-2
    gamma: 0.99
    num_epoch: 3
    buffer_size: 1024
    batch_size: 64
    max_steps: 5.0e5
    summary_freq: 1000
    time_horizon: 64
```

This effectively means that our agent will remember 64 frames or states of input using a memory size of 256. The documentation is unclear as to how much memory a single input takes, so we can only assume that the default visual convolutional encoding network, the original two layer model, requires four per frame. We can assume that, by increasing our convolutional encoding in the previous examples, the agent may have not been able to remember every frame of state. Therefore, let's modify the configuration in the VisualHallway example to account for that increase in memory, and see the effect it has in the following exercise:

1. Open up the VisualHallway example to where we last left it in the previous exercises, with or without pooling enabled. Just be sure to remember if you are or are not using pooling, as this will make a difference to the required memory.

2. Open the `trainer_config.yaml` file located in the `ML-Agents/ml-agents/config` folder.
3. Modify the `VisualHallwayLearning` config section, as follows:

```
VisualHallwayLearning:
    use_recurrent: true
    sequence_length: 128
    num_layers: 1
    hidden_units: 128
    memory_size: 2048 without pooling, 1024 with pooling
    beta: 1.0e-2
    gamma: 0.99
    num_epoch: 3
    buffer_size: 1024
    batch_size: 64
    max_steps: 5.0e5
    summary_freq: 1000
    time_horizon: 64
```

4. We are increasing the agent's memory from 64 to 128 sequences, thus doubling its memory. Then, we are increasing the memory to 2,048 when not using pooling, and 1,024 when using pooling. Remember that pooling collects features and reduces the number of feature maps that are produced at every step of convolution.
5. Save the file after you finish editing it.
6. Open your command or Anaconda window and start training with the following command:

```
mlagents-learn config/trainer_config.yaml --run-id=vh_recurrent --
train
```

7. When prompted, start the training session in the editor by pressing **Play** and watch the action unfold.
8. Wait for the agent to train, like you did for the other examples we ran. You should notice another increase in training performance, as well as the choice of actions the agent makes, which should look better coordinated.

As we can see, a slight tweaking of hyperparameters allowed us to improve the performance of the agent. Understanding the use of the many parameters that are used in training will be critical to your success in building remarkable agents. In the next section, we will look at further exercises you can use to improve your understanding and skill.

Exercises

As always, try and complete a minimum of two to three of these exercises on your own, and for your own benefit. While this is a hands-on book, it always helps to spend a little more time applying your knowledge to new problems.

Complete the following exercises on your own:

1. Go through and explore the **VisualPushBlock** example. This example is quite similar to the **Hallway**, and is a good analog to play with.
2. Modify the Hallway example's **HallwayAgent** script to use more scanning angles, and thus more vector observations.
3. Modify the Hallway example to use a combined sensor sweep and visual observation input. This will require you to modify the learning brain configuration by adding a camera, and possibly updating some hyperparameters.
4. Modify other visual observation environments to use some form of vector observation. A good example to try this on is the **VisualPushBlock** example.
5. Modify the visual observation camera space to be larger or smaller than 84 x 84 pixels, and to use, or not use, gray scaling. This is a good exercise to play with when testing more complex or simpler CNN network architectures.
6. Modify the `create_visual_observation_encoder` convolutional encoding function so that it can use different CNN architectures. These architectures may be as simple or complex as you want.
7. Modify the `create_visual_observation_encoder` convolutional encoding function to use different levels and amounts of pooling layers. Try and use pooling after every convolutional layer to explore its effect on training.
8. Disable and enable recurrent networks on one or two of the other example's environments and explore the effect this has.
9. Play with the `sequence_length` and `memory_size` parameters with recurrent enabled to see the effect that different sequence lengths have on agent performance. Be sure to increase the `memory_size` parameter if you increase the `sequence_length`.
10. Consider adding additional vector or visual observations to the agent. After all, an agent doesn't have to have only a single form of sensory input. An agent could always detect the direction it is in, or perhaps it may have other forms of sensory input, such as being able to listen. We will give an agent the ability to listen in a later chapter, but try and implement this yourself.

Remember, these exercises are provided for your benefit and enjoyment, so be sure to try at least a couple.

Summary

In this chapter, we took a very close look at how the agents in ML-Agents perceive their environment and process input. An agent's perception of the environment is completely in control by the developer, and it is often a fine balance of how much or how little input/state you want to give an agent. We played with many examples in this chapter and started by taking an in-depth look at the Hallway sample and how an agent uses rays to perceive objects in the environment. Then, we looked at how an agent can use visual observations, not unlike us humans, as input or state that it may learn from. From this, we delved into the CNN architecture that ML-Agents uses to encode the visual observations it provides to the agent. We then learned how to modify this architecture by adding or removing convolution or pooling layers. Finally, we looked at the role of memory, or how recurrent sequencing of input state can be used to help with agent training. Recurrent networks allow an agent to add more value to action sequences that provide a reward.

In the next chapter, we will take a closer look at RL and how agents use the PPO algorithm. We will learn more about the foundations of RL along the way, as well as learn about the importance of the many hyperparameters used in training.

8
Understanding PPO

We have avoided going too deep into the more advanced inner workings of the **proximal policy optimization** (**PPO**) algorithm, even going so far as to avoid any policy-versus-model discussion. If you recall, PPO is the **reduced level** (**RL**) method first developed at OpenAI that powers ML-Agents, and is a policy-based algorithm. In this chapter, we will look at the differences between policy-and model-based RL algorithms, as well as the more advanced inner workings of the Unity implementation.

The following is a list of the main topics we will cover in this chapter:

- Marathon reinforcement learning
- The partially observable Markov decision process
- Actor-Critic and continuous action spaces
- Understanding TRPO and PPO
- Tuning PPO with hyperparameters

The content in this chapter is at an advanced level, and assumes that you have covered several previous chapters and exercises. For the purposes of this chapter, we will also assume that you are is able to open and run a learning environment in Unity with ML-Agents without difficulty.

Marathon RL

So far, our focus has been on discrete actions and episodic environments, where the agent often learns to solve a puzzle or accomplish some task. The best examples of such environments are GridWorld, and, of course, the Hallway/VisualHallway samples, where the agent discretely chosses actions such as up, left, down, or right, and, using those actions, has to navigate to some goal. While these are great environments to play with and learn the basic concepts of RL, they can be quite tedious environments to learn from, since results are not often automatic and require extensive exploration. However, in marathon RL environments, the agent is always learning by receiving rewards in the form of control feedback. In fact, this form of RL is analogus to control systems for robotics and simulations. Since these environments are rich with rewards in the form of feedback, they provide us with better immediate feedback when we alter/tune hyperparameters, which will make these types of environments perfect for our own learning purposes.

Unity provides several examples of marathon RL environments, and at the time of writing featured the Crawler, Reacher, Walker, and Humanoid example environments, but these will likely be changed in the future.

Marathon environments are constructed differently, and we should probably understand some of these differences before going any further. Open up the Unity editor and your Python command window of choice, set up to run `mlagents-learn`, and complete the following the exercise:

1. Open the `CrawlerDynamicTarget` example scene from the `Assets/ML-Agents/Examples/Crawler/Scenes` folder. This example features an agent with four movable limbs, each with two joints that can move as well. The goal is for the agent to move toward some dynamic target that keeps changing.
2. Select the **DynamicPlatform** | **Crawler** object in the **Hierarchy** window and take note of the **Crawler Agent** component and **CrawlerDynamicLearning** brain, as shown in the following **screenshot:**

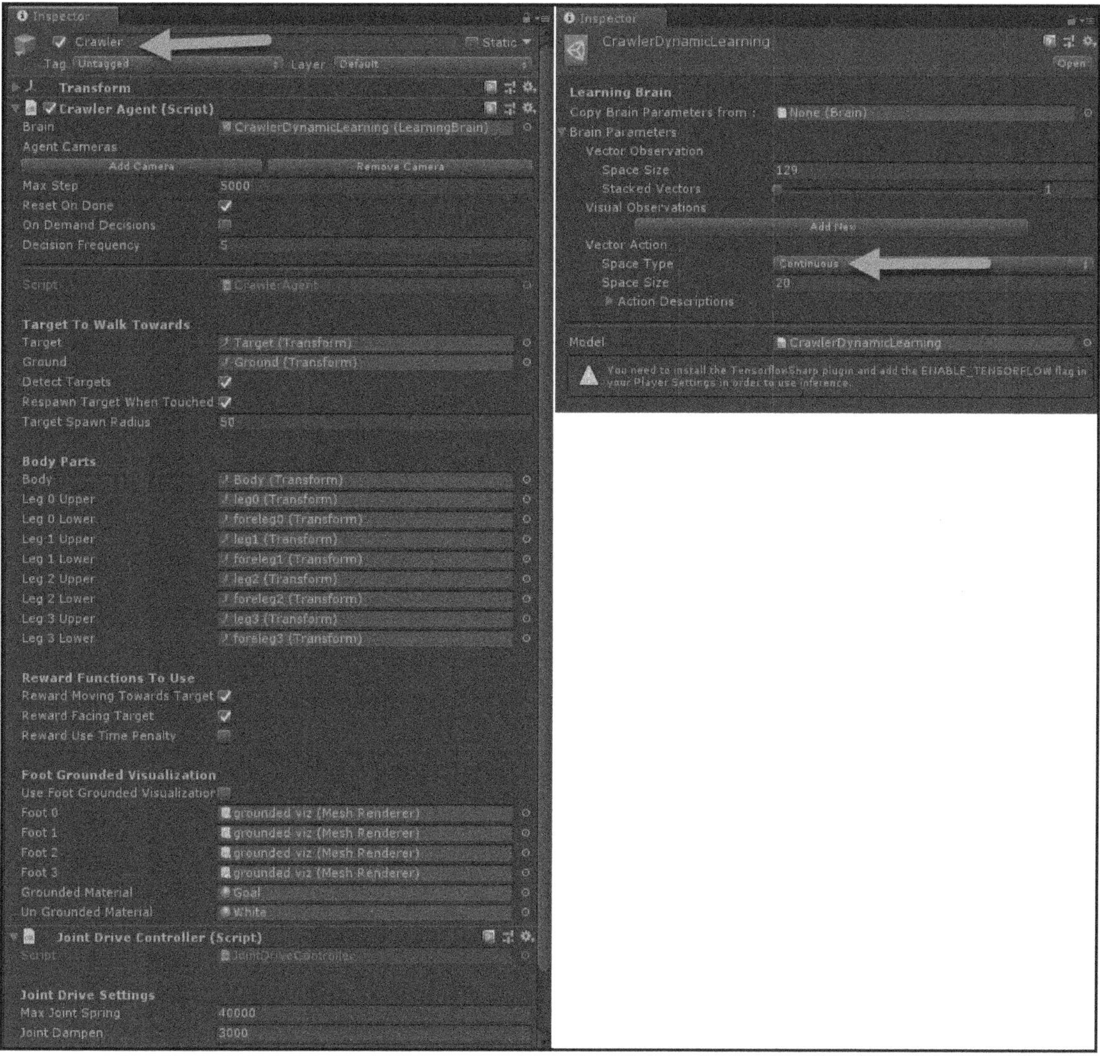

Inspecting the Crawler agent and brain

3. Notice how the space size of the brain is 129 vector observations and 20 continuous actions. A continuous action returns a value that determines the degree to which a joint may rotate, thus allowing the agent to learn how to coordinate these joint actions into movements that will allow it to crawl to a goal.

4. Click the target icon beside the **Crawler Agent** component, and from the context menu, select **Edit Script**.
5. After the script opens, scroll down and look for the `CollectObservations` method:

```
public override void CollectObservations()
{
  jdController.GetCurrentJointForces();

  AddVectorObs(dirToTarget.normalized);
  AddVectorObs(body.transform.position.y);
  AddVectorObs(body.forward);
  AddVectorObs(body.up);
  foreach (var bodyPart in jdController.bodyPartsDict.Values)
  {
    CollectObservationBodyPart(bodyPart);
  }
}
```

6. Again, the code is in C#, but it should be fairly self-explanatory as to what inputs the agent is perceiving. We can first see that the agent takes the direction to target, its up and forward, as well as observations from each body part as input.
7. Select **Academy** in the scene and make sure the **Brain** configuration is set for **Control** (learning).
8. From your previously prepared command window or Anaconda window, run the `mlagents-learn` script as follows:

```
mlagents-learn config/trainer_config.yaml --run-id=crawler --train
```

9. Quite quickly after the training begins, you will see the agent making immediate measurable progress.

This agent can impressively train very quickly, and will be incredibly useful for testing our knowledge of how RL works in the coming sections. Feel free to look through and explore this sample, but avoid tuning any parameters, as we will begin doing that in the next section.

The partially observable Markov decision process

Back in `Chapter 5`, *Introducing DRL*, we learned that a **Markov Decision Process** (**MDP**) is used to define the state/model an agent uses to calculate an action/value from. In the case of Q-learning, we have seen how a table or grid could be used to hold an entire MDP for an environment such as the Frozen Pond or GridWorld. These types of RL are model-based, meaning they completely model every state in the environment—every square in a grid game, for instance. Except, in most complex games and environments, being able to map physical or visual state becomes a partially observable problem, or what we may refer to as a **partially observable Markov decision process** (**POMDP**).

A POMDP defines a process where an agent never has a complete view of its environment, but instead learns to conduct actions based on a derived general policy. This is demonstrated well in the Crawler example, because we can see the agent learning to move using only limited information—the direction to target. The following table outlines the definition of Markov models we generally use for RL:

	No	**Yes**	
All states observable?	**No**	Markov Chain	MDP
	Yes	Hidden Markov Model	POMDP

Since we provide our agent with control over its states in the form of actions, the Markov models we study are the MDP and POMDP. Likewise, these processes will also be often referred to as on or off model, while if an RL algorithm is completely aware of state, we call it a model-based process. Conversely, a POMDP refers to an off-model process, or what we will refer to as a policy-based method. Policy-based algorithms, provide better generalization and have the ability to learn in environments with an unknown or infinite number of observable states. Examples of partially observable states are environments such as the **Hallway**, **VisualHallway**, and, of course, **Crawler**.

Markov models provide a foundation for many aspects of machine learning, and you may encounter their use in more advanced deep learning methods known as deep probabilistic programming. Deep PPL, as it is referred to, is a combination or variational inference and deep learning methods.

Model-free methods typically use an experienced buffer to store a set of experiences that it will use later to learn a general policy from. This buffer is defined by a few hyperparameters, called `time_horizon`, `batch_size`, and `buffer_size`. Definitions of each of these parameters extracted from the ML-Agents documentation are given here:

- `time_horizon`: This corresponds to how many steps of experience to collect per agent before adding them to the experience buffer. When this limit is reached before the end of an episode, a value estimate is used to predict the overall expected reward from the agent's current state. As such, this parameter trades off between a less biased, but higher variance estimate (long time horizon), and a more biased, but less varied estimate (short time horizon). In cases where there are frequent rewards within an episode, or episodes are prohibitively large, a smaller number can be more ideal. This number should be large enough to capture all the important behavior within a sequence of an agent's actions:
    - Typical range: 32 – 2,048
- `buffer_size`: This corresponds to how many experiences (agent observations, actions, and rewards obtained) should be collected before we update the model or do any learning. This should be a multiple of `batch_size`. Typically, a larger `buffer_size` parameter corresponds to more stable training updates.
    - Typical range: 2,048 – 4,09,600
- `batch_size`: This is the number of experiences used for one iteration of a gradient descent update. This should always be a fraction of the `buffer_size` parameter. If you are using a continuous action space, this value should be large (in the order of thousands). If you are using a discrete action space, this value should be smaller (in order of tens).
    - Typical range (continuous): 512 – 5,120
    - Typical range (discrete): 32 – 512

We can see how these values are set by looking at the `CrawlerDynamicLearning` brain configuration, and altering this to see the effect this has on training. Open up the editor and a properly configured Python window to the `CrawlerDynamicTarget` scene and follow this exercise:

1. Open the `trainer_config.yaml` file located in the `ML-Agents/ml-agents/config` folder.

2. Scroll down to the `CrawlerDynamicLearning` brain configuration section:

```
CrawlerDynamicLearning:
  normalize: true
  num_epoch: 3
  time_horizon: 1000
  batch_size: 2024
  buffer_size: 20240
  gamma: 0.995
  max_steps: 1e6
  summary_freq: 3000
  num_layers: 3
  hidden_units: 512
```

3. Note the highlighted lines showing the `time_horizon`, `batch_size`, and `buffer_size` parameters. If you recall from our earlier **Hallway/VisualHallway** examples, the `time_horizon` parameter was only 32 or 64. Since those examples used a discrete action space, we could set a much lower value for `time_horizon`.
4. Double all the parameter values, as shown in the following code excerpt:

```
time_horizon: 2000
batch_size: 4048
buffer_size: 40480
```

5. Essentially, what we are doing here is doubling the amount of experiences the agent will use to build a policy of the environment around it. In essence, we are giving the agent a larger snapshot of experiences to train against.
6. Run the agent in training as you have done so many times before.
7. Let the agent train for as long as you ran the previous base sample. This will give you a good comparison in training performance.

One thing that will become immediately obvious is how much more stable the agent trains, meaning the agent's mean reward will progress more steadily and jump around less. Recall that we want to avoid training jumps, spikes, or wobbles, as this could indicate poor convergence on the part of the network's optimization method. This means that more gradual changes are generally better, and indicate good training performance. By doubling `time_horizon` and associated parameters, we have doubled the amount of experiences the agent used to learn from. This, in turn, had the effect of stabilizing the training, but it is likely that you noticed the agent took longer to train to the same number of iterations.

Partially observable RL algorithms are classed as policy-based, model-free, or off-model, and are a foundation for PPO. In the next section, we will look at the improvements in RL that deal with the additional complexities of managing continuous action spaces better.

Actor-Critic and continuous action spaces

Another complexity we introduced when looking at marathon RL or control learning was the introduction of continuous action spaces. Continuous action spaces represent a set of infinite possible actions an agent could take. Where our agent could previously favor a discrete action, yes or no, it now has to select some points within an infinite space of actions as an action for each joint. This mapping from an infinite action space to an action is not easy to solve—however, we do have neural networks at our disposal, and these provide us with an excellent solution using an architecture not unlike the GANs we looked at in `Chapter 3`, *GAN for Games*.

As we discovered in the chapter on GANs, we could propose a network architecture composed of two competing networks. These competing networks would force each network to learn by competing against each other for the best solution to mapping a random space into a convincing forgery. A similar concept to a GAN can be applied in this case as well, and is called the Actor-Critic model. A diagram of this model is as follows:

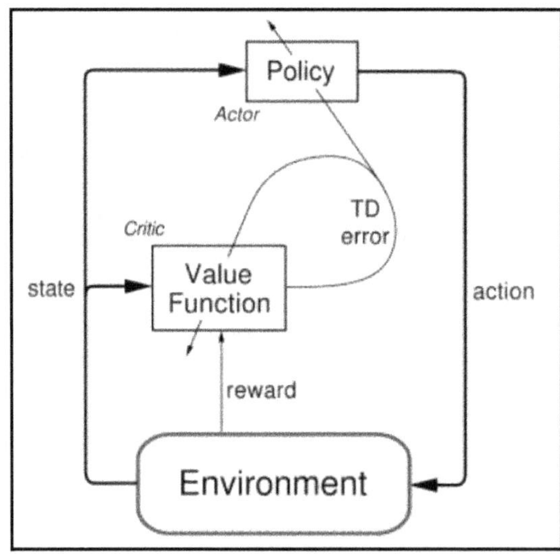

Actor-Critic architecture

What happens here is that the **Actor** selects an **action** from the policy given a **state**. The **state** is first passed through a **Critic**, which values the best action given the current **state**, provided some **error**. More simply put, the **Critic** criticizes each action based on the current **state**, and then the **Actor** chooses the best action given the **state**.

This method of action selection was first explored in an algorithm called **dueling double Q networks** (**DDQN**). It is now the basis for most advanced RL algorithms.

Actor-Critic was essentially required to solve the continuous action space problem, but, given its performance, this method has been incorporated into some advanced discrete algorithms as well. ML-Agents uses an Actor-Critic model for continuous spaces, but does not use one for discrete action spaces.

Using Actor-Critic requires, or works best with, additional layers and neurons in our network, which is something we can configure in ML-Agents. The hyperparameter definitions for these are pulled from the ML-Agents documents, and are as follows:

- `num_layers`: This corresponds to how many hidden layers are present after the observation input, or after the CNN encoding of the visual observation. For simple problems, fewer layers are likely to train faster and more efficiently. More layers may be necessary for more complex control problems:
  - Typical range: 1 – 3
- `hidden_units`: These correspond to how many units are in each fully-connected layer of the neural network. For simple problems where the correct action is a straightforward combination of the observation inputs, this should be small. For problems where the action is a very complex interaction between the observation variables, this should be larger:
  - Typical range: 32 – 512

Let's open up a new ML-Agents marathon or control sample and see what effect modifying these parameters has on training. Follow this exercise to understand the effect of adding layers and neurons (units) to a control problem:

1. Open the **Walker** scene from the `Assets/ML-Agents/Examples/Walker/Scenes` folder. This example features a walking humanoid animation.
2. Locate and select the **WalkerAgent** object in the **Hierarchy** window, and then look to the **Inspector** window and examine the **Agent** and **Brain** settings, as shown in the following screenshot:

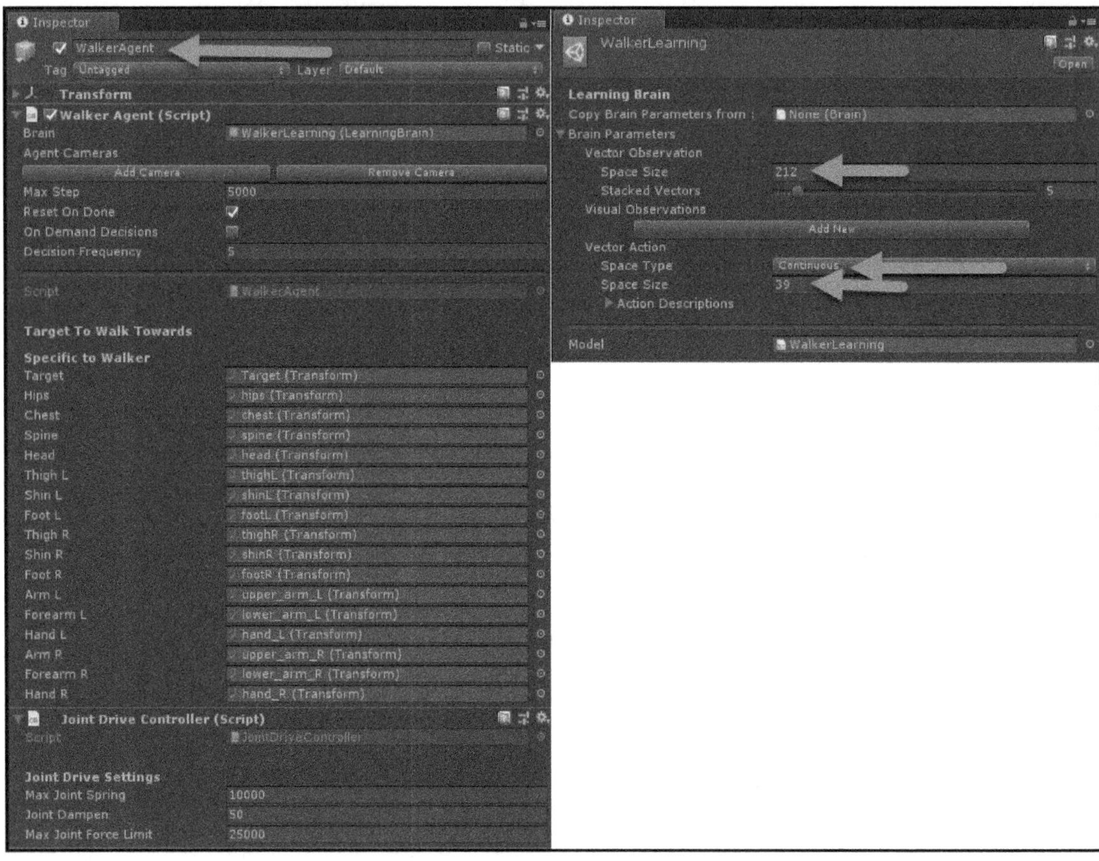

The WalkerAgent and WalkerLearning properties

3. Select `WalkerAcademy` in the **Hierarchy** window and make sure the **Control** option is enabled for the `Brains` parameter.
4. Open the `trainer_config.yaml` file located in the `ML-Agents/ml-agents/config` folder and scroll down to the `WalkerLearning` section as follows:

```
WalkerLearning:
    normalize: true
    num_epoch: 3
    time_horizon: 1000
    batch_size: 2048
    buffer_size: 20480
    gamma: 0.995
    max_steps: 2e6
    summary_freq: 3000
    num_layers: 3
    hidden_units: 512
```

5. Notice how many layers and units this example is using. Is it more or fewer than what we used for the discrete action problems?
6. Save everything and set the sample up for training.
7. Launch a training session from your Python console with the following command:

```
mlagents-learn config/trainer_config.yaml --run-id=walker --train
```

8. This agent may take considerably longer to train, but try and wait for about 100,000 iterations in order to get a good sense of its training progress.

Now that we have a better understanding of Actor-Critic and how it is used in continuous action spaces, we can move on to exploring what effect changing the network size has on training these more complex networks in the next section.

Expanding network architecture

Actor-Critic architectures increase the complexity of the problem, and thus the complexity and size of the networks needed to solve them. This is really no different than the case in our earlier look at PilotNet, the multilayer CNN architecture that was used by Nvidia to self-drive.

What we want to see is the immediate effect that increasing the size of our network has on a complex example such as the Walker example. Open Unity to the `Walker` example and complete the following exercise:

1. Open `trainer_config.yaml` from where it is normally located.
2. Modify the `WalkerLearning` configuration, as shown in the following code:

```
WalkerLearning:
    normalize: true
    num_epoch: 3
    time_horizon: 1000
    batch_size: 2048
    buffer_size: 20480
    gamma: 0.995
    max_steps: 2e6
    summary_freq: 3000
    num_layers: 1
    hidden_units: 128
```

3. Set `num_layers: 1` and `hidden_units: 128`. These are typical values that we would use for discrete action space problems. You can confirm this by looking at another discrete sample, such as the `VisualHallwayLearning` configuration, as follows:

```
VisualHallwayLearning:
    use_recurrent: false
    sequence_length: 64
    num_layers: 1
    hidden_units: 128
    memory_size: 256
    beta: 1.0e-2
    gamma: 0.99
    num_epoch: 3
    buffer_size: 1024
    batch_size: 64
    max_steps: 5.0e5
    summary_freq: 1000
    time_horizon: 64
```

4. This sample uses the same settings as we just set our continuous action problem to.
5. When you are done editing, save everything and get ready for training.
6. Launch a training session, with a new `run-id` parameter. Remember to get in the practice of changing the `run-id` parameter with every run so that it is easier to discern each run in TensorBoard.

7. As always, let the sample run for as long as you did the earlier unaltered run for a good comparison.

One of the things you may immediately notice when running this sample is how stable the training is. The second thing you may notice is that training stability increases, but performance slightly decreases. Remember that a smaller network has less weights and will generally be more stable and quicker to train. However, in this problem, while the training is more stable on the network and promises to be faster, you may notice that training hits a wall. The agent, now limited by network size, is able to optimize the smaller network faster, but without the fine control we have seen before. In fact, this agent will never be as good as the first unaltered run since it is now limited by a smaller network. This is another one of those trade-offs you need to balance when building DRL agents for games/simulations.

In the next section, we take a further look at what we call advantage functions or those used like in Actor-Critic, and will first explore TRPO, and, of course, PPO.

Understanding TRPO and PPO

There are many variations to the policy-and model-free algorithms that have become popular for solving RL problems of optimizing predictions of future rewards. As we have seen, many of these algorithms use an advantage function, such as Actor-Critic, where we have two sides of the problem trying to converge to the optimum solution. In this case, the advantage function is trying to find the maximum expected discounted rewards. TRPO and PPO do this by using an optimization method called a **Minorize-Maximization (MM)** algorithm. An example of how the MM algorithm solves a problem is shown in the following diagram:

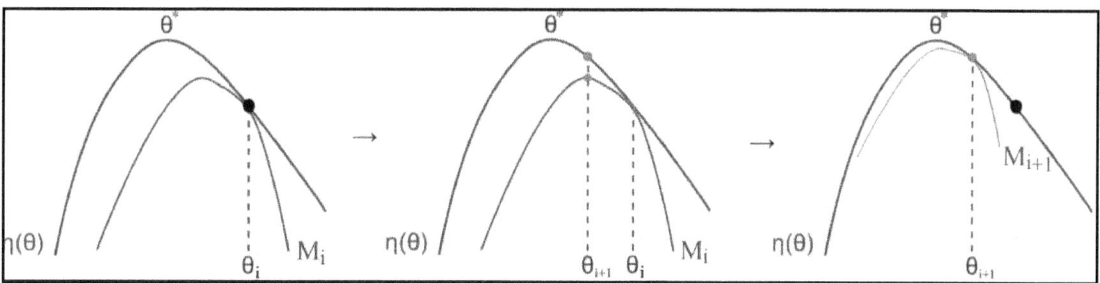

Using the MM algorithm

This diagram was extracted from a series of blogs by Jonathon Hui that elegantly describe the MM algorithm along with the TRPO and PPO methods in much greater detail. See the following link for the source: (`https://medium.com/@jonathan_hui/rl-proximal-policy-optimization-ppo-explained-77f014ec3f12`).

Essentially, the MM algorithm finds the optimum pair function by interactively maximizing and minimizing function parameters until it arrives at a converged solution. In the diagram, the red line denotes the function we are looking to approximate, and the blue line denotes the converging function. You can see the progression as the algorithm picks min/max values that will find a solution.

The problem we encounter when using MM is that the function approximation can sometimes fall off, or down into a valley. In order to understand this better, let's consider this as solving the problem of climbing an uneven hill using a straight line. An example of such a scenario is seen here:

Attempting to climb a hill using linear methods

You can see that using only linear paths to try and navigate this quite treacherous ridge would, in fact, be dangerous. While the danger may not be as real, it is still a big problem when using linear methods to solve MM, as it is if you were hiking up a steep ridge using only a straight fixed path.

TRPO solves the problem of using linear methods by using a quadratic method, and by limiting the amount of steps each iteration can take in a form of trust region. That is, the algorithm makes sure that every position is positive and safe. If we consider our hill climbing example again, we may consider TRPO as placing a path or region of trust, like in the following photo:

A trust region path up the hill

In the preceding photo, the path is shown for example purposes only as a connected set of circles or regions; the real trust path may or may not be closer to the actual peak or ridge. Regardless, this has the effect of allowing the agent to learn at a more gradual and progressive pace. With TRPO, the size of the trust region can be altered and made bigger or smaller to coincide with our preferred policy convergence. The problem with TRPO is that it is quite complex to implement since it requires the second-degree derivation of some complex equations.

PPO addresses this issue by limiting or clipping the Kulbach-Leibler (**KL**) divergence between two policies through each iteration. KL divergence measures the difference in probability distributions and can be described through the following diagram:

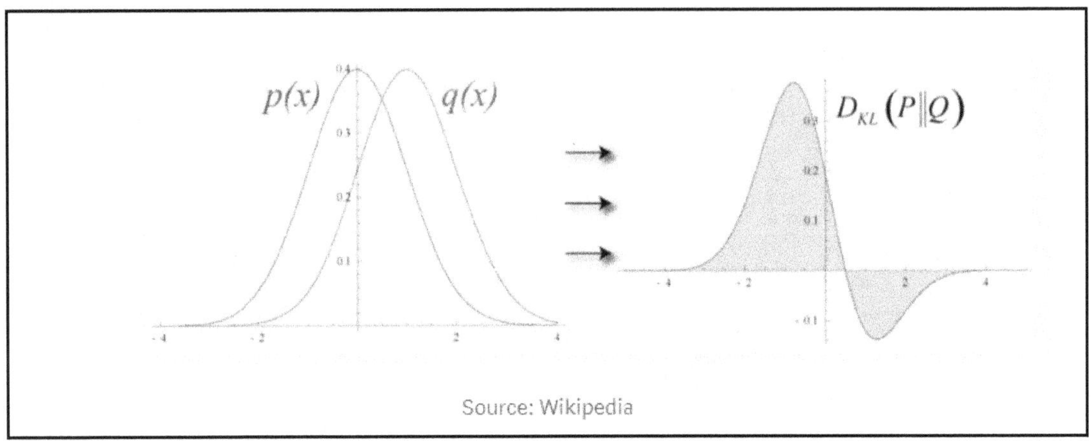

Understanding KL divergence

In the preceding diagram, **p(x)** and **q(x)** each represent a different policy where the KL divergence is measured. The algorithm then, in turn, uses this measure of divergence to limit or clip the amount of policy change that may occur in an iteration. ML-Agents uses two hyperparameters that allow you to control this amount of clipping applied to the objective or function that determines the amount of policy change in an iteration. The following are the definitions for the beta and epsilon parameters, as described in the Unity documentation:

- **Beta**: This corresponds to the strength of the entropy regularization, which makes the policy *more random*. This ensures that agents properly explore the action space during training. Increasing this will ensure that more random actions are taken. This should be adjusted so that the entropy (measurable from TensorBoard) slowly decreases alongside increases in reward. If entropy drops too quickly, increase beta. If entropy drops too slowly, decrease beta:
  - Typical range: 1e-4 – 1e-2
- **Epsilon**: This corresponds to the acceptable threshold of divergence between the old and new policies during gradient descent updating. Setting this value to be small will result in more stable updates, but will also slow the training process:
  - Typical range: 0.1 – 0.3

The key thing to remember about these parameters is that they control how quickly a policy changes from one iteration to the next. If you notice an agent training somewhat erratically, it may be beneficial to tune these parameters to smaller values. The default value for **epsilon** is **.2** and for **beta** is **1.0e-2**, but, of course, we will want to explore how these values may affect training, either in a positive or negative way. In the next exercise, we will modify these policy change parameters and see what effect they have in training:

1. For this example, we will open up the `CrawlerDynamic` scene from the `Assets/ML-Agents/Examples/Crawler/Scenes` folder.
2. Open the `trainer_config.yaml` file located in the `ML-Agents/ml-agents/config` folder. Since we have already evaluated the performance of this sample, there are a couple of ways we will revert the training configuration and make some modification to the beta and epsilon parameters.
3. Scroll down to the `CrawlerDynamicLearning` configuration section and modify it as follows:

```
CrawlerDynamicLearning:
    normalize: true
    num_epoch: 3
    time_horizon: 1000
    batch_size: 1024
    buffer_size: 20240
    gamma: 0.995
    max_steps: 1e6
    summary_freq: 3000
    num_layers: 3
    hidden_units: 512
    epsilon: .1
    beta: .1
```

4. We modified the `epsilon` and `beta` parameters to higher values, meaning that the training will be less stable. If you recall, however, these marathon examples generally train in a more stable manner.
5. Open up a properly configured Python console and run the following command to launch training:

```
mlagents-learn config/trainer_config.yaml --run-id=crawler_policy -
-train
```

6. As usual, wait for a number of training sessions for a good comparison from one example to the next.

What you may find unexpected is that the agent appears to start regressing, and in fact, it is. This is happening because we made those trust regions too large (a large **beta**), and while we allowed the rate of change to be lower (.1 **epsilon**), we can see the **beta** value is more sensitive to training.

Keep in mind that the Unity ML-Agents implementation uses a number of cross-features in tandem, which comprise a powerful RL framework. In the next section, we will take another quick look at a late-comer optimization parameter that Unity has recently added.

Generalized advantage estimate

The area of RL is seeing explosive growth due to constant research that is pushing the envelope on what is possible. With every little advancement comes additional hyperparameters and small tweaks that can be applied to stabilize and/or improve training performance. Unity has recently add a new parameter called lambda, and the definition taken from the documentation is as follows:

- **lambda**: This corresponds to the lambda parameter used when calculating the **Generalized Advantage Estimate** (**GAE**) `https://arxiv.org/abs/1506.02438`. This can be thought of as how much the agent relies on its current value estimate when calculating an updated value estimate. Low values correspond to more reliance on the current value estimate (which can be high bias), and high values correspond to more reliance on the actual rewards received in the environment (which can be high variance). The parameter provides a trade-off between the two, and the right value can lead to a more stable training process:
    - Typical range: 0.9 – 0.95

The GAE paper describes a function parameter called lambda that can be used to shape the reward estimation function, and is best used for control or marathon RL tasks. We won't go too far into details, and interested readers should certainly pull down the paper and review it on their own. However, we will explore how altering this parameter can affect a control sample such as the `Walker` scene in the next exercise:

1. Open the Unity editor to the `Walker` example scene.
2. Select the **Academy** object in the **Hierarchy** and confirm that the scene is still set for training/learning. If it is, you won't have to do anything else. If the scene isn't set up to learn, you know what to do.

3. Open the `trainer_config.yaml` file and modify `WalkerLearning` as follows:

```
WalkerLearning:
    normalize: true
    num_epoch: 3
    time_horizon: 1000
    batch_size: 2048
    buffer_size: 20480
    gamma: 0.995
    max_steps: 2e6
    summary_freq: 3000
    num_layers: 3
    hidden_units: 512
    lambd: .99
```

4. Notice how we are setting the `lambd` parameters and make sure that `num_layers` and `hidden_units` are reset to the original values. In the paper, the authors describe optimum values from `.95` to `.99`, but this differs from the Unity documentation.
5. Save the file when you are done editing.
6. Open up a Python console setup for training and run it with the following command:

```
mlagents-learn config/trainer_config.yaml --run-id=walker_lambd --
train
```

7. Make sure that you let the sample run as long as you have previously to get a good comparison.

One thing you will notice after a log of training is that the agent does indeed train almost 25% slower on this example. What this result tells us is that, by increasing lambda, we are telling the agent to put more value on rewards. Now, this may seem counter-intuitive, but in this sample or this type of environment, the agent is receiving constant small positive rewards. This results in each reward getting skewed, which, as we can see, skews training and impedes agent progress. It may be an interesting exercise for interested readers to try and play with the lambda parameter in the Hallway environment, where the agent only receives a single positive episode reward.

The RL advantage function or functions come in many forms, and are in place to address many of the issues with off-model or policy-driven algorithms such as PPO. In the next section, we round off the chapter by modifying and creating a new sample control/marathon learning environment on our own.

Learning to tune PPO

In this section, we are going to learn to tune a modified/new control learning environment. This will allow us to learn more about some inner workings of the Unity example, but will also show you how to modify a new or modified sample on your own later. Let's begin by opening up the Unity editor so we can complete the following exercise:

1. Open the `Reacher` scene, set it for learning, and run it in training. You should be able to do this part in your sleep now. Let the agent train for a substantial amount of time so you can establish a baseline, as always.
2. From the menu, select `Assets/Import Package/Custom Package`. Locate `Chapter_8_Assets.unitypackage` from the `Chapter08` folder of the books downloaded to the source code.
3. Open up the **Reacher_3_joint** scene from the `Assets/HoDLG/Scenes` folder. This is the modified scene, but we will go through its construction as well.
4. First, notice that there is only a single **Reacher** arm active, but now with three joints, as shown in the following screenshot:

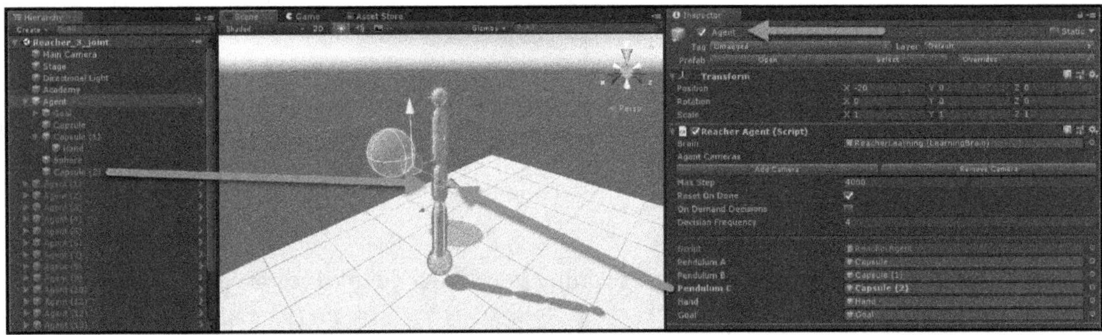

Inspecting the Agent game object

5. Notice how the arm now has three sections, with the new section called **Capsule(2)** and identified as **Pendulum C**. The order of the joints is now out of order, meaning **Pendulum C** is actually the middle pendulum and not the bottom.
6. Select each of the **Capsule** objects and inspect their configuration and placement, as summarized in the following screenshot:

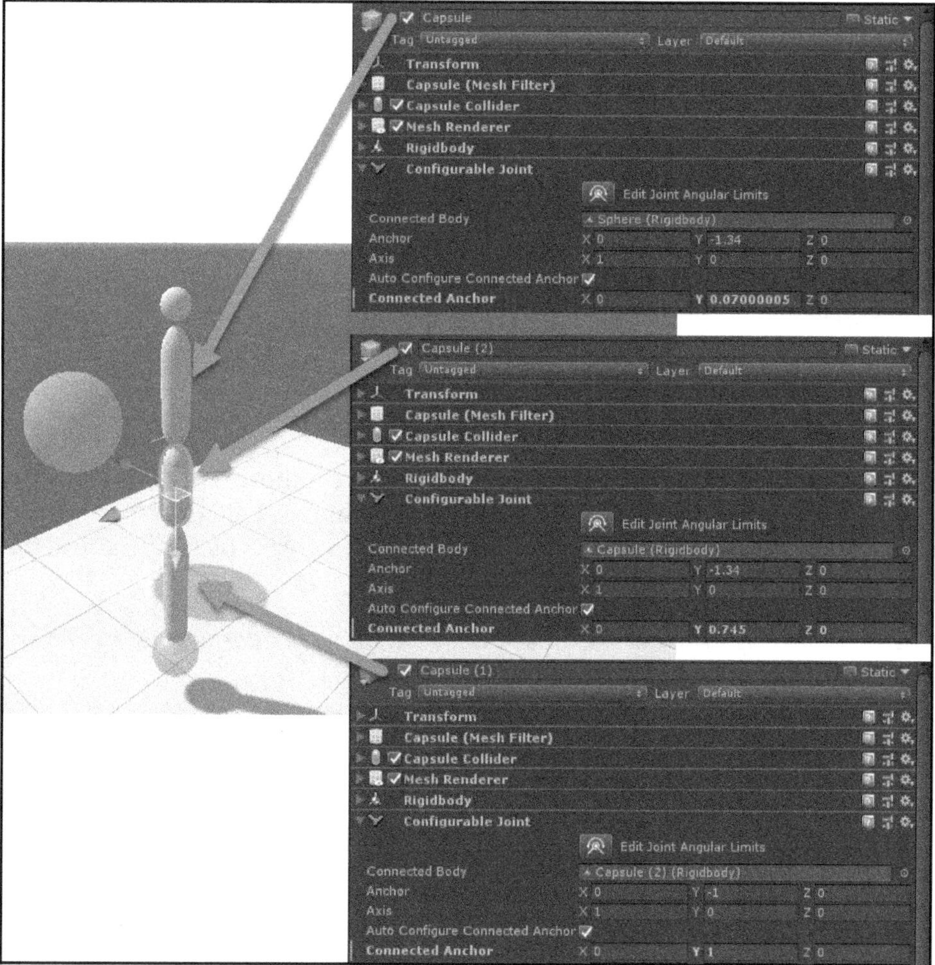

Inspecting the Capsule objects

7. Be sure to note the **Configurable Joint | Connected Body** object for each of the capsules as well. This property sets the body that the object will hinge or join to. There are plenty of other properties on the **Configurable Joint** component that would allow you to mimic this joint interaction in any form, perhaps even biological. For example, you may want to make the joints in this arm to be more human-like by only allowing certain angles of movement. Likewise, if you were designing a robot with limited motion, then you could simulate that with this joint component as well.
8. At this stage, we can set up and run the example. Open and set up for training a Python console or Anaconda window.

9. Run the sample in training and observe the progress of the agent. Let the agent run for enough iterations in order to compare training performance with the baseline.

At this stage, we have our sample up and running and we are ready to start tuning new parameters in to optimize training. However, before we do that, we will step back and take a look at the C# code changes required to make the last sample possible. The next section covers the C# code changes, and is optional for those developers not interested in the code. If you plan to build your own control or marathon environments in Unity, you will need to read the next section.

Coding changes required for control projects

As we already mentioned, this section is optional and is for those curious about getting into the details of building their own control sample using Unity C#. It is also likely that, in the future, no coding changes will be required to modify these types of samples, and that is the other reason this section is optional.

Complete the following exercise to go through the coding changes needed to add a joint in the Reacher control example:

1. Select the **Agent** object in the **Hierarchy** window and then, in the **Inspector** window, note the **Reacher Agent_3** component. This is the modified script that we will be inspecting.
2. Click the target icon beside the **Reach Agent_3** component, and from the context menu, select **Edit Script**.
3. This will open the `ReacherAgent_3.cs` script in your C# code editor of choice.
4. The first thing to note under the declarations is the addition of new variables, highlighted in bold as follows:

```
public GameObject pendulumA;
public GameObject pendulumB;
public GameObject pendulumC;
public GameObject hand;
public GameObject goal;
private ReacherAcademy myAcademy;
float goalDegree;
private Rigidbody rbA;
private Rigidbody rbB;
private Rigidbody rbC;
private float goalSpeed;
private float goalSize;
```

5. Two new variables, `pendulumC` and `rbC`, are added for holding the new joints GameObject and RigidBody. Now, `Rigidbody` in Unity physics denotes an object that can be moved or manipulated by the physics engine.
   Unity is in the process of performing an upgrade to their physics engine that will alter some of the teachings here. The current version of ML-Agents uses the old physics system, so this example will as well.
6. The next thing of importance to note is the addition of additional agent observations, as shown in the following `CollectObservations` method:

```
public override void CollectObservations()
    {
        AddVectorObs(pendulumA.transform.localPosition);
        AddVectorObs(pendulumA.transform.rotation);
        AddVectorObs(rbA.angularVelocity);
        AddVectorObs(rbA.velocity);

        AddVectorObs(pendulumB.transform.localPosition);
        AddVectorObs(pendulumB.transform.rotation);
        AddVectorObs(rbB.angularVelocity);
        AddVectorObs(rbB.velocity);

        AddVectorObs(pendulumC.transform.localPosition);
        AddVectorObs(pendulumC.transform.rotation);
        AddVectorObs(rbC.angularVelocity);
        AddVectorObs(rbC.velocity);

        AddVectorObs(goal.transform.localPosition);
        AddVectorObs(hand.transform.localPosition);
        AddVectorObs(goalSpeed);
   }
```

7. The section in bold is adding the new observations for `pendulumC` and `rbC`, which total another 13 vectors. Recall that this means we also needed to switch our brain from 33 vector observations to **46** observations, as shown in the following screenshot:

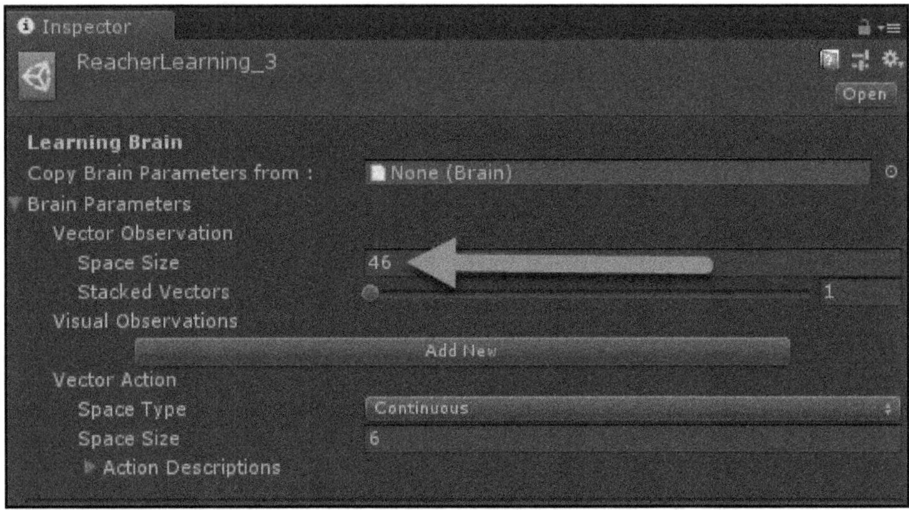

Inspecting the update ReacherLearning_3 brain

8. Next, we will look to the `AgentAction` method; this is where the Python trainer code calls the agent and tells it what movements it makes, and is as follows:

```
public override void AgentAction(float[] vectorAction, string
textAction)
  {
        goalDegree += goalSpeed;
        UpdateGoalPosition();

        var torqueX = Mathf.Clamp(vectorAction[0], -1f, 1f) * 150f;
        var torqueZ = Mathf.Clamp(vectorAction[1], -1f, 1f) * 150f;
        rbA.AddTorque(new Vector3(torqueX, 0f, torqueZ));

        torqueX = Mathf.Clamp(vectorAction[2], -1f, 1f) * 150f;
        torqueZ = Mathf.Clamp(vectorAction[3], -1f, 1f) * 150f;
        rbB.AddTorque(new Vector3(torqueX, 0f, torqueZ));

        torqueX = Mathf.Clamp(vectorAction[3], -1f, 1f) * 150f;
        torqueZ = Mathf.Clamp(vectorAction[4], -1f, 1f) * 150f;
        rbC.AddTorque(new Vector3(torqueX, 0f, torqueZ));
  }
```

9. In this method, we are extending the code to allow the agent to move the new joint in the form of `rigidbody rbC`. Did you notice that the new learning brain also added more action space?
10. Lastly, we look at the `AgentReset` method to see how the agent will reset itself with the new limb, as follows:

```
public override void AgentReset()
    {
        pendulumA.transform.position = new Vector3(0f, -4f, 0f) +
transform.position;
        pendulumA.transform.rotation = Quaternion.Euler(180f, 0f,
0f);
        rbA.velocity = Vector3.zero;
        rbA.angularVelocity = Vector3.zero;

        pendulumB.transform.position = new Vector3(0f, -10f, 0f) +
transform.position;
        pendulumB.transform.rotation = Quaternion.Euler(180f, 0f,
0f);
        rbB.velocity = Vector3.zero;
        rbB.angularVelocity = Vector3.zero;

        pendulumC.transform.position = new Vector3(0f, -6f, 0f) +
transform.position;
        pendulumC.transform.rotation = Quaternion.Euler(180f, 0f,
0f);
        rbC.velocity = Vector3.zero;
        rbC.angularVelocity = Vector3.zero;

        goalDegree = Random.Range(0, 360);
        UpdateGoalPosition();

        goalSize = myAcademy.goalSize;
        goalSpeed = Random.Range(-1f, 1f) * myAcademy.goalSpeed;

        goal.transform.localScale = new Vector3(goalSize, goalSize,
goalSize);
    }
```

11. All this code does is reset the position of the arm to its original position and stop all movement.

That covers the only required code changes for this example. Fortunately, only one script needed to be modified. It is likely that in the future you won't have to modify these scripts at all. In the next section, we will follow up by refining the sample's training by tuning extra parameters and introducing another training optimization for policy learning methods.

Multiple agent policy

In this section, we are going to look at how policy or off-model based methods such as PPO can be improved on by introducing multiple agents to train the same policy. The example exercise you will use in this section will be completely up to you, and should be one that you are familiar with and/or interested in. For our purposes, we will explore a sample that we have looked at extensively—the Hallway/VisualHallway. If you have been following most of the exercises in this book, you should be more than capable of adapting this example. However, note that, for this exercise, we want to use a sample that is set up to use multiple agents for training.

Previously, we avoided discussing the multiple agents; we avoided this aspect of training before because it may complicate the discussion of on-model versus off-model. Now that you understand the differences and reasons for using a policy-based method, you can better appreciate that since our agents are using a policy-based method, we can simultaneously train multiple agents against the same policy. However, this can have repercussions for other training parameters and configuration, as you may well imagine.

Open up the Unity editor to the `Hallway/VisualHallway` example scene, or one of your choosing, and complete the following exercise:

1. Open up a Python or Anaconda console window and get it ready to train.
2. Select and enable the **HallwayArea**, selecting areas (1) to (19) so they become active and viewable in the scene.
3. Select the **Agent** object in each **HallwayArea**, and make sure that **Hallway Agent | Brain** is set to **HallwayLearning** and not **HallwayPlayer**. This will turn on all the additional training areas.
4. Depending on your previous experience, you may or may not want to modify the sample back to the original. Recall that in an earlier exercise, we modified the **HallwayAgent** script to only scan a smaller section of angles. This may also require you to alter the **brain** parameters as well.
5. After you have the scene set up, save it and the project.

6. Run the scene in training using a unique `run-id` and wait for a number of training iterations. This sample may train substantially slower, or even faster, depending on your hardware.

Now that we have established a new baseline for the Hallway environment, we can now determine what effect modifying some hyperparameters has on discrete action samples. The two parameters we will revisit are the `num_epochs` (number of training epochs) and `batch_size` (experiences per training epoch) parameters that we looked at earlier with the continuous action (control) sample. In the documentation, we noted that a larger batch size was preferred when training control agents.

Before we continue, let's open the `trainer_config.yaml` file and inspect the **HallwayLearning** configuration section as follows:

```
HallwayLearning:
    use_recurrent: true
    sequence_length: 64
    num_layers: 2
    hidden_units: 128
    memory_size: 256
    beta: 1.0e-2
    gamma: 0.99
    num_epoch: 3
    buffer_size: 1024
    batch_size: 128
    max_steps: 5.0e5
    summary_freq: 1000
    time_horizon: 64
```

In the Unity documentation, it specifically mentions only increasing the number of epochs when increasing the batch size, and this is in order to account for additional training experiences. We learned that control examples generally benefit from a larger batch size, and, consequently, a larger epoch size. However, one last thing we want to determine is the effect of altering the `batch_size` and `num_epoch` parameters in a discrete action example with multiple agents feeding into and learning from the same policy.

For the purposes of this exercise, we are only going to modify `batch_size` and `num_epoch` to values as follows:

1. Update the `HallwayLearning` or brain configuration you are using to use the following parameters:

```
HallwayLearning:
    use_recurrent: true
    sequence_length: 64
```

```
num_layers: 2
hidden_units: 128
memory_size: 256
beta: 1.0e-2
gamma: 0.99
num_epoch: 10
buffer_size: 1024
batch_size: 1000
max_steps: 5.0e5
summary_freq: 1000
time_horizon: 64
```

2. We set `num_epoch` to 10 and `batch_size` to `1000`. These settings are typical for a control sample, as we have previously seen, but now we want to see the effect in a discrete action example with multiple agents training the same policy.
3. Prepare the sample for training, and get the Python console ready and open.
4. Run the training session with the following command:

```
mlagents-learn config/trainer_config.yaml --run-id=hallway_e10b1000
--train
```

5. Notice how we have set `run-id` using a helper prefix to name the iteration. We used `e10` to represent that the `num_epoch` parameter is set to `10`, and `b1000` represents the `batch_size` value of `1000`. This type of naming scheme can be helpful, and is one we will continue using through this book.

As the agent trains, try and answer the following questions:

- Does the agent train better or worse than you expected?
- Why do you think that is?

It will be up to you to run the sample in order to learn the answer to those questions. In the next section, we will look at helpful exercises you can do on your own to help your understanding of these complex topics.

Exercises

Attempt one or two of the following exercises on your own:

1. Run the **CrawlerStaticTarget** example scene and compare its performance to the dynamic sample.

2. Double the `time_horizon`, `batch_size`, and `buffer_size` brain hyperparameters in one of the other control examples:

```
time_horizon: 2000
batch_size: 4048
buffer_size: 40480
```

3. Perform the same modification of `time_horizon`, `batch_size`, and `buffer_size` on another control sample and observe the combined effect.
4. Modify the `num_layers` and `hidden_units` brain hyperparameters to values we used in a control sample and apply them to a discrete action example, such as the **Hallway** example, as shown in the following code. How did it affect training?

```
num_layers: 3
hidden_units: 512
```

5. Alter the `num_layers` and `hidden_units` hyperparameters on another continuous or discrete action example and combine it with other parameter modifications.
6. Modify the lambda `lambd` brain hyperparameter in a discrete action example to a value of `.99`. Remember that this will have the effect of strengthening the rewards:

```
lambd: .99
```

7. Create your own control creature with joints and limbs. A good place to start is using the Crawler example and modifying that.
8. Modify one of the control samples by adding new limbs or joints.
9. Modify the **Walker** control example to give the agent a weapon and a target. You will have to combine elements of the **Walker** and **Reacher** examples.
10. Run the **VisualHallwayLearning** sample scene with altered `num_epoch` and `batch_size` parameters. Are the results what you expected?

As we progress through the book, these exercises may become more and more tedious, especially if you run them on an older and slower system. However, it is important to understand how these parameters can alter an agent's training.

When speaking to deep learning and RL practitioners, they will often compare the subtlely of training to the difference between being a good or great cook. A good cook may make things taste good and serve a completely acceptable meal, but it takes a great cook, and their attention to detail, to make you an exceptional meal that you will remember.

Summary

In this chapter, we dug in and learned more of the inner workings of RL by understanding the differences between model-based versus off-model and/or policy-based algorithms. As we learned, Unity ML-Agents uses the PPO algorithm, a powerful and flexible policy learning model that works exceptionally well when training control, or what is sometimes referred to as marathon RL. After learning more basics, we jumped into other RL improvements in the form of Actor-Critic, or advantage training, and what options ML-Agents supports. Next, we looked at the evolution of PPO and its predecessor, the TRPO algorithm, how they work at a basic level, and how they affect training. This is where we learned how to modify one of the control samples to create a new joint on the Reacher arm. We finished the chapter by looking at how multi-agent policy training can be improved on, again by tuning hyperparameters.

We have covered many aspects and details of RL and how agents train, but we have left the most important part of training, rewards, to the next chapter. In the next chapter, we look into rewards, reward functions, and how rewards can even be simulated.

9
Rewards and Reinforcement Learning

Rewards are a fundamental aspect of reinforcement learning, and the concept is easy to grasp. After all, we partly teach and train others—dogs and children, for instance—with reinforcement through rewards. The concept of implementing rewards or a `reward` function in a simulation can be somewhat difficult, and prone to a lot of trial and error. This is the reason for waiting until a later and more advanced chapter to talk about rewards, building `reward` functions, and reward assistance methods such as Curriculum Learning, Backplay, Curiosity Learning, and Imitation Learning / Behavioral Cloning.

Here is a quick summary of the concepts we will cover in this chapter:

- Rewards and `reward` functions
- Sparsity of rewards
- Curriculum Learning
- Understanding Backplay
- Curiosity Learning

While this is an advanced chapter, it is also an essential one and not something you want to skip over. Likewise, many of the top-performing RL demos, such as AlphaStar from DeepMind, use the advanced algorithms in this chapter to teach agents to do tasks that were previously not thought possible.

Rewards and reward functions

We often face this preconceived notion of rewards-based learning or training as comprising of an action being completed, followed by a reward, be it good or bad. While this notion of RL works completely fine for a single action-based task, such as the old multi-arm bandit problem we looked at earlier, or teaching a dog a trick, recall that reinforcement learning is really about an agent learning the value of actions by anticipating future rewards through a series of actions. At each action step, when the agent is not exploring, the agent will determine its next course of action based on what it perceives as having the best reward. What is not always so clear is what those rewards should represent numerically, and to what extent that matters. Therefore, it is often helpful to map out a simple set of `reward` functions that describe the learning behavior we want our agent to train on.

Let's open up the Unity editor to the **GridWorld** example and learn how to create a set of `reward` functions and mappings that describe that training, as follows:

1. Open up the `GridWorld` example from the **Assets** | **ML-Agents** | **Examples** | **GridWorld** | **Scenes** folder.
2. Select the **trueAgent** object in the **Hierarchy** and then switch the agent's brain, at **Grid Agent** | **Brain**, to **GridWorldLearning**.
3. Select the **GridAcademy** and set the **Grid Academy** | **Brains** | **Control** option to enabled.
4. Select and disable the **Main Camera** in the scene. This will make the agent's camera the primary camera, and the one we can view the scene with.
5. Open up and prepare a Python or Anaconda window for training. Check previous chapters or the Unity documentation if you need to remember how to do this.
6. Save the scene and project.
7. Launch the sample into training using the following command at the Python/Anaconda window:

```
mlagents-learn config/trainer_config.yaml --run-id=gridworld --
train
```

8. One of the first things you will appreciate about this sample is how quickly it trains. Remember that the primary reason the agent trains so quickly is because the state space is so small; 5x5 in this example. An example of the simulation running is shown in the following screenshot:

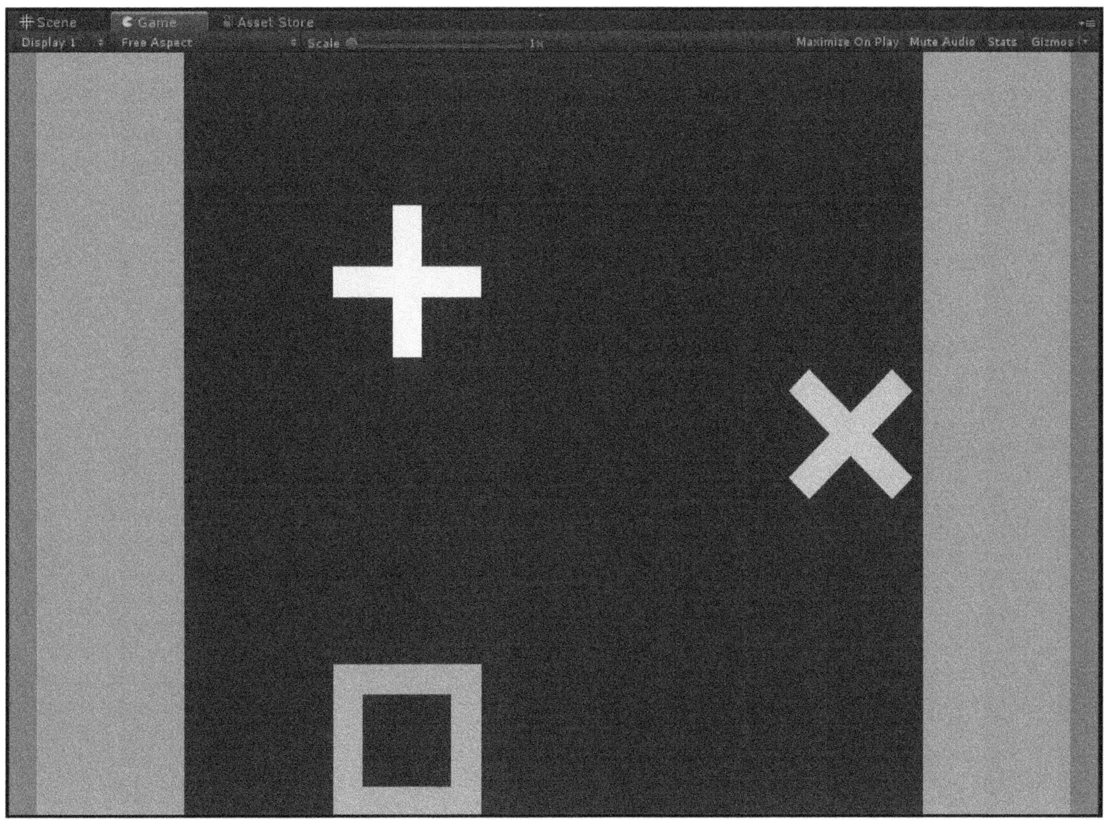

GridWorld example running on 5x5 grid

9. Run the sample until completion. It does not take long to run, even on older systems.

Notice how the agent quickly goes from a negative reward to a positive reward as it learns to place the cube over the green +. However, did you notice that the agent starts training from a negative mean reward? The agent starts with a zero reward value, so let's examine where the negative reward is coming from. In the next section, we look at how to build the `reward` functions by looking at the code.

Building reward functions

Building `reward` functions can be quite simple, as this one will be, or extremely complex, as you may well imagine. While this step is optional for training these examples, it is almost mandatory when you go to build your own environments. It can also identify problems in your training, and ways of enhancing or easing training as well.

Open up the Unity editor and follow this exercise to build these sample `reward` functions:

1. Select the **trueAgent** object in the **Hierarchy** window and then click the target icon beside the **Grid Agent** component.
2. Select **Edit Script** from the **Contact** menu.
3. After the script opens in your editor, scroll down to the `AgentAction` method as follows:

```
public override void AgentAction(float[] vectorAction, string
textAction)
{
  AddReward(-0.01f);
  int action = Mathf.FloorToInt(vectorAction[0]);

  ... // omitted for brevity

  Collider[] blockTest = Physics.OverlapBox(targetPos, new
Vector3(0.3f, 0.3f, 0.3f));
  if (blockTest.Where(col =>
col.gameObject.CompareTag("wall")).ToArray().Length == 0)
  {
    transform.position = targetPos;
    if (blockTest.Where(col =>
col.gameObject.CompareTag("goal")).ToArray().Length == 1)
    {
      Done();
      SetReward(1f);
    }
    if (blockTest.Where(col =>
col.gameObject.CompareTag("pit")).ToArray().Length == 1)
    {
      Done();
      SetReward(-1f);
    }
  }
}
```

4. We want to focus on the highlighted lines, `AddReward` and `SetReward`:
    - `AddReward(-.1f)`: This first line denotes a step reward. Every step the agent takes will cost the agent a negative reward. This is the reason we see the agent show negative rewards until it finds the positive reward.
    - `SetReward(1f)`: This the final positive reward the agent receives, and it is set to the maximum value of `1`. In these types of training scenarios, we prefer to use a range of rewards from -1 to +1.
    - `SetReward(-1f)`: This is the pit of death reward, and a final negative reward.
5. Using each of the previous statements, we can map these to `reward` functions as follows:
    - `AddReward(-.1f)` = $R(s_t) = R(s_{t-1}) + 0.1$
    - `SetReward(1f)` = $R(s) = 1$
    - `SetReward(-1f)` = $R(s) = -1$
6. One thing to notice here is that `AddReward` is an incremental reward, while `SetReward` sets the final value. So, the agent only ever sees a positive reward by reaching the final goal.

By mapping these `reward` functions, we can see that the only way an agent can learn a positive reward is by finding its way to a goal. This is the reason the agent begins with a negative reward, it essentially only first learns to avoid wasting time or moves until it randomly encounters the goal. From there, the agent can quickly assign value to states based on previous positive rewards received. The issue is that the agent first needs to encounter a positive reward before we begin with the actual training. We discuss this particular problem in the next section.

Sparsity of rewards

We call the situation where an agent does not get enough, or any, positive rewards, a sparsity of rewards. The simplest way to show how a sparsity of rewards can happen is by example, and fortunately, the **GridWorld** example can easily demonstrate this for us. Open the editor to the **GridWorld** example and follow this exercise:

1. Open the **GridWorld** sample scene from where we left it in the last exercise. For the purposes of this exercise, it is also helpful to have trained the original sample to completion. **GridWorld** is one of those nice compact examples that train quickly and is an excellent place to test basic concepts, or even hyperparameters.

2. Select the **GridAcademy** and change the **Grid Academy** | **Reset Parameters** | **gridSize** to `25`, as shown in the following screen excerpt:

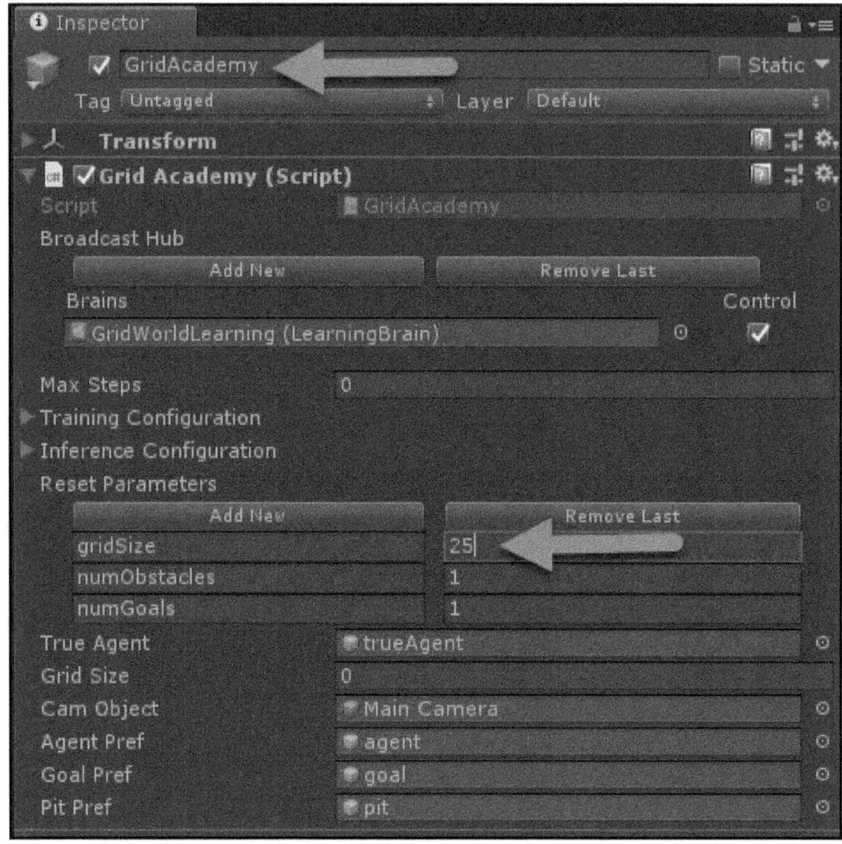

Setting the GridAcademy gridSize parameter

3. Save the scene and the project.
4. Launch the sample into training with the following command from your Python/Anaconda window:

```
mlagents-learn config/trainer_config.yaml --run-id=grid25x25 --
train
```

5. This will launch the sample and, assuming you still have the **agentCam** as the main camera, you should see the following in the **Game** window:

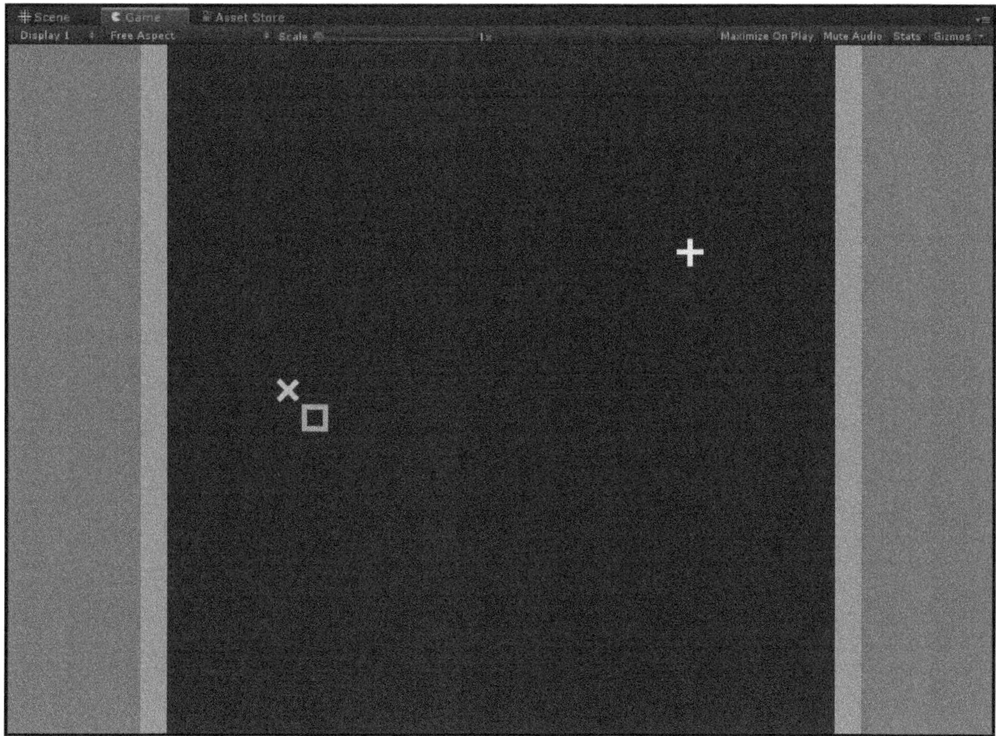

The GridWorld with a grid size of 25x25

6. We have extended the game play space from a 5x5 grid to a 25x25 grid, making the goal (+) symbol much more difficult for the agent to randomly find.
7. What you will quickly notice after a few reported iterations is how poorly the agent is performing in some cases even, reporting less than a -1 mean reward. What's more, the agent could continue training like this for a long time. In fact, it is possible the agent could never discover a reward within 100, 200, 1,000, or more iterations. Now, this may appear to be a problem of state, and, in some ways, you may think of it that way. However, remember that the input state into our agent is the same camera view, a state of 84x84 pixels image, and we have not changed that. So, for the purposes of this example, think of state in the policy RL algorithm as remaining fixed. Therefore, our best course of action in order to fix the problem is to increase the rewards.

8. Stop the training example from the Python/Anaconda window by typing *Ctrl* + *C*. In order to be fair, we will increase the number of rewards for goals and deaths equally.
9. Back in the editor, select the **GridAcademy** and increase the **numObstacles** and **numGoals** on the **Grid Academy** | **Reset Parameters** component properties, as shown in the following excerpt:

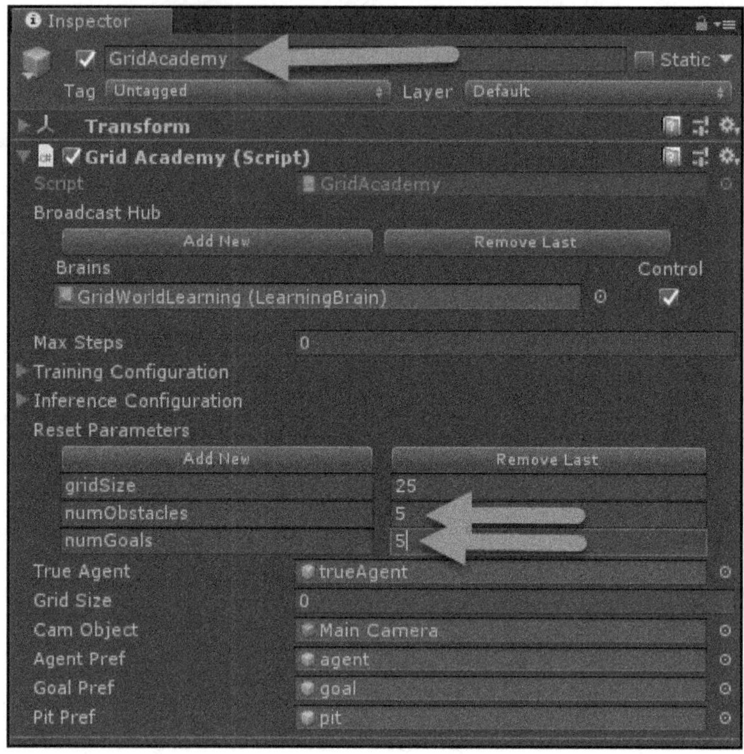

Updating the number of Obstacles and Goals

10. Save the scene and the project.
11. Launch the training session with the following code:

```
mlagents-learn config/trainer_config.yaml --run-id=grid25x25x5 --train
```

12. This is to denote that we are running the sample with five times the number of obstacles and goals.
13. Let the agent train for 25,000 iterations and notice the performance increase. Let the agent train to completion and compare the results to our first run.

The problem of sparsity of rewards is generally encountered more frequently in discrete action tasks, such as **GridWorld/Hallway** and so on. because the `reward` function is often absolute. In continuous learning tasks, the `reward` function is often more gradual and is typically measured by some progress to a goal, and not just the goal itself.

By increasing the number of obstacles and goals—the negative and positive rewards—we are able to train the agent much more quickly, although it is likely you will see very erratic cycles of training, and the agent never truly gets as good as the original. In fact, the training actually may diverge at some point later on. The reason for this is partly because of its limited vision, and we have only partially corrected the sparse rewards problem. We can, of course, fix the issue of sparse rewards in this example by simply increasing the number of goals and obstacles. You can go back and try a value of 25 for the number of obstacles and rewards and see much more stable, long-term results.

Of course, in many RL problems, an increasing number of rewards is not an option, and we need to look at cleverer methods, as we will see in the next section. Fortunately, a number of methods have arisen, in very brief time, looking to address the problem of sparse or difficult rewards. Unity, being at the top, quickly jumped on and implemented a number of methods, the first of which we will look at is called Curriculum Learning, which we will discuss in the next section.

Curriculum Learning

Curriculum Learning allows for an agent to progressively learn a difficult task by stepping up the `reward` function. While the reward remains absolute, the agent finds or achieves the goal in a simpler manner, and so learns the purpose of the reward. Then, as the training progresses and as the agent learns, the difficulty of receiving a reward increases, which, in turn, forces the agent to learn.

Unity, of course, has a few samples of this, and we will look at the `WallJump` example of how a Curriculum Learning sample is set up in the following exercise:

1. Open the **WallJump** scene from the **Assets** | **ML-Agents** | **Examples** | **WallJump** | **Scenes** folder.
2. Select the **Academy** object in the **Hierarchy** window.
3. Click both **Control** options on **Wall Jump Academy** | **Brains** | **Control** parameter as shown in the following excerpt:

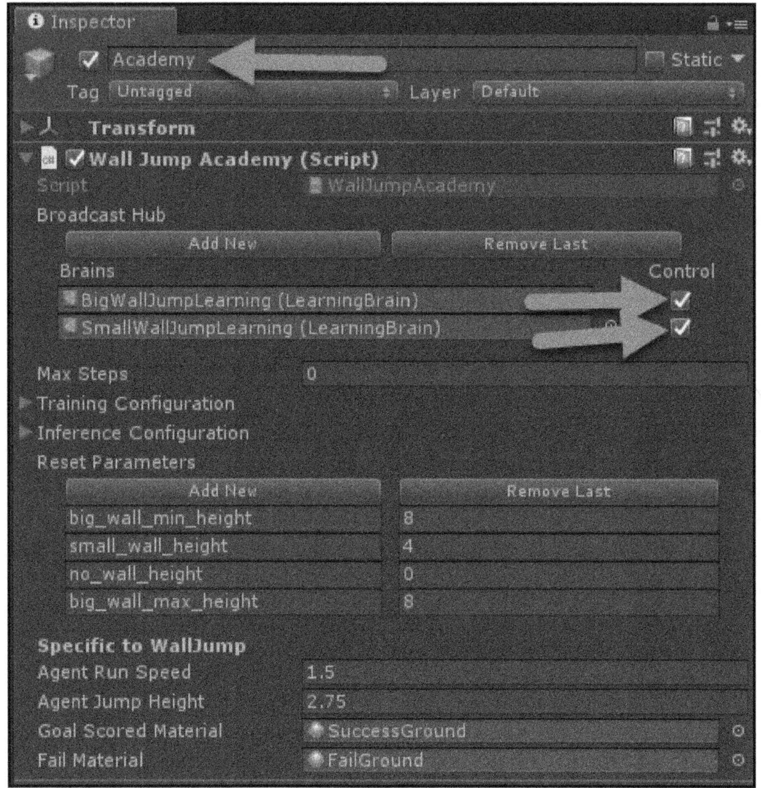

Setting the multiple brains to learning

4. This sample uses multiple brains in order to better separate the learning by task. In fact, all the brains will be trained in tandem.
5. Curriculum Learning uses a second configuration file to describe the curriculum or steps of learning the agent will undergo.
6. Open the `ML-Agents/ml-agents/config/curricul/wall-jump` folder.
7. Open the `SmallWallJumpLearning.json` file in a text editor. The file is shown for reference as follows:

```
{
    "measure" : "progress",
    "thresholds" : [0.1, 0.3, 0.5],
    "min_lesson_length": 100,
    "signal_smoothing" : true,
    "parameters" :
    {
        "small_wall_height" : [1.5, 2.0, 2.5, 4.0]
    }
}
```

8. This JSON file defines the configuration the **SmallWallJumpLearning** brain will take as part of its curriculum or steps to learning. The definition for all these parameters are well documented in the Unity documentation, but we will take a look at parameters from the documentation as follows:
    - `measure` – What to measure learning progress, and advancement in lessons by:
        - reward – Uses a measure received reward.
        - progress – Uses ratio of steps/max_steps.
    - `thresholds` (float array) – Points in value of measure where the lesson should be increased.
    - `min_lesson_length` (int) – The minimum number of episodes that should be completed before the lesson can change. If a measure is set to reward, the average cumulative reward of the last `min_lesson_length` episodes will be used to determine if the lesson should change. Must be non-negative.

9. What we can see by reading this file is that there are three lessons set by a `measure` of `progress` defined by the number of episodes. The episode boundaries are defined at `.1` or 10%, `.3` or 30%, and `.5` or 50% of the total episodes. With each lesson, we set parameters defined by boundaries, and in this example the parameter is `small_wall_height` with a first lesson boundary of `1.5` to `2.0`, a second lesson boundary of `2.0` to `2.5`, and a third lesson at `2.5` to `4.0`.
10. Open up a Python/Anaconda window and prepare it for training.
11. Launch the training session with the following command:

```
mlagents-learn config/trainer_config.yaml --
curriculum=config/curricula/wall-jump/ --run-id=wall-jump-
curriculum --train
```

12. The extra bit that is highlighted adds the folder to the secondary curriculum configuration.
13. You will need to wait for at least half of the full training steps to run in order to see all three levels of training.

This example introduced one technique we can use to solve the problem of sparse or difficult to achieve rewards. In the next section, we look at a specialized form of Curriculum Training called Backplay.

Understanding Backplay

In late 2018, Cinjon Resnick released an innovative paper, titled *Backplay: Man muss immer umkehren*, (`https://arxiv.org/abs/1807.06919`) that introduced a refined form of Curriculum Learning called Backplay. The basic premise is that you start the agent more or less at the goal, and then progressively move the agent back during training. This method may not work for all situations, but we will use this method with Curriculum Training to see how we can improve the **VisualHallway** example in the following exercise:

1. Open the **VisualHallway** scene from the **Assets** | **ML-Agents** | **Examples** | **Hallway** | **Scenes** folder.
2. Make sure the scene is reset to the default starting point. If you need to, pull down the source from ML-Agents again.
3. Set the scene for learning using the **VisualHallwayLearning** brain, and make sure that the agent is just using the default visual observations of 84x84.

4. Select the **Academy** object and in the **Inspector** window add a new **Hallway Academy** | **Reset Parameter** called `distance`, as shown in the following excerpt:

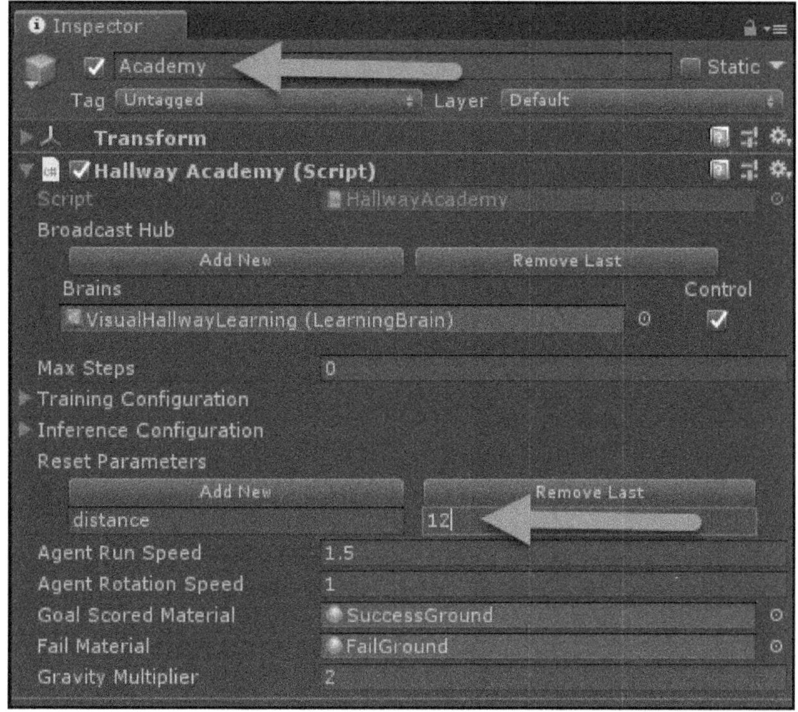

Setting a new Reset Parameter on the Academy

5. You can use **Reset Parameters** for more than just Curriculum Learning, as they can help you easily configure training parameters within the editor. The parameter we are defining here is going to set the distance, the agent is away from the back goal region. This sample is intended to show the concept of Backplay, and in order to properly implement it we would need to move the agent right in front of the proper goal—we will defer from doing this for now.
6. Select the **VisualHallwayArea** | **Agent** and open the **Hallway Academy** script in your code editor of choice.

7. Scroll down to the `AgentReset` method and adjust the top line to that shown as follows:

```
public override void AgentReset()
{
  float agentOffset = academy.resetParameters["distance"];
  float blockOffset = 0f;
  // ... rest removed for brevity
```

8. This single line of code will adjust the starting offset of the agent to the now preset **Reset Parameters** of the **Academy**. Likewise, as the **Academy** updates those parameters during training, the agent will also see updated values.
9. Save the file and return to the editor. The editor will recompile your code changes and let you know if everything is okay. A red error in the console will typically mean you have a compiler error, likely caused by incorrect syntax.
10. Open a prepared Python/Anaconda window and run the training session with the following command:

```
mlagents-learn config/trainer_config.yaml --run-id=vh_backplay --train
```

11. This will run the session in regular mode, without Curriculum Learning, but it will adjust the starting position of the agent to be closer to the goals. Let this sample run and see how well the agent performs now that it starts so close to the goals.

Let the training run for a while and observe the difference in training from the original. One thing you will notice is that the agent can't help but run into the reward now, which is what we are after. The next piece we need to implement is the Curriculum Learning part, where we will move the agent back as it learns to find the reward in the next section.

Implementing Backplay through Curriculum Learning

In the last section, we implemented the first part of Backplay, which is having the agent start next to, or very close to the goal. The next part we need to accomplish is progressively moving the agent back to its intended starting point using Curriculum Learning. Open up the Unity editor to the **VisualHallway** scene again and follow these steps:

1. Open the `ML-Agents/ml-agents/config` folder with a file explorer or command shell.

2. Create a new folder called `hallway` and navigate to the new folder.
3. Open a text editor or create a new JSON text file called `VisualHallwayLearning.json` in the new directory. **JavaScript Object Notation** (**JSON**) is intended to describe objects in JavaScript, it has become a standard for configuration settings as well.
4. Enter the following JSON text in the new file:

```
{
    "measure" : "rewards",
    "thresholds" : [0.1, 0.2, 0.3, 0.4, 0.5, 0.6, 0.7],
    "min_lesson_length": 100,
    "signal_smoothing" : true,
    "parameters" :
    {
        "distance" : [12, 8, 4, 2, -2, -4, -8, -12]
    }
```

5. This configuration file defines a curriculum that we will use to train an agent on Backplay. The file defines a `measure` of `rewards` and `thresholds` that define when the agent will advance to the next level of training. When a reward threshold is hit for a minimum episode length of `100` steps, than the training will advance to the next `distance` parameter. Notice how we define the distance parameter with `12`, representing a distance close to the goals, and then decreasing. You could, of course, create a function that maps different range values, but we will leave that up to you.
6. Save the file after you are done editing.
7. Launch a training session from a Python/Anaconda window with the following command:

```
mlagents-learn config/trainer_config.yaml --
curriculum=config/curricula/hallway/ --run-id=hallway-curriculum --
train
```

8. After the training starts, notice how the curriculum is getting set in the Python/Anaconda window, as shown in the following screenshot:

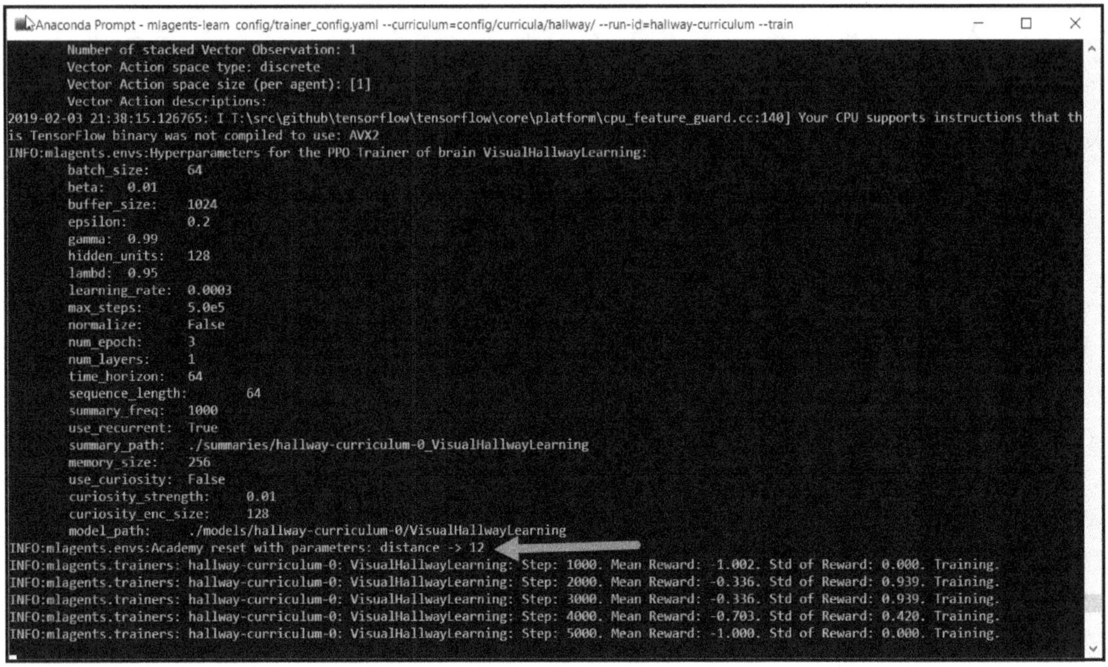

```
Anaconda Prompt - mlagents-learn config/trainer_config.yaml --curriculum=config/curricula/hallway/ --run-id=hallway-curriculum --train
        Number of stacked Vector Observation: 1
        Vector Action space type: discrete
        Vector Action space size (per agent): [1]
        Vector Action descriptions:
2019-02-03 21:38:15.126765: I T:\src\github\tensorflow\tensorflow\core\platform\cpu_feature_guard.cc:140] Your CPU supports instructions that th
is TensorFlow binary was not compiled to use: AVX2
INFO:mlagents.envs:Hyperparameters for the PPO Trainer of brain VisualHallwayLearning:
        batch_size:     64
        beta:   0.01
        buffer_size:    1024
        epsilon:        0.2
        gamma:  0.99
        hidden_units:   128
        lambd:  0.95
        learning_rate:  0.0003
        max_steps:      5.0e5
        normalize:      False
        num_epoch:      3
        num_layers:     1
        time_horizon:   64
        sequence_length:        64
        summary_freq:   1000
        use_recurrent:  True
        summary_path:   ./summaries/hallway-curriculum-0_VisualHallwayLearning
        memory_size:    256
        use_curiosity:  False
        curiosity_strength:     0.01
        curiosity_enc_size:     128
        model_path:     ./models/hallway-curriculum-0/VisualHallwayLearning
INFO:mlagents.envs:Academy reset with parameters: distance -> 12
INFO:mlagents.trainers: hallway-curriculum-0: VisualHallwayLearning: Step: 1000. Mean Reward: -1.002. Std of Reward: 0.000. Training.
INFO:mlagents.trainers: hallway-curriculum-0: VisualHallwayLearning: Step: 2000. Mean Reward: -0.336. Std of Reward: 0.939. Training.
INFO:mlagents.trainers: hallway-curriculum-0: VisualHallwayLearning: Step: 3000. Mean Reward: -0.336. Std of Reward: 0.939. Training.
INFO:mlagents.trainers: hallway-curriculum-0: VisualHallwayLearning: Step: 4000. Mean Reward: -0.703. Std of Reward: 0.420. Training.
INFO:mlagents.trainers: hallway-curriculum-0: VisualHallwayLearning: Step: 5000. Mean Reward: -1.000. Std of Reward: 0.000. Training.
```

Watching the curriculum parameters getting set in training

9. Wait for the agent to train, and see how many levels of training it can accomplish before the end of the session.

Now, one thing we need to come clean about is that this sample is more an innovative example than a true example of Backplay. Actual Backplay is described as putting the agent at the goal and working backward. In this example, we are putting the agent almost at the goal and working backward. The difference is subtle, but, by now, hopefully you can appreciate that, in terms of training, it could be significant.

Curiosity Learning

Up until now, we have considered just the extrinsic or external rewards an agent may receive in an environment. The **Hallway** example, for instance, gives a +1 external reward when the agent reaches the goal, and a -1 external reward if it gets the wrong goal. However, real animals like us can actually learn based on internal motivations, or by using an internal `reward` function. A great example of this is a baby (a cat, a human, or whatever) that has an obvious natural motivation to be curious through play. The curiosity of playing provides the baby with an internal or intrinsic reward, but the actual act itself gives it a negative external or extrinsic reward. After all, the baby is expending energy, a negative external reward, yet it plays on and on in order to learn more general information about its environment. This, in turn, allows it to explore more of the environment and ultimately attain some very difficult goal, such as hunting, or going to work.

This form of internal or intrinsic reward modeling falls into a subclass of RL, called Motivated Reinforcement Learning. As you may well imagine, this whole arc of learning could have huge applications in gaming, from creating NPCs to more believable opponents that actually get motivated by some personality trait or emotion. Imagine having a computer opponent that can get angry, or even, compassionate? Of course, we are a long way from getting there, but in the interim, Unity has added an intrinsic reward system in order to model agent curiosity, and this is called Curiosity Learning.

Curiosity Learning (**CL**) was first developed by researchers at the University of California, Berkley, in a paper called *Curiosity-Driven Exploration by Self-Supervised Prediction,* which you can find at `https://pathak22.github.io/noreward-rl/`. The paper goes on to describe a system of solving sparse rewards problems using forward and inverse neural networks. They called the system an **Intrinsic Curiosity Module** (**ICM**), with the intent for it to be used as a layer or module on top of other RL systems. This is exactly what Unity did, and they have added this as a module to ML-Agents.

The Lead Researcher at Unity, Dr. Arthur Juliani, has an excellent blog post on their implementation that can be found at `https://blogs.unity3d.com/2018/06/26/solving-sparse-reward-tasks-with-curiosity/`.

ICM works by using an inverse neural network that is trained using the current and next observation of the agent. It uses an encoder to encode a prediction on what the action was between the two states, current and next. Then, the forward network is trained on the current observation and action in which it encodes to the next observation. The difference is then taken between the real and predicted encodings from the inverse and forward models. In this case, the bigger the difference, the bigger the surprise, and the more intrinsic the rewards. A diagram extracted from Dr. Juliani's blog is shown as follows, describing how this works:

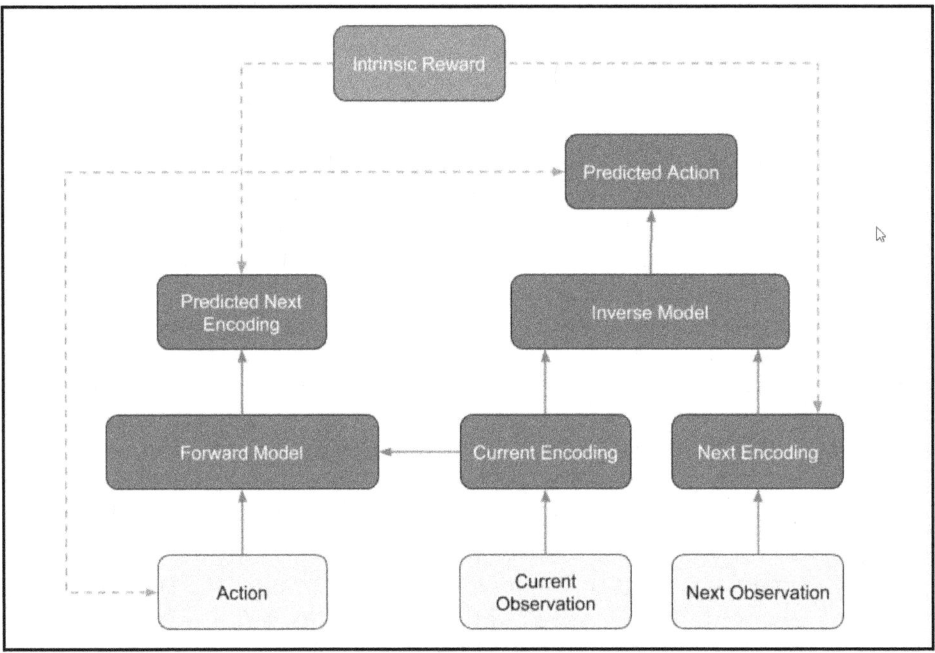

Inner workings of the Curiosity Learning Module

The diagram shows the depiction of the two models and layers in blue, forward and inverse, with the blue lines depicting network flow, the green box representing the intrinsic model calculation, and the reward output in the form of the green dotted lines.

Well, that's enough theory, its time to see how this CL works in practice. Fortunately, Unity has a very well developed environment that features this new module that is called Pyramids. Let's open Unity and follow the next exercise to see this environment in action:

1. Open the **Pyramid** scene from the **Assets** | **ML-Agents** | **Examples** | **Pyramids** | **Scenes** folder.

2. Select the **AreaPB(1)** to **AreaPB(15)** in the **Hierarchy** window and then deactivate these objects in the **Inspector** window.
3. Leave the scene in player mode. For the first time, we want you to play the scene on your own and figure out the goal. Even if you read the blog or played the scene, try again, but this time, think what reward functions would need to be in place.
4. Press **Play** in the editor and start playing the game in **Player** mode. If you have not played the game before or understand the premise, don't be surprised if it takes you a while to solve the puzzle.

Now, for those of you that didn't read or play ahead, here is the premise. The scene starts where the agent is randomly placed into an area of rooms with pyramids of stone in which one has a switch. The goal of the agent is to activate the switch that then spawns a pyramid of sand boxes with a large gold box on top. The switch turns from red to green after it is activated. After the pyramid appears, the agent then needs to knock the pyramid over and retrieve the gold box. It certainly is not the most complex of puzzles, but one that does require a bit of exploration and curiosity.

Imagine if we tried to model this form of curiosity, or need to explore, with a set of `reward` functions. We would need a `reward` function for activating the button, moving to rooms, knocking over blocks, and, of course, getting the gold box. Then we would have to determine the value of each of those objectives, perhaps using some form of **Inverse Reinforcement Learning** (**IRL**). However, with Curiosity Learning, we can create the reward function for just the end goal of getting the box (+1), and perhaps a small negative step goal (.0001), then use intrinsic curiosity rewards to let the agent learn the remaining steps. Quite a clever trick, and we will see how this works in the next section.

The Curiosity Intrinsic module in action

With our appreciation of the difficulty of the **Pyramids** task, we can move on to training the agent with curiosity in the following exercise:

1. Open the **Pyramids** scene in the editor.
2. Select the **AreaRB** | **Agent** object in the **Hierarchy** window.
3. Switch the **Pyramid Agent** | **Brain** for the **PyramidsLearning** brain.
4. Select the **Academy** object in the **Hierarchy** window.

5. Enable the **Control** option on the **Academy** | **Pyramid Academy** | **Brains** | **Control** property, as shown in the following screenshot:

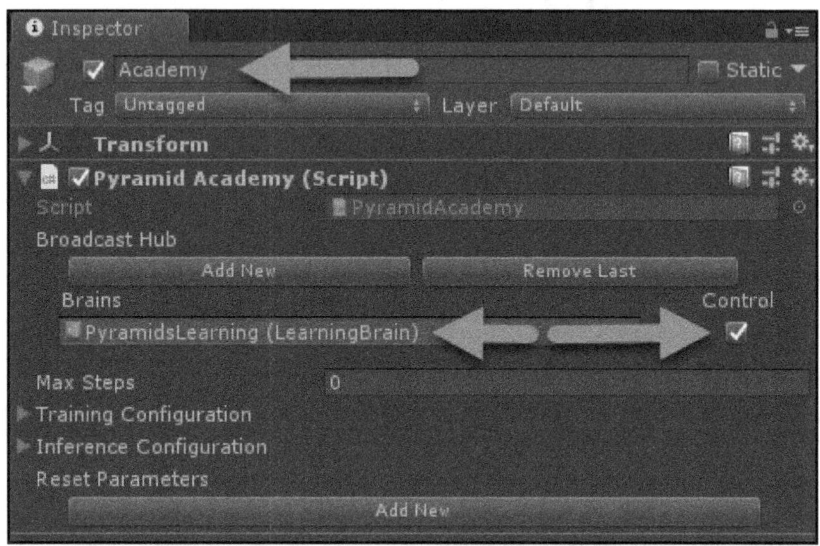

Setting the Academy to Control

6. Open a Python or Anaconda console and prepare it for training.
7. Open the `trainer_config.yaml` file located in the `ML-Agents/ml-agents/config` folder.
8. Scroll down to the `PyramidsLearning` configuration section, as follows:

```
PyramidsLearning:
    use_curiosity: true
    summary_freq: 2000
    curiosity_strength: 0.01
    curiosity_enc_size: 256
    time_horizon: 128
    batch_size: 128
    buffer_size: 2048
    hidden_units: 512
    num_layers: 2
    beta: 1.0e-2
    max_steps: 5.0e5
    num_epoch: 3
```

9. There are three new configuration parameters highlighted in bold:
    - `use_curiosity`: Set this to `true` to use the module, but it is generally `false` by default.
    - `curiosity_strength`: This is how strongly the agent values the intrinsic reward of curiosity over the extrinsic ones.
    - `curiosity_enc_size`: This is the size of the encoded layer we compress the network to. If you think back to autoencoders, you can see the size of 256 is quite large, but also consider the size of the state space or observation space you may be encoding.

Leave the parameters at the values they are set.

10. Launch the training session with the following command:

```
mlagents-learn config/trainer_config.yaml --run-id=pyramids --train
```

While this training session may take a while, it can be entertaining to watch how the agent explores. Even with the current settings, using only one training area, you may be able to see the agent solve the puzzle on a few iterations.

Since ICM is a module, it can quickly be activated for any other example we want to see the effects on, which is what we will do in the next section.

Trying ICM on Hallway/VisualHallway

Not unlike the agents we train, we learn quite well from trial and error. This is the reason we practice, practice, and practice more of those very difficult tasks such as dancing, singing, or playing an instrument. RL is no different and requires the practitioner to learn the ins and outs training through the rigors of trial, error, and further exploration. Therefore, in this next exercise, we are going to combine Backplay (Curriculum Learning) and Curiosity Learning together into our old friend, the Hallway, and see what effect it has, as follows:

1. Open the **Hallway** or **VisualHallway** scene (your preference) as we last left it, with Curriculum Learning enabled and set to simulate Backplay.
2. Open the `trainer_config.yaml` configuration file location in the `ML-Agents/ml-agents/config` folder.

3. Scroll down to the `HallwayLearning` or `VisualHallwayLearning` brain configuration parameters and add the following additional configuration lines:

```
HallwayLearning:
    use_curiosity: true
    curiosity_strength: 0.01
    curiosity_enc_size: 256
    use_recurrent: true
    sequence_length: 64
    num_layers: 2
    hidden_units: 128
    memory_size: 256
    beta: 1.0e-2
    gamma: 0.99
    num_epoch: 10
    buffer_size: 1024
    batch_size: 1000
    max_steps: 5.0e5
    summary_freq: 1000
    time_horizon: 64
```

4. This will enable the curiosity module for this example. We use the same settings for curiosity as we used for the last **Pyrmarids** example.
5. Make sure this sample is prepared for curriculum Backplay as we configured it in that section. If you need to, go back and review that section and add the capability to this example before continuing.

This may require you to create a new curricula file that uses the same parameters as we did previously. Remember that the curricula file needs to have the same name as the brain it is being used against.

6. Open a Python/Anaconda window prepared for training and start training with the following command:

```
mlagents-learn config/trainer_config.yaml --
curriculum=config/curricula/hallway/ --run-id=hallway_bp_cl --train
```

7. Let the training run until completion, as the results can be interesting and show some of the powerful possibilities of layering learning enhancements for extrinsic and intrinsic rewards.

This exercise showed how to run an agent with both Curriculum Learning simulating Backplay, and Curiosity Learning adding an aspect of agent motivation to the learning. As you may well imagine, intrinsic reward learning and the whole field of Motivated Reinforcement Learning may lead to some interesting advances and enhancements to our DRL.

In the next section, we will review a number of helpful exercises that should help you learn more about these concepts.

Exercises

While your motivation may vary as to why you are reading this book, hopefully by now you can appreciate the value of just doing things on your own. As always, we present these exercises for your enjoyment and learning, and hope you have fun completing them:

1. Select another sample scene that uses discrete actions and write the reward functions that go with it. Yes, that means you will need to open up and look at the code.
2. Select a continuous action scene and try writing the reward functions for it. While this one may be difficult, it is essential if you want to build your own control training agent.
3. Add Curriculum Learning to one of the other discrete action samples we have explored. Decide on how you can break the training into levels of difficulty and create parameters for controlling the evolution of the training.
4. Add Curriculum Learning to a continuous action sample. This is more difficult, and you likely want to perform exercise number two first.
5. Implement actual Backplay on the Hallway environment by placing the agent starting at the goal and then, as the agent trains, move it back to the desired start with Curriculum Learning.
6. Implement Backplay on another discrete action example you have run and see the effect it has on training.
7. Implement Curiosity Learning on the **VisualPyramids** example and notice the difference in training.
8. Implement Curiosity Learning on a continuous action example and notice the effect it has on training. Is it what you expected?
9. Disable Curiosity Learning on the **Pyramids** example and see what effect this has on agent training.
10. Think of a way in which you could add Backplay to the **VisualPyramids** example. You'll get bonus points if you actually build it.

As you can see, the exercises are getting more demanding as we progress through the book. Remember, even completing one or two of these exercises will make a difference in your take-away knowledge.

Summary

In this chapter, we looked at a fundamental component of RL, and that is rewards. We learned that, when building training environments, it was best that we defined a set of `reward` functions our agent will live by. By understanding these equations, we get a better sense of how frequent or sparse rewards can negatively affect training. We then looked at a few methods, the first of which is called Curriculum Learning, that could be used to ease or step the agent's extrinsic rewards. After that, we explored another technique, called Backplay, that used a reverse play technique and Curriculum Training to enhance an agent's training. Finally, we looked at internal or intrinsic rewards, and the concept of Motivated Reinforcement Learning. We then learned that the first intrinsic reward system developed into ML-Agents was to give an agent a motivation for curiosity. We looked at how to use Curiosity Learning on a few examples, and even incorporated it with Backplay via Curriculum Learning.

In the next chapter, we look to more reward helper solutions in the form of Imitation and Transfer Learning, where we will learn how a human's gameplay experience can be mapped to a form of learning called Imitation Learning or Behavioral Cloning.

10
Imitation and Transfer Learning

At the time of writing, a new AI called AlphaStar, a **deep reinforcement learning** (**DRL**) agent, used **imitation learning** (**IL**) to beat a human opponent five-nil playing the real-time strategy game StarCraft II. AlphaStar was the continuation of David Silver and Google DeepMind's work to build a smarter and more intelligent AI. The specific techniques AlphaStar used to win could fill a book, and IL and the use of learning to copy human play is now of keen interest. Fortunately, Unity has already implemented IL in the form of offline and online training scenarios. While we won't make it to the level of AlphaStar in this chapter, we still will learn about the underlying technologies of IL and other forms of transfer learning.

In this chapter, we will look at the implementation of IL in ML-Agents and then look to other applications of transfer learning. We will cover the following topics in this chapter:

- IL or behavioral cloning
- Online training
- Offline training
- Transfer Learning
- Imitation Transfer Learning

While AlphaStar performed a stunning tactical victory against a human pro player in an RTS game, it has still come under scrutiny for the type of play and actions it used. Many human players stated that the AI's tactical abilities were clearly superior, but the overall strategy and planning were abysmal. It should be interesting to see how Google DeepMind approaches this criticism.

This will be an exciting chapter, and will provide you with plenty of training possibilities for your future developments, which all starts in the next section.

IL, or behavioral cloning

IL, or behavioral cloning, is the process by which observations and actions are captured from a human, or perhaps another AI, and used as input into training an agent. The agent essentially becomes guided by the human and learns by their actions and observations. A set of learning observations can be received by real-time play (online) or be extracted from saved games (offline). This provides the ability to capture play from multiple agents and train them in tandem or individually. IL provides the ability to train or, in effect, program agents for tasks you may find impossible to train for using regular RL, and because of this, it will likely become a key RL technique that we use for most tasks in the near future.

It is hard to gauge the value something gives you until you see what things are like without it. With that in mind, we will first start by looking at an example that uses no IL, but certainly could benefit from it. Open up the Unity editor and follow this exercise:

1. Open up the **Tennis** scene from the **Assets** | **ML-Agents** | **Examples** | **Tennis** | **Scenes** folder.
2. Select and disable the extra agent training areas, **TennisArea(1)** to **TennisArea(17)**.
3. Select **AgentA** and make sure **Tennis Agent** | **Brain** is set to **TennisLearning**. We want each agent to be against the other agent in this example.
4. Select **AgentB** and make sure **Tennis Agent** | **Brain** is set to **TennisLearning**. In this example, for a brief instance, we are training multiple agents in the same environment. We will cover more scenarios where agents play other agents as a way of learning in `Chapter 11`, *Building Multi-Agent Environments*.
5. Select **Academy** and make sure that **Tennis Academy** | **Brains** is set to **TennisLearning** and the **Control** option is enabled, as shown in the following screenshot:

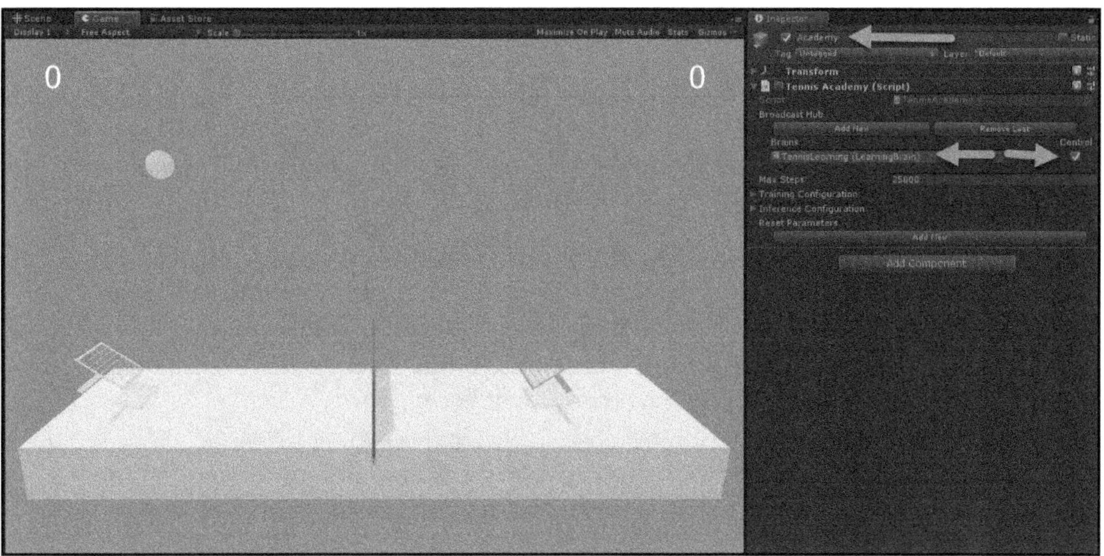

Setting Control to enabled on Academy

6. Open a Python/Anaconda window and prepare it for training. We will launch training with the following command:

```
mlagents-learn config/trainer_config.yaml --run-id=tennis --train
```

7. Watch the training for several thousand iterations, enough to convince yourself the agents are not going to learn this task easily. When you are convinced, stop the training and move on.

You can see by just looking at this first example that ordinary training and the other advanced methods we looked at, such as Curriculum and Curiosity Learning, would be difficult to implement, and in this case could be counterproductive. In the next section, we look at how to run this example with IL in online training mode.

Online training

Online Imitation Learning is where you teach the agent to learn the observations of a player or another agent in real time. It also is one of the most fun and engaging ways to train agents or bots. Let's jump in and set up the tennis environment for online Imitation Learning in the next exercise:

1. Select the **TennisArea** | **AgentA** object and set **Tennis Agent** | **Brain** to **TennisPlayer**. In this IL scenario, we have one brain acting as a teacher, the player, and a second brain acting as the student, the learner.
2. Select the **AgentB** object and make sure **Tennis Agent** | **Brain** is set to **TennisLearning**. This will be the student brain.
3. Open the `online_bc_config.yaml` file from the `ML-Agents/ml-agents/config` folder. IL does not use the same configuration as PPO so the parameters will have similar names but may not respond to what you have become used to.
4. Scroll down in the file to the `TennisLearning` brain configuration as shown in the following code snippet:

```
TennisLearning:
    trainer: online_bc
    max_steps: 10000
    summary_freq: 1000
    brain_to_imitate: TennisPlayer
    batch_size: 16
    batches_per_epoch: 5
    num_layers: 4
    hidden_units: 64
    use_recurrent: false
    sequence_length: 16
```

5. Looking over the hyperparameters, we can see there are two new parameters of interest. A summary of those parameters is as follows:
    - `trainer`: `online_` *or* `offline_bc`—using online or offline Behavioral Cloning. In this case, we are performing online.
    - `brain_to_imitate`: `TennisPlayer`—this sets the brain that the learning brain should attempt to imitate.
      We won't make any changes to the file at this point.
6. Open your prepared Python/Anaconda window and launch training with the following command:

```
mlagents-learn config/online_bc_config.yaml --run-id=tennis_il --
train --slow
```

7. After you press **Play** in the editor, you will be able to control the left paddle with the *W*, *A*, *S*, *D* keys. Play the game, and you may be surprised at how quickly the agent learns and can get quite good. The following is an example of the game being played:

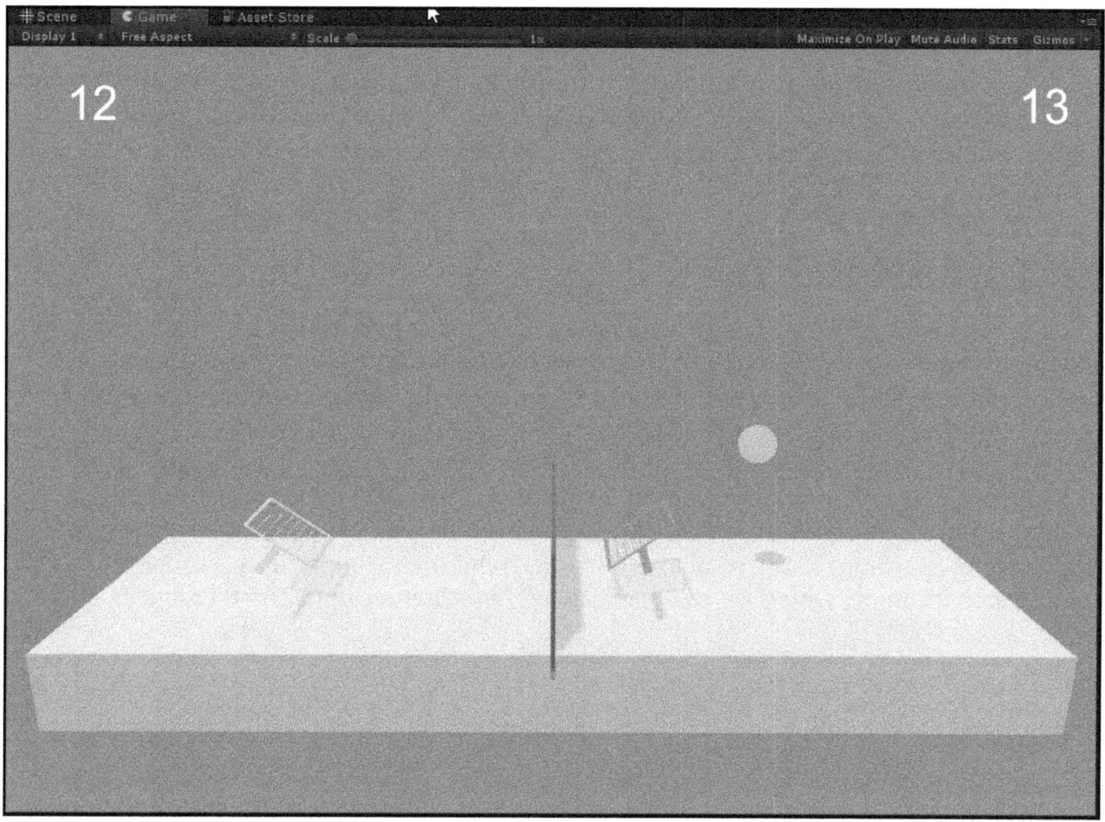

Playing and teaching the agent with IL

8. Keep playing the example until completion if you like. It can also be interesting to switch players during a game, or even train the brain and use the trained model to play against later. You do remember how to run a trained model, right?

At some point while playing through the last exercise, you may have wondered why we don't we train all RL agents this way. A good question, but as you can imagine, it depends. While IL is very powerful, and quite a capable learner, it doesn't always do what we expect it to do. Also, an IL agent is only going to learn the search space (observations) it is shown and remain within those limitations. In the case of AlphaStar, IL was the main input for training, but the team also mentioned that the AI did have plenty of time to self-play, which likely accounted for many of its winning strategies. So, while IL is cool and powerful, it is not the golden goose that will solve all our RL problems. However, you are likely to have a new and greater appreciation for RL, and in particular IL, after this exercise. In the next section, we explore using offline IL.

Offline training

Offline training is where a recorded gameplay file is generated from a player or agent playing a game or performing a task, and is then fed back as training observations to help an agent learn later on. While online learning certainly is more fun, and in some ways more applicable to the Tennis scene or other multiplayer games, it is less practical. After all, you generally need to play an agent in real time for several hours before an agent will become good. Likewise, in online training scenarios, you are typically limited to single agent training, whereas in offline training a demo playback can be fed to multiple agents for better overall learning. This also allows us to perform interesting training scenarios, similar to AlphaStar training, where we can teach an agent so that it can teach other agents.

We will learn more about multi-agent gameplay in `Chapter 11`, *Building Multi-Agent Environments*.

For this next exercise, we are going to revisit our old friend the **Hallway/VisualHallway** example. Again, we are doing this so we can compare our results to the previous sample exercises we ran with this environment. Follow this exercise to set up a new offline training session:

1. Clone and download the ML-Agents code to a new folder, perhaps choosing `ml-agents_b`, `ml-agents_c`, or some other name. The reason we do this is to make sure that we run these new exercises with a clean environment. Also, it can sometimes help to go back to old environments and recall settings or configuration that you may forget to update.
2. Launch Unity and open the **UnitySDK** project and the **Hallway** or **VisualHallway** scene, your choice.

3. The scene should be set to run in **Player** mode. Just confirm this. If you need to change it, then do so.
4. Disable any additional agent training environments in the scene if others are active.
5. Select **HallwayArea** | **Agent** in the **Hierarchy** window.
6. Click the **Add Component** button at the bottom of the **Inspector** window, type `demo`, and select the **Demonstration Recorder** component as shown in the following screenshot:

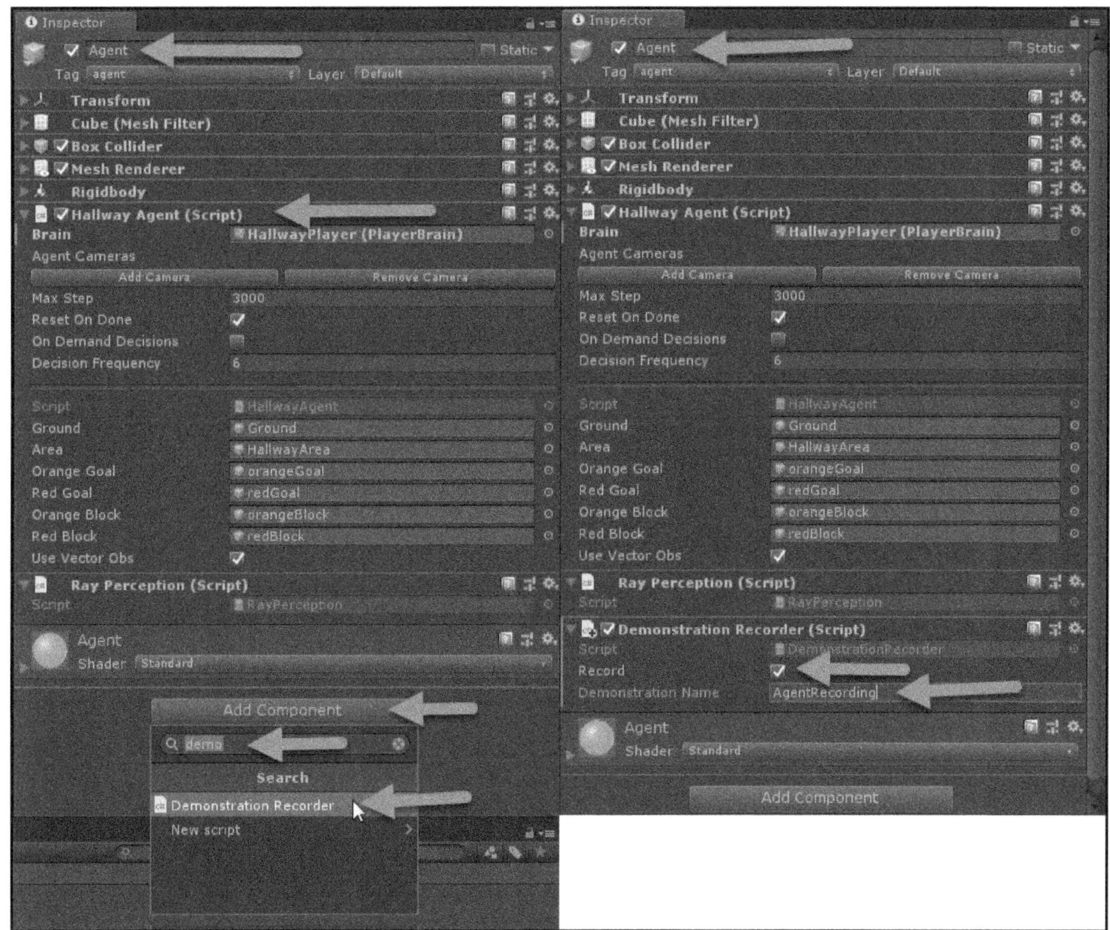

Adding a Demonstration Recorder

7. Click **Record** on the new **Demonstration Recorder** component, as shown in the preceding screenshot, check throughout. Also, fill in the **Demonstration Name** property of the recording, which is also shown.
8. Save the scene and project.
9. Press **Play** and play the scene for a fair amount of time, more than a few minutes but perhaps less than hours. Of course, how well you play will also determine how well the agent learns. If you play poorly, so will the agent.
10. After you think enough time has passed, and you have played as well as you could, stop the game.

After playing the game, you should see a new folder called **Demonstrations** created in the **Assets** root folder in your **Project** window. Inside the folder will be your demonstration recording. This is the recording we will feed the agent in the next section.

Setting up for training

Now that we have our demonstration recording, we can do more on the training part. This time, however, we will play back our observation file to multiple agents in multiple environments. Open the **Hallway/VisualHallway** sample scene and follow the next exercise to set up for training:

1. Select and enable all the **HallwayArea** training environments **HallwayArea(1)** to **HallwayArea(15)**
2. Select **HallwayArea** | **Agent** in the **Hierarchy** and then switch **Hallway Agent** | **Brain** to **HallwayLearning**, as shown in the following screenshot:

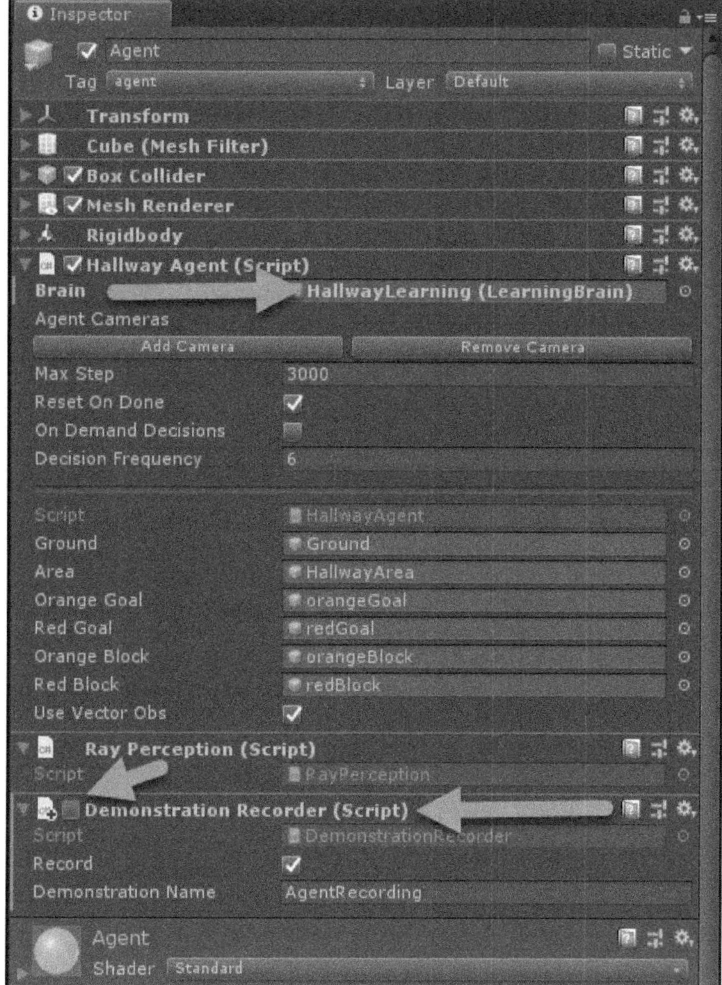

Setting the agent components

3. Also, select and disable the **Demonstration Recording** component as shown in the preceding screen excerpt
4. Make sure all the agents in the scene are using **HallwayLearning** brains

5. Select **Academy** in the **Hierarchy** and then enable the **Hallway Academy** | **Brains** | **Control** option as shown in the following screenshot:

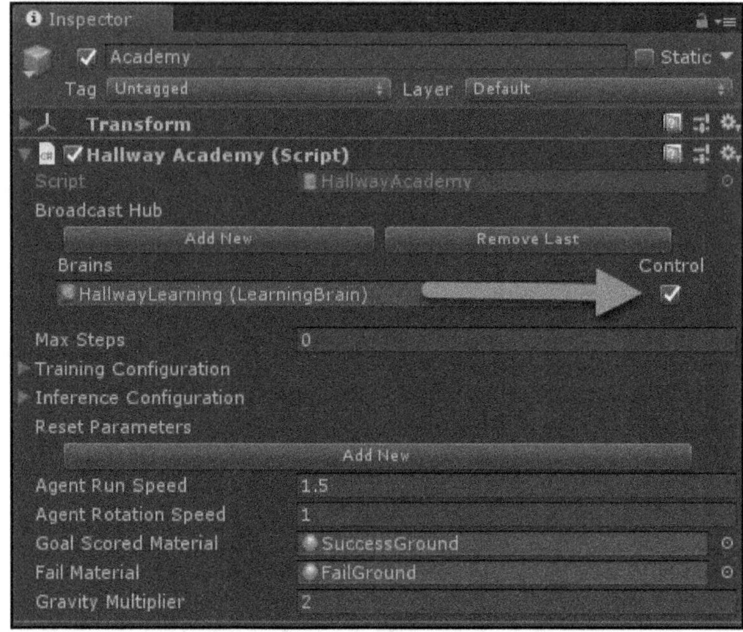

Enabling Academy to Control the Brains

6. Save the scene and project

Now that we have the scene configured for agent learning, we can move on to feeding the agent in the next section.

Feeding the agent

When we performed online IL, we only fed one agent at a time in the tennis scene. This time, however, we are going to train multiple agents from the same demonstration recording in order to improve training performance.

We have already set up for training, so let's start feeding the agent in the following exercise:

1. Open a Python/Anaconda window and set it up for training from the new `ML-Agents` folder. You did reclone the source, right?
2. Open the `offline_bc_config.yaml` file from the `ML-Agents/ml-agents_b/config` folder. The contents of the file are as follows for reference:

```
default:
    trainer: offline_bc
    batch_size: 64
    summary_freq: 1000
    max_steps: 5.0e4
    batches_per_epoch: 10
    use_recurrent: false
    hidden_units: 128
    learning_rate: 3.0e-4
    num_layers: 2
    sequence_length: 32
    memory_size: 256
    demo_path:
./UnitySDK/Assets/Demonstrations/<Your_Demo_File>.demo

HallwayLearning:
    trainer: offline_bc
    max_steps: 5.0e5
    num_epoch: 5
    batch_size: 64
    batches_per_epoch: 5
    num_layers: 2
    hidden_units: 128
    sequence_length: 16
    use_recurrent: true
    memory_size: 256
    sequence_length: 32
    demo_path: ./UnitySDK/Assets/Demonstrations/demo.demo
```

3. Change the last line of the `HallwayLearning` or `VisualHallwayLearning` brain to the following:

```
HallwayLearning:
    trainer: offline_bc
    max_steps: 5.0e5
    num_epoch: 5
    batch_size: 64
    batches_per_epoch: 5
    num_layers: 2
    hidden_units: 128
```

```
sequence_length: 16
use_recurrent: true
memory_size: 256
sequence_length: 32
demo_path: ./UnitySDK/Assets/Demonstrations/AgentRecording.demo
```

4. Note that if you are using the `VisualHallwayLearning` brain, you will need to also change the name in the preceding config script.
5. Save your changes when you are done editing.
6. Go back to your Python/Anaconda window and launch training with the following command:

```
mlagents-learn config/offline_bc_config.yaml --run-id=hallway_il --
train
```

7. When prompted, press **Play** in the editor and watch the training unfold. You will see the agent play using very similar moves to yourself, and if you played well, the agent will quickly start learning and you should see some impressive training, all thanks to IL.

RL can be thought of as the brute-force approach to learning, while the refinement of Imitation Learning and training by observation will clearly dominate the future of agent training. Of course, is it really any wonder? After all, we simple humans learn that way.

In the next section, we look at another exciting area of deep learning, transfer learning, and how it applies to games and DRL.

Transfer learning

Imitation Learning, by definition, falls into a category of **Transfer Learning** (**TL**). We can define Transfer Learning as the process by which an agent or DL network is trained by transference of experiences from one to the other. This could be as simple as the observation training we just performed, or as complex as swapping layers/layer weights in an agent's brain, or just training an agent on a similar task.

Intransfer learningwe need to make sure the experiences or previous weights we use are generalized. Through the foundational chapters in this book (chapters 1-3), we learned the value of generalization using techniques such as dropout and batch normalization. We learned that these techniques are important for more general training; the form of training that allows the agent/network better inference on test data. This is no different than if we were to use an agent trained on one task to learn on another task. A more general agent will, in effect, be able to transfer knowledge more readily than a specialist agent could, if at all.

We can demonstrate this in a quick example starting with training the following simple exercise:

1. Open up the **VisualHallway** scene in the Unity editor.
2. Disable any additional training areas.
3. Confirm that **Academy** is in **Control** of the **Brain**.
4. Select the **VisualHallwayLearning** brain from the **Hallway/Brains** folder and set **Vector Action** | **Branches Size** | **Branch 0 Size** to `7`, as shown in the following screenshot:

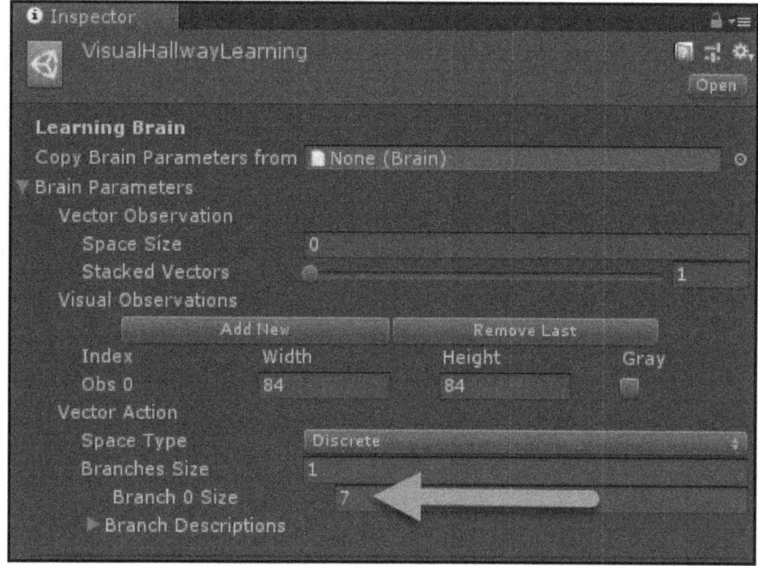

Increasing the vector action space of the agent

5. We increase the action space for the brain so that it is compatible with the required action space for our transfer learning environment, which we will get to later.
6. Save the scene and project.
7. Open a Python/Anaconda window that is prepared for training.
8. Launch a training session with the following code:

```
mlagents-learn config/trainer_config.yaml --run-id=vishall --train
--save-freq=10000
```

9. Here, we have introduced a new parameter that controls the frequency at which model checkpoints are created. The default is currently set to 50,000, but we just don't want to wait that long.
10. Run the agent in training in the editor for at least one model checkpoint save, as shown in the following screen excerpt:

```
is TensorFlow binary was not compiled to use: AVX2
INFO:mlagents.envs:Hyperparameters for the PPO Trainer of brain VisualHallwayLearning:
        batch_size:     64
        beta:   0.01
        buffer_size:    1024
        epsilon:        0.2
        gamma:  0.99
        hidden_units:   128
        lambd:  0.95
        learning_rate:  0.0003
        max_steps:      5.0e5
        normalize:      False
        num_epoch:      3
        num_layers:     1
        time_horizon:   64
        sequence_length:        64
        summary_freq:   1000
        use_recurrent:  True
        summary_path:   ./summaries/visualhallwaylearning-0_VisualHallwayLearning
        memory_size:    256
        use_curiosity:  False
        curiosity_strength:     0.01
        curiosity_enc_size:     128
        model_path:     ./models/visualhallwaylearning-0/VisualHallwayLearning
INFO:mlagents.trainers: visualhallwaylearning-0: VisualHallwayLearning: Step: 1000. Mean Reward: -1.002. Std of Reward: 0.000. Training.
INFO:mlagents.trainers: visualhallwaylearning-0: VisualHallwayLearning: Step: 2000. Mean Reward: -1.000. Std of Reward: 0.000. Training.
INFO:mlagents.trainers: visualhallwaylearning-0: VisualHallwayLearning: Step: 3000. Mean Reward: -1.000. Std of Reward: 0.000. Training.
INFO:mlagents.trainers: visualhallwaylearning-0: VisualHallwayLearning: Step: 4000. Mean Reward: -1.000. Std of Reward: 0.000. Training.
INFO:mlagents.trainers: visualhallwaylearning-0: VisualHallwayLearning: Step: 5000. Mean Reward: -1.000. Std of Reward: 0.000. Training.
INFO:mlagents.trainers: visualhallwaylearning-0: VisualHallwayLearning: Step: 6000. Mean Reward: -1.000. Std of Reward: 0.000. Training.
INFO:mlagents.trainers: visualhallwaylearning-0: VisualHallwayLearning: Step: 7000. Mean Reward: -1.000. Std of Reward: 0.000. Training.
INFO:mlagents.trainers: visualhallwaylearning-0: VisualHallwayLearning: Step: 8000. Mean Reward: -1.000. Std of Reward: 0.000. Training.
INFO:mlagents.trainers: visualhallwaylearning-0: VisualHallwayLearning: Step: 9000. Mean Reward: -1.000. Std of Reward: 0.000. Training.
INFO:mlagents.envs:Saved Model
INFO:mlagents.trainers: visualhallwaylearning-0: VisualHallwayLearning: Step: 10000. Mean Reward: -1.000. Std of Reward: 0.000. Training.
```

The ML-Agents trainer creating a checkpoint

11. Checkpoints are a way of taking snapshots of a brain and saving them for later. This allows you to go back and continue training where you left off.
12. Let the agent train to a checkpoint and then terminate training by pressing *Ctrl* + *C* or *command* + *C* on Mac in the Python/Anaconda window.

When you have terminated training, it is time to try this saved brain on another learning environment in the next section.

Transferring a brain

We now want to take the brain we have just been training and reuse it in a new, but similar, environment. Since our agent uses visual observations, this makes our task easier, but you could try and perform this example with other agents as well.

Let's open Unity and navigate to the **VisualPushBlock** example scene and follow this exercise:

1. Select **Academy** and enable it for **Control** of the **Brains.**
2. Select the **Agent** and set it to use the **VisualPushBlockLearning** brain. You should also confirm that this brain is configured in the same way as the **VisualHallwayLearning** brain we just ran, meaning that the **Visual Observation** and **Vector Action** spaces match.
3. Open the `ML-Agents/ml-agents_b/models/vishall-0` folder in File Explorer or another file explorer.
4. Change the name of the file and folder from `VisualHallwayLearning` to `VisualPushBlockLearning` as shown in the following screenshot:

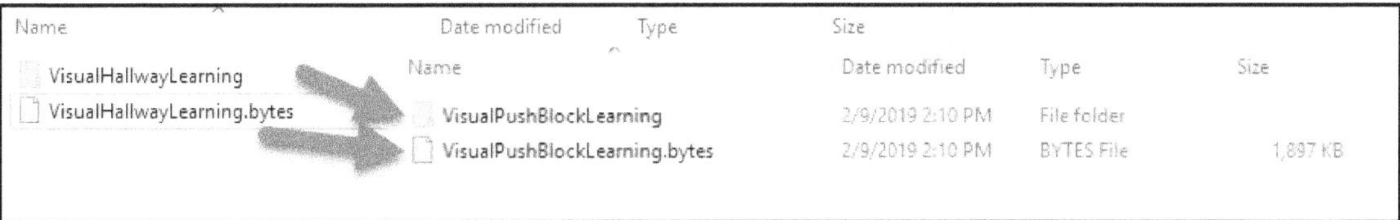

Changing the model path manually

5. By changing the name of the folder, we are essentially telling the model loading system to restore our **VisualHallway** brain as **VisualPushBlockBrain**. The trick here is making sure that both brains have all the same hyperparameters and configuration settings.

6. Speaking of hyperparameters, open the `trainer_config.yaml` file and make sure that the **VisualHallwayLearning** and **VisualPushBlockLearning** parameters are the same. The configuration for both is shown in the following code snippet for reference:

```
VisualHallwayLearning:
    use_recurrent: true
    sequence_length: 64
    num_layers: 1
    hidden_units: 128
    memory_size: 256
    beta: 1.0e-2
    gamma: 0.99
    num_epoch: 3
    buffer_size: 1024
    batch_size: 64
    max_steps: 5.0e5
    summary_freq: 1000
    time_horizon: 64

VisualPushBlockLearning:
    use_recurrent: true
    sequence_length: 64
    num_layers: 1
    hidden_units: 128
    memory_size: 256
    beta: 1.0e-2
    gamma: 0.99
    num_epoch: 3
    buffer_size: 1024
    batch_size: 64
    max_steps: 5.0e5
    summary_freq: 1000
    time_horizon: 64
```

7. Save the configuration file when you are done editing.
8. Open your Python/Anaconda window and launch training with the following code:

```
mlagents-learn config/trainer_config.yaml --run-id=vishall --train
--save-freq=10000 --load
```

9. The previous code is not a misprint; it is the exact same command we used to run the **VisualHallway** example, except with `--load` appended on the end. This should launch the training and prompt you to run the editor.
10. Feel free to run the training for as long as you like, but keep in mind that we barely trained the original agent.

Now, in this example, even if we had trained the agent to complete **VisualHallway**, this likely would not have been very effective in transferring that knowledge to **VisualPushBlock**. For the purposes of this example, we chose both since they are quite similar, and transferring one trained brain to the other was less complicated. For your own purposes, being able to transfer trained brains may be more about retraining agents on new or modified levels, perhaps even allowing the agents to train on progressively more difficult levels.

Depending on your version of ML-Agents, this example may or may not work so well. The particular problem is the complexity of the model, number of hyperparameters, input space, and reward system that we are running. Keeping all of these factors the same also requires keen attention to detail. In the next section, we will take a short diversion to explore how complex these models are.

Exploring TensorFlow checkpoints

TensorFlow is quickly becoming the underlying graph calculation engine that is powering most deep learning infrastructure. While we haven't covered how these graph engines are constructed in much detail, it can be helpful to review these TensorFlow models visually. Not only can we start to appreciate the complexity of these systems better, but a good visual is often worth a thousand words. Let's open up a web browser and follow the next exercise:

1. Search for the phrase `netron tensorflow` in your browser with your favorite search engine. Netron is an OpenSource TensorFlow model viewer that is perfect for our needs.
2. Find a link to the **GitHub** page and on the page the links to download the binary installers. Select the installer for your platform and click **Download**. This will take you to another download page where you can select the file for download.
3. Use the installer for your platform to install the **Netron** application. On Windows, this is as simple as downloading the exe installer and running it.

4. Run the **Netron** application, and after it launches, you will see the following:

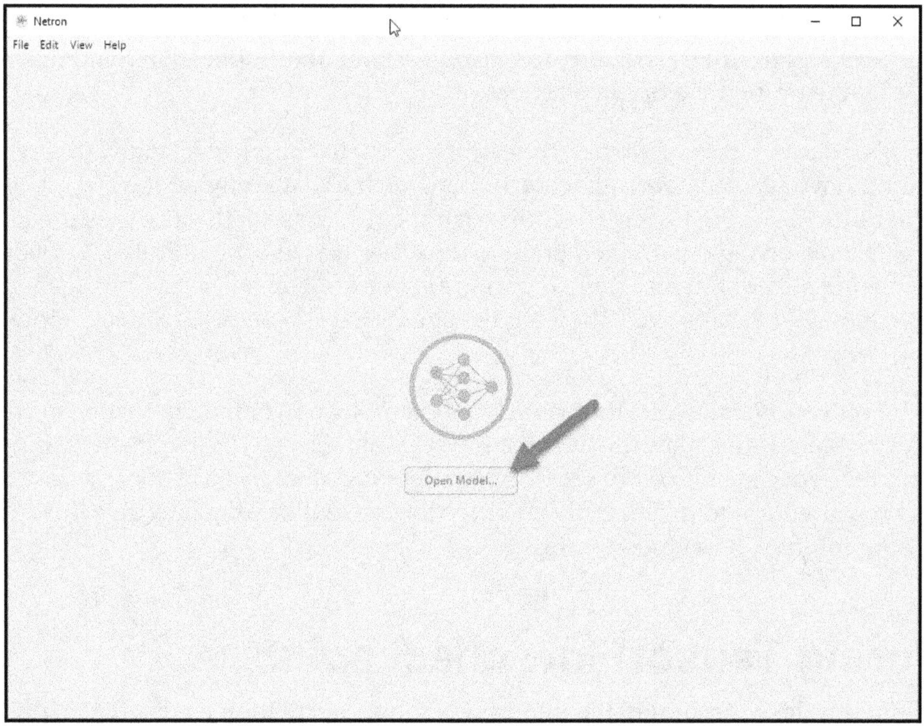

The Netron application

5. Click the **Open Model...** button in the middle of the window

6. Use File Explorer to locate the `ML-Agents/ml-agents/models/vishall-0\VisualHallwayLearning` folder, and locate the `raw_graph.def` file as shown in the following screenshot:

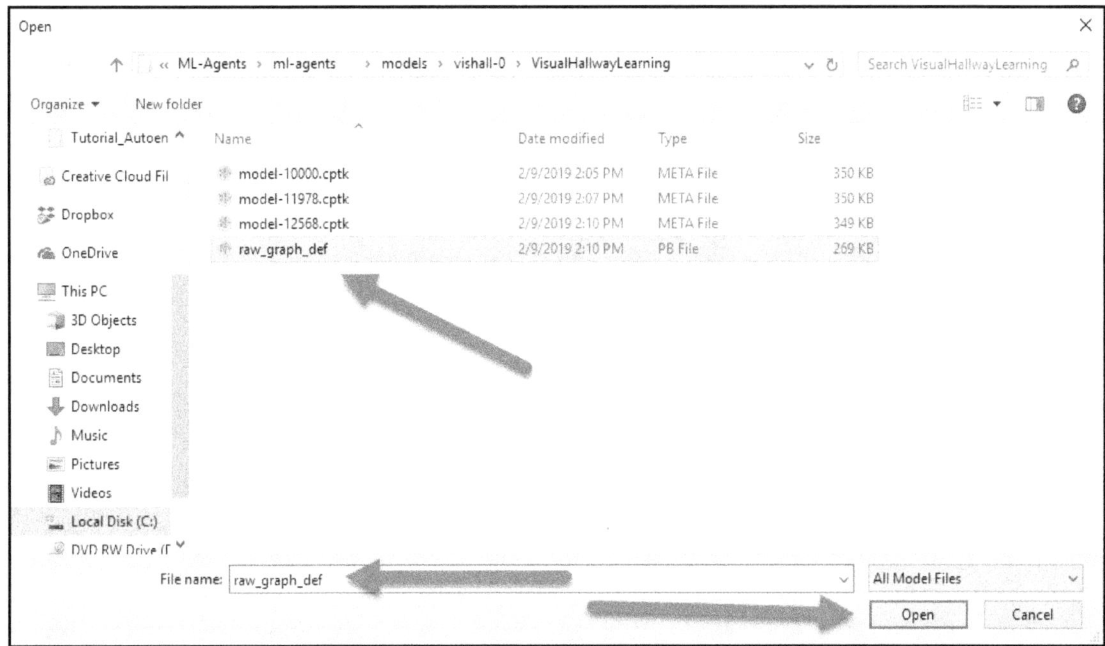

Selecting the model graph definition to load

7. After loading the graph, use the - button in the top-right to zoom the view as far out as you can, similar to the following screenshot:

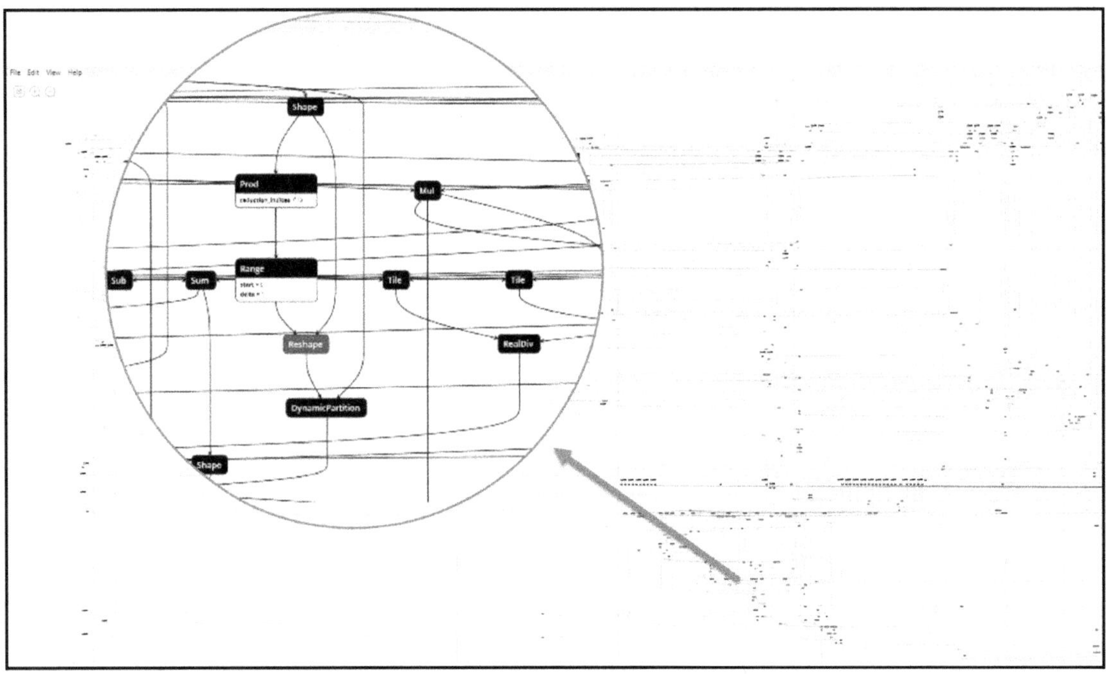

The TensorFlow graph model of our agent's brain

8. As the inset shows, this graph is beyond complex, and not something we would be easily able to make sense of. However, it can be interesting to look through and see how the model/graph is constructed.

9. Scroll to the top of the graph and find a node called **advantages**, then select the node and note the **Graph** and **Inputs**, model properties as shown in the following screenshot:

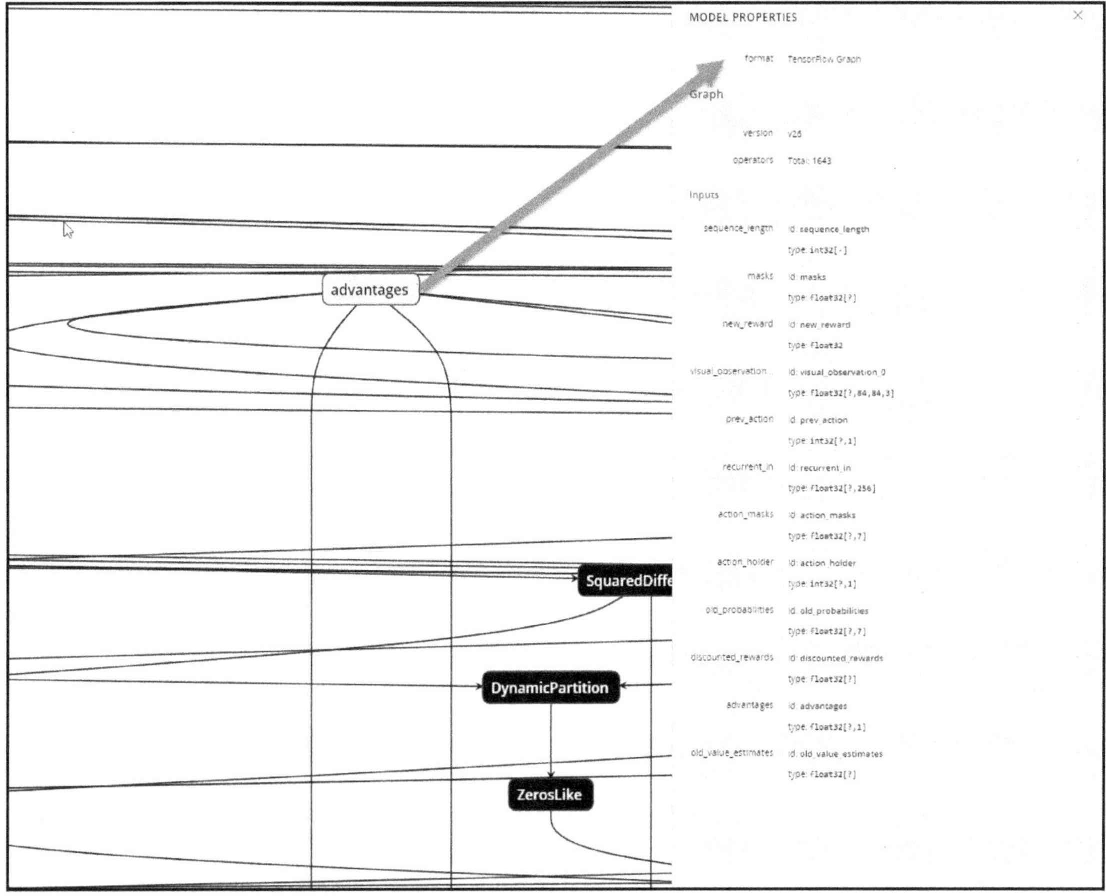

Properties of the advantages graph model

10. Within the properties view of this model, you should be able to see some very familiar terms and settings, such as **visual_observation_0**, for instance, which shows the model input is a tensor of shape [84,84,3].

When you are done, feel free to look over other models, and perhaps even explore with other models even outside Unity. While this tool isn't quite capable of summarizing a complex model like we have, it does show how powerful these types of tools are becoming. What's more, if you can find your way around, you can even export variables for later inspection or use.

Imitation Transfer Learning

One of the problems with Imitation Learning is that it often focuses the agent down a path that limits its possible future moves. This isn't unlike you being shown the improper way to perform a task and then doing it that way, perhaps without thinking, only to find out later that there was a better way. Humanity, in fact, has been prone to this type of problem over and over again throughout history. Perhaps you learned as a child that swimming right after eating was dangerous, only to learn later in life through your own experimentation, or just common knowledge, that that was just a myth, a myth that was taken as fact for a very long time. Training an agent through observation is no different you limit the agent's vision in many ways to a narrow focus that is limited by what it was taught. However, there is a way to allow an agent to revert back to the partial brute-force or trial-and error exploration in order to expand its training.

With ML-Agents we can combine IL with a form oftransfer learningin order to allow an agent to learn first from observation, then by furthering its training by learning from the once student. This form of IL chaining, if you will, allows you to train an agent to auto-train multiple agents. Let's open up Unity to the **TennisIL** scene and follow the next exercise:

1. Select the **TennisArea** | **Agent** object and in the **Inspector**, disable the **BC Teacher Helper** component, and then add a new **Demonstration Recorder** as shown in the following screenshot:

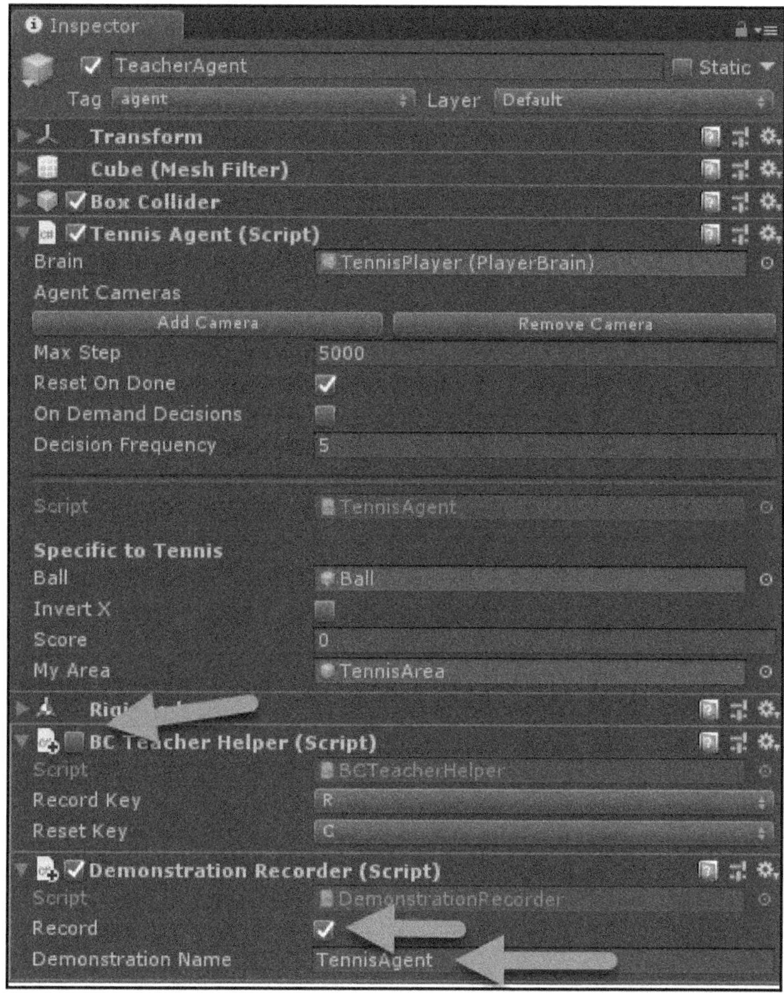

Checking that the BC Teacher is attached to the Agent

2. **BC Teacher Helper** is a recorder that works just like the **Demonstration Recorder**. The BC recorder allows you to turn the recording on and off as the agent runs, which is perfect for online training, but at the time of writing, the component was not working.

3. Make sure **Academy** is set to **Control** the **TennisLearning** brain.
4. Save the scene and project.
5. Open a Python/Anaconda window and launch training with the following command:

```
mlagents-learn config/online_bc_config.yaml --run-id=tennis_il --
train --slow
```

6. Press **Play** when prompted to run the game in the editor. Control the blue paddle with the *W*, *A*, *S*, *D* keys and play for a few seconds to warm up.
7. After you are warmed up, press the *R* key to begin recording a demo observation. Play the game for several minutes and let the agent become capable. After the agent is able to return the ball, stop the training session.

This will not only train the agent, which is fine, but it will also create a demo recording playback we can use to further train the agents to learn how to play each other in a similar way to how AlphaStar was trained. We will set up our tennis scene to now run in offline training mode with multiple agents in the next section.

Training multiple agents with one demonstration

Now, with the recording of us playing tennis, we can use this to feed into the training of multiple agents all feeding back into one policy. Open Unity to the tennis scene, the one with the multiple environments, and follow the next exercise:

1. Type `agent` into the Filter bar at the top of the **Hierarchy** window as shown in the following screenshot:

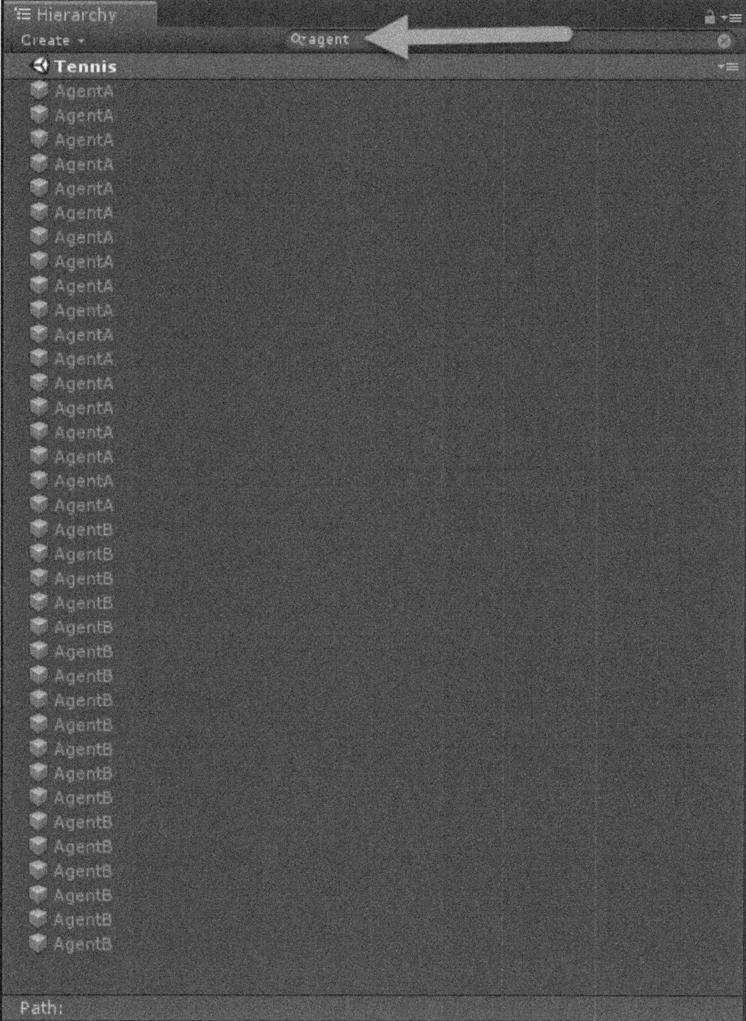

Searching for all the agents in the scene

2. Select all the agent objects in the scene and bulk change their **Brain** to use **TennisLearning** and not **TennisPlayer**.
3. Select **Academy** and make sure to enable it to control the brains.
4. Open the `config/offline_bc_config.yaml` file.

5. Add the following new section for the `TennisLearning` brain at the bottom:

```
TennisLearning:
    trainer: offline_bc
    max_steps: 5.0e5
    num_epoch: 5
    batch_size: 64
    batches_per_epoch: 5
    num_layers: 2
    hidden_units: 128
    sequence_length: 16
    use_recurrent: true
    memory_size: 256
    sequence_length: 32
    demo_path: ./UnitySDK/Assets/Demonstrations/TennisAgent.demo
```

6. Save the scene and the project.
7. Open the Python/Anaconda window and run training with the following code:

```
mlagents-learn config/offline_bc_config.yaml --run-id=tennis_ma --
train
```

8. You may want to add the `--slow` switch in order to watch the training, but it should not be required.
9. Let the agents train for some time and notice its improved progress. Even with a short observation recording input, the agent becomes a capable player rather quickly.

There are multiple ways to perform this type of IL andtransfer learningchaining that will allow your agent some flexibility in training. You could even use the trained model's checkpoint without IL and run the agents with transfer learning as we did earlier. The possibilities are limitless, and it remains to be seen what will emerge as best practices.

In the next section, we'll provide some exercises that you can use for your own personal learning.

Exercises

The exercises at the end of this chapter could likely provide several hours of fun. Try and only complete one or two exercises, as we still need to finish the book:

1. Set up and run the **PyramidsIL** scene to run online IL.
2. Set up and run the **PushBlockIL** scene to run online IL.
3. Set up and run the **WallJump** scene to run with online IL. This requires you to modify the scene.
4. Set up and run the **VisualPyramids** scene to use offline recording. Record a training session then train an agent.
5. Set up and run the **VisualPushBlock** scene to use offline recording. Use offline IL to train the agent.
6. Set up the **PushBlockIL** scene to record an observation demo. Then use this offline training to train multiple agents in the regular **PushBlock** scene.
7. Set up the **PyramidsIL** scene to record a demo recording. Then use this for offline training to train multiple agents in the regular **Pyramids** scene.
8. Train an agent in the **VisualHallway** scene using any form of learning you like. After training, modify the **VisualHallway** scene to use different materials on the walls and floor. Changing materials on Unity objects is quite easy. Then, use the technique of swapping model checkpoints as a way of transfer learning the previously trained brain into a new environment.
9. Do exercise eight, but using the **VisualPyramids** scene. You could also add other objects or blocks in this scene.
10. Do exercise eight, but using the **VisualPushBlock** scene. Try adding other blocks or other objects that the agent may have to work around.

Just remember that, if you are attempting any of the Transfer Learning exercises, attention to detail is important when matching the complex graphs. In the next section, we summarize what we have covered in this chapter.

Summary

In this chapter, we covered an emerging technique in RL called Imitation Learning or Behavioral Cloning. This technique, as we learned, takes the captured observations of a player playing a game and then uses those observations in an online or offline setting to further train the agent. We further learned that IL is just a form of Transfer Learning. We then covered a technique with ML-Agents that will allow you to transfer brains across environments. Finally, we looked at how to chain IL andtransfer learningas a way of stimulating the agent's training into developing new strategies on its own.

In the next chapter, we will further our understanding of DRL in games by looking at multiple agent training scenarios.

11
Building Multi-Agent Environments

With our single-agent experiences under our belt, we can move on to the more complex but equally entertaining world of working in multi-agent environments, training multiple agents to work in the same environment in a co-operative or competitive fashion. This also opens up several new opportunities for training agents with adversarial self-play, cooperative self-play, competitive self-play, and more. The possibilities become endless here, and this may be the true holy grail of AI.

In this chapter, we are going to cover several aspects of multi-agent training environments and the main section topics are highlighted here:

- Adversarial and cooperative self-play
- Competitive self-play
- Multi-brain play
- Adding individuality with intrinsic rewards
- Extrinsic rewards for individuality

This chapter assumes you have covered the three previous chapters and completed some exercises in each. In the next section, we begin to cover the various self-play scenarios.

It is best to start this chapter with a new clone of the ML-Agents repository. We do this as a way of cleaning up our environment and making sure no errant configuration was unintentionally saved. If you need help with this, then consult one of the earlier chapters.

Adversarial and cooperative self-play

The term *self-play* can, of course, mean many things to many people, but in this case, we mean the brain is competing (adversarial) or cooperating with itself by manipulating multiple agents. In the case of ML-Agents, this may mean having a single brain manipulating multiple agents in the same environment. There is an excellent example of this in ML-Agents, so open up Unity and follow the next exercise to get this scene ready for multi-agent training:

1. Open the **SoccerTwos** scene from the **Assets** | **ML-Agents** | **Examples** | **Soccer** | **Scenes** folder. The scene is set to run, by default, in player mode, but we need to convert it back to learning mode.
2. Select and disable all the **SoccerFieldTwos(1)** to **SoccerFieldTwos(7)** areas. We won't use those yet.
3. Select and expand the remaining active **SoccerFieldTwos** object. This will reveal the play area with four agents, two marked **RedStriker** and **BlueStriker** and two marked **RedGoalie** and **BlueGoalie**.
4. Inspect the agents and set each one's brain to **StrikerLearning** or **GoalieLearning** as appropriate, as shown here:

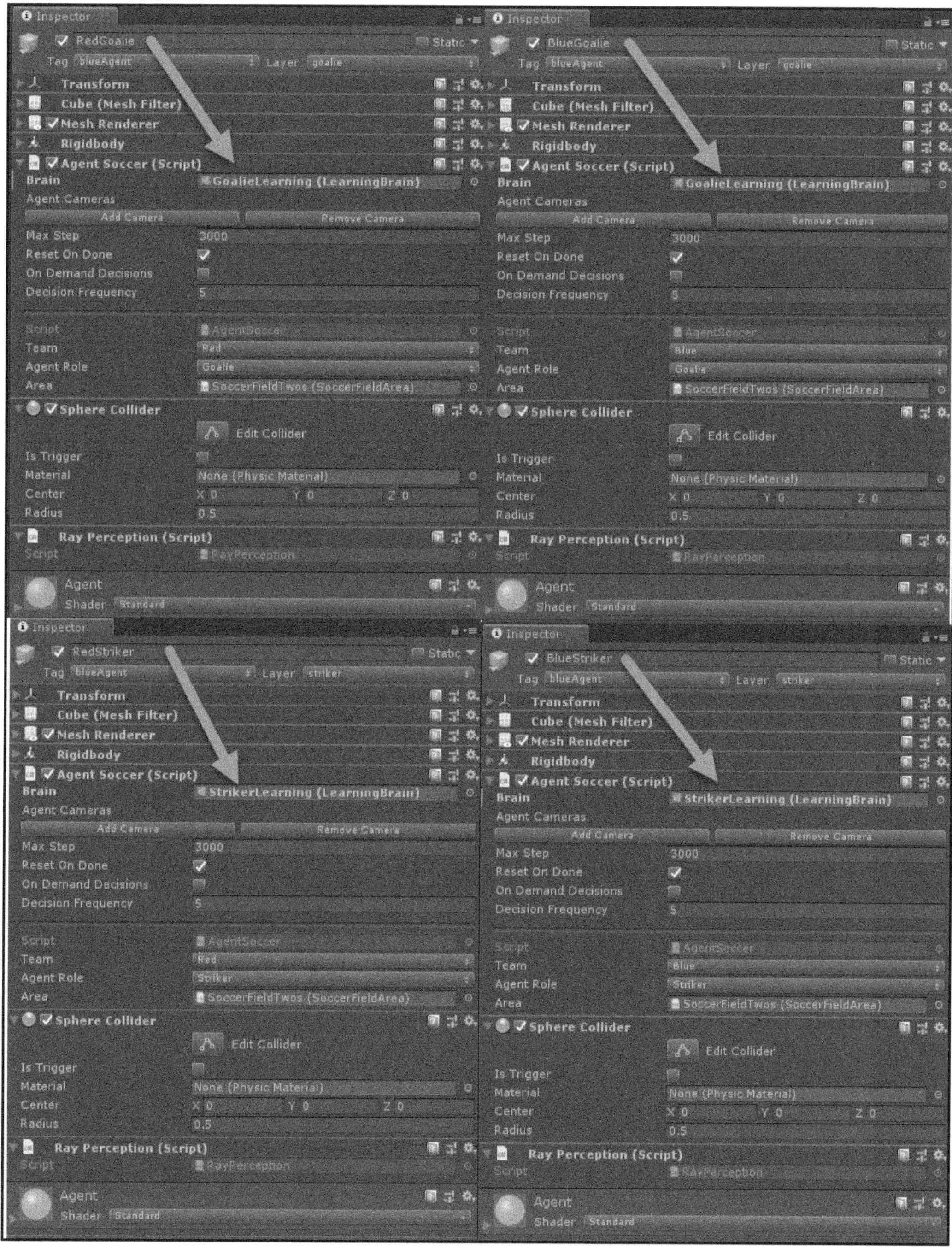

Setting the learning brains on the agents

5. We have four agents in this environment being controlled by brains that are both cooperating with and competing against each other. To be honest, this example is brilliant and demonstrates incredibly well the whole concept of cooperative and competitive self-play. If you are still struggling with some concepts, consider this diagram, which shows how this is put together:

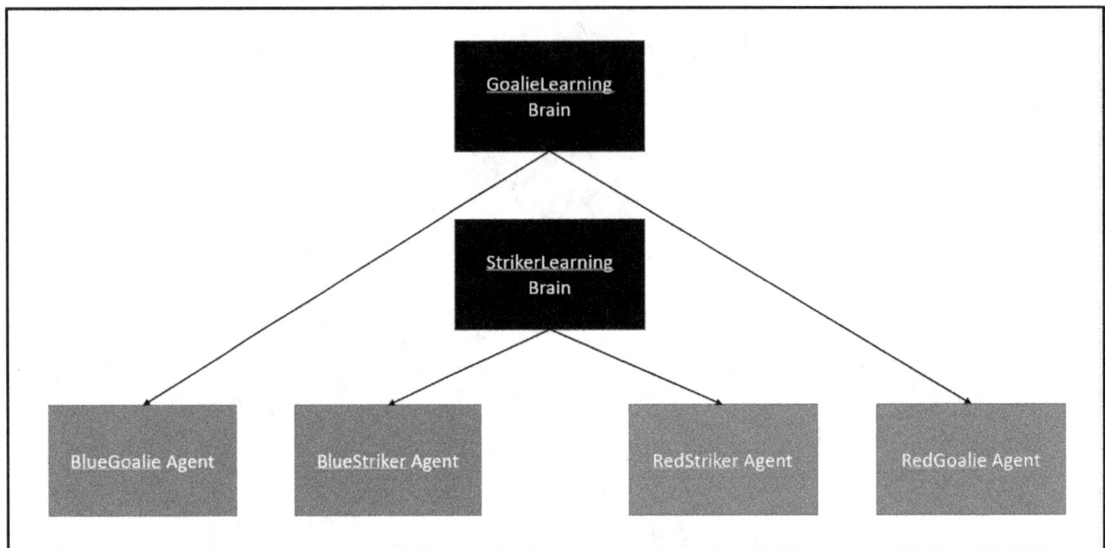

The SoccerTwos brain architecture

6. As we can see, we have two brains controlling four agents: two strikers and two goalies. The striker's job is to score against the goalie, and, of course, the goalie's job is to block goals.
7. Select the **Academy** and set the **Soccer Academy** | **Brains** | **Control** enabled for both brains, as shown:

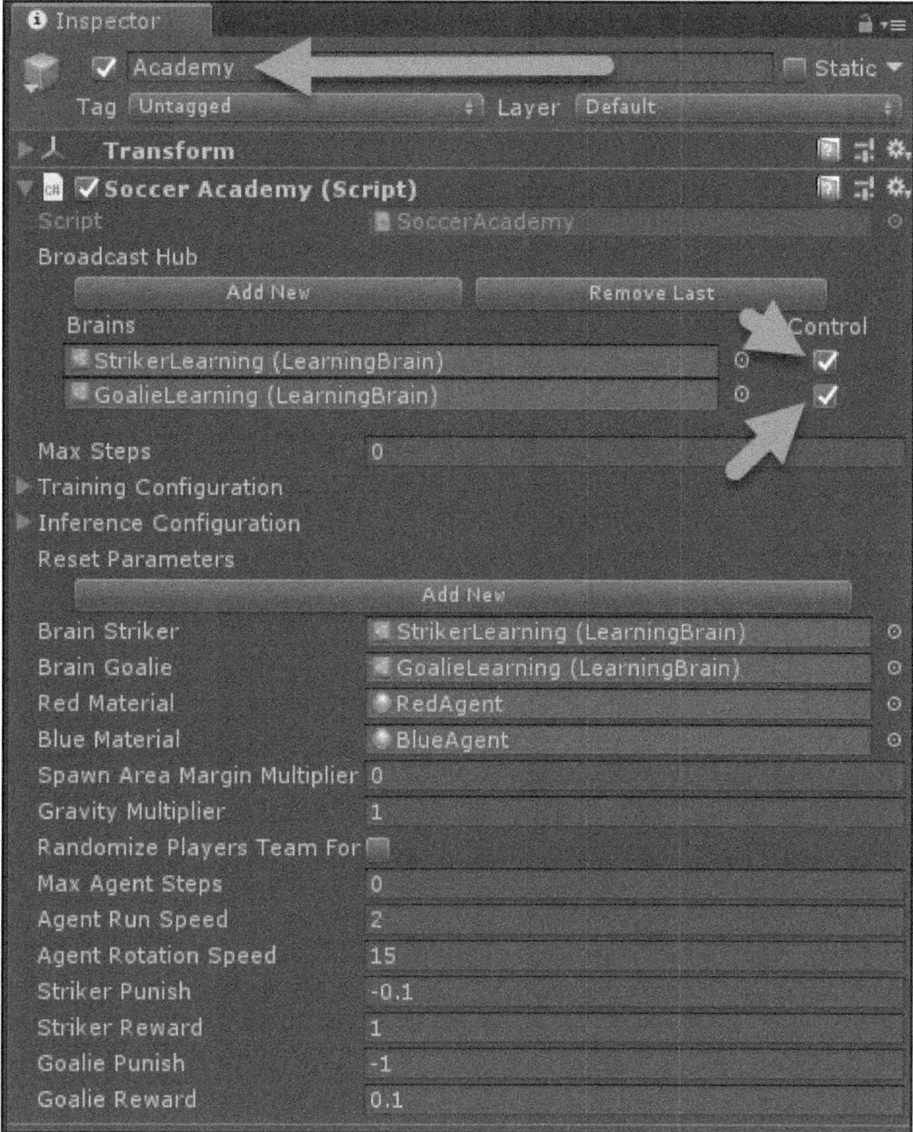

Setting the Brains to control in the Academy

8. Also, note the **Striker**, **Goalie Reward**, and **Punish** settings at the bottom of the **Soccer Academy** component. It is important to also note the way the `reward` functions for each brain. The following are the `reward` functions described mathematically for this sample:

$$R_{striker}(goal) = 1$$
$$R_{striker}(-goal) = -0.1$$
$$R_{goalie}(goal) = 0.1$$
$$R_{goalie}(-goal) = -1$$

9. That means, when a goal is scored, each of the four agents gets a reward based on its position and team. Thus, if red scored, the **Red Striker** would get a `+1` reward, the **Blue Striker** a `-0.1` reward, the **Red Goalie** a `+0.1` reward, and the poor **Blue Goalie** a `-1` reward. Now, you may think this could cause overlap, but remember that each agent's view of a state or an observation will be different. Thus, the reward will be applied to the policy for that state or observation. In essence, the agent is learning based on its current view of the environment, which will change based on which agent is sending that observation.
10. Save the scene and project when you are done editing.

That sets up our scene for multi-agent training using two brains and four agents, using both competitive and cooperative self-play. In the next section, we complete the external configuration and start training the scene.

Training self-play environments

Training these types of self-play environments opens up further possibilities for not only enhanced training possibilities but also for fun gaming environments. In some ways, these types of training environments can be just as much fun to watch, as we will see at the end of this chapter.

For now, though, we are going to jump back and continue setting up the configuration we need to train our **SoccerTwos** multi-agent environment in the next exercise:

1. Open the `ML-Agents/ml-agents/config/trainer_config.yaml` file and inspect the `StrikerLearning` and `GoalieLearning` config sections, as shown:

```
StrikerLearning:
    max_steps: 5.0e5
    learning_rate: 1e-3
    batch_size: 128
    num_epoch: 3
    buffer_size: 2000
    beta: 1.0e-2
    hidden_units: 256
    summary_freq: 2000
    time_horizon: 128
    num_layers: 2
    normalize: false

GoalieLearning:
    max_steps: 5.0e5
    learning_rate: 1e-3
    batch_size: 320
    num_epoch: 3
    buffer_size: 2000
    beta: 1.0e-2
    hidden_units: 256
    summary_freq: 2000
    time_horizon: 128
    num_layers: 2
    normalize: false
```

2. The obvious thought is that the brains should have a similar configuration, and you may start that way, yes. However, note that even in this example the `batch_size` parameter is set differently for each brain.
3. Open a Python/Anaconda window and switch to your ML-Agents virtual environment and then launch the following command from the `ML-Agents/ml-agents` folder:

```
mlagents-learn config/trainer_config.yaml --run-id=soccer --train
```

4. Press **Play** when prompted, and you should see the following training session running:

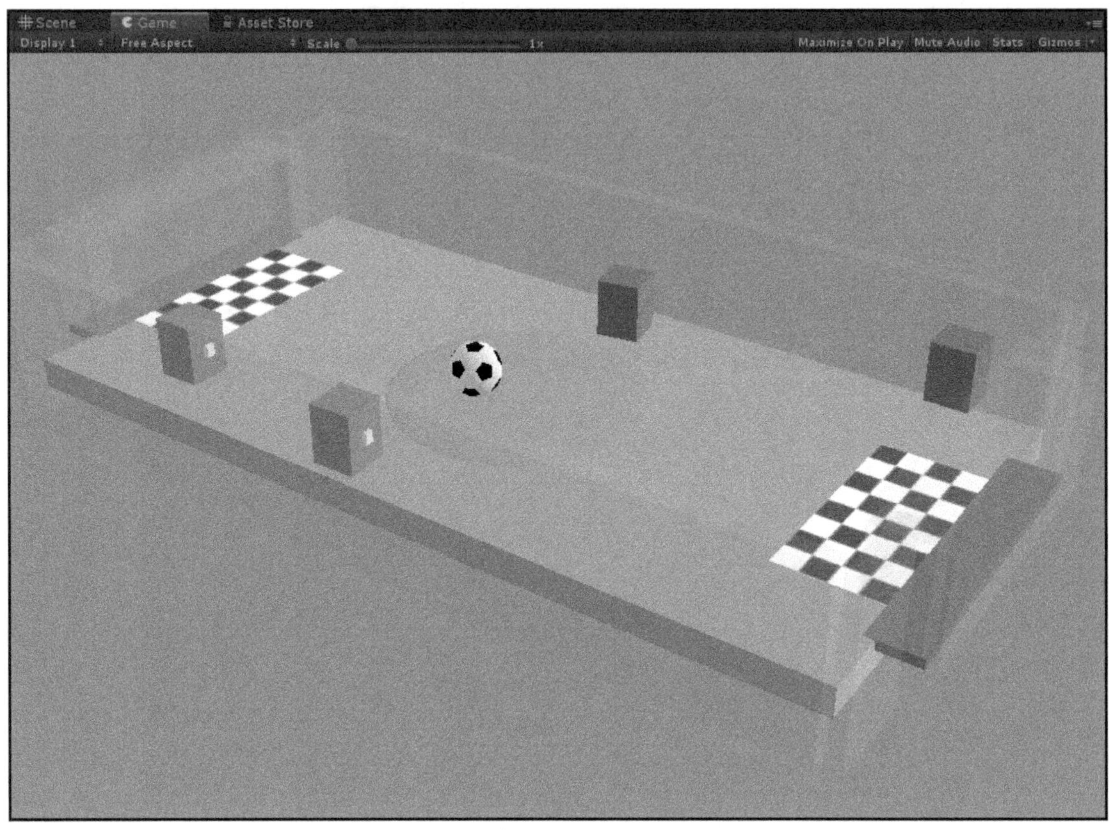

The SoccerTwos scene running in training mode

5. As has been said, this can be a very entertaining sample to watch, and it trains surprisingly quickly.

6. Open up the Python/Anaconda console after some amount of training, and note how you are getting stats on two brains now, **StrikerLearning** and **GoalieLearning**, as shown in the following screenshot:

```
Anaconda Prompt - mlagents-learn config/trainer_config.yaml --run-id=soccer --train
        epsilon:        0.2
        gamma:  0.99
        hidden_units:   256
        lambd:  0.95
        learning_rate:  1e-3
        max_steps:      5.0e5
        normalize:      False
        num_epoch:      3
        num_layers:     2
        time_horizon:   128
        sequence_length:        64
        summary_freq:   2000
        use_recurrent:  False
        summary_path:   ./summaries/soccer-0_GoalieLearning
        memory_size:    256
        use_curiosity:  False
        curiosity_strength:     0.01
        curiosity_enc_size:     128
        model_path:     ./models/soccer-0/GoalieLearning
INFO:mlagents.trainers: soccer-0: StrikerLearning: Step: 2000. Mean Reward: -0.240. Std of Reward: 0.708. Training.
INFO:mlagents.trainers: soccer-0: GoalieLearning: Step: 2000. Mean Reward: 0.240. Std of Reward: 0.708. Training.
INFO:mlagents.trainers: soccer-0: StrikerLearning: Step: 4000. Mean Reward: -0.755. Std of Reward: 0.505. Training.
INFO:mlagents.trainers: soccer-0: GoalieLearning: Step: 4000. Mean Reward: 0.755. Std of Reward: 0.505. Training.
INFO:mlagents.trainers: soccer-0: StrikerLearning: Step: 6000. Mean Reward: -0.482. Std of Reward: 0.724. Training.
INFO:mlagents.trainers: soccer-0: GoalieLearning: Step: 6000. Mean Reward: 0.482. Std of Reward: 0.724. Training.
INFO:mlagents.trainers: soccer-0: StrikerLearning: Step: 8000. Mean Reward: -0.822. Std of Reward: 0.406. Training.
INFO:mlagents.trainers: soccer-0: GoalieLearning: Step: 8000. Mean Reward: 0.822. Std of Reward: 0.406. Training.
INFO:mlagents.trainers: soccer-0: StrikerLearning: Step: 10000. Mean Reward: -1.000. Std of Reward: 0.000. Training.
INFO:mlagents.trainers: soccer-0: GoalieLearning: Step: 10000. Mean Reward: 1.000. Std of Reward: 0.000. Training.
INFO:mlagents.trainers: soccer-0: StrikerLearning: Step: 12000. Mean Reward: -0.545. Std of Reward: 0.718. Training.
INFO:mlagents.trainers: soccer-0: GoalieLearning: Step: 12000. Mean Reward: 0.545. Std of Reward: 0.718. Training.
INFO:mlagents.trainers: soccer-0: StrikerLearning: Step: 14000. Mean Reward: -0.198. Std of Reward: 0.749. Training.
INFO:mlagents.trainers: soccer-0: GoalieLearning: Step: 14000. Mean Reward: 0.198. Std of Reward: 0.749. Training.
INFO:mlagents.trainers: soccer-0: StrikerLearning: Step: 16000. Mean Reward: -0.788. Std of Reward: 0.437. Training.
INFO:mlagents.trainers: soccer-0: GoalieLearning: Step: 16000. Mean Reward: 0.788. Std of Reward: 0.437. Training.
```

Console output showing stats from two brains

7. Note how **StrikerLearning** and **GoalieLearning** are returning opposite rewards to each other. This means, in order for these agents to be trained, they must balance their mean reward to 0 for both agents. As the agents train, you will notice their rewards start to converge to 0, the optimum reward for this example.
8. Let the sample run to completion. You can easily get lost watching these environments, so you may not even notice the time go by.

This example showed how we can harness the power of multi-agent training through self-play to teach two brains how to both compete and cooperate at the same time. In the next section, we look at multiple agents competing against one another in self-play.

Adversarial self-play

In the previous example, we saw an example of both cooperative and competitive self-play where multiple agents functioned almost symbiotically. While this was a great example, it still tied the functionality of one brain to another through their reward functions, hence our observation of the agents being in an almost rewards-opposite scenario. Instead, we now want to look at an environment that can train a brain with multiple agents using just adversarial self-play. Of course, ML-Agents has such an environment, called **Banana**, which comprises several agents that randomly wander the scene and collect bananas. The agents also have a laser pointer, which allows them to disable an opposing agent for several seconds if they are hit. This is the scene we will look at in the next exercise:

1. Open the **Banana** scene from the **Assets** | **ML-Agents** | **Examples** | **BananaCollectors** | **Scenes** folder.
2. Select and disable the additional training areas **RLArea(1)** to **RLArea(3)**.
3. Select the five agents (**Agent**, **Agent(1)**, **Agent(2)**, **Agent(3)**, **Agent(4)**) in the **RLArea**.
4. Swap the **Banana Agent** | **Brain** from **BananaPlayer** to **BananaLearning**.
5. Select the **Academy** and set the **Banana Academy** | **Brains** | **Control** property to **Enabled**.
6. Select the **Banana Agent** component (**Script**) in the editor, and open it in your code editor of choice. If you scroll down to the bottom, you can see the `OnCollisionEnter` method as shown:

```
void OnCollisionEnter(Collision collision)
{
  if (collision.gameObject.CompareTag("banana"))
  {
    Satiate();
    collision.gameObject.GetComponent<BananaLogic>().OnEaten();
    AddReward(1f);
    bananas += 1;
    if (contribute)
    {
      myAcademy.totalScore += 1;
    }
  }
```

```
    if (collision.gameObject.CompareTag("badBanana"))
    {
      Poison();
      collision.gameObject.GetComponent<BananaLogic>().OnEaten();

      AddReward(-1f);
      if (contribute)
      {
        myAcademy.totalScore -= 1;
      }
    }
  }
```

7. Reading the preceding code, we can summarize our `reward` functions to the following:

$$R_{collector}(banana_{good}) = 1$$

$$R_{collector}(banana_{bad}) = -1$$

   This simply means the agents only receive a reward for eating bananas. Interestingly, there is no reward for disabling an opponent with a laser or by being disabled.

8. Save the scene and the project.
9. Open a prepared Python/Anaconda console and start training with the following command:

```
mlagents-learn config/trainer_config.yaml --run-id=banana --train
```

10. Press **Play** in the editor when prompted, and watch the action unfold as shown in the next screenshot:

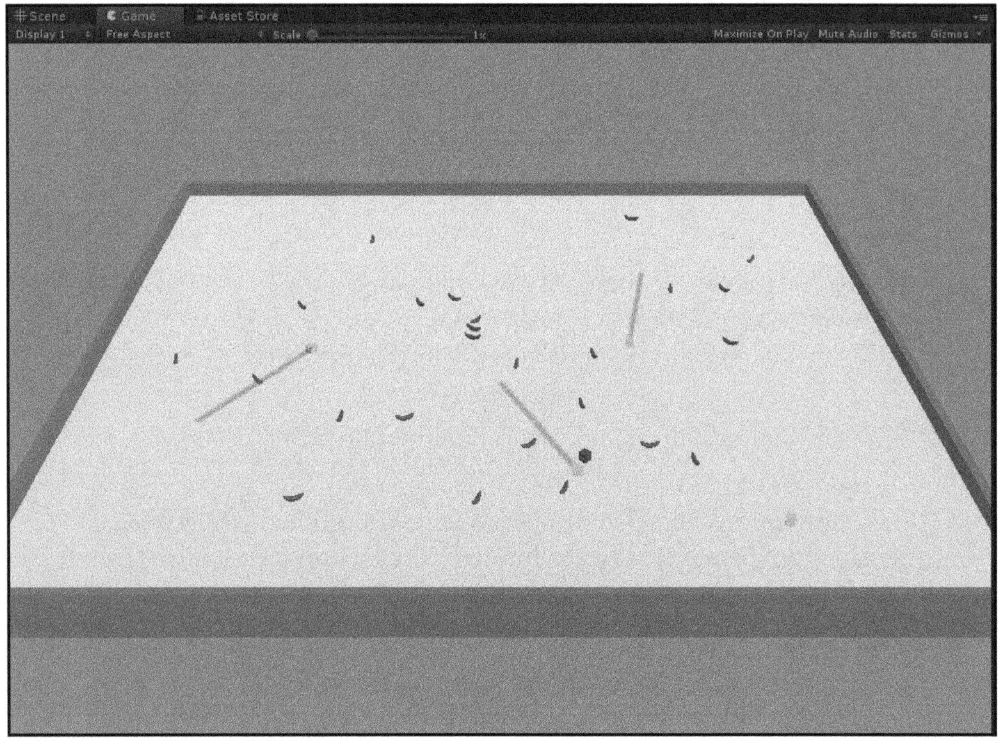

The Banana Collector agents doing their work

11. Let the scene run for as long as you like.

This scene is an excellent example of how agents learn to use a secondary game mechanic that returns no rewards, but, like the laser, is still used to immobilize adversarial collectors and obtain more bananas, all while only receiving rewards for eating only bananas. This example shows some of the true power of RL and how it can be used to find secondary strategies in order to solve problems. While this is a very entertaining aspect and fun to watch in a game, consider the grander implications of this. RL has been shown to optimize everything from networking to recommender systems using **adversarial self-play**, and it will be interesting to see what this method of learning is capable of accomplishing in the near future.

Multi-brain play

One of the truly great things about the ML-Agents kit is the ability to add multiple agents powered by multiple brains quickly. This in turns gives us the ability to build more complex game environments or scenarios with fun agents/AI to play both with and against. Let's see how easy it is to convert our soccer example to let the agents all use individual brains:

1. Open up the editor to the **SoccerTwos** scene we looked at earlier.
2. Locate the `Brains` folder for the example at **Assets** | **ML-Agents** | **Examples** | **Soccer** | **Brains**.
3. Click the **Create** menu in the upper right corner of the window and from the **Context** menu, and select **ML-Agents** | **Learning Brain**:

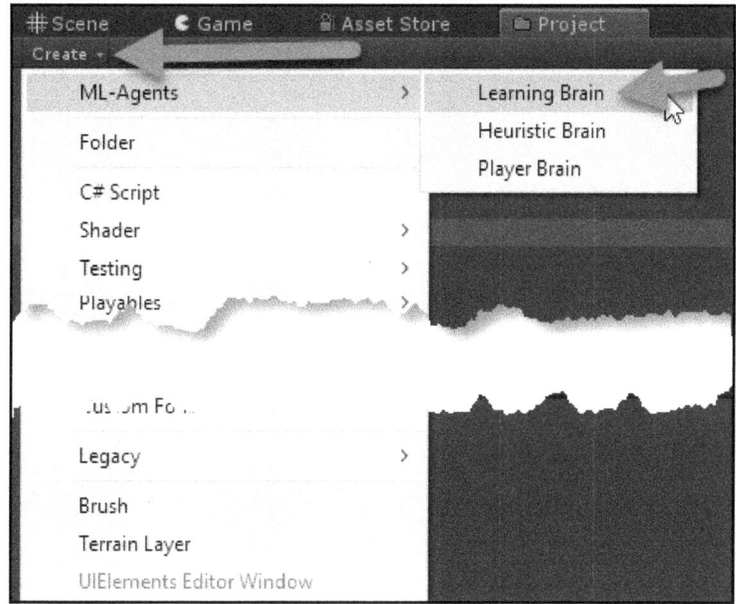

Creating a new learning brain

4. Name the new brain `RedStrikerLearning`. Create three more new brains named `RedGoalieLearning`, `BlueGoalieLearning`, and `BlueStrikerLearning` in the same folder.

5. Select **RedStrikerLearning**. Then select and drag the **StrikerLearning** brain and drop it into the **Copy Brain Parameters from** slot:

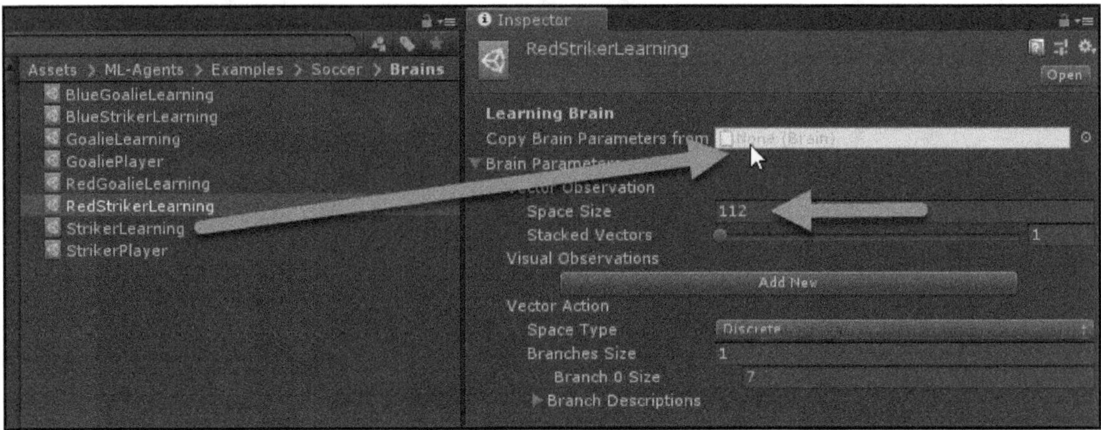

Copying brain parameters from another brain

6. Do this for **BlueStrikerLearning**, copying parameters from **StrikerLearning**. Then do the same for the **RedGoalieLearning** and **BlueGoalieLearning**, copying parameters from **GoalieLearning**.
7. Select the **RedAgent** in the **Hierarchy** window and set the **Agent Soccer | Brain** to **RedStrikerLearning**. Do this for each of the other agents, matching the color with a position. **BlueGoalie -> BlueGoalieLearning**.
8. Select **Academy** and remove all the current **Brains** from the **Soccer Academy | Brains** list. Then add all the new brains we just created back into the list using the **Add New** button and set them to **Control**:

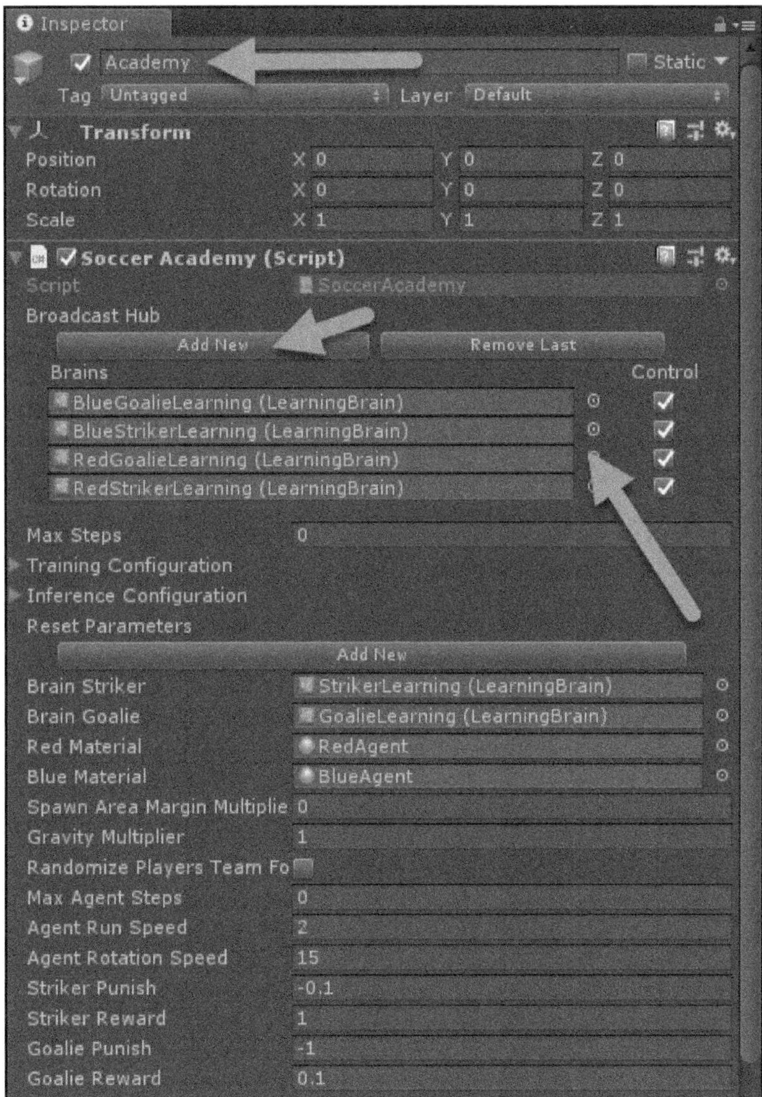

Adding the new brains to Academy

9. Save the scene and the project. Now, we just swapped the example from using two concurrent brains in self-play mode to be individual agents on teams.
10. Open a Python/Anaconda window set up for training and launch with it the following:

```
mlagents-learn config/trainer_config.yaml --run-id=soccer_mb --
train
```

11. Let the training run and note how the agents start off playing just as well as they did previously. Take a look at the console output as well. You will see it now reports for four agents, but the agents are still somewhat symbiotic, as the red striker is opposite the blue goalie. However, they now train much more slowly, due in part to each brain seeing only half the observations now. Remember that we had both striker agents feeding to a single brain previously, and, as we learned, this additional input of state can expedite training substantially.

At this point, we have four agents with four individual brains playing a game of soccer. Of course, since the agents are still training symbiotically by sharing a reward function, we can't really describe them as individuals. Except, as we know, individuals who play on teams are often influenced by their own internal or intrinsic reward system. We will look at how the application of intrinsic rewards can make this last exercise more interesting in the next section.

Adding individuality with intrinsic rewards

As we learned in `Chapter 9`, *Rewards and Reinforcement Learning*, intrinsic reward systems and the concept of agent motivation is currently implemented as just **curiosity learning** in ML-Agents. This whole area of applying intrinsic rewards or motivation combined with RL has wide applications to gaming and interpersonal applications such as **servant agents**.

In the next exercise, we are going to add intrinsic rewards to a couple of our agents and see what effect this has on the game. Open up the scene from the previous exercise and follow these steps:

1. Open up the `ML-Agents/ml-agents/config/trainer_config.yaml` file in a text editor. We never did add any specialized configuration to our agents, but we are going to rectify that now and add some extra configurations.

2. Add the following four new brain configurations to the file:

```
BlueStrikerLearning:
    max_steps: 5.0e5
    learning_rate: 1e-3
    batch_size: 128
    num_epoch: 3
    buffer_size: 2000
    beta: 1.0e-2
    hidden_units: 256
    summary_freq: 2000
    time_horizon: 128
    num_layers: 2
    normalize: false

BlueGoalieLearning:
    use_curiosity: true
    summary_freq: 1000
    curiosity_strength: 0.01
    curiosity_enc_size: 256
    max_steps: 5.0e5
    learning_rate: 1e-3
    batch_size: 320
    num_epoch: 3
    buffer_size: 2000
    beta: 1.0e-2
    hidden_units: 256
    time_horizon: 128
    num_layers: 2
    normalize: false

RedStrikerLearning:
    use_curiosity: true
    summary_freq: 1000
    curiosity_strength: 0.01
    curiosity_enc_size: 256
    max_steps: 5.0e5
    learning_rate: 1e-3
    batch_size: 128
    num_epoch: 3
    buffer_size: 2000
    beta: 1.0e-2
    hidden_units: 256
    time_horizon: 128
    num_layers: 2
    normalize: false

RedGoalieLearning:
```

```
max_steps: 5.0e5
learning_rate: 1e-3
batch_size: 320
num_epoch: 3
buffer_size: 2000
beta: 1.0e-2
hidden_units: 256
summary_freq: 2000
time_horizon: 128
num_layers: 2
normalize: false
```

3. Note how we have also enabled `use_curiosity: true` on the `BlueGoalieLearning` and `RedStrikerLearning` brains. You can copy and paste most of this from the original `GoalieLearning` and `StrikerLearning` brain configurations already in the file; just pay attention to the details.
4. Save the file when you are done editing.
5. Open your Python/Anaconda console and start training with the following command:

```
mlagents-learn config/trainer_config.yaml --run-id=soccer_icl --
train
```

6. Let the agents train for a while, and you will notice that, while they do appear to work more like individuals, their training ability is still subpar, while any improvement we do see in training is likely the cause of giving a couple of agents curiosity.

This ability to add individuality to an agent with intrinsic rewards or motivation will certainly mature as DRL does for games and other potential applications and will hopefully provide other intrinsic reward modules that may not be entirely focused on learning. However, intrinsic rewards can really do much to encourage individuality, so in the next section, we introduce extrinsic rewards to our modified example.

Another excellent application of transfer learning would be the ability to add intrinsic reward modules after agents have been trained on general tasks.

Extrinsic rewards for individuality

We have looked extensively at external or extrinsic rewards for several chapters now and how techniques can be used to optimize and encourage them for agents. Now, it may seem like the easy way to go in order to modify an agent's behavior is by altering its extrinsic rewards or in essence its reward functions. However, this can be prone to difficulties, and this can often alter training performance for the worse, which is what we witnessed when we added **Curriculum Learning** (**CL**) to a couple of agents in the previous section. Of course, even if we make the training worse, we now have a number of techniques up our sleeves such as **Transfer Learning** (**TL**), also known as **Imitation Learning** (**IL**); **Curiosity**; and CL, to help us correct things.

In the next exercise, we are going to look to add further individuality to our agents by adding additional extrinsic rewards. Open up the previous exercise example we were just working on and follow along:

1. From the menu, select **Window** | **Asset Store**. This will take you to the Unity Asset Store, which is an excellent resource for helper assets. While most of these assets are paid, honestly, the price compared to comparable developer tools is minimal, and there are several free and very excellent assets that you can start using to enhance your training environments. The Asset Store is one of the best and worst things about Unity, so if you do purchase assets, be sure to read the reviews and forum posts. Any good asset will typically have its own forum if it is developer-focused, artistic assets much less so.
2. In the search bar, enter `toony tiny people` and press the *Enter* key or click the **Search** button. This will display the search results.

We would like to thank **Polygon Blacksmith** for their support in allowing us to distribute their Toony Tiny People Demo asset with the book's source. Also, their collection of character assets is very well done and simple to use. The price is also at an excellent starting point for some of the larger asset packages if you decide you want to build a full game or enhanced demo.

3. Select the result called **Toony Tiny People Demo** by **Polygon Blacksmith** and select it. It will appear as shown in this screenshot:

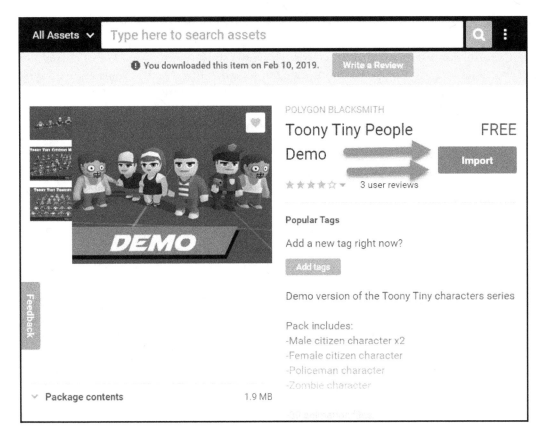

The Toony Tiny People Demo asset from Polygon Blacksmith

4. Click the red **Download** button and, after the asset has downloaded, the button will change to **Import**, as shown in the preceding screenshot. Click the **Import** button to import the assets. When you are prompted by the **Import** dialog, make sure everything is selected and click **Import**.

These types of low polygon or toon assets are perfect for making a simple game or simulation more entertaining and fun to watch. It may not seem like much, but you can spend a lot of time watching these training sims run, and it helps if they look appealing.

5. Select and expand all the agent objects in **Hierarchy**. This includes **RedStriker**, **BlueStriker**, **RedGoalie**, and **BlueGoalie**.
6. Open the **Assets** | **TooyTinyPeople** | **TT_demo** | **prefabs** folder in the **Project** window.
7. Select and drag the **TT_demo_Female** prefab from the preceding folder and drop it into the **RedStriker** agent object in the **Hierarchy** window. Select the cube object just beneath the agent and disable it in the inspector. Continue to do this for the other agents according to the following list:
    - **TT_demo_female -> RedStriker**
    - **TT_demo_male_A -> BlueStriker**
    - **TT_demo_police -> BlueGoalie**
    - **TT_demo_zombie -> RedGoalie**

This is further demonstrated in this screenshot:

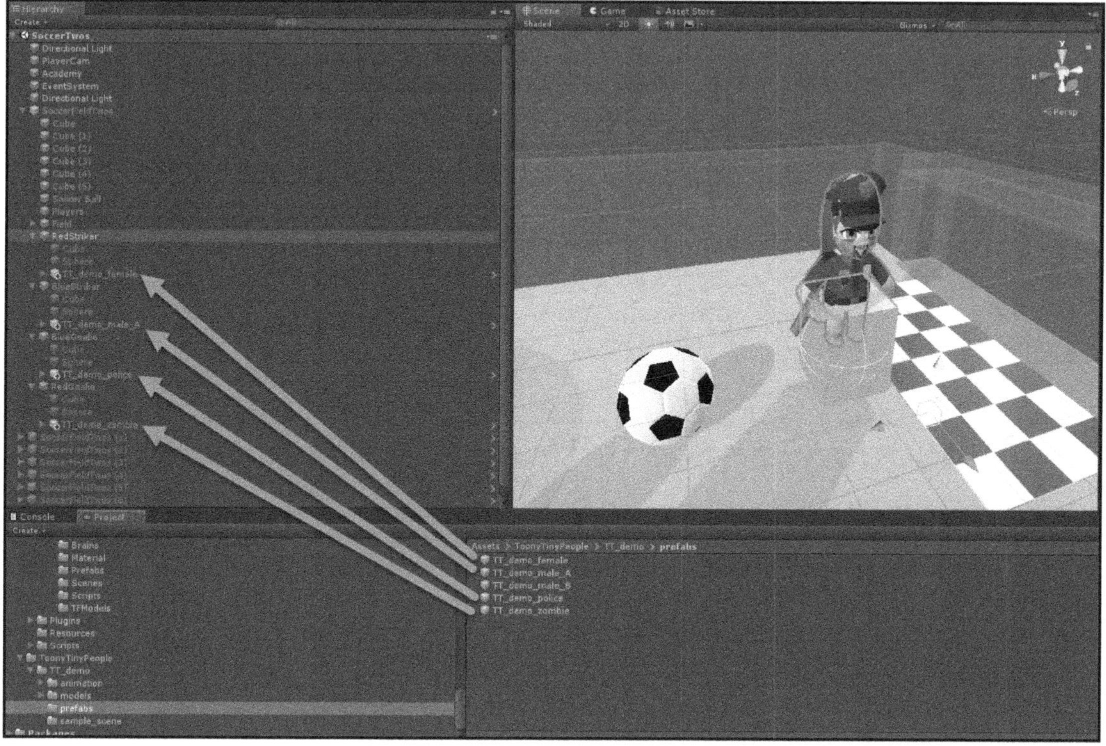

Setting the new agent bodies

8. Make sure to also reset the new agent model's **Transform Position** and **Orientation** to `[0,0,0]`, as shown in the following screenshot:

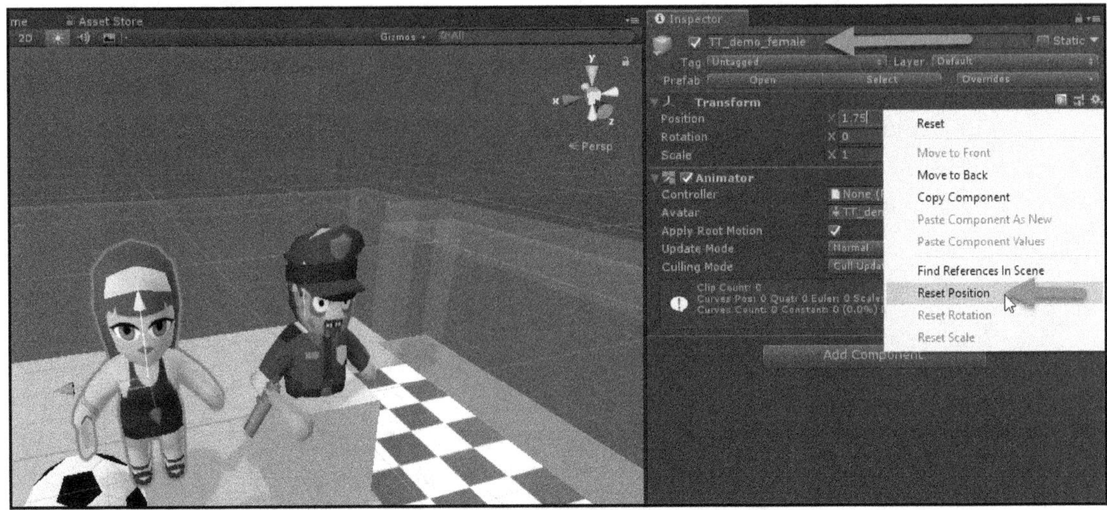

Resetting the orientation and position of dragged prefabs

9. Save the scene and project.

At this point, you can run the scene in training and watch the new agent models move around, but there isn't much point. The agents will still act the same, so what we need to do next is set additional extrinsic rewards based on some arbitrary personality, which we will define in the next section.

Creating uniqueness with customized reward functions

We managed to have some success in making our agents unique by adding intrinsic rewards, although the results may have been not as unique as we would have liked. This means we now want to look at modifying the agents' extrinsic rewards in the hopes of making their behavior more unique and ultimately more entertaining for the game.

The best way for us to start doing that is to look at the `SoccerTwos` reward functions we described earlier; these are listed here, for reference:

$$R_{striker}(goal) = 1$$
$$R_{striker}(-goal) = -0.1$$
$$R_{goalie}(goal) = 0.1$$
$$R_{goalie}(-goal) = -1$$

What we want to do now is apply some individualistic modification to the rewards function based on the current character. We will do this by simply chaining the functions with a modification based on the character type, as shown:

$$R_{girl}(goal) = R_{striker}(goal) * 1.25 \text{ or } R_{girl}(-goal) = R_{striker}(-goal) * 1.25$$
$$R_{boy}(goal) = R_{striker}(goal) * .95 \text{ or } R_{boy}(-goal) = R_{striker}(-goal) * .95$$
$$R_{police}(goal) = R_{goalie}(goal) \text{ or } R_{police}(-goal) = R_{goalie}(-goal)$$
$$R_{zombie}(goal) = R_{goalie}(goal) * .5 \text{ or } R_{zombie}(-goal) = R_{goalie}(-goal) * .5$$

All we are doing here with these reward functions is simply modifying the reward value by some personality modification. For the girl, we give her a bonus of 1.25 x the rewards, reflecting that she may be excited. The boy is less excited, so we modify his rewards by .95 times, which reduces them slightly. The policeman, who is always calm and in control, remains constant with no rewards modifications. Finally, we introduce a bit of a wildcard, the half-dead zombie. In order to characterize it as half-dead, we also decrease all of its rewards by half as well.

You could, of course, modify these functions in any way you please, according to your game mechanics, but it is important to note that the effect of the personality modification you are applying could hinder training. Be sure to take a mental note of that as we get into training this example as well.

A girl, a boy, a zombie, and a policeman enter the soccer field.

Now that we understand the new reward functions, we want to add to our example that it is time to open Unity and code them. This example will require some slight modifications to the C# files, but the code is quite simple and should be readily understood by any programmer with experience of a C-based language.

Open up Unity to the scene we were modifying in the previous example, and follow the next exercise:

1. Locate the **RedStriker** agent in the **Hierarchy** window and select it.

2. From **Inspector**, click the gear icon beside the **Agent Soccer** component and, from the **Context** menu, select **Edit Script**. This will open the script and solution in your editor.
3. Add a new `enum` called `PersonRole` at the top of the file right after the current `enum AgentRole` and as shown in the code:

```
public enum AgentRole
{
  striker,goalie
} //after this line
public enum PersonRole
{
  girl, boy, police, zombie
}
```

4. This creates a new role, for, in essence, the personality we want to apply to each brain.
5. Add another new variable to the class, as shown:

```
public AgentRole agentRole; //after this line
public PersonRole playerRole;
```

6. That adds the new `PersonRole` to the agent. Now we want to also add the new type to the setup by adding a single line to the `InitializeAgent` method, shown here:

```
public override void InitializeAgent()
{
  base.InitializeAgent();
  agentRenderer = GetComponent<Renderer>();
  rayPer = GetComponent<RayPerception>();
  academy = FindObjectOfType<SoccerAcademy>();
  PlayerState playerState = new PlayerState();
  playerState.agentRB = GetComponent<Rigidbody>();
  agentRB = GetComponent<Rigidbody>();
  agentRB.maxAngularVelocity = 500;
  playerState.startingPos = transform.position;
  playerState.agentScript = this;
  area.playerStates.Add(playerState);
  playerIndex = area.playerStates.IndexOf(playerState);
  playerState.playerIndex = playerIndex;
  playerState.personRole = personRole;  //add this line
}
```

7. You should likely see an error now in the line. That is because we also need to add the new `personRole` property to `PlayerState`. Open the `PlayerState` class and add the property as shown:

```
[System.Serializable]
public class PlayerState
{
  public int playerIndex;
  public Rigidbody agentRB;
  public Vector3 startingPos;
  public AgentSoccer agentScript;
  public float ballPosReward;
  public string position;
  public AgentSoccer.PersonRole personRole { get; set; }  //add me
}
```

8. You should now be in the `SoccerFieldArea.cs` file. Scroll to the `RewardOrPunishPlayer` method and modify it as shown:

```
public void RewardOrPunishPlayer(PlayerState ps, float striker,
float goalie)
{
  if (ps.agentScript.agentRole == AgentSoccer.AgentRole.striker)
  {
    RewardOrPunishPerson(ps, striker);  //new line
  }
  if (ps.agentScript.agentRole == AgentSoccer.AgentRole.goalie)
  {
    RewardOrPunishPerson(ps, striker); //new line
  }
  ps.agentScript.Done(); //all agents need to be reset
}
```

9. What we are doing here is injecting another reward function, `RewardOrPunishPerson`, in order to add our extrinsic personality rewards. Next, add a new `RewardOrPunishPerson` method, as shown:

```
private void RewardOrPunishPerson(PlayerState ps, float reward)
{
  switch (ps.personRole)
  {
    case AgentSoccer.PersonRole.boy:
      ps.agentScript.AddReward(reward * .95f);
      break;

    case AgentSoccer.PersonRole.girl:
      ps.agentScript.AddReward(reward*1.25f);
```

```
            break;

          case AgentSoccer.PersonRole.police:
            ps.agentScript.AddReward(reward);
            break;

          case AgentSoccer.PersonRole.zombie:
            ps.agentScript.AddReward(reward * .5f);
            break;
        }
      }
```

10. That code does exactly what our earlier customized reward functions do. When you are done editing, save all your files and return to the Unity editor. If there are any errors or compiler warnings, they will be shown in the console. If you need to go back and fix any (red) error issues, do so.

As you can see, with very little code, we are able to add our extrinsic personality rewards. You could, of course, enhance this system in any number of ways and even make it more generic and parameter-driven. In the next section, we look to put all this together and get our agents training individually.

Configuring the agents' personalities

With all the code set up, we can now continue back in the editor and set up the agents to match the personality we want to apply to them. Open up the editor again, and follow the next exercise to apply the personalities to the agents and start training:

1. Select **RedStriker** in **Hierarchy** and set the **Agent Soccer** | **Person Role** parameter we just created to **Girl**, as shown:

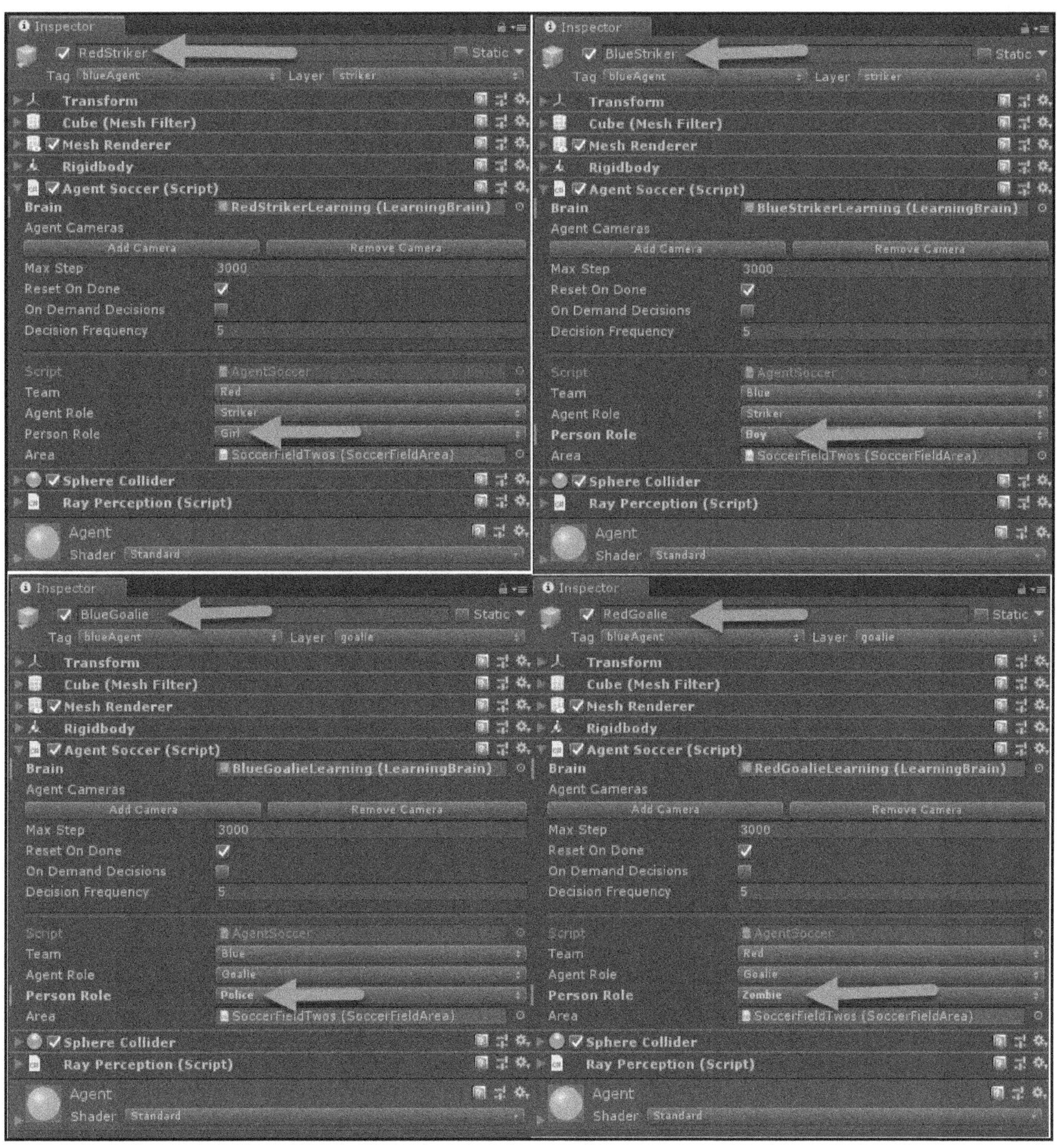

Setting the personalities on each of the agents

2. Update all the agents with the relevant personality that matches the model we assigned earlier: **BlueStriker**-> **Boy**, **BlueGoalie** -> **Police**, and **RedGoalie** -> **Zombie**, as shown in the preceding screenshot.
3. Save the scene and project.
4. Now, at this point, if you wanted it to be more detailed, you may want to go back and update each of the agent brain names to reflect their personalities, such as **GirlStrikerLearning** or **PoliceGoalieLearning**, and you can omit the team colors. Be sure to also add the new brain configuration settings to your `trainer_config.yaml` file.
5. Open your Python/Anaconda training console and start training with the following command:

```
mlagents-learn config/trainer_config.yaml --run-id=soccer_peeps --
train
```

6. Now, this can be very entertaining to watch, as you can see in the following screenshot:

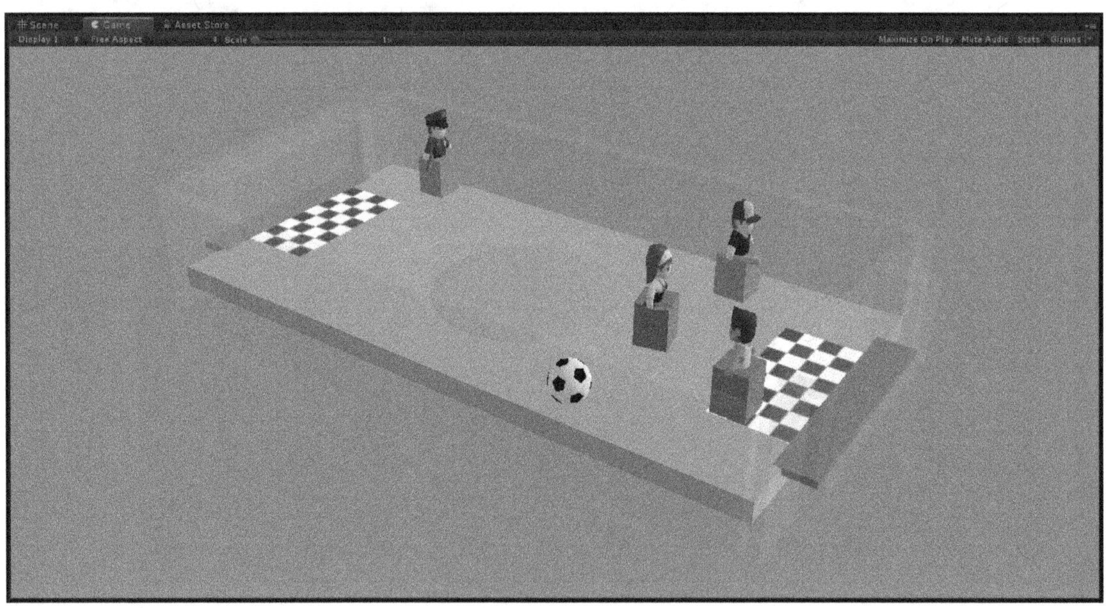

Watching individual personalities play soccer

7. Note how we kept the team color cubes active in order to show which team each individual agent is on.

8. Let the agents train for several thousand iterations and then open the console; note how the agents now look less symbiotic. In our example, they are still paired with each other, since we only applied a simple linear transformation to the rewards. You could, of course, apply more complex functions that are non-linear and not inversely related that describe some other motivation or personality for your agents.
9. Finally, let's open up TensorBoard and look at a better comparison of our multi-agent training. Open another Python/Anaconda console to the `ML-Agents/ml-agents` folder you are currently working in and run the following command:

```
tensorboard --logdir=summaries
```

10. Use your browser to open the TensorBoard interface and examine the results. Be sure to disable any extra results and just focus on the four brains in our current training run. The three main plots we want to focus on are shown merged together in this diagram:

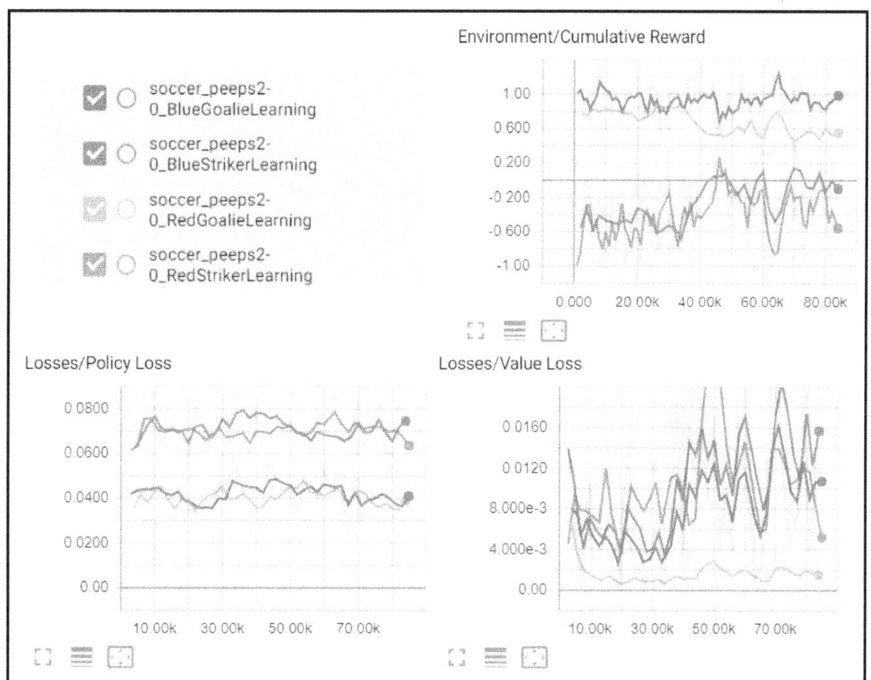

TensorBoard Plots showing results of training four brains

As you can see from the TensorBoard results, the agents are not training very well. We could enhance that, of course, by adding additional training areas and feeding more observations in order to train the policy. However, if you look at the **Policy Loss** plot, the results show the agents' competition is causing minimal policy change, which is a bad thing this early in training. If anything, the zombie agent appears to be the agent learning the best from these results.

There are plenty of other ways you can, of course, modify your extrinsic reward function in order to encourage some behavioral aspect in multi-agent training scenarios. Some of these techniques work well and some not so well. We are still in the early days of developing this tech and best practices still need to emerge.

In the next section, we look to further exercises you can work on in order to reinforce your knowledge of all the material we covered in this chapter.

Exercises

As always, try at least one or two of the following exercises on your own for your own enjoyment and learning:

1. Open the **BananaCollectors** example **Banana** scene and run it in training mode.
2. Modify the **BananaCollectors** | **Banana** scene so that it uses five separate learning brains and then run it in training mode.
3. Modify the reward functions in the last **SoccerTwos** exercise to use exponential or logarithmic functions.
4. Modify the reward function in the last **SoccerTwos** exercise to use non-inverse related and non-linear functions. This way, the mean modifying the positive and negative rewards is different for each personality.
5. Modify the **SoccerTwos** scene with different characters and personalities. Model new rewards functions as well, and then train the agents.
6. Modify the **BananaCollectors** example **Banana** scene to use the same personalities and custom reward functions as we did with the **SoccerTwos** example.
7. Do exercise 3 with the **BananaCollectors** example.
8. Do exercise 4 with the **BananaCollectors** example.
9. Do exercise 5 with the **BananaCollectors** example.
10. Build a new multi-agent environment using one of the current samples as a template or create your own. This last exercise could very likely turn into your very own game.

You may have noticed by now that as we progress through the book, the exercises become more time-consuming and difficult. Please try for your own personal benefit to complete at least a couple of the exercises.

Summary

In this chapter, we explored a world of possibilities with multi-agent training environments. We first looked at how we could set up environments using self-play, where a single brain may control multiple brains that both compete and cooperate with one another. Then we looked at how we could add personality with intrinsic rewards in the form of curiosity using the ML-Agents curiosity learning system. Next, we looked at how extrinsic rewards could be used to model an agent's personality and influence training. We did this by adding a free asset for style and then applied custom extrinsic rewards through reward function chaining. Finally, we trained the environment and were entertained by the results of the boy agent solidly thrashing the zombie; you will see this if you watch the training to completion.

In the next chapter, we will look at another novel application of DRL for debugging and testing already constructed games.

3
Section 3: Building Games

In this final section, we will explore the various ways that deep learning can be implemented in games right now, and we'll also look to the future of deep learning in games.

In this section, we will include the following chapters:

- `Chapter 12`, *Debugging/Testing a Game with DRL*
- `Chapter 13`, *Obstacle Tower Challenge and Beyond*

12
Debugging/Testing a Game with DRL

While the ML-Agents framework provides powerful capabilities for building AI agents for your games, it also provides automation for debugging and testing. The development of any complex software needs to be tied to extensive product testing and review by talented quality assurance teams. Testing every aspect, every possible combination, and every level can be extremely time-consuming and expensive. Therefore, in this chapter, we will look at using ML-Agents as an automated way to test a simple game. As we change or modify the game, our automated testing system can inform us of any issues or possible changes that may have broken the test. We can also take this further with ML-Agents, for instance, to evaluate training performance.

The following is a brief summary of what we will cover in this chapter:

- Introducing the game
- Setting up ML-Agents
- Overriding the Unity input system
- Testing through imitation
- Analyzing the testing process

In this chapter, we will assume that you have sound knowledge of the ML-Agents toolkit and are somewhat familiar with the Unity game engine. You should also have a good grasp of reward functions and the use of imitation learning with ML-Agents.

In the next section, we will start by downloading and importing the game; we will teach ML-Agents to play in the following section. This should be considered an advanced chapter, even for experienced users of Unity. Therefore, if you are relatively new to Unity and/or C#, just take your time and slowly work through the exercises. By the end of this chapter, if you have completed all the exercises, you should be on your way to being a Unity pro.

Introducing the game

The game that we are going to look at is a demo sample asset that is free and is an excellent example of a typical game. The game that we'll test will use discrete control mechanics and a first-person perspective, like the games that we have looked at in the past. The technique that we will show you here is how to map/hack into a game's controller so that it can be powered by ML-Agents. Using this technique should allow you to attach ML-Agents to any existing game, although different controllers, such as third-person or top-down, may require a slightly altered approach.

If you consider yourself an experienced Unity user and have your own project that uses an FPS system, then you should go ahead and try to adapt this sample to your own game or example.

You will generally find a lack of good sample game projects for Unity, due to a somewhat questionable technique called **asset flipping**. Essentially, some developers will take a sample project and quickly skin it as their own game, and then resell it. This practice has primarily been frowned upon in the Unity community, since it generally casts this excellent game engine in a negative light. The quick games, meant only as samples, are often of very poor quality and are unsupported, not to mention that these developers only use the free license, which means that these poorly designed games are also shipped with *Made with Unity*.

We want to illustrate how ML-Agents can be incorporated into a working game for testing, debugging, and/or as an AI enhancement. Let's start by importing the base project and setting up the game to run in the editor. Along the way, we may have to tweak a few things in order to get things working, but that is our intent. Open up the Unity editor and follow the exercises in the next section to set up the base game project:

1. Create a new project called `HoDLG` (or another name of your preference). Wait for the empty project to load. Again, if you feel qualified, use your own project.
2. From the menu, select **Window** | **Asset Store**.

3. In the search pane, type `ms vehicle system` and hit *Enter* or click on the **Search** button. We are going to look at a free asset called **MS Vehicle System**, which has a fun little environment that we can play with. It is often difficult to find free environments such as this (for the reasons mentioned earlier), but, generally, well-made commercial (not free) asset packages will provide good demo environments such as this one. Unity has a number of tutorial environments as well, but they tend to become dated quickly, and they may not always upgrade that easily.
4. Click on the **MS Vehicle System** card and wait for the asset page to load, as shown in the following screenshot:

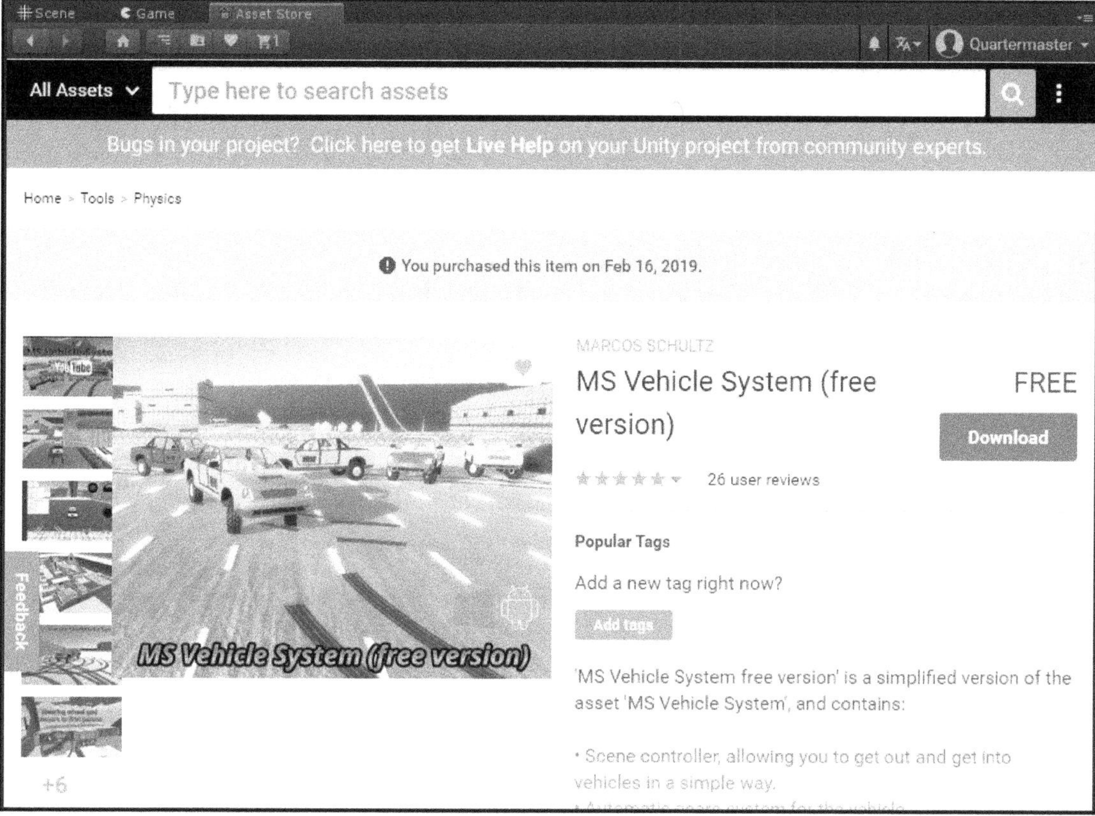

Selecting the asset package to download

5. Click on the **Download** button to download the asset, and then click on **Import** to import the asset into the project. Follow the import dialogues to import all of the assets into the project.
6. Locate the **MainScene** scene in the **Assets** | **MSVehicleSystem (FreeVersion)** folder, and open it.
7. Press **Play** to run the scene in the editor, and use the controls to drive the vehicles around. Notice how you can switch vehicles and camera controls. When you are done testing (playing), stop the scene by pressing **Play**.
8. Type `canvas` in the **Hierarchy** filter field and just select all of the **Canvas** objects in the scene, as shown in the following screenshot:

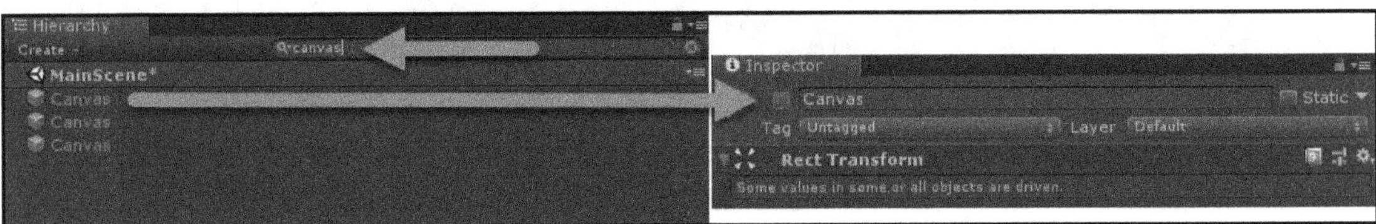

Disabling the Canvas UI in the scene

9. That will disable the UI in the scene; we won't need it for testing, and in this case, it isn't important. If this were a real game, there might have been more colorful visuals to denote scores, and you could always add those, of course.
10. Click on the **X** beside the filter input to clear it and return the scene to normal.
11. Play the scene again, and explore several areas. Look for an area that you think may make a suitable goal; remember, don't make it too difficult initially. The following is an example of a spot that might make an interesting goal; see whether you can find the location:

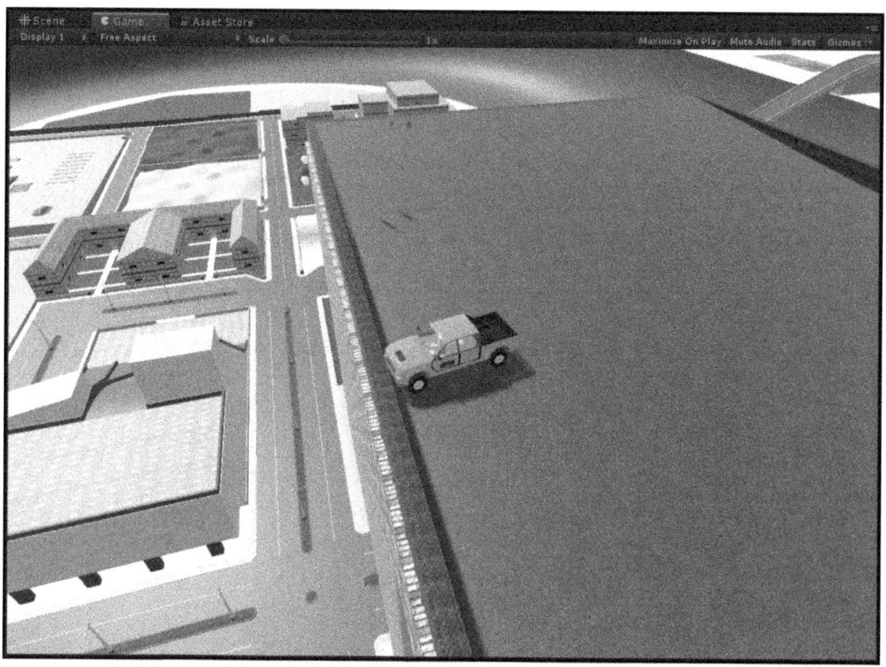

Finding a good place for our goal

Even if you can't find the specific spot, locate an area that is difficult to get to. That way, the agent will have to explore the level extensively in order to find the goal (or goals). In our case, we will drop random goal squares on to the level and encourage the agent to look for those. That way, we can also map out areas that get explored by how often it happens, and then determine how to cover other areas for testing. Before we get to that, we will add ML-Agents, in the next section.

Setting up ML-Agents

At the time of writing this book, ML-Agents is developed and shipped as a GitHub project. It is likely that as the product matures, it will be shipped as its own asset package, but currently, it is not.

Therefore, we first need to export ML-Agents as an asset package. Open up a new Unity Editor session to an ML-Agents or Unity SDK project, and follow these steps:

1. Locate the **ML-Agents** folder in the **Project** window, and select it.
2. From the menu, select **Assets** | **Export Package**.
3. Be sure that all of the folder contents are highlighted, as shown in the following **Exporting package** dialog excerpt:

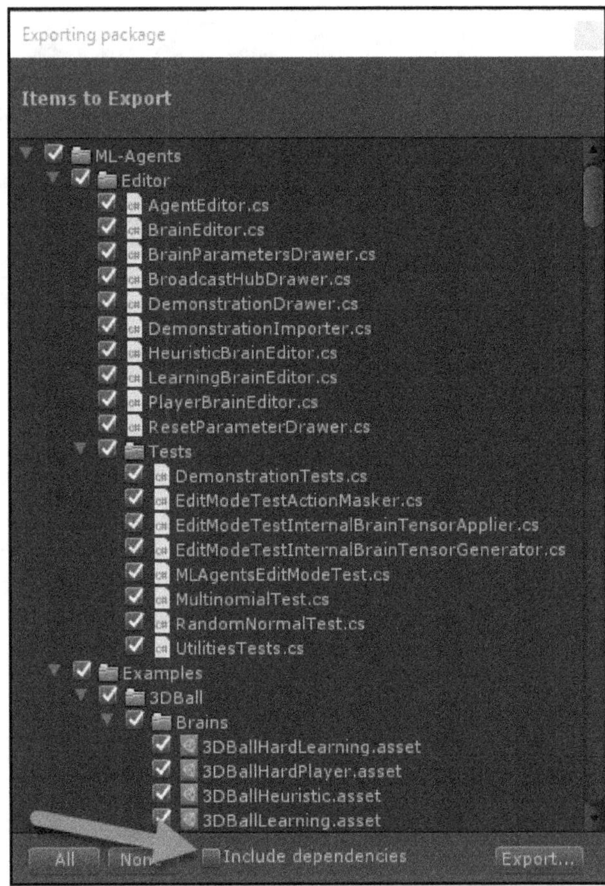

Exporting ML-Agents as an asset package

4. Be sure to uncheck the **Include dependencies** checkbox, as shown in the preceding excerpt. As long as you have the proper root folder selected, all of the dependencies that we need should get packaged.
5. Click on the **Export...** button in the dialog, and then choose and save the asset file to a location that you will easily be able to find later.
6. Open the Unity Editor to the project that we started in the last exercise.
7. From the menu, select **Assets** | **Import Package** | **Custom Package**. Locate the package that we just exported and import it into the new test project.
8. Locate the project window and create a new folder called `HoDLG` in the **Assets** root, and, then, inside that new folder, create new folders called `Brains`, `Prefabs`, and `Scripts`, as shown in the following screenshot:

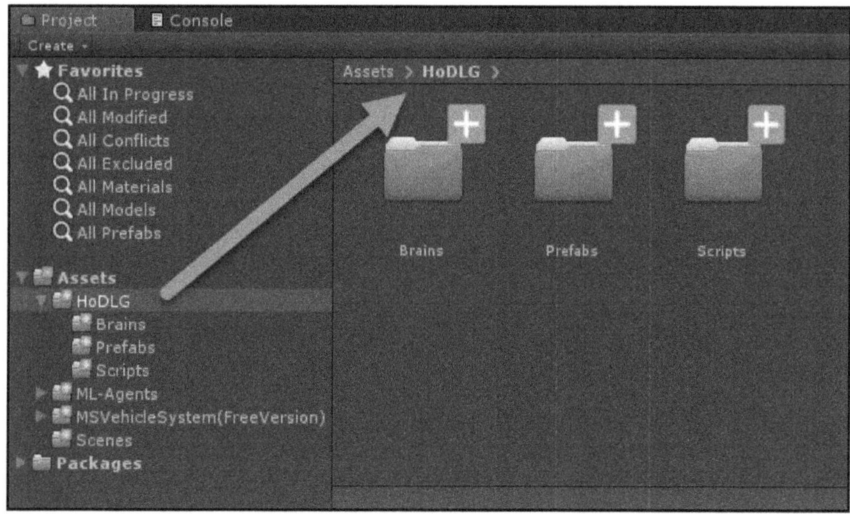

Creating new project folders

9. Creating these folders is the standard way of laying the foundation for a new asset, example, or project. You can now close the old ML-Agents Unity SDK project, as we no longer need it.

Now that we have ML-Agents imported and the foundations laid for our test game, we can move on to adding the learning parts of ML-Agents for testing.

Introducing rewards to the game

The scene currently has no well-defined goal. There are plenty of open worlds and exploration-style games where the goal is very loosely defined. For our purposes, however, we only really want the agent to test-play the whole game level, and hopefully identify any game flaws or perhaps strategies that we never foresaw. Of course, that doesn't mean that if the car-driving agents became good, we could also use them as game opponents. The bottom line is that our agent needs to learn, and it does that through rewards; therefore, we need to make some reward functions.

Let's first define a reward function for our goal, as follows:

$$R(goal) = 1$$

It's pretty simple; whenever the agent encounters a goal, they will score a reward of 1 . Now, to avoid the agent taking too long, we will also introduce a standard step reward, as follows:

$$R(step) = -1/Max_{steps}$$

This means that we apply a step reward of -1 divided by the maximum number of steps, per agent action. This is quite standard (our **Hallway** agent used it, for instance), so there is nothing new here. So, our reward functions will be quite simple, which is good.

In many cases, your game may have well-defined goals that you can use to give rewards with. A driving game, for example, would have a clear goal that we could map for our agent. In this case, in our open-world game, it makes sense to add goals for the agent to locate. How you implement your reward structure does matter, of course, but use what makes sense for your situation.

With the reward functions defined, it is time to introduce the concept of a goal into our game. We want to keep this system somewhat generic, so we will build a goal deployment system into a new object called `TestingAcademy`. That way, you can take this academy and drop it into any similar FPS or third-person controlled worlds, and it will work the same.

First-person shooter (**FPS**) refers to a type of game, but also a type of control/camera system. We are interested in the latter, since it is the method by which we control our car.

Open the editor to the new combined project, and follow the next exercise to build the `TestingAcademy` object:

1. Click in the **Hierarchy** window, and from the menu, select **GameObject** | **Create Empty**. Name the new object `TestingAcademy`.
2. Locate and click inside the **HoDLG** | **Scripts** folder, and then open the **Create** sub-menu in the **Project** window.
3. From the **Create** menu, select **C# Script**. Rename the script `TestingAcademy`.
4. Open the new **TestingAcademy** script and enter the following code:

```
using MLAgents;
using UnityEngine;

namespace Packt.HoDLG
{
  public class TestingAcademy : Academy
  {
    public GameObject goal;
    public int numGoals;
    public Vector3 goalSize;
    public Vector3 goalCenter;
    public TestingAgent[] agents;
    public GameObject[] goals;
  }
}
```

All of the code for this chapter's exercise is included in the `Chapter_12_Code.assetpackage` included with the book's source code.

5. This code defines our class and imports by using the required namespaces. Then, we define our own namespace, `Packt.HoDLG`, and the class is extended from `Academy`, an ML-Agents base class. Next comes the declaration of several variables for defining the goal deployment cube. Think of this as a virtual cube in space that will spawn the goals. The idea is to let physics do the rest and let the goal just drop to the ground.

Namespaces are optional in Unity, but it is highly recommended to put your code within a namespace in order to avoid most naming issues, which can be a common problem if you are using many assets or if you find yourself modifying existing assets, as we are doing here.

6. Next, we will define the standard `Academy` class setup method, `InitializeAcademy`. This method is called automatically, and is shown as follows:

```
public override void InitializeAcademy()
{
  agents = FindObjectsOfType<TestingAgent>();
  goals = new GameObject[numGoals];
}
```

7. This method is called as a part of the ML-Agents setup, and it essentially starts the whole SDK. By adding the `Academy` (`TestingAcademy`), we will effectively be enabling ML-Agents. Next, we will add the final method, called when the academy is reset at the end of all of the agent episodes, as follows:

```
public override void AcademyReset()
{
  if (goalSize.magnitude > 0)
  {
    for(int i = 0; i < numGoals; i++)
    {
    if(goals[i] != null && goals[i].activeSelf)
      Destroy(goals[i]);
    }
    for(int i = 0; i < numGoals; i++)
    {
      var x = Random.Range(-goalSize.x / 2 + goalCenter.x,
goalSize.x / 2 + goalCenter.x);
      var y = Random.Range(-goalSize.y / 2 + goalCenter.y,
goalSize.y / 2 + goalCenter.y);
      var z = Random.Range(-goalSize.z / 2 + goalCenter.z,
goalSize.z / 2 + goalCenter.z);
     goals[i] = Instantiate(goal, new Vector3(x, y, z),
```

```
        Quaternion.identity, transform);
            }
          }
        }
```

8. This code just spawns the goals randomly within the virtual cube bounds. Before it does this, however, it first clears the old goals by using the `Destroy` method. `Destroy` removes an object from the game. Then, the code loops again and creates new goals at random locations within the virtual cube. The line that actually creates the goal in the game is highlighted and uses the `Instantiate` method. `Instantiate` creates an object in the game at the specified location and rotation.
9. Save the file and return to the editor. Don't worry about any compiler errors at this time. If you are writing the code from scratch, you will be missing some types, which we will define later.

With the new `TestingAcademy` script created, we can move on to adding the component to the game object and setting up the academy in the next section.

Setting up TestingAcademy

With the `TestingAcademy` script created, it is time to add it to the game object via the following steps:

1. Drag the new **TestingAcademy** script file from the **Scripts** folder and drop it on to the **TestingAcademy** object in the **Hierarchy** window. This will add the component to the object. We want to create a few other components before we complete the academy.
2. Click in the **Hierarchy** window, and in the menu, select **Game Object** | **3D Object** | **Cube**. Rename the new object `goal`.

3. Select the object and change the **Tag** to `goal`. Then, swap its material by clicking on the **Target** icon and selecting the **v46**, or another flashy material of your choice, as shown in the following screenshot:

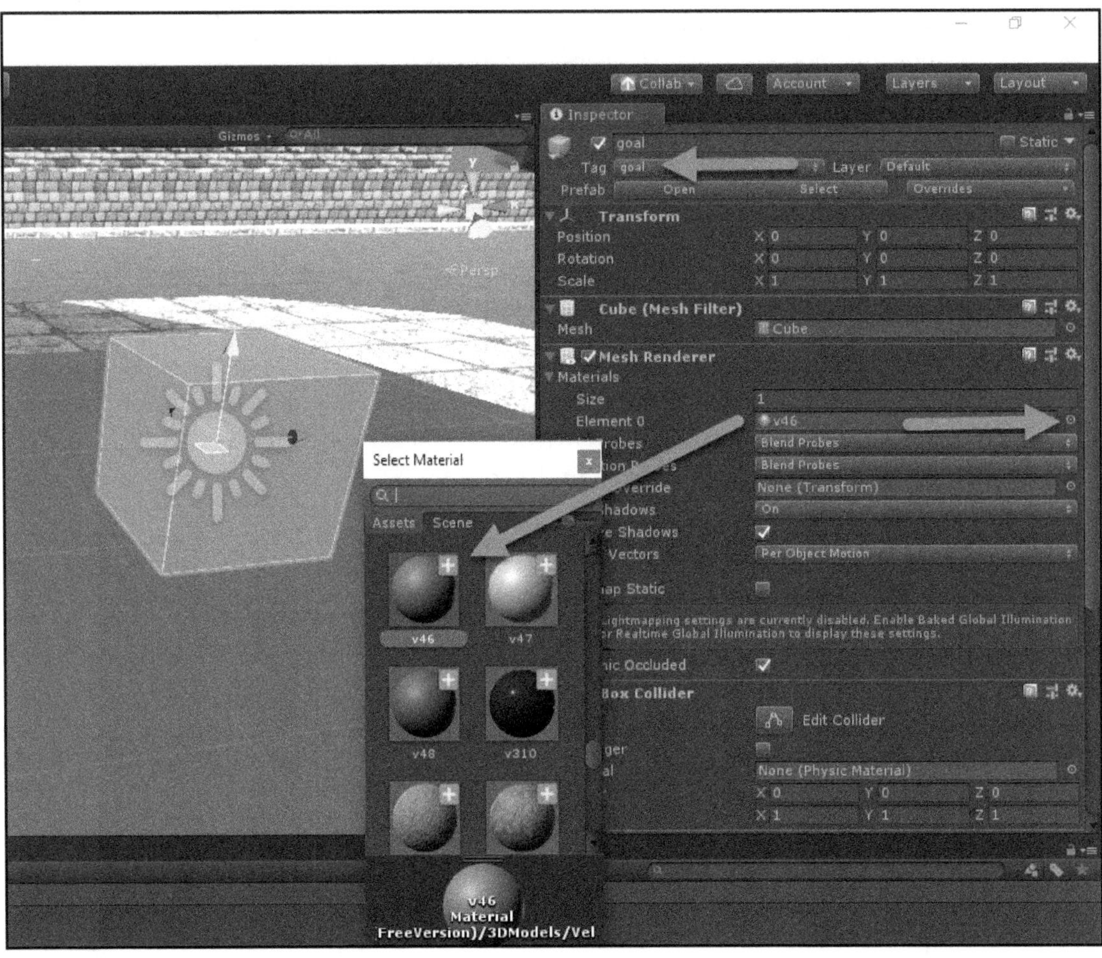

Swapping the goal object's materials

4. With the **goal** object selected from the menu, select **Component** | **Physics** | **Rigidbody**. This will add a physics system component called a **Rigidbody**. By adding the **Rigidbody** to the object, we allow it to be controlled by the physics system.

5. Drag and drop the **goal** object into the **HoDLG | Prefabs** folder in the **Project** window. This will turn the goal object into a **Prefab**. Prefabs are self-contained objects that contain their own hierarchies. A prefab can contain an entire scene, or just one object, as we have here.
6. Select and delete the **goal** object from the **Hierarchy** window. In the future, we will programmatically instantiate the **goal** from the **Academy** by using its **Prefab**.
7. Click inside the **HoDLG | Brains** folder, and click to open the **Create** menu. From the menu, select **ML-Agents | LearningBrain**. Name the new brain `TestingLearningBrain`, and then create a new player brain called `TestingPlayerBrain`. Don't worry about configuring the brains just yet.
8. Select the **TestingAcademy** object in the **Hierarchy** window, and then update the values of the **Testing Academy** component, as shown in the following screenshot:

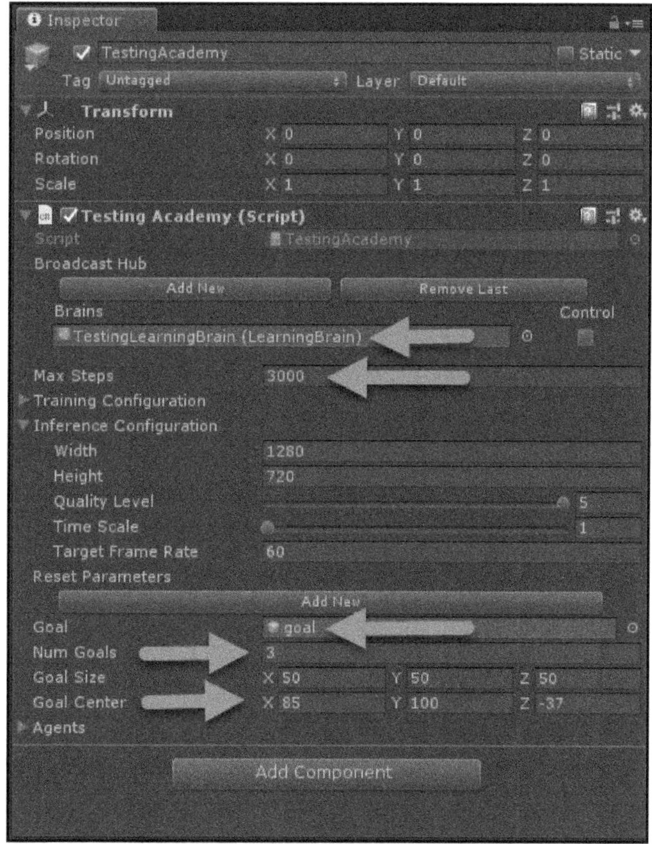

Setting up TestingAcademy

9. Notice that we are setting up the following properties in the **TestingAcademy** script:
    - **Brains**: **TestingLearningBrain**
    - **Max Steps**: **3000**
    - **Goal**: Goal set by dragging the prefab from the folder
    - **Num Goals**: **3** (number of goals dropped from the box)
    - **Goal Size**: (**50**, **50**, **50**) (determines maximum bounds of the goal box)
    - **Goal Center**: (**85**, **110**, **-37**) (the center point of the goal box)

You may be tempted to run the project at this point; you can if you have just downloaded the code, but hold off until we define the `TestingAgent` in the next section.

Scripting the TestingAgent

Of course, our testing (or however far we want to take this simulation) won't do much without an agent to interact with the environment and learn. In the next exercise, we will define the script that describes the `TestingAgent` component:

1. Click inside the **HoDLG** | **Scripts** folder, and click on the **Create** button to open the menu.
2. From the menu, select **C# Script** and name the script `TestingAgent`.
3. Open the script in your editor and start to script it with the following code:

```
using MLAgents;
using UnityEngine;

namespace Packt.HoDLG
{
  public class TestingAgent : Agent
  {
    public string[] axisAction;
    protected Vector3 resetPos;
    protected Quaternion resetRot;
  }
}
```

4. This starts our class; this time, it's extended from `Agent`, another base class. Then, we define some base fields for setting variables and recording the agent's start position and rotation.

5. Next, we move on to define the `InitializeAgent` method. This method is called once, to set up the agent and make sure that the action lengths are the same; we will get to that shortly. We remember the position/rotation from which the agent started, so that we can restore it later. The code is as follows:

```
public override void InitializeAgent()
{
  base.InitializeAgent();
  if (axisAction.Length !=
brain.brainParameters.vectorActionSize[0])
    throw new MLAgents.UnityAgentsException("Axis actions must
match agent actions");

  resetPos = transform.position;
  resetRot = transform.rotation;
}
```

6. Next, we define an empty method called `CollectObservations`. This is typically where the agent observes the environment; since we plan to use visual observations, we can leave this empty. The code is as follows:

```
public override void CollectObservations(){  }
```

7. Next, we define another required method: `AgentAction`. This is the method where we add the negative step reward and move the agent, as shown in the following code snippet:

```
public override void AgentAction(float[] vectorAction, string
textAction)
{
  AddReward(-1f / agentParameters.maxStep);
  MoveAgent(vectorAction);
}

public void MoveAgent(float[] act)
{
  for(int i=0;i<act.Length;i++)
  {
    var val = Mathf.Clamp(act[i], -1f, 1f);
    TestingInput.Instance.setAxis(val,axisAction[i]);
  }
}
```

8. The code here is what deciphers the actions from the brain and injects them back into a new class (which we will build shortly), called `TestingInput`. `TestingInput` is a helper class that we will use to override the input system of the game.
9. Save the script, and, again, ignore any compiler errors. Again, we have a new dependency, `TestingInput`, that we will define shortly.

With the new script in hand, we can begin to set up the `TestingAgent` component in the next section.

Setting up the TestingAgent

Now, the system that we are building here is fairly generic, and it's intended to be used in multiple environments. Keep that in mind as we set things up, especially if some concepts seem a bit abstract. Open up the editor, and let's add the `TestingAgent` script to an object:

1. Select **Vehicle1**, **Vehicle3**, **Vehicle4,** and **Vehicle5** in the scene, and disable them. We currently only want to give our agent the ability to drive, and not to switch vehicles; therefore, we only need the default **Vehicle2**.
2. Select the **TestingAgent** script from the **HoDLG | Scripts** folder and drag it on to the **Vehicle2** object. This will add the **TestingAgent** component to our **Vehicle2**, and will make it an agent (well, almost).
3. Open **Vehicle2 | Cameras** in the **Hierarchy** window and choose the view that you want the agent to use. We will select **Camera2** for this exercise, but the options for each of the five cameras are shown in the following screenshot:

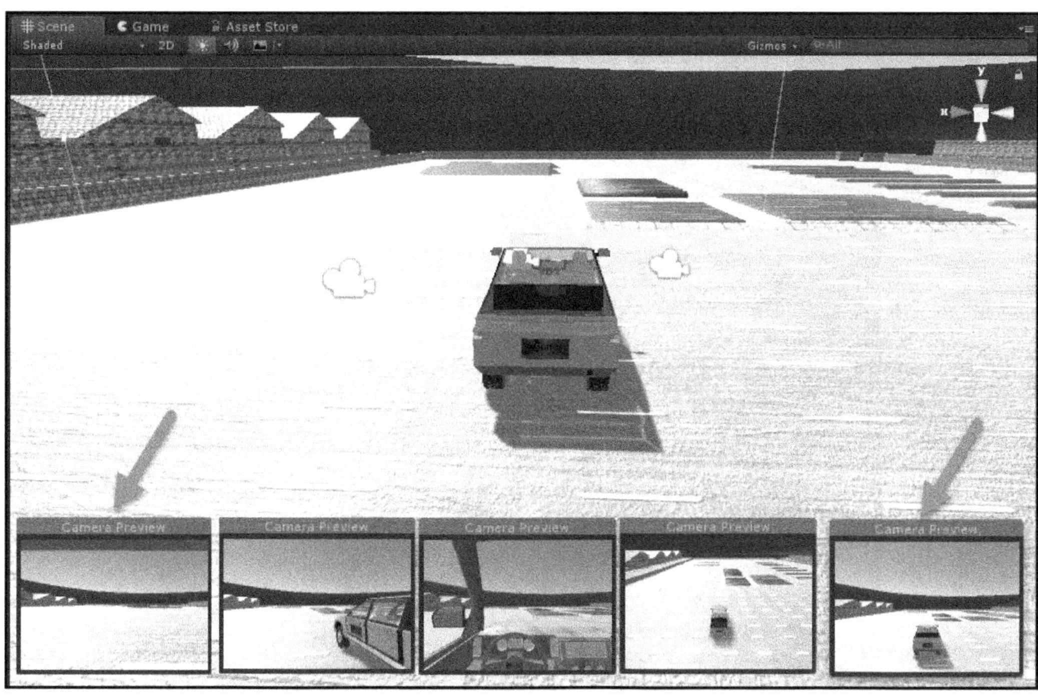

Selecting the visual observation camera to use as an input to the agent

4. The best options are either **Camera1** or **Camera5**, as shown in the preceding screenshot. Note that the cameras are ordered in reverse, with **1** starting at the far right, not the left. Of course, that leaves plenty of opportunity to play with other visual input in the future.

5. Select **Vehicle2** and drag the selected **TestingPlayerBrain** and **Camera1** into the required slots, as shown in the following screenshot:

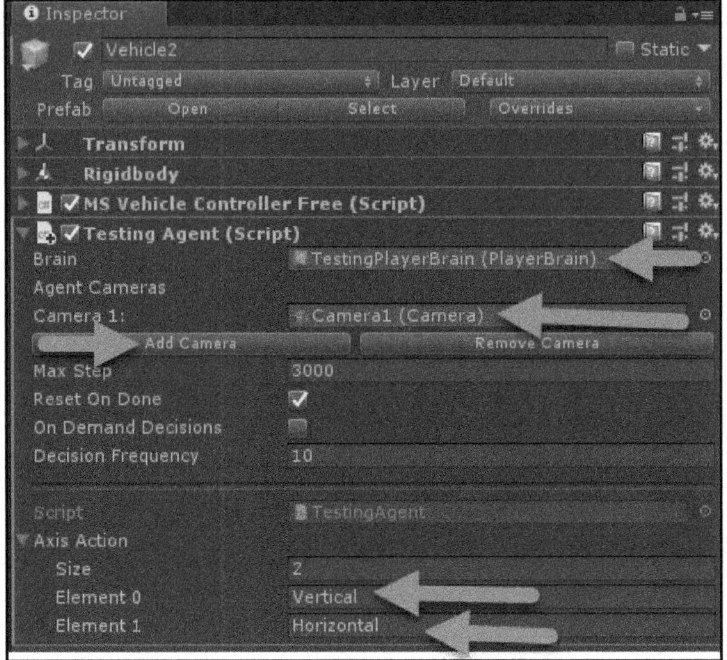

Setting up the TestingAgent component

6. You will also need to define additional properties, which are summarized as follows:
    - **Brain**: **TestingPlayerBrain.**
    - **Camera 1**: Click on **Add Camera** to add a new camera, and then select **Camera1** from the **Vehicle2** cameras.
    - **Decision Frequency**: `10` (this determines how often the agent makes decisions; `10` is a good starting point for this game. It will vary, and you will likely have to tune it to your needs)

- **Axis Action: 2**:
    - **Element 0**: **Vertical** (denotes the axis we will be overriding to allow the agent to control the game. We will get more into axis descriptions shortly)
    - **Element 1**: **Horizontal** (same as the preceding)

7. Save the project and the scene, and, again, ignore any compiler errors.

That completes the set up of the `TestingAgent`; as you can see, there isn't a whole lot of configuration or code required to get this running. In the future, you will likely see more advanced ways of testing/debugging or building agents this way. For now, however, we need to complete our example by injecting into the Unity input system, which we will do in the next section.

Overriding the Unity input system

One of Unity's most compelling features is its ability to be cross-platform across any system, and with that comes several helpful layers of abstraction that we can use to inject our code into. However, the game in question needs to be following the Unity best practices in order to make this injection easy. That isn't to say that we couldn't do it by overriding the game's input system; it just wouldn't be as easy.

Before we get into describing how the injection works, let's take a step back and look at the best practices for using the Unity input system. Over the years, the Unity input system has evolved from a simple query that the device uses for inputs to the more cross-platform system that it uses now. However, many developers, including Unity itself, still use input methods that query a particular key code, for instance. The best practice is to define a set of axes (input channels) that define the input for the game.

We can easily see how it is currently defined in the game by following this exercise:

1. From the editor menu, select **Edit | Project Settings**.
2. Select the **Input** tab and then expand **Axes | Horizontal** and **Axes | Vertical**, as shown in the following screenshot:

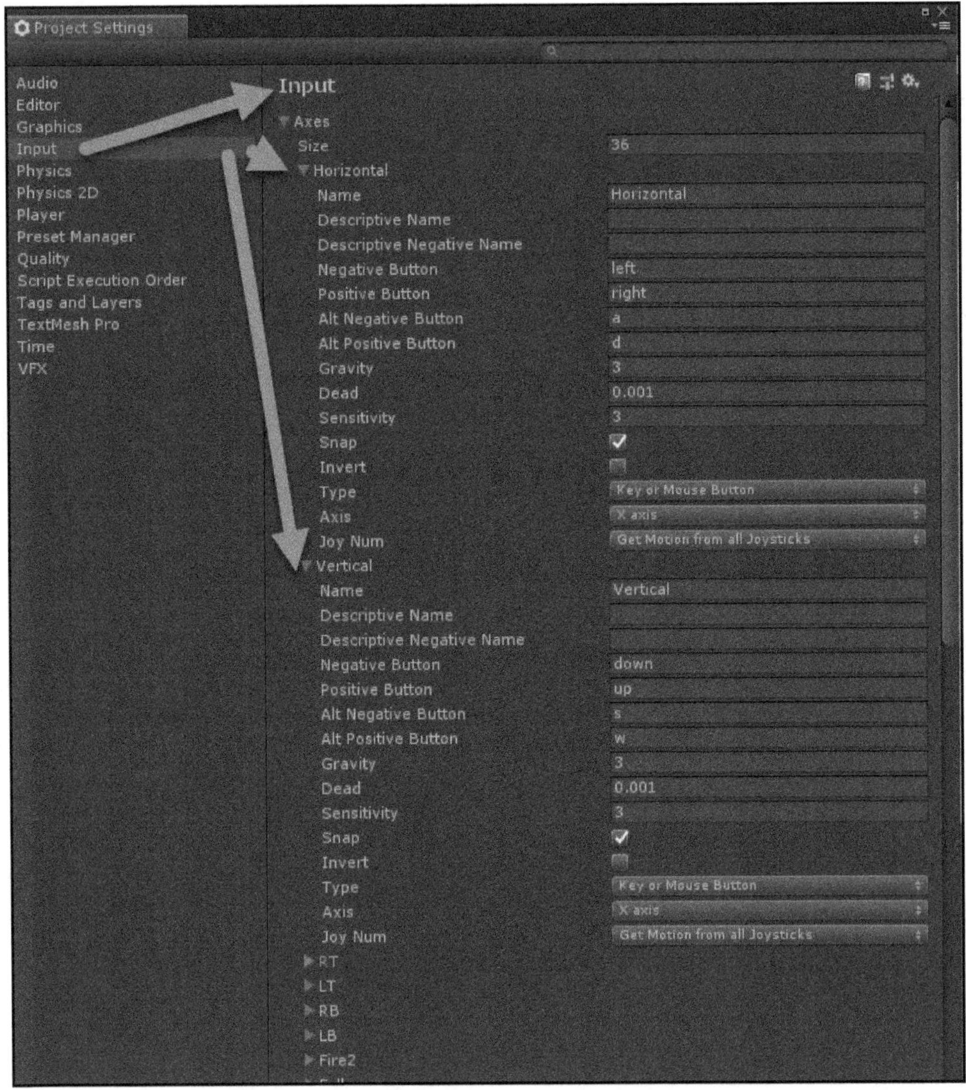

Inspecting the Input Axes settings

3. The **Vertical** and **Horizontal** axes define the input that will be used to control the game. By defining them in this tab, we can control the input across platforms by querying the axes. Notice that the axis input allows us to define both the button and joystick (touch) input. The output of a query to the input system with `getAxis` returns a value from `-1` to `+1`, or continuous output. This means that we can take any discrete form of input, such as a keystroke, and immediately convert it to a continuous value automatically. For example, if a user presses the *W* key, the input system coverts that to a positive 1 value on the **Vertical Axis**, and conversely, a press on the *S* key generates a negative 1 value, again on the **Vertical Axis.** Likewise, the *A* and *D* keys control the **Horizontal Axis**.

As you have seen in a few chapters in this book, using the .6 version of ML-Agents, the current discrete action solution is not nearly as good as the continuous action. Therefore, it will be our preference going forward.

At this point, you may be wondering why we used discrete actions at all; that is a good question. It remains to be seen how Unity will handle this dichotomy in the future. In the next section, we will look at how to inject into the input system.

Building the TestingInput

We are going to use a pattern called a **Singleton** in order to implement a class that we can access from anywhere in our code, much like the input class from Unity that is currently used. Unity has the benefit of making the input completely static, but for our purposes, we will use the well-defined scripting version. Open the editor and follow the next exercise to build the `TestingInput` script and object:

1. Select the **HoDLG | Scripts** folder and open the **Create** menu.
2. From the **Create** menu, select **C# Script**. Name the new script `Singleton`. This script is the standard pattern script from `http://wiki.unity3d.com/index.php/Singleton`; the script is shown as follows:

```
using UnityEngine;

namespace Packt.HoDLG
{
  /// <summary>
  /// Inherit from this base class to create a singleton.
  /// e.g. public class MyClassName : Singleton<MyClassName> {}
  /// </summary>
  public class Singleton<T> : MonoBehaviour where T : MonoBehaviour
```

```
    {
      // Check to see if we're about to be destroyed.
      private static bool m_ShuttingDown = false;
      private static object m_Lock = new object();
      private static T m_Instance;
      /// <summary>
      /// Access singleton instance through this propriety.
      /// </summary>
      public static T Instance
      {
        get
        {
          if (m_ShuttingDown)
          {
            Debug.LogWarning("[Singleton] Instance '" + typeof(T) +
               "' already destroyed. Returning null.");
            return null;
          }
          lock (m_Lock)
          {
            if (m_Instance == null)
            {
              // Search for existing instance.
              m_Instance = (T)FindObjectOfType(typeof(T));
              // Create new instance if one doesn't already exist.
              if (m_Instance == null)
              {
                // Need to create a new GameObject to attach the
singleton to.
                var singletonObject = new GameObject();
                m_Instance = singletonObject.AddComponent<T>();
                singletonObject.name = typeof(T).ToString() + "
(Singleton)";
                // Make instance persistent.
                DontDestroyOnLoad(singletonObject);
              }
            }
            return m_Instance;
          }
        }
      }
      private void OnApplicationQuit()
      {
        m_ShuttingDown = true;
      }
      private void OnDestroy()
      {
        m_ShuttingDown = true;
```

```
        }
      }
    }
```

3. Enter the preceding code, or just use the code downloaded from the book's source. A singleton allows us to define one thread-safe instance of a specific class that all of the objects can refer to. A typical static class will not be thread-safe, and may cause corruption or memory issues.
4. Create a new script called `TestingInput` in the **HoDLG** | **Scripts** folder and open it for editing.
5. We will start the class with the following code:

```
using System.Collections.Generic;
using System.Linq;
using UnityEngine;

namespace Packt.HoDLG
{
  public class TestingInput : Singleton<TestingInput>
  {
    public string[] axes;
    public bool isPlayer;
  }
}
```

6. Notice the highlighted line, and how we declare the class to extend from the type `Singleton` that wraps the type `TestingInput`. This form of recursive typing, which uses generics, is perfect for the singleton. Don't worry if this is a little unclear; the only thing that you need to remember is that we can now access the instance of this class from anywhere in our code. Notice that we mentioned an instance and not a class, meaning that we can also persist the state within our `TestingInput` class. The variables that we declare here, `axes` and `isPlayer`, are either set in the editor or defined in the `Start` method, as follows:

```
void Start()
{
  axisValues = new Dictionary<string, float>();
  //reset the axes to zero
  foreach(var axis in axes)
  {
    axisValues.Add(axis, 0);
  }
}
```

7. Inside the `Start` method, we define a `Dictionary` to hold the axis and values that we want this component to override. This allows us to control which input we want to override. Then, we build the collection of name/value pairs.
8. Next, we will define a couple methods that will allow us to both mimic and set the axis values of our input system. Unity has no direct way to set the value of an axis. Currently, the `Input` system queries the hardware directly in order to read the input state, and provides no way to override this for testing. While this is a feature that has long been requested by the community, it remains to be seen whether it will ever be implemented.
9. We then enter a `setAxis` and `getAxis` method, as follows:

```
public void setAxis(float value, string axisName)
{
  if (isPlayer == false && axes.Contains(axisName)) //don't if
player mode
  {
    axisValues[axisName] = value;
  }
}
public float getAxis(string axisName)
{
  if (isPlayer)
  {
    return Input.GetAxis(axisName);
  }
  else if(axes.Contains(axisName))
  {
    return axisValues[axisName];
  }
  else
  { return 0; }
}
```

10. That completes the script; if you have been adding the code as you go, save the file and return to Unity. At this point, you should see no compiler errors, as all of the required types should be present and accounted for.

That sets up the `TestingInput` script; now, we need to move on to the next section to add it to the scene.

Adding TestingInput to the scene

Singletons can be called from anywhere and everywhere, and they actually don't need a game object in the scene. However, by adding the object to the scene, we become more self-aware of the required dependency, as it allows us to set required parameters for a particular scene. Open the Unity editor and follow the next exercise to add the `TestingInput` component to the scene:

1. Click in the **Hierarchy** window, and from the menu, select **Game Object** | **Create Empty**. Rename the object `TestingInput`.
2. Drag the **TestingInput** script from the **HoDLG** | **Scripts** folder in the **Project** window to the new **TestingInput** object in the **Hierarchy** window.
3. Select the **TestingInput** object, and then set the required **Axes**, as shown in the following screenshot:

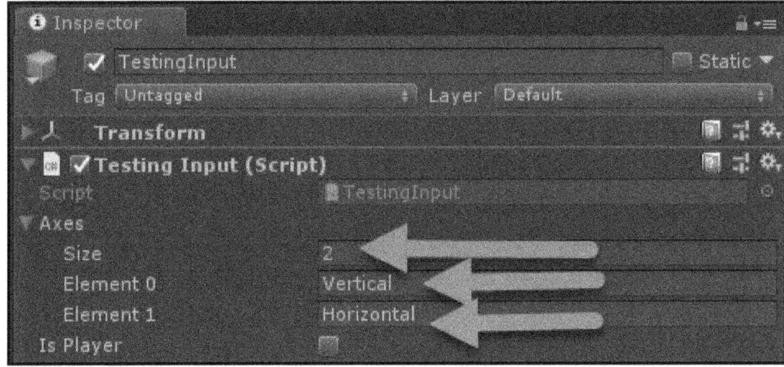

Setting the axes to override

4. We need to define two **Axes** that we want to override. In this case, we are only overriding the **Vertical** (*S* and *W*) and **Horizontal** (*A* and *D*) keys. You could, of course, override any axis that you wanted, but in this case, we are only overriding two.
5. Save the project and the scene.

At this point, you can't really run the project, since the actual input system isn't overriding anything just yet. We complete that final injection in the next section.

Overriding the game input

At this point, we have a complete testing system in place; we just need to complete the last parts of the injection. This bit of surgery can require a keen eye and a little digging through code. Fortunately, there are some good, clear indicators that you can use to spot places for injection. Open the editor and follow the next steps to complete the injection:

1. Select the **Control** object in the **Hierarchy** window.
2. Locate the **MS Scene Controller Free** component in the **Inspector** window and use the **Context** menu to open the script in your code editor.
3. Locate the following block of code, around line **286** (about halfway in), as follows:

```
case ControlTypeFree.windows:
  verticalInput = Input.GetAxis (_verticalInput);
  horizontalInput = Input.GetAxis (_horizontalInput);
  mouseXInput = Input.GetAxis (_mouseXInput);
  mouseYInput = Input.GetAxis (_mouseYInput);
  mouseScrollWheelInput = Input.GetAxis (_mouseScrollWheelInput);
  break;
}
```

4. This is where the game is querying the `GetAxis` method, in order to return the values of the respective input axis. As we have discussed, we are only interested in the vertical and horizontal axes for this example. You can, of course, override other axes, as you see fit.
5. Modify the lines where the `verticalInput` and `horizontalInput` are being set, as follows:

```
verticalInput = TestingInput.Instance.getAxis(_verticalInput);
horizontalInput = TestingInput.Instance.getAxis(_horizontalInput);
```

6. Notice that we call `TestingInput.Instance`, in order to access the singleton instance of our class. This allows us to query that class for the current input values. The `TestingInput` object can now be the source of truth (as far as this class is concerned), with respect to the input.

7. Previously, we quickly went over the agent code that sets the input, but here it is again for reference:

```
public void MoveAgent(float[] act)
{
  for(int i=0;i<act.Length;i++)
  {
    var val = Mathf.Clamp(act[i], -1f, 1f);
    TestingInput.Instance.setAxis(val,axisAction[i]);
  }
}
```

8. Notice the highlighted line in the `TestingAgent` `MoveAgent` method. This is where we override the input by the agent and inject the values back into the game.
9. Save the code and return to the editor. Make sure to fix any compiler issues now.

Unfortunately, we are still unable to run the scene, as we have one last configuration step to tend to. In the next section, we will complete the configuration by setting up the brains.

Configuring the required brains

The last piece of the puzzle is to configure the brains that we quickly built earlier. ML-Agents requires that the brains be configured with the required input and observation space, in order to work correctly. We will set up the `TestingPlayerBrain` and `TestingLearningBrain` in the next exercise:

1. Open the Unity editor and select **TestingLearningBrain** from the **HoDLG | Brains** folder to open it in the **Inspector**.

2. Set the **Brain** parameters, as shown in the following screenshot:

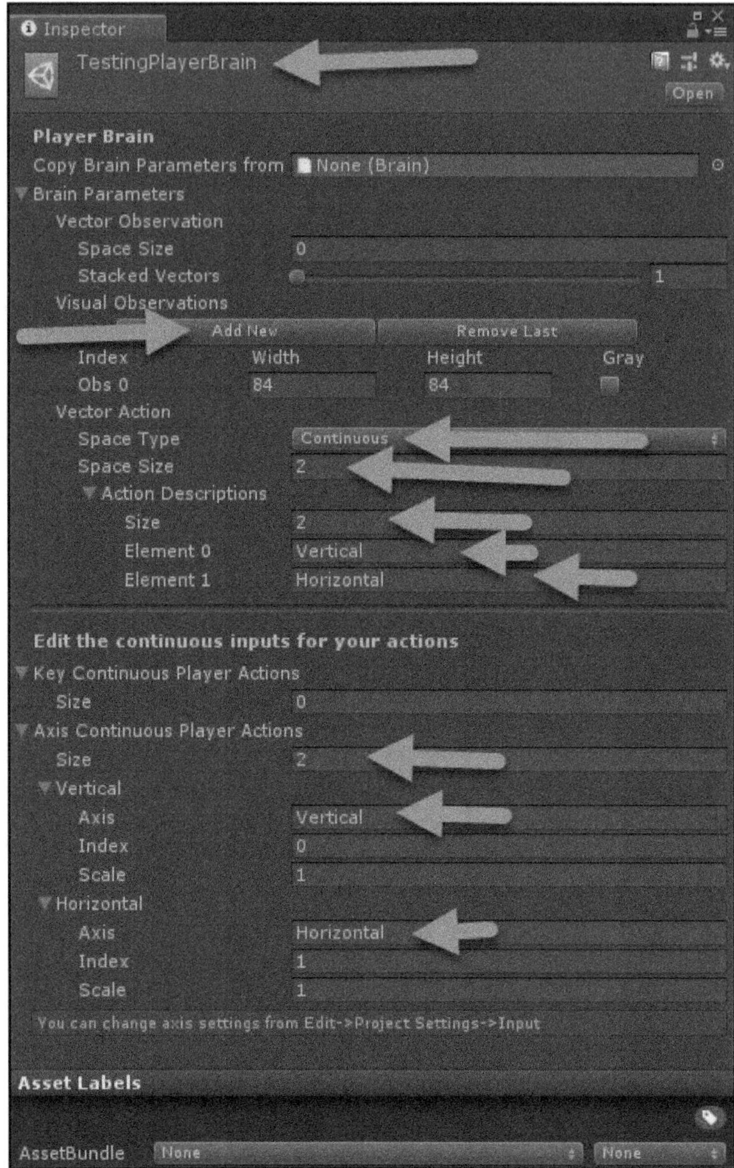

Setting the parameters for the TestingPlayerBrain

3. There are several parameters to set; they are summarized as follows:
    - **Visual Observations**: `84` x `84` and no grayscale
    - **Vector Action:**
        - **Space Type: Continuous**
        - **Space Size:** `2`
        - **Action Descriptions:**
            - **Size:** `2`
            - **Element 0: Vertical**
            - **Element 1: Horizontal**
    - **Axis Continuous Player Actions:**
        - **Size:** `2`
        - **Vertical:**
            - **Axis: Vertical**
            - **Index:** `0`
            - **Scale:** `1`
        - **Horizontal:**
            - **Axis: Horizontal**
            - **Index:** `1`
            - **Scale:** `1`

4. Select **TestingLearningBrain** and configure it the same, but for learning, as shown in the following screenshot:

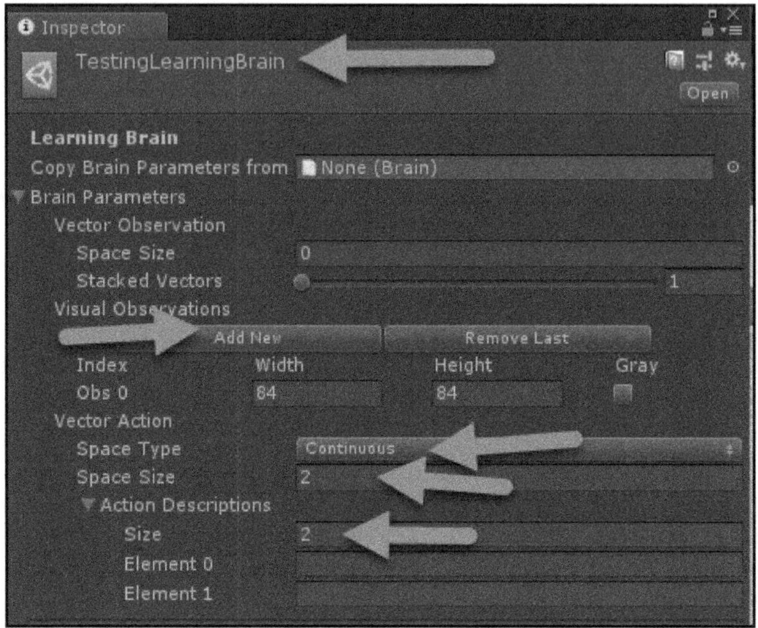

Configuring the TestingLearningBrain

5. The configuration for the learning brain is much simpler, but it is also still required, even when running the sample in player mode (which, if you recall, it is set up to do).
6. Save the scene and project. Finally, we have completed our required configuration.
7. Press **Play** to run the scene and play the game in player mode. We are controlling the game through the ML-Agents system. After a few seconds, you should see some goals drop nearby.

8. Control the vehicle and drive into a goal, as shown in the following screenshot:

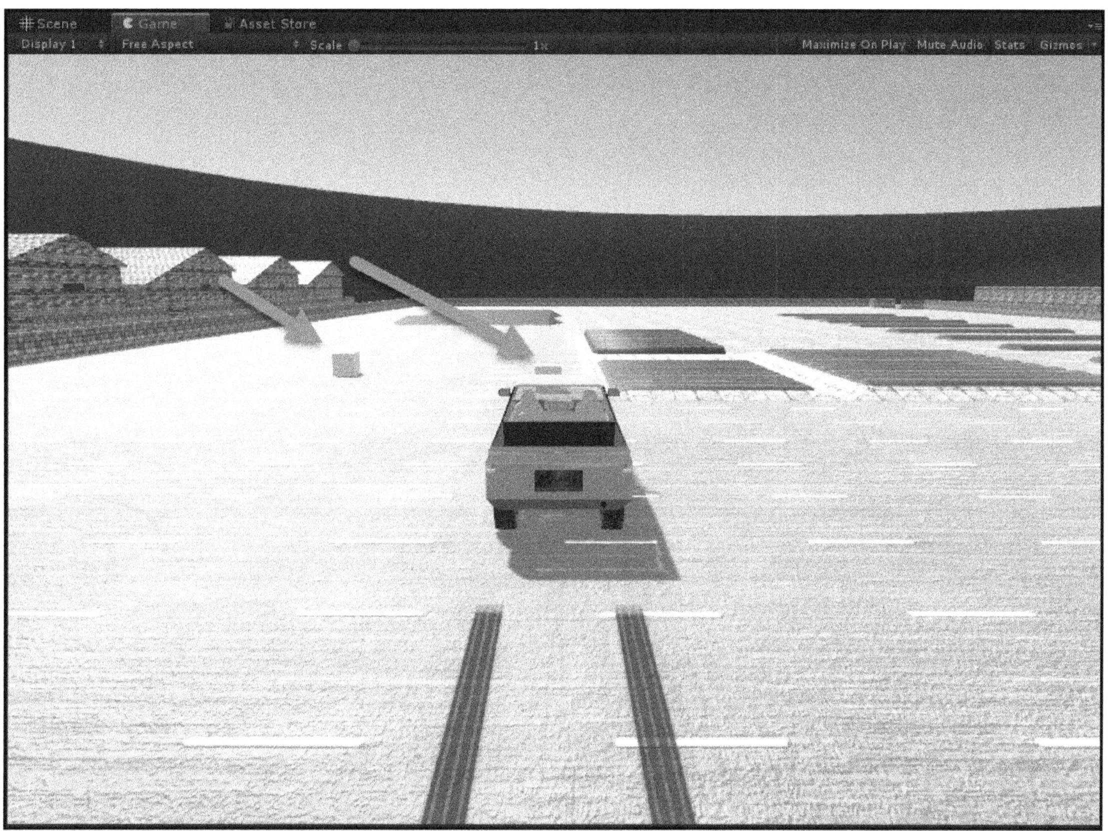

Driving into the goals

9. When you are done playing, stop the game.

Now that we are able to play the game through ML-Agents by using a configured player brain, we will switch to a learning brain and let an agent take control in the next section.

Time for training

However we decide to use this platform, whether for training or testing, we now need to do the last brain configuration step, in order to set any custom hyperparameters that we may decide to use for training. Open a Python/Anaconda console and prepare it for training, and then follow these steps:

1. Open the `trainer_config.yaml` file located in the `ML-Agents/ml-agents/config` folder.
2. We will add a new configuration section to the config file, modeled after one of the other visual environments. Add the new configuration, as follows:

```
TestingLearningBrain:
    use_recurrent: true
    sequence_length: 64
    num_layers: 1
    hidden_units: 128
    memory_size: 256
    beta: 1.0e-2
    gamma: 0.99
    num_epoch: 3
    buffer_size: 1024
    batch_size: 64
    max_steps: 5.0e5
    summary_freq: 1000
    time_horizon: 64
```

3. Notice that we added the word `brain`, in order to differentiate it from the other brains. This brain is modeled after the `VisualHallwayBrain` that we spent some time exploring previously. Keep in mind, however, that we are running a continuous action problem now, and this can affect some parameters.
4. Save the file and return to the Unity editor.
5. Locate the `TestingAcademy` object, swap its `Brains` for a `TestingLearningBrain`, and set it to `Control`, as you have done so many times before.

6. Save the scene and project and return to the Python/Anaconda console.
7. Start a training/learning/testing session by running the following command:

```
mlagents-learn config/trainer_config.yaml --run-id=testing --train
```

8. Watch the training session and the agent play the game. The agent will run, and depending on how long you train, it may become good at finding the goals.

At this point, you can let the agent go and just run through your level on its own, exploring. However, what we want to do is control or nudge the testing agent to the right path by using imitation learning, which we will discuss in the next section.

Testing through imitation

At this point in your learning, you have learned several strategies that we can apply to help our testing agent learn and find the goals. We can use curiosity or curriculum learning fairly easily, and we will leave that as an exercise for the reader. What we want is a way to control some of the testing process, and we don't really want our agent to randomly test everything (at least not at this stage). Sure, there are places where completely random testing works well. (By the way, this random form of testing is called **monkey testing**, because it resembles a monkey just mashing keys or input.) However, in a space such as our game, exploring every possible combination could take a very long time. Therefore, the best alternative is to capture player recordings and use them for our testing agent as a source for imitation learning.

With everything set up and with our ability to now route the input events through ML-Agents, we can capture player input in the form that an agent needs to learn from. Let's open a backup Unity and set up the scene to capture player recordings, as follows:

1. Select the **Vehicle2** object in the **Hierarchy** window. Recall that this is where the **TestingAgent** script is attached.
2. Use the **Add Component** button at the bottom of the **Inspector** window to add a **Demonstration Recorder** component to the agent.

3. Set the **Demonstration Recorder** to **Record** and the **Demonstration Name** to **Testing**, and change the brain to **TestingPlayerBrain**, as shown in the following screenshot:

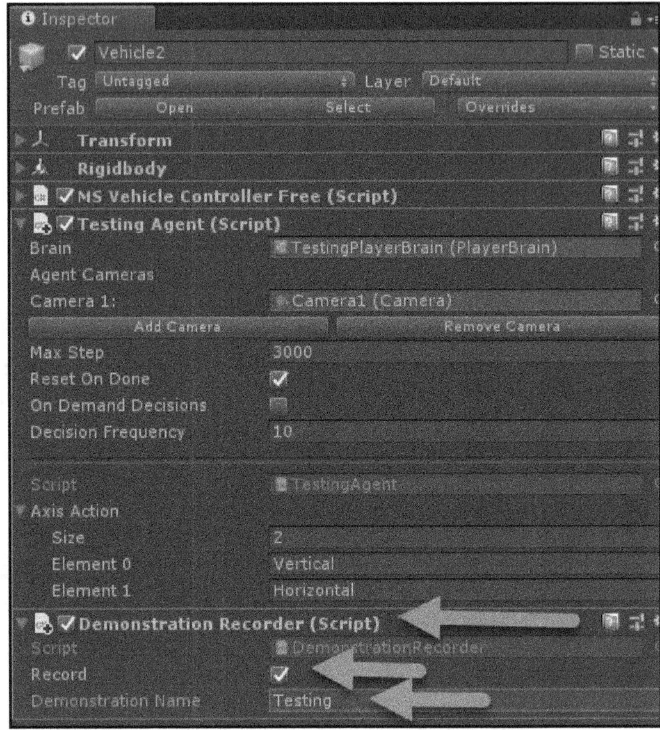

Adding a Demonstration Recorder to the agent

4. Select the **TestingAcademy** object, and make sure to disable the **Control** option on the **Brain**. We want the player to control the agent when recording.
5. Press **Play** and run the game. Use the *WASD* controls keys on your keyboard to drive the vehicle over the goals. Play for a little while, in order to generate a decent recording.
6. When you are done, check the `Assets` folder for a new folder called `Demonstrations` that contains your `Testing.demo` recording file.

Now, with the player recording in play, we can set up and run the agent, using imitation learning to test the level.

Configuring the agent to use IL

We have already run through the process of setting up and running an offline **imitation learning (IL)** session, but let's review the process in the next exercise:

1. Open the Unity editor to the same project and locate the **Vehicle2** object containing the agent.
2. Switch the agent's brain from **TestingPlayerBrain** to **TestingLearningBrain**.
3. Select the **TestingAcademy** and enable the **Control** property on the **Testing Academy | Brains** component property.
4. Save the scene and project.
5. Open the `config/offline_bc_config.yaml` file in a text or code editor.
6. Add the following section (a modified copy of `HallwayLearning`):

```
TestingLearningBrain:
    trainer: offline_bc
    max_steps: 5.0e5
    num_epoch: 5
    batch_size: 64
    batches_per_epoch: 5
    num_layers: 2
    hidden_units: 128
    sequence_length: 16
    use_recurrent: true
    memory_size: 256
    sequence_length: 32
    demo_path: ./UnitySDK/Assets/Demonstrations/Testing.demo
```

7. Save the file when you are done editing it.
8. Open a Python/Anaconda console that is ready for training, and enter the following command:

```
mlagents-learn config/offline_bc_config.yaml --run-id=testing_il --
train
```

9. Note a couple of modifications, highlighted in bold. After the training starts, watch the agent drive the car in the same manner that you trained it (or at least, it will try to).
10. Let the agent play the game, and watch how well it performs and/or gets into trouble.

This demo/game is quite stable and is not prone to any obvious issues, which makes testing it for obvious issues difficult. However, hopefully, you can appreciate that if this type of system is implemented very early in a game, even just for testing, it provides the ability to quickly find bugs and other issues. Of course, currently, our only method to identify any issues is to watch the agent play, which doesn't save us any time. What we need is a way to track agent activity and determine whether (and when) the agent finds itself in trouble. Fortunately, we can easily add this form of tracking by adding analytics, which we will cover in the next section.

Analyzing the testing process

One of the key features that ML-Agents is currently missing is extra training analytics (beyond what is provided by the console and TensorBoard). A key feature that could be crucial (and which is not difficult to add) is training analytics. This could be implemented with the Unity Analytics service that is free to try with all games. Since this isn't a current feature in ML-Agents, it is one that we will add in the next exercise, by adding our own training analytics system:

1. Open the Unity editor, and from the menu, select **Window | General | Services**. This will open a new window called **Services**, usually over the top of the **Inspector** window.
2. Click on the **Analytics** service in the newly opened **Services** window. You will need to progress through a couple of screens, asking for your preferences and acknowledgment, as shown in the following screenshot:

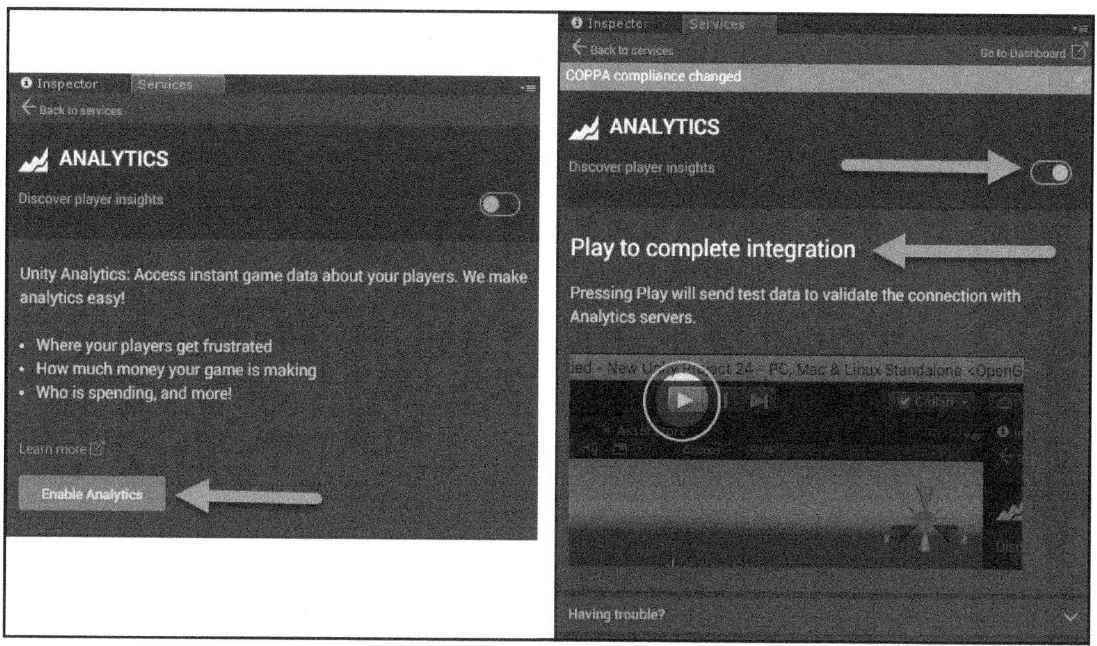

Setting up analytics for your project

3. Click on the button to enable **Google Analytics**. Then, select the **Discover player insights** switch, and you will be prompted to press **Play** in your editor.
4. Press **Play** in the editor, and let the game run for only a few seconds.

5. Return to the **Services** window and the **Analytics** page, and at the top, you should see a button called **Go to Dashboard**. Click on the button, as shown in the following screenshot:

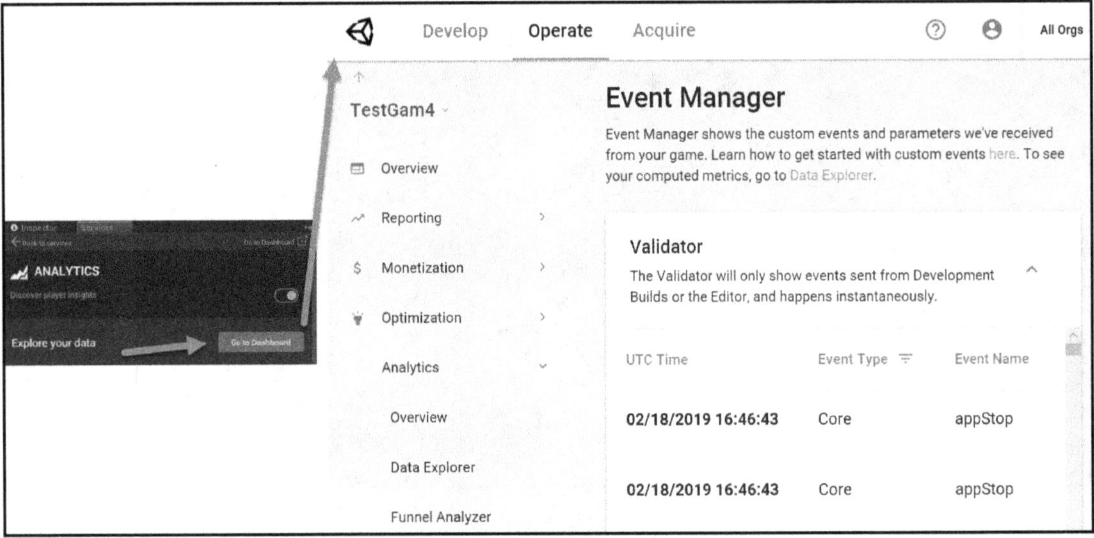

Exploring your data using the dashboard

6. This will open your default web browser to your project analytics page, and you should see some events, such as **appStart** and **appStop**.

That completes the setup of the analytics service, and, as you have seen, it is quite easy. However, as with everything, we need to customize some of the reporting data that we will send to the analytics service. You will learn how to send your own custom analytics in the next section.

Sending custom analytics

If you have used the analytics service previously, you may have your own best practices for how to track your game usage; if so, feel free to use that. The method that we will present here is intended as a start for how you can go about setting up and sending custom analytics for training, or even for tracking player usage.

Let's begin by opening the Unity editor and following the next exercise:

1. Create a new C# script called `TestingAnalytics` in the `HoDLG Scripts` folder.
2. Open and edit the `TestingAnalytics` script in your editor, and enter the following code:

```
using UnityEngine;

namespace Packt.HoDLG
{
 public class TestingAnalytics : Singleton<TestingAnalytics>
 {
 private TestingAcademy academy;
 private TestingAgent[] agents;
 private void Start()
 {
 academy = FindObjectOfType<TestingAcademy>();
 agents = FindObjectsOfType<TestingAgent>();
 }
 public string CurrentGameState
 {
 get
 {
 var state = string.Empty;
 foreach (var agent in agents)
 {
 foreach (var goal in academy.goals)
 {
 var distance = Vector3.Distance(goal.transform.position,
agent.transform.position);
 state += agent.name + " distance to goal " + distance + "/n";
 }
 }
 return state;
 }
 }
 }
}
```

3. All this code does is collect the current position of the goals and how close they are to the agents. That is what we care about currently. Also, notice that we made this a **public property,** so that it can be called like a method, and not just a field. This will be important later on.
4. Save the file and return to the editor. Confirm that there are no compiler errors.

5. Create a new empty game object in the scene, and call it `TestingAnalytics`. Drag the new `TestingAnalytics` script on to the object to set it as a scene component. While the class is a singleton, we still want to add it as a dependency in the scene (essentially, as a reminder). However, there is another trick that we can also use to program prefabs.
6. Drag the **TestingAnalytics** object into the **HoDLG | Prefabs** folder. This will make the object a prefab, which is now accessible by all of the other prefabs.
7. Double-click on the **goal** prefab located in the **HoDLG | Prefabs** folder to open the object in its own mini editor.
8. Use the **Add Component** button to add an **Analytics Event Tracker** component to the object and configure it, as shown in the following screenshot:

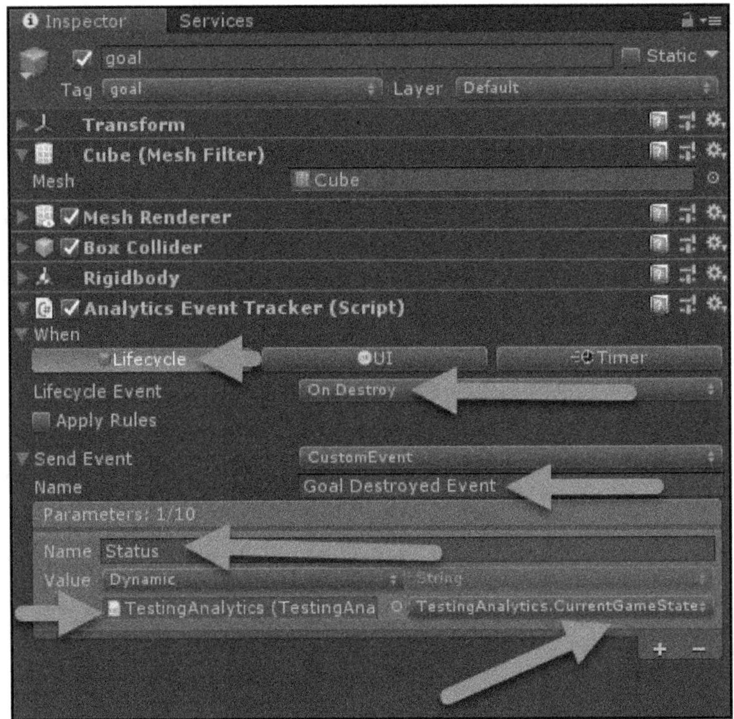

Setting up the Analytics Event Tracker

9. Configure the component as follows:
    - **When: Lifecycle**
    - **Lifecycle Event: On Destroy**
    - **Send Event:**
        - **Name: Goal Destroyed Event**
        - **Parameters: 1/10:**
            - **Name: Status**
            - **Value: Dynamic**
            - **Object: TestingAnalytics (Prefab)**
            - **Method: CurrentGameState**
10. Switch the scene back to the player mode by altering the **Academy** and **Agent** configuration.
11. Save the scene and the project.
12. Run the scene by pressing **Play**, and drive over a goal. As you hit the goal, check the **Analytics** dashboard and note how the event is tracked.

At this stage, the analytics only report when a goal is destroyed, and they report how close each agent is to a goal. So, for one agent and three goals, they would report three distances when a goal was destroyed by driving over it or when the object was reset. By following these stats, you can generally view how each agent testing session is going overall, for better or for worse. Of course, you can add any manner of analytics that you want; it is easy to get carried away. Who knows; in the future, Unity may offer a self-testing platform driven by ML-Agents that provides testing analytics.

We are coming to the end of another chapter, and, of course, we are approaching your favorite section, Exercises.

Exercises

The exercises in this chapter are a mix of working with ML-Agents and building your own testing analysis platform. As such, choose one or two exercises that make sense for you to complete on your own from the following list:

1. Configure the **TestingAgent** to use a different camera for its visual observation input.
2. Enable **Curiosity Learning** on the agent's brain.
3. Set up the **TestingAgent** to control a different vehicle.

4. Set up the **TestingAgent** to run on another vehicle and let ML-Agents control both of the agents simultaneously.
5. Add additional tracking analytics custom events for the agents. Perhaps track the distance that the agent travels versus its lifetime. This will provide a speed factor that can also denote the agent's efficiency. An agent that hits a goal quicker will have a better speed factor.
6. Enable online imitation learning by adding a second vehicle with a learning agent. If you need to, go back and review the setup of the tennis scene.
7. Set up the **Academy** to use curriculum learning. Perhaps allow the virtual goal deployment box to grow in size over training iterations (by 10%, or some other factor). This will allow the goals to disperse farther and make it more difficult for the agent to find.
8. Modify the visual observation input that the brains are using to `184` x `184`, the new standard, and see what effect this has on agent training.
9. Modify the visual observation convolutional encoding network, as we did in `Chapter 7`, *Agents and the Environment*, to use more layers and/or different filtering.
10. Apply this testing framework to your own game. Be sure to also add the analytics, so that you can track training and player usage.

These exercises are more involved than those in the previous chapters, since this is a big and important chapter. In the next section, we will review what you learned and covered in this chapter.

Summary

Of all the chapters in this book, this may be the most useful if you are in the process of developing your own game. Game testing is one of those things that requires so much time and attention, it has to be up for some form of automation. While it makes sense for DRL to work well in this area for almost any game, it remains to be seen whether that is one of the niches for this new learning phenomena. One thing that's for sure, however, is that ML-Agents is more than capable of working as a testing harness, and we are sure that it will only get better over time.

In this chapter, we looked at building a generic testing platform, powered by ML-Agents, that we can use to test any game automatically. We first looked at each of the components that we needed to adapt, the academy and the agent, and how they could be generalized for testing. Then, we looked at how we could inject into the Unity input system and use our `TestingAgent` to override the game's input and learn how to control it on its own. After that, we looked at how to better set up our testing by using offline IL and recording a demo file that we could use to train the agent later. Finally, in order to see how well our testing was doing, we added analytics and customized them to our needs.

The next chapter will be our final chapter and our last discussion of deep learning for games; appropriately enough, we will look at what the future holds for ML-Agents and DRL.

13
Obstacle Tower Challenge and Beyond

In this chapter, our final one, we will take a look at the current and future state of **deep learning** (**DL**) and **deep reinforcement learning** (**DRL**) for games. We take an honest and candid look to see whether these technologies are ready for prime-time commercial games or whether they are just novelties. Are we poised to see DRL agents beating human players at every game imaginable a few years from now? While that remains to be seen, and things are changing quickly, the question really is this: is DL ready for your game? It likely is a question you are asking yourself at this very moment, and it is hopefully one we will answer in this chapter.

This chapter will be a mix of hands-on exercises and general discussions with unfortunately no exercises. Well, there is one big exercise, but we will get to that shortly. Here is what we will cover in this chapter:

- The Unity Obstacle Tower challenge
- Deep Learning for your game?
- Building your game
- More foundations of learning

This chapter assumes you have covered numerous exercises in this book in order to understand the context. We will refer to those sections in order to remind the reader, but please don't jump to this chapter first.

The Unity Obstacle Tower Challenge

The **Unity Obstacle Tower Challenge** was introduced in February 2019 as a discrete visual learning problem. As we have seen before, this is the holy grail of learning for games, robotics, and other simulations. What makes it more interesting is this challenge was introduced outside of ML-Agents and requires the challenger to write their own Python code from scratch to control the game—something we have come close to learning how to do in this book, but we omitted the technical details. Instead, we focused on the fundamentals of tuning hyperparameters, understanding rewards, and the agent state. All of these fundamentals will come in handy if you decide to tackle the tower challenge.

At the time this book was written, the ML-Agents version used for developing was `0.6`. If you have run all the exercises to completion, you will have noticed that all of the visual learning environments using a discrete action space suffer from a vanishing or exploding gradient problem. What you will see happen is the agent essentially learning nothing and performing random actions; this often takes several hundred thousand iterations to see. But we don't see this problem in environments with a smaller state space using vector observations. In visual environments with a large input state, though, the problem can be seen quite regularly. This means that, essentially, at the time of writing anyway, you would not want to use the Unity code; it currently is a poor visual learner of discrete actions.

At the time of writing, the Unity Obstacle Tower Challenge has just started, and early metrics are already being reported. The current leading algorithm from Google, DeepMind, not surprisingly, is an algorithm called **Rainbow**. In short, Rainbow is the culmination of many different DRL algorithms and techniques all combined to better learn the discrete action visual-learning space that the tower so well defines.

Now that we have established that you likely want to write your own code, we will understand the high-level critical pieces your agent needs to address. It likely would take another book to explain how to do the coding and other technical aspects of that, so we will instead talk about the overall challenges and the critical elements you need to address. Also, the winners will more than likely need to use more probabilistic methods in order to address the problem, and that is currently not covered very well anywhere.

Let's set up the challenge and get it running in the next exercise:

1. Download the Obstacle Tower Environment as a binary from `https://github.com/Unity-Technologies/obstacle-tower-env`.
2. Follow the instructions and download the zip file for your environment as directed. On most systems, this just requires downloading and unzipping the file into a folder you will execute from later.
3. Unzip the file into a well-known folder.

4. Launch the program by double-clicking on it (Windows) to enter the name in a console. After you launch the challenge, you can actually play it as a human. Play the game and see how many floors you can climb. An example of the running challenge is shown in the following screenshot:

The Obstacle Tower Challenge in player mode

One of the first things you will learn as you progress through the game is that the game starts out quite simply, but on the later floors, it gets quite difficult, even for a human.

Now, as we mentioned, solving this challenge is well beyond the scope of this book, but hopefully you can now appreciate some of the complexities that currently stifle the field of deep reinforcement learning. We have reviewed the major challenges that you will face when undertaking this method in the following table:

Problem	**Chapter**	**Current Status**	**Future**
Visual observation state—you will need to build a complex enough CNN and possibly recurrent networks to encode enough details in the visual state.	`Chapter` 7, *Agent and the Environment*	The current Unity visual encoder is far from acceptable.	Fortunately, there is plenty of work always being done with CNN and recurrent networks for analysis of videos. Remember, you don't just want to capture static images; you also want to encode the sequence of the images.

DQN, DDQN, or Rainbow	`Chapter 5`, *Introducing DRL*	Rainbow is currently the best, and it is available on the GCP.	As we have seen in this book, PPO only performs well on continuous action spaces. In order to tackle the discrete action space, we look back to more fundamental methods such as DQN or the newcomer Rainbow, which is the summation of all base methods. We will also discuss future ways in which further use of deep probabilistic methods may be the answer.
Intrinsic rewards	`Chapter 9`, *Rewards and Reinforcement Learning*	The use of an intrinsic reward system shows promise for exploration.	Being able to introduce intrinsic reward systems such as **Curiosity Learning** allows the agent to explore new environments based on some expectation of state. This method will be essential for any algorithm that plans to reach the higher levels of the tower.
Understanding	`Chapter 6`, *Unity ML-Agents*	Unity provides an excellent sample environment to build and test models on.	You can easily build and test a similar environment in Unity quite quickly and on your own. It is no wonder Unity never released the raw Unity environment as a project. This was more than likely because this would have attracted many novices, thinking they could overcome the problem with just training. Sometimes, training is just not the answer.
Sparse rewards	`Chapter 9`, *Rewards and Reinforcement Learning* `Chapter 10`, *Imitation and Transfer Learning*	Could implement Curriculum or Imitation Learning.	We have already covered many examples of ways to manage the sparse rewards problem. It will be interesting to see how much the winners depend on one of these methods, such as IL, to win.
Discrete actions	`Chapter 8`, *Understanding PPO*	We learned how PPO allowed continuous action problems to learn, using stochastic methods.	As we alluded to before, it will likely take new work into more deep probabilistic methods and techniques to work around some of the current problems. This will likely require the development of new techniques using new algorithms, and how long that takes remains to be seen.

Each of the problems highlighted in the preceding table will likely need to be solved in part or wholly in order to get an agent from floor 1 to 100 to complete the entire challenge. It remains to be seen how this will play out for Unity, the winner, and DRL as a whole. In the next section, we discuss the practical applications of DL and DRL, and how they can be used for your game.

Deep Learning for your game?

It's likely the reason you picked this book up was to learn about DL and DLR for games in the hope of landing your dream job or completing your dream game. In either case, we come to a point where you decide whether this technology is worth including in your own game and to what extent. The following is a list of ten questions you can use to determine whether DL is right for your game:

1. Have you already made the decision and need to build the game with DL or DRL?
    - Yes – 10 points
    - No – 0 points
2. Will your game benefit from some form of automation, either through testing or managing repetitious player tasks?
    - Yes – 10 points
    - No – 0 points
3. Do you want to make training and AI or another similar activity part of the game?
    - Yes – (-5) points. *You may be better off using a more robust from of AI to simulate the training. Training DRL takes too many iterations and samples to be effective as an inline game-training tool, at least for now.*
    - No – 0 points.
4. Do you want cutting-edge AI to feature in your game?
    - Yes – 10 points. *There are certainly ways of layering AI technologies and making a DRL solution work. When it comes to current AI, there really is no better cutting-edge technology.*
    - No – 0 points.
5. Do you have hours of time to train an AI?
    - Yes – 10 points
    - No – (-10) points
6. Have you read a good portion of this book and completed at least a few of the exercises?
    - Yes – 10 points, +5 if you completed more than 50%
    - No – (-10) points; thanks for the honesty
7. Do you have a background or affinity for math?
    - Yes – 10 points
    - No – (-10) points

8. How many papers have you read on reinforcement learning at an academic level?
    - 10+ – 25 points
    - 5–10 – 10 points
    - 1–5 – 5 points
    - 0 – 0 points
9. What is your completion timeline?
    - 1–3 months – (-10) points
    - 3–6 months – 0 points
    - 6–12 months – 10 points
    - 1–2+ years – 25 points
10. What is the size of your team?
    - Solo – (-10) points
    - 2–5 – 0 points
    - 6–10 – 10 points
    - 11+ – 25 points

Answer all the questions and score your points to determine your full readiness score. Consult the following to determine how ready you and/or your team are:

- **<0 points** - How did you even make it this far into the book? You're not ready, and it's best you just put this book down.
- **0-50** - You certainly show promise, but you are going to need some more help; check out the following section on next steps and further areas of learning.
- **50-100** - You certainly are on your way to building the knowledge base and implementing some fun DRL in games, but you may still need a little help. Check the section on next steps and further areas of learning.
- **100+** - You are well beyond ready, and we appreciate you taking the time to read this book. Perhaps take some of your own personal time and pass your own or your team members' knowledge on to people you know.

Of course, there are no absolute rules to the results of the preceding test, and you may find that you score quite low but then go on to make the next great AI game. How you approach the results is up to you, and how you take your next steps is also entirely up to you.

In the next section, we look at the next steps you can take to learn more about DRL and how to build better automation and AI in games.

Building your game

Now that you have decided to use deep learning and/or deep reinforcement learning for your game, it is time to determine how you plan to implement various functionality in your game. In order to do that, we are going to go through a table outlining the steps you need to go through in order to build your game's AI agent:

Step	Action	Summary
Start	Determine at what level you want the AI in the game to operate, from basic, perhaps for just testing and simple automation, to advanced, where the AI will complete against the player.	Determine the level of AI.
Resourcing	Determine the amount of resources. Basic AI or automation could be handled within the team itself, whereas more complex AI may require one or many experienced members of staff.	Team requirements.
Knowledge	Determine the level of knowledge the team possesses and what will be required. It is a given that any team implementing new AI will need to learn new skills.	Knowledge-gap analysis.
Demonstration	Always start by building a simple but workable proof of concept that demonstrates all critical aspects of the system.	Demonstrate the team can complete the basic premise.
Implementation	Build the actual system in a way that is simplistic and maintainable. Keep all the things you know simple and clean.	Build the system.
Testing	Test the system over and over again. It is critical that the system is tested thoroughly, and of course what better way to do that than with a DRL automated test system.	Test the system.
Fix	As anyone who has developed software for more than a few weeks will tell you, the process is build, test, fix, and repeat. That essentially is the software development process, so try not to add too many other bells and whistles to distract from that.	Fixing the system.
Release	Releasing software to users/players is absolutely critical to a successful game or software product of any kind. You will always want to release early and often, which means your players must be encouraged to test, and to provide feedback.	Let the bugs out.
Repeat	The cycle is endless and will continue as long as your product/game makes money.	Support the system.

The preceding process is the basic premise and will work for most of your development needs. In most cases, you may want to track individual work items such as features or bugs on a work or task board. You may want to use a more defined process such as Scrum, but often keeping things simple is your best course of action.

Scrum and other software development processes are great examples to learn from, but unless you have formally trained staff, it's better to avoid trying to implement these yourself. There are often subtle rules that need to be enforced in these processes for them to work as they claim to. Even trained Scrum Masters may need to battle daily to enforce these rules in many organizations, and in the end their value becomes more management-driven than developer-focused. Use the previous table as a guide for the steps you take in building your next game, and always remember that build, release, fix, and repeat is the key to good software.

In the next section, we will look at other things you can use to expand your learning.

More foundations of learning

There is an ever-growing resource for learning about machine learning, DL, and of course DLR. The list is becoming very large, and there are many materials to choose from. For that reason, we will now summarize the areas we feel show the most promise for developing AI and DL for games:

- **Basic Data Science Course**: If you have never taken a basic fundamentals course on data science, then you certainly should. The foundations of understanding the qualities of data, statistics, probability, and variability are too numerous to mention. Be sure to cover this foundation first.
- **Probabilistic Programming**: This is a combination of various variational inference methods by which to answer problems given a probability of events with an answer of the probability that some event may occur. These types of models and languages have been used to analyze financial information and risk for years, but they are now coming to the forefront in ML technologies.
- **Deep Probabilistic Programming**: This is the combination of variational inference and DL models. Variational inference is the process by which you answer a question with a probability given the input of possibly multiple probabilities. So, instead of using a series of weights to train a network, we use a series of probability distributions. This method has proven to be very effective and has recently performed visual image classification tasks with a modified probabilistic CNN model.

- **Visual state classification and encoding**: A critical aspect to a DL system is the development of CNN models to classify images. You will need to understand this space very well in order to build the networks for your game environment. Recall that different environments may require CNN models.
- **Memory**: Memory can of course come in all forms, but the primary one of interest is the **recurrent neural network** (**RNN**). Early on in this book, we looked at the current standard recurrent network model we use called the **long short-term memory** (**LSTM**) **block**. Even at the time of writing, there is a renewed interest in the **gated recurrent unit** (**GRU**), a more complex recurrent network that has been shown to handle the vanishing gradient problem better. There is always an interest in cloud or other supported technologies and how they may interact with new DL technologies.
- **DL as a Service**: Companies such as Google, Amazon, Microsoft, OpenAI, and others who claim to be all about openness are often far from it. In most cases, if you want to incorporate these technologies into your game, you will need to subscribe to their service—which of course has its own pluses and minuses. The major problem is that if your game becomes popular and if you rely heavily on the DL service, your profits will be tied to it. Fortunately, Unity has yet to take this approach, but that does remain to be seen depending on how easily the community solves the Obstacle Tower Challenge.
- **Math**: In general, you will want to always advance your math skills whether you plan to dig deep into building your own models or not. In the end, your gut understanding of the math will provide you with the insights you need to overcome these complex technologies.
- **Perseverance**: Learn to fail, and then move on. This is critical and something many new developers often get disgruntled with and then move on to something easier, simpler, and less rewarding. Be happy when you fail, as failing is learning to understand. If you never fail, you really never learn, so learn to fail.

A hard-coded list of learning resources would likely get out of date before this book is even printed or released. Use the preceding list to generalize your learning and broaden your basic machine learning and data science knowledge as well. First and foremost, DL is a data science pursuit that serves respect to the data; never forget that as well.

In the next section for our final chapter, we will summarize this chapter and the book.

Summary

In this chapter, we took a short tour of many basic concepts involving your next steps in DL and DRL; perhaps you will decide to pursue the Unity Obstacle Tower Challenge and complete that or just use DRL in your own project. We looked at simple quizzes in order to evaluate your potential for diving in and using DRL in a game. From there, we looked at the next steps in development, and then finally we looked at other areas of learning may want to focus on.

This book was an exercise in understanding how effective DL can be when applied to your game project in the future. We explored many areas of basic DL principles early on and looked at more specific network types such as CNN and LSTM. Then, we looked at how these basics network forms could be applied to applications for driving and building a chatbot. From there, we looked at the current king of machine learning algorithms, reinforcement and deep reinforcement learning. We then looked at one of the current leaders, Unity ML-Agents, and how to implement this technology, over several chapters by looking at how simple environments are built to more complex multi-agent environments. This also allowed us to explore different forms of intrinsic/extrinsic rewards and learning systems, including curriculum, curiosity, imitation, and transfer learning.

Finally, before finishing this chapter, we completed a long exercise regarding using DRL for automatic testing and debugging with the added option of using IL as a way of enhancing testing.

Other Books You May Enjoy

If you enjoyed this book, you may be interested in these other books by Packt:

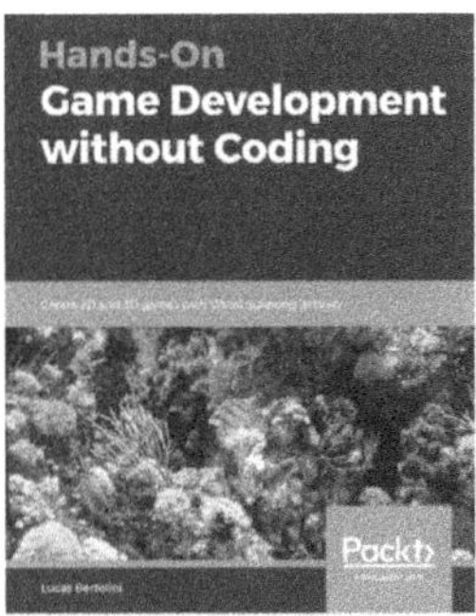

Hands-On Game Development without Coding
Lucas Bertolini

ISBN: 9781789538335

- Understanding the Interface and kit flow.
- Comprehend the virtual space and its rules.
- Learning the behaviours and roles each component must have in order to make a videogame.
- Learn about videogame development
- Creating a videogame without the need of learning any programming language
- Create your own gameplay HUD to display player and Enemy information

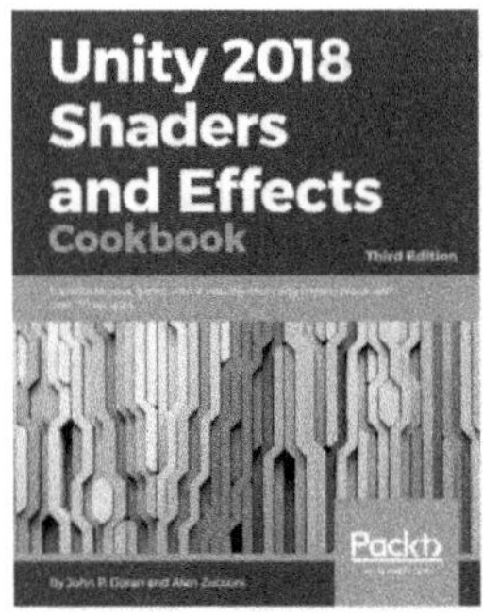

Unity 2018 Shaders and Effects Cookbook - Third Edition
John P. Doran, Alan Zucconi

ISBN: 9781788396233

- Understand physically based rendering to fit the aesthetic of your game
- Write shaders from scratch in ShaderLab and HLSL/Cg
- Combine shader programming with interactive scripts to add life to your materials
- Design efficient shaders for mobile platforms without sacrificing their realism
- Use state-of-the-art techniques, such as volumetric explosions and fur shading
- Master the math and algorithms behind the most used lighting models
- Understand how shader models have evolved and how you can create your own

Leave a review - let other readers know what you think

Please share your thoughts on this book with others by leaving a review on the site that you bought it from. If you purchased the book from Amazon, please leave us an honest review on this book's Amazon page. This is vital so that other potential readers can see and use your unbiased opinion to make purchasing decisions, we can understand what our customers think about our products, and our authors can see your feedback on the title that they have worked with Packt to create. It will only take a few minutes of your time, but is valuable to other potential customers, our authors, and Packt. Thank you!

Index

A

B

C

D

E

F

G

H

I

Q

R

S

T

U

V

W

www.ingramcontent.com/pod-product-compliance
Lightning Source LLC
LaVergne TN
LVHW081512050326
832903LV00025B/1466

* 9 7 8 1 7 8 8 9 9 4 0 7 1 *